Lecture Notes of the Institute for Computer Sciences, Social Informatics and Telecommunications Engineering 428

More information about this series at https://link.springer.com/bookseries/8197

Wei Bao · Xingliang Yuan · Longxiang Gao ·
Tom H. Luan · David Bong Jun Choi (Eds.)

Ad Hoc Networks and Tools for IT

13th EAI International Conference, ADHOCNETS 2021
Virtual Event, December 6–7, 2021
and 16th EAI International Conference, TRIDENTCOM 2021
Virtual Event, November 24, 2021
Proceedings

 Springer

Editors
Wei Bao 🄳
School of Computer Science
University of Sydney
Camperdown, NSW, Australia

Longxiang Gao 🄳
School of Information Technology
Deakin University
Mont Albert, VIC, Australia

David Bong Jun Choi 🄳
School of Electronic Engineering, School
of Computer Science and Engineering
Soongsil University
Dongjak, Seoul, Korea (Republic of)

Xingliang Yuan 🄳
Monash University
Clayton, VIC, Australia

Tom H. Luan 🄳
School of Cyber Engineering
Xidian University
Xi'an, China

ISSN 1867-8211   ISSN 1867-822X (electronic)
Lecture Notes of the Institute for Computer Sciences, Social Informatics
and Telecommunications Engineering
ISBN 978-3-030-98004-7   ISBN 978-3-030-98005-4 (eBook)
https://doi.org/10.1007/978-3-030-98005-4

This Springer imprint is published by the registered company Springer Nature Switzerland AG
The registered company address is: Gewerbestrasse 11, 6330 Cham, Switzerland

Preface

We are delighted to introduce the proceedings of the 13th edition of the European Alliance for Innovation (EAI) International Conference on Ad Hoc Networks (ADHOC-NETS 2021). This conference brought together researchers, developers, and practitioners around the world to disseminate, exchange, and discuss all recent advances related to ad hoc networks.

The technical program of ADHOCNETS 2021 consisted of 15 full papers, which were selected from 29 submitted papers. Aside from the high-quality technical paper presentations, the technical program also featured a keynote speech given by Tao Gu from the School of Computing at Macquarie University, Australia.

Coordination with the steering committee, Imrich Chlamtac, Shiwen Mao, and Jun Zheng, was essential for the success of the conference. We sincerely appreciate their constant support and guidance. It was also a great pleasure to work with such an excellent organizing committee team for their hard work in organizing and supporting the conference. Moreover, we would like to thank the Technical Program Committee who completed the peer-review process for technical papers and helped to put together a high-quality technical program. We are also grateful to Conference Manager Karolina Marcinova for her support and all the authors who submitted their papers to the ADHOCNETS 2021 conference and workshops.

We strongly believe that ADHOCNETS provides a good forum for all researchers, developers, and practitioners to discuss all science and technology aspects that are relevant to ad hoc networks. We also expect that the future editions of the ADHOCNETS conference will be as successful and simulating, as indicated by the contributions presented in this volume.

December 2021

Wei Bao
Xingliang Yuan
Albert Zomaya

Organization

Steering Committee

Imrich Chlamtac (Chair) University of Trento, Italy
Shiwen Mao Auburn University, USA
Jun Zheng Southeast University, China

Organizing Committee

General Chair

Albert Y. Zomaya University of Sydney, Australia

Technical Program Committee Chairs

Wei Bao University of Sydney, Australia
Xingliang Yuan Monash University, Australia

Publicity and Social Media Chair

Ibrahim Khalil Royal Melbourne Institute of Technology
  (RMIT), Australia

Sponsorship and Exhibits Chair

Xiao Liu Deakin University, Australia

Publications Chair

Young Choon Lee Macquarie University, Australia

Web Chair

Zhengjie Yang University of Sydney, Australia

Local Chair

Kanchana Thilakarathna University of Sydney, Australia

Technical Program Committee

Chengjun Cai	City University of Hong Kong, China
Xiao Chen	Monash University, Australia
Helei Cui	Northwestern Polytechnical University, China
Wibowo Hardjawana	University of Sydney, Australia
Qiang He	Swinburne University of Technology, Australia
Chuang Hu	Hong Kong Polytechnic University, Hong Kong
Hazem Ibrahim	York University, Canada
Honghao Ju	Southwest Jiaotong University, China
Salil Kanhere	University of New South Wales, Australia
Avadh Kumari	Indian Institute of Technology, Roorkee, India
Shangqi Lai	Monash University, Australia
Young Choon Lee	Macquarie University, Australia
Nour Moustafa	University of New South Wales, Australia
Dinh Nguyen	Deakin University, Australia
Abubakar Sadiq Sani	University of New South Wales, Australia
Viet Vo	Monash University, Australia
Hao Wang	Louisiana State University, USA
Lei Xu	Nanjing University of Science and Technology, China
Dong Yuan	University of Sydney, Australia
Xuyun Zhang	Macquarie University, Australia
Yifeng Zheng	Harbin Institute of Technology, China
Bing Bing Zhou	University of Sydney, Australia
Cong Zuo	Nanyang Technological University, Singapore

Preface

We are delighted to introduce the proceedings of the sixteenth edition of the European Alliance for Innovation (EAI) International Conference on Tools for Design, Implementation and Verification of Emerging Information Technologies TRIDENTCOM 2021. This conference brought together technical experts and researchers from academia and industry worldwide to discuss the emerging technologies such as blockchain, deep learning, edge computing, cyber-physical systems, cybersecurity, and computer communications.

The technical program of TRIDENTCOM 2021 consisted of eight full papers, which were presented in two sessions. Aside from the high-quality technical paper presentations, the technical program also featured two keynote speeches given by Ying-Dar Lin from National Chiao Tung University (NCTU) and Jaideep Vaidya from Rutgers University.

Coordination with the general chairs, Yong Xiang and Song Guo, was essential for the success of the conference. We sincerely appreciate their constant support and guidance. It was also a great pleasure to work with such an excellent organizing committee team for their hard work in organizing and supporting the conference. In particular, we are grateful to the Technical Program Committee who completed the peer-review process for technical papers and helped to put together a high-quality technical program. We are also grateful to Conference Managers Jacqueline Sirotová and Aleksandra Sledziejowska for their support and all the authors who submitted their papers to the TRIDENTCOM 2021 conference.

We strongly believe that TRIDENTCOM provides a good forum for all researchers, developers, and practitioners to discuss all science and technology aspects that are relevant to blockchain, deep learning, edge computing, cyber-physical systems, cybersecurity, and computer communications. We also expect that the future editions of the TRIDENTCOM conference will be as successful and stimulating, as indicated by the contributions presented in this volume.

Longxiang Gao
Tom H. Luan
David Choi

Organization

Steering Committee

Imrich Chlamtac   University of Trento, Italy
Victor C. M. Leung   University of British Columbia, Canada

Organizing Committee

General Chair

Yong Xiang   Deakin University, Australia

General Co-chair

Song Guo   Hong Kong Polytechnic University, Hong Kong

Technical Program Committee Chairs

Longxiang Gao   Deakin University, Australia
Tom H. Luan   Xidian University, China
David Choi   Soongsil University, South Korea

Sponsorship and Exhibit Chair

Bruce Gu   Victoria University, Australia

Local Chair

Xiaodong Wang   Deakin University, Australia

Workshops Chair

Yuan Jin   Monash University, Australia

Publicity and Social Media Chairs

Mohamad Khattar Awad   Kuwait University, Kuwait
Youyang Qu   Deakin University, Australia

Publications Chair

Lianhua Chi   La Trobe University, Australia

Web Chair

Di Wu   Deakin University, Australia

Demos Chair

Alessio Bonti   Deakin University, Australia

Technical Program Committee

Miao Wang   Miami University, USA
Ning Lu   Queen's University, Canada
Saurabh Garg   University of Tasmania, Australia
Ning Zhang   University of Windsor, Canada
Keshav Sood   Deakin University, Australia
Ping Wang   York University, Canada
Jiong Jin   Swinburne University, Australia
Sungguk Yoon   Soongsil University, South Korea
Yujie Tang   Algoma University, Canada
Qiang Ye   Minnesota State University, USA
Yonghoon Choi   Kwangwoon University, South Korea
Ajit Kumar   Soongsil University, South Korea
Xiaohui Liang   University of Massachusetts Boston, USA
Kuan Zhang   University of Nebraska–Lincoln, USA
Nizar Alsharif   Al-Baha University, Saudi Arabia
Yuan Wu   Macau University, Macau
Sangkyun Lee   Korea University, South Korea
Neetesh Saxena   Cardiff University, UK
Jaesung Park   Kwangwoon University, South Korea
Dhananjay Singh   Hankuk University of Foreign Studies,
                                       South Korea
Yuan Zhang   Southwest University, China
Chao Chen   James Cook University, Australia
Anfeng Liu   Central South University, China
Wesley De Neve   Ghent University, Belgium

Contents

Network Applications (ADHOCNETS 2021)

Main Track (TRIDENTCOM 2021)

Network Routing (ADHOCNETS 2021)

Analysis of Routing Attacks in FANETs

Ozlem Ceviz[1,2](✉) ⓘ, Pinar Sadioglu[2] ⓘ, and Sevil Sen[2] ⓘ

[1] Department of Computer Engineering, Sivas University of Science and Technology,
Sivas, Turkey
ozlemceviz@sivas.edu.tr
[2] WISE Laboratory, Department of Computer Engineering, Hacettepe University,
Ankara, Turkey
{n19249120,ssen}@cs.hacettepe.edu.tr

Abstract. Nowadays, Unmanned Aerial Vehicles (UAV) are widely used in a variety of fields, especially in military and industrial applications. However, the usage of a single UAV has begun to be insufficient in most missions. A single UAV may not complete its mission in cases of rapid depletion of its batteries, limited field of view, long-term performance of a task, a fall or a malfunction in the system due to an external effect. In such cases, Flying Ad Hoc Networks (FANETs) that allow more than one UAV to participate in a common network and execute complex tasks in an organized manner is recommended. However, FANETS are target of attacks due to being used in critical applications. Moreover, they are vulnerable to a variety of attacks due to their very nature and the cooperative routing protocols they use. Moreover, FANETs requires new security solutions or adaptation of existing security solutions of Mobile Ad Hoc Networks (MANETs), since it has much higher mobility than MANETs. Since mobility could affect security in different ways, at first attacks against FANETs should be analyzed. This is the main aim of this study. In this paper, various attacks against FANETs, namely dropping, blackhole, sinkhole, flooding attacks are analyzed. This is the first study that presents a comprehensive attack analysis in FANETs by simulating realistic network scenarios, where UAVs move in 3D as in real life.

Keywords: FANET · UAV · AODV · Routing attacks · Blackhole attack · Flooding attack · Dropping attack

1 Introduction

Unmanned aerial vehicle (UAV) systems have started to be used in many areas with the rapid development of technology. They are already frequently used in military, industrial and civilian applications. Especially, UAVs being work as a group without human intervention has led to further expansion of their research areas. However, in order to work in groups, they need to set up a communication network among themselves at first. Ad hoc networks, which can be formed without the need of human intervention, resolve faults and organize

W. Bao et al. (Eds.): ADHOCNETS 2021/TridentCom 2021, LNICST 428, pp. 3–17, 2022.
https://doi.org/10.1007/978-3-030-98005-4_1

themselves, are suitable for providing network connectivity between UAVs [14]. However, high speeds and mobility of UAVs, in contrast to many other type of ad hoc networks, results in the topology to change very dynamically. Therefore, a new type of ad hoc networks called Flying Ad Hoc Networks (FANETs) has emerged and becomes one of the popular research areas [13]. FANETs have been used in many applications in order to execute specialized tasks such as monitoring, surveillance and reconnaissance, environmental surveillance. In such applications, nodes could report their findings to ground controller systems or designated nodes in the network [12,25].

FANETs are used in many applications, especially mission-critical ones, which make them the target of new attacks. First of all, the use of wireless links makes the network susceptible to eavesdropping and active interference attacks. Furthermore, routing protocols designed for ad hoc networks rely on the cooperativeness of nodes, which makes insider attacks to be very effective in such networks. Although AODV protocol is a popular routing protocol for FANETs, it is vulnerable to attacks [10]. High mobility of such networks could also affect security in different ways. On the one hand, mobility allows attackers to evade from security solutions while damaging the network. On the other hand, the effect of attacks could be limited on highly mobile targets. Controller systems in the network can be the target of attacks such as Denial of Service (DoS) attacks, and hence the availability of the network can be compromised.

New security solutions should be improved for FANETs. While there are many security proposals for MANETs in the literature, they are not directly applicable to FANETs due to their high level mobility. Furthermore, the existence of ground controller systems allows to use such nodes in security solutions. On the other hand, there is no central points in typical MANETs and all data are distributed in MANETs. Furthermore, UAVs move in 3D contrary to nodes in MANETs and VANETs. Moreover, they might have different mobility models than other type of ad hoc networks. For example, in order to complete some missions, they might fly together in one direction as a group and move periodically towards to the controller ground system. Therefore, new security solutions and architectures should be developed for FANETs or the existing solutions proposed for ad hoc networks should be adapted to FANETs. This requires attacks against FANETs to be thoroughly analyzed, which is the main aim of the current study.

In this study, the effects of various routing attacks against FANETs are analyzed. AODV, which is one of the most popular routing protocols for ad hoc networks, are used. AODV is also a popular protocol in FANETs due to its simplicity and low overhead [23]. Attacks, namely dropping, flooding, blackole and sikhole are analyzed on networks with varying percentage of attackers from 5% to 20%. The 3D Gaussian Markov Model is used as the mobility model in order to simulate flying nodes. While studies in the literature still use 2D mobility models such Random Waypoint Mobility Model and low node speeds such as 20 m/s that is suitable for MANETs applications [17,21], here realistic network scenarios for FANETs are simulated by using Ns-3 [16]. To the best of the authors' knowledge, this is the first study that rigorously analyze attacks against FANET on realistic network scenarios. The effects of attacks on simulated networks are evaluated by using packet delivery ratio, overhead and end-to-end delay.

The rest of this paper is organized as follows. Section 2 summarizes the related studies in the literature. Section 3 makes a brief introduction to the AODV protocol at first, then introduces the mobility model and attacks simulated in this study. Section 4 gives details about the experimental settings, and presents the attack analysis results. Finally, Sect. 5 concludes the paper.

2   Related Work

Although there are many studies on MANETs security in the literature, research on FANETs security is still immature even though they have been started to use in many applications. There are quite a number of studies that analyze attacks against AODV on mobile ad hoc networks in the literature [9,11,15,19]. In [15], both atomic and composite attacks against AODV are systematically presented. Jain et al. [11] and Dokurer et al. [9], not only analyze blackhole attacks, but also propose solutions for blackhole attacks by improving AODV. Both approaches show similarity since they ignore the firstly arrived RREP message to the source node based on the assumption this reply packet is from the attacker node. In [19], again, the effect of blackhole attacks are evaluated on networks using different routing protocols, AODV and OLSR. The results show that the AODV protocol shows better performance than the OLSR protocol. However if there is no attack in the network, OLSR provides higher throughput on small networks.

UAVs can be a potential target for attackers, whether they are part of a group as in ad hoc networks or single, in order to damage the device and/or access the data it contains. The impact of such threats targeting its privacy, security and physical integrity can severely affect both for the mission of UAV or to the network it is included in [2,3]. Moreover, multi-UAV communication is exposed to additional threats for trust establishment and secure communication mechanisms. FANETs have higher levels of node mobility and hence more frequent changes in network topology than traditional MANETs. In [4,20], authors discuss the unique characteristics of FANETs and their challenges. Bekmezci et al. [5] address security requirements of FANETs and possible threats against these highly networks. Furthermore, the authors present well-known ad hoc network attacks and discuss security solutions for such attacks on FANETs.

There are a few security solutions proposed for FANETs in the literature. Some studies [6,24] propose solutions for sybil attacks. Walia et al. [24] proposes a mutual authentication technique in order to detect sybil attack. In this method, each node checks its neighbor nodes and if there are different neighbors with the same ID, the node is marked as malicious and monitored. If this marked node changes its identity, it is assumed to be malicious. The proposed method has maximum throughput, minimum overhead and packet loss compared to other methods. Another proposed solution from Bhatia et al. [6] consists of monitoring, detection and isolation steps to identify malicious nodes triggering the sybil attack. In another study [8], a hybrid intrusion detection system is proposed.

The proposed method consist of two steps. Firstly, the spectral analysis is used to generate a specific traffic signature which offers a basic degree of knowledge regarding the type of intrusion in the network. Secondly, with the output of the first step, the controller/observer-based estimation step evaluates the level of attack observed in the network.

To sum up, even though routing attacks against AODV are extensively studied in the literature, different characteristics of FANETs such as having nodes with higher speeds, moving in 3D requires a new analysis of attacks on these highly mobile networks. The lack of such an analysis also negatively impacts the development of security solutions for FANETs.

3 Background

3.1 Routing Protocol: AODV

AODV is widely used in ad hoc networks, where FANETs are no exception. Since there is high mobility in FANETs, routing protocols proposed for them seek to establish and maintain communication between end points in such dynamic topologies. AODV is a reactive and multi-hop routing protocol that responds to this request. AODV enables the rapid discovery of routes to a new destination and cancels out inactive routes [18]. Due to high speeds of UAVs, FANETs experience frequent link breakages and disconnection problems.

AODV has two main mechanisms: route discovery and route maintenance. In the route discovery phase, the source node, who does not have a valid route to the destination node in its routing table, broadcasts route request (RREQ) packets. Any node having a valid route to the destination could send a unicast route reply (RREP) packet to the source node. The source node selects the freshest and the shortest path (having minimum number of hops) to the destination. In the route maintenance mechanism, locally detected broken links are announced to other nodes by using route error (RERR) packets. These packets are frequently broadcast to the whole network.

3.2 Attacks

Four type of attacks against AODV are analyzed in this study.

Sinkhole Attack. In this attack scenario, the malicious node aims to attract network traffic to itself by advertising a better route to the destination. This attack often lays the foundation for further attacks such as selective dropping, modification attacks.

In this study, when the attacker receives a RREQ message, it replies with a fake RREP that claims that it is one hop away from the destination node, hence it increases its chance to be selected as the shortest path. Moreover, it advertises itself as the freshest route to the destination by increasing the destination sequence number, hence in this case it guarantees to be selected as the route to

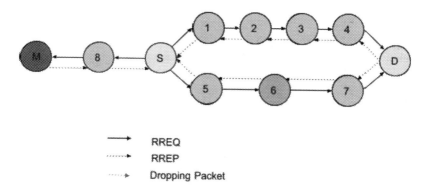

Fig. 1. Blackhole attack

the destination. When this route is selected, the attacker listens to all communication between the source and the destination nodes, therefore it is called as the sinkhole attack.

Dropping Attack. In this simple attack scenario, the attacker simply drops packets it received. It could selectively drop packets such as packets destined to a particular destination. Or he could randomly drop some packets in order to be more evasive, however in this case the effect of the attack is expected to be more limited. Besides data packets, the attacker could also drop routing control packets. In this case, active routes might not be built or inactive routes might not be announced in time. Such cases result in re-initiating the route discovery mechanism, which might consume network resources, cause congestion and delays. In this study, the attacker drops all data packets it received.

BlackHole Attack. Blackhole attack is a composite attack that performs sinkhole and dropping/modification attacks consecutively. Firstly it directs the network traffic to itself by advertising it has the best route to the destination, then it performs other attacks on the network traffic it receives such as modification, dropping, fabrication attacks. In the simulations here, in the first phase of the attack, the sinkhole attack is carried out as defined above, then only the dropping attack is performed in the second phase of this attack.

In Fig. 1, a blackhole attack is demonstrated. The source node (S) wants to discover a route to the destination node (D) by broadcasting a RREQ message. When the malicious node (M) receives one of these RREQ messages, it replies with a fake RREP. As shown in the figure, even M is not in the route to the destination, it receives data packets sent from S to D, since it claims itself to be in the shortest path to the destination.

Ad Hoc Flooding Attack. In this attack scenario, the attacker takes the advantage of high number of messages sent in the route discovery mechanism in order to overwhelm the network. In this DoS attack, malicious nodes send a large number of RREQ messages for the selected nodes. This attack results in increasing the network traffic, consuming network and nodes resources, breaking the connection between nodes, and interrupting data transmitting. In the simulations, a random destination node is selected and 20 new RREQ messages are sent to discover routes to this destination node. The attack is repeated every 3 s for another destination node that is randomly selected.

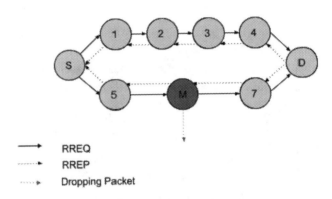

Fig. 2. Dropping attack in AODV protocol

3.3   Gauss-Markov (GM) Mobility Model

In order to simulate the mobility of UAVs in a realistic way, a three-dimensional mobility model should be used in the experiments. For that reason, 3D Gauss-Markov (GM) Mobility Model, which is a time-based mobility model designed with a single adjustment parameter to prevent sharp motion changes and to integrate various randomness adaptations [22] is used in this study. Since the movements of a node between its consecutive positions must be harmonious [7], the model keeps the previous movements in its memory. The mobility behaviour of nodes are adjusted by the α parameter, which takes values between zero and one. While α is 0, it corresponds to a memory-free model (i.e. random mobility). While it gets closer to 1, the motion becomes more predictable.

4   Attack Analysis

The main purpose of this study is to analyze routing attacks against FANETs. Therefore, a number of networks is simulated firstly without attacks, and then with the attacks described above. Finally, the performance of all simulated networks is analyzed. Here, the simulation environment is introduced below at first, then the effect of attacks on these simulated networks are discussed in the subsequent sections.

4.1   Simulation Settings

In this study, the well-known network simulator, Ns-3 [16] is employed to simulate networks and attacks against FANETs. In order to see the multi-hop characteristics of AODV, each network consists of 25 nodes, where one of them is a mobile server node. Each network is run without attacks, then run with blackhole, sinkhole, dropping and ad hoc flooding attacks separately. Different ratios of attackers are applied from 5% to 20% and the position of attackers are selected randomly five times for each network topology. Hence 70 (14×5) network topologies are executed for each attack type and ratio, and the average of performance metrics on these 70 networks are given in the results. As noted above, 3D Gaussian Markov Model is used in order to represent nodes' mobility in 3D. α value is started from 0.495 in order to keep the balance between random mobility and predictable mobility and, each time it is increased by 0.001 for simulating a different network topology. The speeds of nodes are set to 720 km/h as in real life. In order to be compatible with FANETs, the 802.11n MAC protocol is used at 5 GHz [1]. The transmission range of the nodes is determined as 250 m for the given network area. Each node sends 1024-byte 15 UDP packets to the server node every 0.5 s. All simulation parameters are summarized in Table 1.

The following performance metrics are employed in order to see the effects of attacks on networks: packet delivery ratio, end-to-end delay, and overhead metrics. Packet delivery ratio (PDR) is the average of the ratio of the total number of packets received by all nodes in the network to the total number of packets destined for the same nodes. End-to-end (E2E) delay is the measurement in seconds, of the average of all delays that occur in the network during data transmission between end communication points. Overhead is the ratio of the total control packets generated by the routing protocol to the received data packets.

4.2   Experimental Results

In the experiments, firstly 14 networks with varying network topologies are executed without no attacker. Then, different attack types are applied to the same topologies with different ratio of attackers. Firstly, the effects of sinkhole attack is given in Table 2 and Fig. 3. Table 2 shows the average values of performance metrics on networks with different attack ratios. Figure 3 emphasizes on PDR by using the box plot representation. As defined above, the attacker does not drop data packets deliberately in this attack scenario. However, due to the attacker of building inactive routes, the data packets might not be reached to the destination as shown in the results. The attacker might not be even in a route between the source and the destination.

Table 1. Simulation parameters used in Ns-3

Parameter	Value
Routing protocol	AODV
MAC protocol	IEEE 802.11n
Frequency band	5 GHz
Simulation time	900 s
Area	1700 m × 1700 m × 1500 m
Number of nodes	25
Node speed	720 km/h
Transmission range	250 m
Traffic type	UDP
Packet size	1024 bytes
Packet count	15
Bandwidth	6 Mbps
Ratio of malicious node	No attack, 5%, 10%, 15%, 20%
Mobility model	GM model
Bounds for GM	X: [−70; 70], Y: [−70; 70], Z: [0; 70]
α for GM	[0.495–0.509]

Table 2. Average performance metrics of networks under sinkhole attack

Attackers (%)	PDR (%)	E2E delay (s)	Overhead
0%	91,43	0,0253	12,5
5%	84,94	0,031	6,98
10%	84,01	0,036	11,04
15%	70,11	0,018	42,16
20%	56,60	0,017	111,14

The effect of dropping attack is given in Table 3 and Fig. 4. Even though the attacker positions are selected randomly, the same set of attackers are used in each topology for different attack scenarios. Therefore, the same data packets pass through attackers in each attack scenario. In addition, more data packets could be directed to the malicious node in sinkhole attack. Please also note that the attacker size is increased by covering already existing attacker nodes on networks with less number of attackers for each topology. As shown in the results, as the number of attacker increases, its effect becomes more evident in the network.

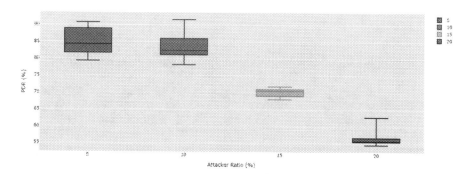

Fig. 3. PDR of networks under sinkhole attack

Table 3. Average performance metrics of networks under dropping attack

Attackers (%)	PDR (%)	E2E delay (s)	Overhead
0%	91,43	0,0253	12,29
5%	88,47	0,024	5,61
10%	81,84	0,036	11,87
15%	70,14	0,023	42,17
20%	56,72	0,018	110,02

Table 4 shows the average of performance metrics on simulated networks under blackchole attack. In order to see PDR more closely, Fig. 5 shows the box plot for this performance metric. As shown in the results, the network is affected worse as the number of attackers increases. Especially when the attacker ratio reaches to 15%, PDR decreases down to approximately 70%. When the attacker rate is 20%, PDR reaches to an unacceptable level. However such attacks are not very effective on networks having a lower density of attackers due to high mobility. Since all the attacks analyzed so far causes data packets to drop, and hence the route discovery mechanism is re-initiated, the number of routing control packets on networks increases with the number of attackers.

Blackhole attack reduces PDR slightly more than sinkhole attack on networks where more than 5% of nodes are attackers. Even though both attacks take control of the route to the destination node, in some cases the attackers could be in a route between the source and the destination nodes. In such cases only, data packets are forwarded in sinkhole attacks, which explains the small differences between PDR of networks under sinkhole and blackhole attacks.

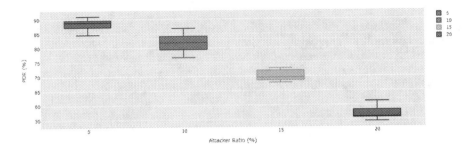

Fig. 4. PDR of networks under dropping attack

Table 4. Average performance metrics of networks under blackhole attack

Attackers (%)	PDR (%)	E2E delay (s)	Overhead
0%	91,43	0,0253	6,64
5%	88,04	0,0254	5,91
10%	82,53	0,0334	11,68
15%	69,34	0,0191	43,58
20%	56,81	0,0170	72,77

Finally, a DoS attack type is analyzed. The performance results of networks under ad hoc flooding attacks is given in Table 5 and Fig. 6. As expected, the overhead increases considerably. The high number of routing control messages also cause data packets to drop due to network congestion.

The effects of attacks are compared with each other by using PDR, E2E delay, and overhead in Figs. 7, 8, 9 respectively. As shown in Fig. 7, even though blackhole attack is a combination of sinkhole and dropping attacks, the difference between the effects of those attacks is not very notable, not as much as being expected. Hence, the attackers could decrease PDR considerably even by only performing the simplest attack in these small networks, dropping, so it does not need even need to attract the traffic through itself. This may be due to other factors analyzed in depth in the ongoing study. On the other hand, ad hoc flooding attack causes more packets to drop than dropping attacks due to congestion it has created in the network. Even in the presence of one attacker (5%), ad hoc flooding attack shows a considerable decrease in PDR.

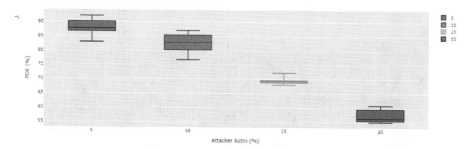

Fig. 5. PDR of networks under blackHole attack

Table 5. Average performance metrics of networks under ad hoc flooding attack

Attackers (%)	PDR (%)	E2E delay (s)	Overhead
0%	91,43	0,0253	12,29
5%	76,53	0,065	5,59
10%	76,46	0,063	5,00
15%	69,30	0,028	40,66
20%	57,01	0,018	107,76

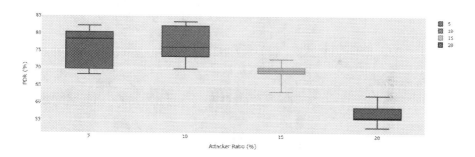

Fig. 6. PDR of networks under ad hoc flooding attack

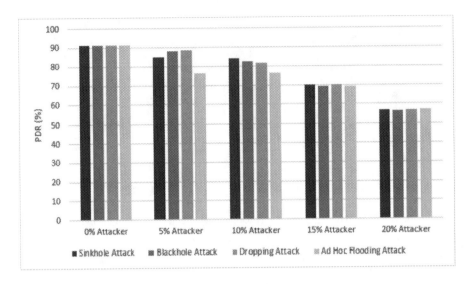

Fig. 7. Comparison of PDR on networks under different attack types

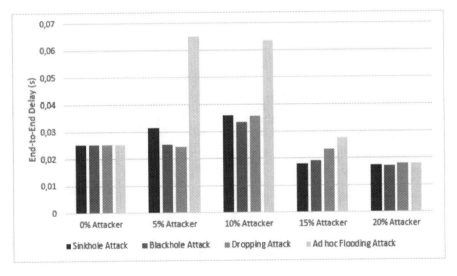

Fig. 8. Comparison of E2E delay on networks under different attack types

As shown in Fig. 8, E2E delay increases until the density of attackers reaches to 10% of nodes. Since the network resources are still available until this point, packet delay increases proportionally to the increase in the number of attackers. However, as the number of attackers in the network continues to increase, the overhead also increases considerably due to re-initiating of the route discovery mechanism as shown in Fig. 9. This increase is very dramatic for ad hoc flooding attacks as expected. Because of the overhead, and so the network congestion, packets have started to be dropped. Moreover, since data packets in shorter routes have higher chance to be forwarded than data packets in longer routes, this might still affect the E2E delay positively on networks under high number of attackers.

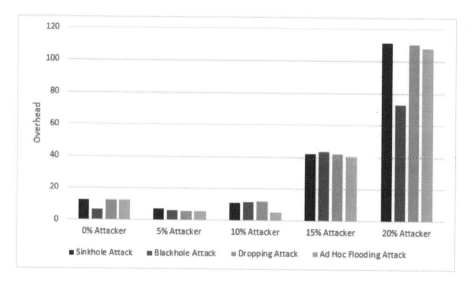

Fig. 9. Comparison of overhead on networks under different attack types

5 Conclusion

This paper analyzes how various attacks against FANETs affect network performance. Particularly routing attacks targeting AODV, namely sinkhole, dropping, blackhole and ad hoc flooding attacks are taken into consideration. The experimental results show that all attacks degrade the performance of the network, especially when the ratio of attackers has exceed 15%. When the density of attackers below that, the network can still run smoothly. In such cases, the effects of such attacks might be limited due to high mobility. Furthermore, it is shown sinkhole, dropping and blackhole attacks affect the network in a similar way when the attackers are placed in the same positions. Hence, the attackers could decrease the PDR by performing the simplest attack, dropping, so it does not need even need to attract the traffic through itself in small networks. Only ad hoc flooding attack could results in a sharper decrease in PDR even in the existence of one attacker (5%) due to its very nature.

To the best of the authors' knowledge, this is the first attack analysis on FANETs with realistic simulation parameters. The studies in the literature still use the 2D mobility models. Hence, it is believed that this study could accelerate studies on FANETs security. Researchers could use the network parameters here in order to simulate attacks that could really affect FANETs, so they could propose solutions for mitigating/detecting such attacks. In the future, more complex attack scenarios in larger networks are planned to be analyzed.

References

1. Abraham, S., Meylan, A., Nanda, S.: 802.11n MAC design and system performance. In: IEEE International Conference on Communications, vol. 5, pp. 2957–2961. IEEE (2005). https://doi.org/10.1109/icc.2005.1494932
2. Akram, R.N., et al.: Security, privacy and safety evaluation of dynamic and static fleets of drones. In: 2017 IEEE/AIAA 36th Digital Avionics Systems Conference (DASC), pp. 1–12 (2017). https://doi.org/10.1109/DASC.2017.8101984
3. Altawy, R., Youssef, A.M.: Security, privacy, and safety aspects of civilian drones: a survey. ACM Trans. Cyber-Phys. Syst. 1(2), 1–25 (2016). https://doi.org/10.1145/3001836
4. Bekmezci, I., Sahingoz, O.K., Temel, S.: Flying AD-HOC networks (FANETS): a survey. AD Hoc Networks 11(3), 1254–1270 (2013). https://doi.org/10.1016/j.adhoc.2012.12.004
5. Bekmezci, I., Şentürk, E., Türker, T.: Security issues in flying AD-HOC networks (FANETS). J. Aero. Space Technol. 9(2), 13–21 (2016). http://jast.hezarfen.msu.edu.tr/index.php/JAST/article/view/32
6. Bhatia, V., Walia, E., Singla, P.: VANET and FANET under the impact of the security attack. Int. J. Innov. Technol. Explor. Eng. 8(9), 390–397 (2019). https://doi.org/10.35940/ijitee.I1062.0789S19
7. Broyles, D., Jabbar, A., Sterbenz, J.P.: Design and analysis of a 3-D gauss-markov mobility model for highly dynamic airborne networks. In: Proceedings of the International Telemetering Conference, p. 46 January 2010
8. Condomines, J.P., Zhang, R., Larrieu, N.: Network intrusion detection system for UAV AD-HOC communication: from methodology design to real test validation. Ad Hoc Networks 90, 101759 (2019). https://doi.org/10.1016/j.adhoc.2018.09.004
9. Dokurer, S., Erten, Y.M., Acar, C.E.: Performance analysis of ad-hoc networks under black hole attacks. In: Conference Proceedings of IEEE SOUTHEASTCON, pp. 148–153 (2007). https://doi.org/10.1109/SECON.2007.342872
10. El-Semary, A.M., Diab, H.: BP-AODV: blackhole protected AODV routing protocol for MANETs based on chaotic map. IEEE Access 7, 95197–95211 (2019). https://doi.org/10.1109/ACCESS.2019.2928804
11. Jain, A.K., Tokekar, V.: Mitigating the effects of Black hole attacks on AODV routing protocol in mobile AD Hoc networks. In: 2015 International Conference on Pervasive Computing ICPC 2015 (2015). https://doi.org/10.1109/PERVASIVE.2015.7087174
12. Ladosz, P., Oh, H., Chen, W.H.: Optimal positioning of communication relay unmanned aerial vehicles in urban environments. In: 2016 International Conference on Unmanned Aircraft Systems (ICUAS), pp. 1140–1147 (2016). https://doi.org/10.1109/ICUAS.2016.7502562
13. Mahmud, I., Cho, Y.Z.: Adaptive hello interval in FANET routing protocols for green UAVs. IEEE Access 7, 63004–63015 (2019). https://doi.org/10.1109/ACCESS.2019.2917075
14. Maxa, J.a., Mahmoud, M.s.B., Larrieu, N.: Extended Verification of Secure UAANET Routing Protocol To cite this version : HAL Id : hal-01365933 Extended Verification of Secure UAANET Routing Protocol (2016)

15. Ning, P., Sun, K.: How to misuse AODV: a case study of insider attacks against mobile ad-hoc routing protocols. Ad Hoc Networks **3**(6), 795–819 (2005)
16. The ns-3 network simulator (2021). http://www.nsnam.org/
17. Ochola, E.O., Mejaele, L.F., Eloff, M.M., Van Der Poll, J.A.: Manet reactive routing protocols node mobility variation effect in analysing the impact of black hole attack. SAIEE Africa Res. J. **108**(2), 80–92 (2017). https://doi.org/10.23919/saiee.2017.8531629
18. Perkings, C., Belding-Royer, E., Das, S.: Ad hoc On-Demand Distance Vector (AODV) Routing. Ietf Rfc 3561 (2003)
19. Praveen, K.S., Gururaj, H.L., Ramesh, B.: Comparative analysis of black hole attack in Ad Hoc network using AODV and OLSR Protocols. Proc. Comput. Sci. **85**, 325–330 (2016). https://doi.org/10.1016/j.procs.2016.05.240
20. Sahingoz, O.K.: Networking models in flying AD-HOC networks (FANETS): concepts and challenges. J. Intell. Robot. Syst. **74**(1), 513–527 (2014). https://doi.org/10.1007/s10846-013-9959-7
21. Sen, J., Koilakonda, S., Ukil, A.: A mechanism for detection of cooperative black hole attack in mobile AD Hoc networks. In: Proceedings - 2011 2nd International Conference on Intelligent Systems, Modelling and Simulation, ISMS 2011, pp. 338–343 (2011). https://doi.org/10.1109/ISMS.2011.58
22. Shumeye Lakew, D., Sa'Ad, U., Dao, N.N., Na, W., Cho, S.: Routing in flying Ad Hoc networks: a comprehensive survey. IEEE Commun. Surv. Tutorials **22**(2), 1071–1120 (2020). https://doi.org/10.1109/COMST.2020.2982452
23. Tan, X., Zuo, Z., Su, S., Guo, X., Sun, X.: Research of security routing protocol for UAV communication network based on AODV. Electronics **9**(8), 1–18 (2020). https://doi.org/10.3390/electronics9081185
24. Walia, E., Bhatia, V., Kaur, G.: Detection of malicious nodes in flying Ad-HOC networks (FANET). Int. J. Electron. Commun. Eng. **5**(9), 6–12 (2018). https://doi.org/10.14445/23488549/ijece-v5i9p102
25. Xu, Z., Huo, J., Wang, Y., Yuan, J., Shan, X., Feng, Z.: Analyzing two connectivities in UAV-ground mobile AD HOC networks. In: 2011 IEEE International Conference on Computer Science and Automation Engineering, vol. 2, pp. 158–162 (2011). https://doi.org/10.1109/CSAE.2011.5952445

Context-Aware Routing and Forwarding Model for NDN-Based VANET

Elídio da Silva[1,2]([✉]) [iD], Joaquim Macedo[2] [iD], and António Costa[2] [iD]

[1] Lurio University, Pemba, Mozambique
id6644@alunos.uminho.pt
[2] Algoritmi Centre, University of Minho, Braga, Portugal
{macedo,costa}@di.uminho.pt
https://algoritmi.uminho.pt/

Abstract. Routing in Vehicular Ad hoc Networks (VANET) is a challenging topic due to the links intermittency, which in turn makes it difficult to manage routing tables. One solution is routing table management avoidance and the adoption of flooding. This solution is adopted by many state-of-art proposals. However, it can degenerate to broadcast storm problems. Some proposals leverage the characteristics of Named Data Networking (NDN) to improve VANET. They use the Forwarding Information Base (FIB) to manage routes, but flooding is still the main mechanism used to update FIB when nodes move from one to another location. These solutions neither take advantage of the in-network caching, nor adapt routing to VANET context.

Each VANET context presents different routing requirements, thus, a context-aware routing and forwarding model that uses FIB to manage routes is proposed. A mobility prediction mechanism is adopted to update FIB and the list of neighbor. Additionally, all overheard packets are processed in order to update the neighbors list and, thus, avoid frequent broadcasts. To take advantage of the in-network caching, nodes share their list of cached contents when responding to a special request from RSU, querying for new content sources. To attain this objective, modifications of the NDN structures are performed.

An improved performance of VANET is expected, at a cost of an increased computational overhead due to the processing of all overheard packets, and the mobility prediction.

Keywords: Caching · Named Data Networking · Routing · Vehicular Ad hoc Networks

1 Introduction

The development of Intelligent Transportation Systems (ITS) [18] is intimately attached to the development of vehicular communications, and particularly Vehicular Ad Hoc Networks (VANET). In turn, the development of vehicular communications presents specific challenges due to their intrinsic characteristics

W. Bao et al. (Eds.): ADHOCNETS 2021/TridentCom 2021, LNICST 428, pp. 18–32, 2022.
https://doi.org/10.1007/978-3-030-98005-4_2

such as frequent network partitioning, highly dynamic topology, and short-lived links between nodes.

State-of-the-art routing and forwarding in VANET are mainly geographic or topology based. Topology-based solutions resort to flooding in order to acquire topological information. Geographical solutions also resort to flooding when the content source moves. Network flooding is a solution that should be avoided, because it is ineffective in terms of resource management and can result in the broadcast storm problem, compromising the traffic and the network efficiency.

Named Data Networking (NDN) [29], a new Internet architecture, identifies the contents by their names instead of their relative location (i.e., the IP addresses). This characteristic (i.e., name-based content identification and routing) brings another important architectural advantage of NDN - the in-network data caching that augment the sharing capacity of the nodes. Additionally, NDN forwarding plane is stateful and adaptive [26], giving this architecture the capacity of controlling and avoiding packet loop.

A context-aware NDN-based routing and forwarding mechanism for VANET is proposed in this paper. The context-awareness is based on the application type and the communication model in use. Additionally, the model distinguishes pull- and push-based messages. We propose a hybrid (geographic and topology-based) routing model, in the sense that the model will leverage all overheard packets to extract topological information and the geographical location of the node will be used to forward packet to specific nodes in the network. To further avoid or reduce the need of flooding, a mobility prediction algorithm will be used. The main task of the mentioned algorithm is to predict routes of the moving nodes, avoiding frequent broadcast of beacon messages. The internals of the mobility prediction mechanism are not discussed here. Whereas the routing mechanism will be responsible of proactively maintaining an updated Forwarding Information Base (FIB) for a relatively long-term base, the proposed forwarding strategy will maintain updated the list of neighbors and will take advantage of in-network data caching to avoid flooding. Differently from studies such as [8], which allow caching of all unsolicited Data, we select unsolicited Data based on their application type: push-based, safety, and all short-lived messages are not cached.

To attain these objectives, the following NDN main structures are modified: Pending Interest table (PIT) to include the previous node forwarding the packet; the FIB, to include Node Mobility Status Information - NMSI (i.e., the node ID, node speed, node geographical coordinates, direction, and timestamp); the NDNLPv2 [16] packet (LpPacket) headers are extended to include the node mobility status information (for Interest and Data packets). This information is extracted in each node receiving the packet and is used to update the list of neighbors; a link adaptation layer is proposed to incorporate the specificities of the ad hoc vehicular network.

The remaining of this paper is organized as follows: Sect. 2 presents the related work. Section 3 presents the model design including the proposed mechanism for content discovery, the forwarding strategy, and the routing protocol. Section 5 presents the summary and discussion of contributions.

2   Related Work

The high mobility of VANET nodes results in an highly dynamic topology and intermittent connectivity. These are the main constraints that make it difficult or even infeasible to run a routing protocol in VANET [8]. Several efforts, however, have been put forward to overcome such difficulties and develop routing solutions for VANET.

Authors in [8] use a complex mapping of geofaces and geographical areas, where to forward the Interests towards the corresponding contents. Having reached the geographical area, the Interest is then flooded.

Authors in [28] propose a proactive opportunistic routing mechanism that keeps track of content locations using last encounter information location. The vehicles periodically advertise to one-hop neighbors to collect the summary of all contents in the node. The same authors propose in [24], a vehicular information network architecture with a push-based mechanism, for content dissemination. The study also proposes a naming scheme and a proactive location-based routing.

Taking advantage of computing, caching and communicating vehicle capabilities, [15] proposed a routing mechanism that confines the broadcast of Interest/Data to most important vehicles. In this way, the information is be available within the vehicles with higher centrality score. To identify important vehicles, which are responsible for efficient content distribution, the authors use their previously proposed mechanisms that enable each vehicle to autonomously find its own importance in the network.

In [12], the authors propose a routing protocol that initially floods the network to populate FIB, and then forwards packets based on the previously populated FIB. This mechanism is somehow similar to the solution proposed by [20] for wired networks. An Interest is periodically broadcasted in order to discover new paths and new content sources. The proposed solution identifies nodes by their MAC address, and in [13] they extend the previous solution, extracting the Face MAC address from the NDN strategy layer. In [9], the same authors propose a V2I communication architecture also based on NDN, which is then extended to support V2V communications. The proposed solution works in two different routing approaches, one where requests are forwarded to the RSU and another where the RSU is defined as a backup network component. Additionally, they propose in [10], a routing protocol that assumes each vehicle having a set of unidirectional antennas, used in unicast transmissions to forward the messages in a specific direction. To support vehicle mobility, the solution includes a forwarding mechanism that uses timers in each vehicle to identify unsatisfied requests. When a timer elapses, the vehicle re-transmits its request through another path. In [11] they present the details of [10], including its performance evaluation.

A routing protocol is proposed in [23]. The solution combines data-name-based routing and host-ID-based routing to address the mobility issue and the broadcast storm problem from NDN flooding solutions. In the referred work, nodes request data by their content name, then, knowing the content location, the ID-based routing is triggered. Using the corresponding position the protocol computes the route towards the destination host. When the content provider is unknown, a flooding process takes place.

In [4] a protocol that reduces broadcast storm by using a defer timer (packet holding time) is proposed. The protocol prioritizes Interest transmissions among neighbor nodes, avoiding packet re-transmissions.

In [6], the authors propose a model in which vehicles periodically notify neighbors about their cached content and maintain a local table containing neighbors' cached contents. When a route disruption occurs, the solution resort to a distance prediction algorithm to calculate the next hop. The presented protocol is topology-based and works proactively.

A reactive routing protocol is presented in [27]. The proposed solution categorizes Information-Centric Networking (ICN) content into: 1) popular public data services, 2) popular private data services, and 3) unpopular data services. Arguing that for each of these categories, it may be necessary to choose an appropriate routing design, the authors designed a Bloom Filter (BF) based routing protocol for popular data services (1 and 2). The nodes in the corresponding clusters periodically summarize the content to create their own BF (content digests), which are then used to advertise (by flooding) the local content of the partition where they belong to.

As shown above, the majority of these proposals resort to flooding for content discovery, dissemination, and for recovering from route disruption. Additionally, they resort to constant broadcast of beacon messages to create and maintain a list of neighbors. To maintain an updated list of neighbors a protocol should increase the frequency of beacon broadcast, which results in an increased network traffic, and consequently collisions and delays in delivering packets.

The result of a literature review performed in [21] indicates that although some proposals applied NDN-based routing and forwarding for VANET, none of the surveyed solutions considers the different network scenarios (e.g., highway, rural or urban environment), the different applications (e.g., safety/emergency, efficiency or entertainment) and do not adapt the solution to the network characteristics where the model is applied, i.e., they are not context-aware. In addition, none of them included mobility prediction to help updating the list of neighbors and in selecting better relay nodes for packet forwarding, in order to avoid or reduce broadcast. Moreover, these solutions do not leverage the in-network data caching for routing decisions. Actually, the study by [6] considers the use of in-network caching for content discovery but, does so by allowing each vehicle in the network to perform flooding, requesting each other node to share the list of their cached content, a solution that can overload the network traffic.

Table 1 presents the comparison summary of state-of-the-art solution, and the main difference with the solution proposed in this work.

Table 1. Main contributions and differences from state-of-the-art solutions

Propriety	References	Existing solution	Our contributions
Content discovery	[4, 10, 12, 13, 15, 23, 24, 27, 28]	Flooding	Flooding (rural scenario); RSU beaconing (urban scenario), flood if no route to RSU, and no corresponding entry in *Cached Content Table* (CCT)
	[9]	Flooding (decentralized approach); RSU beaconing (centralized approach), wait if no route to RSU or to the content source	
Neighbor status	[4, 10, 12, 13, 15, 23, 24, 27, 28]	Maintained by 1-hop beacon broadcast, from all nodes	Maintained by 3-hop beacon broadcast, from RSU (urban scenario), and 1-hop beacon broadcast from all nodes (rural scenario). Normal traffic leveraged to gather neighbor status, by including control information onto the Interest/Data NDNLP packet header
Routing enhance-ment feature	[6]	Caching (periodic beacon broadcast from 1-hop nodes, to share cached content list), and distance prediction method (reference to this method is unreachable)	Caching (Sharing of cached content list from any node), and mobility prediction
Context awareness	[9]	Communication mode (V2V, V2I)	Dissemination mode (push-, pull-based); application type (active safety, efficiency, comfort, interactive-entertainment); network density (rural, urban); and communication model (V2V, V2I)
Content caching	[7]	Cache all content (including all unsolicited Data)	Selective unsolicited Data caching, depending on application type (*drops*: all push-based, *caches*: (1) solicited safety, (2) comfort, and (3) some long-lived interactive-entertainment application)
Beacon broadcast	All	Periodic (frequent) from all nodes	Periodic (less frequent) from all nodes (rural scenario), only RSU (urban scenario). All overheard traffic (not dedicated beacons) leveraged to distribute control information, and reduce the frequency of beacon broadcast

3 Proposed Model Design

In this work, a context-aware routing and forwarding model designed to take mobility prediction in consideration, is proposed. The main goal is to forward packets to specific nodes which trajectories are known, and avoid broadcast whenever possible. In-network content caching is also explored by means of an process initiated by the RSU, in which all nodes along the forwarding path, from the RSU to the content source, share their list of cached content.

The context-awareness is firstly based on the type of communication (i.e., pull- or push-based). Based on the classification adapted from [5], four classes of VANET applications are considered: active safety, efficiency, comfort and interactive-entertainment. These classes are grouped by communication model (i.e., V2I or V2V), region of interest (i.e., small, medium or large), delay sensitivity (i.e., delay tolerant/sensitive), frequency of message transmission, traffic volume, and content validity period. Communication requirements for each of the aforementioned grouping classes are different, thus requiring different routing/forwarding mechanisms.

3.1 Main Modifications to the NDN Structures

The wireless channel is broadcast-based by nature, i.e., each node within the communication range of the sender node will overhear the sent packets. This characteristic can be exploited to reduce the need of broadcast in updating the list of neighbors, as it is done by several state-of-the-art studies, and to learn about new content sources. In order to take advantage of the overheard packets, all NDN packets will be extended to carry additional (optional) control information (i.e., the node mobility status information, mentioned earlier). The inclusion of this information is optional in the sense that whenever necessary, the model can fallback to the normal NDN operational mode, flooding the network to discover new neighbors and new content sources. This information is appended to all (Interest and Data) NDNLP packet header, see Fig. 1a, instead of modifying the network layer packet header.

In wired NDN, when a solicited Data is received, PIT is searched in order to find the Face where to forward this Data to. The Face unambiguously identifies the next hop where the packet should be forwarded to. VANET is essentially based on wireless communications. In this network when a node sends a given packet, the packet is overheard by all nodes within the sender's communication range. Thus, the Face-based communication mechanism does not work for wireless channel. To overcome this, and be able to identify the node where to forward the packet to, the ID of the node is included in the corresponding PIT entry, alongside the Face, see Fig. 1b. A good candidate for node identification is the Mac address of the Faces (i.e., net devices) installed on these nodes. Some representative studies that use MAC addresses to identify nodes, include [9,13,14,17].

Similarly, FIB is extended with the NMSI, see Fig. 1b, that will lately be updated by a mobility prediction algorithm - a topic for future work.

Figure 1 shows how the aforementioned three structures are modified.

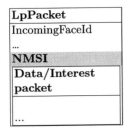
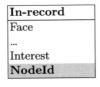

(a) Inclusion of NMSI into   (b) Inclusion of Node ID   (c) Inclusion of NMSI into
LpPacket header   into PIT's In-Record field   FIB's NextHop field

Fig. 1. Modifications to the NDN structures

A new table - Cached Content Table (CCT) - is added to the NDN structure. The table is used in each node to catalog all cached Data, complementing the CS functionality. Each CCT entry is composed by the Data prefix and the node mobility status information. The node mobility status information refers to the status of the last node from where the packet was received.

Given that NDN is designed for wired networks, besides the aforementioned modifications and to complement them, a link adaptation layer between the network layer (NDN) and the Data-link layer is developed, in order to accommodate the specificities of VANET. This adaptation layer is responsible for building and maintaining the list of neighbor, from all the overheard packets, as explained latter. In addition, the NMSI is attached to the outgoing packets at this layer.

3.2   Content Discovery Mechanism

When FIB in each node is empty, or when new content still not registered in FIB is solicited, a content discovery process takes place. This process populates FIB differently for rural and urban environments.

Discovery in Urban Environments. Urban environments are characterized by static infrastructures, which can be the Road-side Unit (RSU) or Base Stations (BS). The geographical location of these nodes are persistently stored in the FIB of all nodes in the network.

Periodically, each RSU broadcasts a beacon message to query new content sources. On response to this beacon, the content sources advertise their contents via a special packet - sData, which is sent back to the RSU. sData is destined to the RSU but all the intermediate nodes receiving this packet register the announced prefix and the list of cached content from the previous node, and then append their own list of cached contents. That is, the in-network caching is leveraged but, instead of allowing all vehicles to broadcast their list of cached content, as proposed in [6], for instance, a request-based mechanism from the RSU is adopted and only the vehicles on the path from the content source to the RSU will be allowed to share their list of cached contents.

The periodicity of the RSU beacon broadcast will be defined based on the periodicity of the updates performed by the mobility prediction algorithm. This way, the frequency of broadcast will be fixed lower than the state-of-the-art solutions.

Discovery in Rural Environments. Rural and other environments not equipped with static nodes, can not efficiently benefit from the mechanism proposed for the urban ones. In these environments a content source producing a new content will immediately announce this content. Additionally, content sources announce content whenever a predefined timer elapses. The timer is set to an ideal value resulting from the experiments, and it will be based on the periodicity of the RSU beacon broadcast. For instance, the timer can be equal to 3 times de periodicity of beacon broadcast. If a packet form RSU is not received during 3 times the fixed periodicity of RSU broadcast, vehicles in rural environment announce their prefixes.

3.3   Forwarding Strategy

For packet forwarding, NDN forwarding plane uses the information stored in FIB. However, differently form TCP/IP networks, NDN forwarding plane is stateful and intelligent, in the sense that it is able to make per node decisions about the preference and the usage of existing routes based on their performance and status. Although NDN-based local networks can work without a routing protocol given the intelligence of the forwarding plane - which can detect and recover by itself from any situation of network failure [29] - the need for routing is exhaustively investigated and justified in [25]. In our design, depending on the message type, the forwarding plane can process the received message without using routing, as explained in the next sections.

The following sections present incoming Data and incoming Interest processing in each NDN node.

Processing for Incoming Data. As presented in Algorithm 1, on packet reception the model verifies if it is a solicited Data or not. Unsolicited Data can be either an overheard pull-based or push-based message. The push-based messages belongs to the safety/emergency class, and in this case the Data is broadcasted after its validity is verified. This type of messages is not processed in PIT or FIB, and is not stored in cache. The reasoning behind this, is the fact that these messages are urgent and short-lived.

Efficiency related messages are generally solicited and also short-lived, therefore are broadcasted and not stored in cache. Comfort and Interactive-entertainment related messages are processed as usual in NDN. In addition, we propose the registration of the received Data in the CCT. This way, future requests for the same Data can be redirected to the nodes holding the Data, based on the information held by this table.

Other unsolicited Data, but not push-based, is stored in cache only if it is classified as long-lived. Otherwise, the Data is discarded.

Algorithm 1: Incoming Data processing

Input   : destId: *Next hop node ID*;
             NMSI: *Node Mobility Status Information*

1 **if** *(Push-based Data)* **then**
2 | **if** *(Data still valid)* **then**
3 | | Broadcast (Data)
4 | **else**
5 | | Discard_Data ()

6 **else**
7 | **if** *(Corresponding Interest exists in PIT)* **then**
8 | | **if** *(Efficiency-related Data)* **then**
9 | | | Broadcast (Data)
10 | | **else**
11 | | | Forward (Data, destId)
12 | | | Add_To_CS (Data)
13 | | | Update_CCT (Data-Prefix, NMSI)

14 | **else**
15 | | **if** *(Long-lived Data)* **then**
16 | | | Add_To_CS (Data)
17 | | | Update_CCT (Data-Prefix, NMSI)
18 | | **else**
19 | | | Discard_Data ()

We propose a scheme where all safety-related content, which is also push-based, will be based on the following prefix:

/push-based/info-type/sender-ID/sender-geo-coordinates/

The first component is used to identify the type of content as being push-based, and destined to broadcast. There can be different types of push-based content. For instance, besides the active safety content there is the content related to road efficiency. The latter is longer-lived than the former, thus, they can be treated differently. This is the reasoning behind the distinction provided by the second component. The third component is the identification of the sender, and the last component is the geographical location of the sender. It is important to have the geographical coordinates of the sender, given that safety content is location-dependent. The broadcast information is only important a hundreds of meters away from the location where it has been sent (i.e., it has a medium region of interest), therefore the model fixes the hop limit to 1.

Processing for Incoming Interest. When an Interest is received, a CS lookup procedure takes place like in the standard NDN. When no corresponding Data is found in CS, a PIT lookup procedure is performed. If a PIT entry exists but from a different incoming Face, the new request is aggregated to the existing pending Interest. If no pending Interest is found, the new Interest is added to PIT. If the Interest is related to the efficiency application class, then it is broadcasted, as it deals with the delay-sensitive content.

If the received packet is related to the comfort or interactive-entertainment application class, then a FIB match is performed. In case that the Interest matches a FIB entry, it is forwarded using the predicted routes, as presented in Sect. 3.4. Otherwise, its corresponding content still needs to be discovered. Apart the mechanism presented in Sect. 3.2, when a new content discovery is to be performed, the following procedure takes place.

In urban environments and for comfort and interactive-entertainment applications classes, the model follows a mechanism similar to the proposed in [9], where the Interest is forwarded towards the RSU which is supposed to have a broader knowledge about other existing routes. However, differently from that study, our solution does not awaits the creation of FIB entry, it broadcasts the Interest. Before the Interest is broadcasted however, a last feature is explored - the usage of known cached contents from other nodes. In this procedure, a CCT lookup is performed and when a match is found the Interest is forwarded accordingly. When no match is found, the Interest is broadcasted.

Algorithm 2 describes the intermediate node processing for an incoming Interest.

3.4   Routing Protocol

Routing protocols are responsible for initiating and maintaining routes to facilitate multi-hop communication. Routing populates and keeps FIB updated.

Several forwarding proposals for NDN-based VANET are based on flooding (blind flooding), and include a particular scheme to control the rebroadcast, e.g., resorting to distances to the content provider, and timers to defer the subsequent broadcast. This mechanism have the advantage of simplicity, does not require the knowledge about the neighbor nodes, and does not require the usage of FIB. However, it generally results in problems such as the traffic congestion, packet collisions, or delivery delays due to the broadcast storm problem [7,19,22].

A relatively more intelligent alternative apart the broadcast and the use of defer timers and distances, is the identification and selection of possible relay nodes by using unicast communications [2,3,9,11,12,17]. This approach requires an updated knowledge of the node's neighbors geographical location, from which the better relay between the current node and the content source can be selected. This mechanism can reduce the traffic congestion, collision and delivery delays, as demonstrated in [1], for specific case of MANET. However, some kind of beacon broadcast is still necessary to maintain an updated list of the neighborhood, as used by the majority of state-of-the-art proposals, see Table 1. We claim, as

---

Algorithm 2: Incoming Interest processing

Input : prevId: *Previous node ID*;
destId: *Next hop node ID*;

1 **if** *(Data exists in CS)* **then**
2 | *ReturnToRequester* (Data, destId)

3 **else**
4 | **if** *(Interest exists in PIT)* **then**
5 | | *Aggregate* (Interest)

6 | **else**
7 | | *AddToPITEntry* (Interest, prevId)
8 | | **if** *(Efficiency-related Interest)* **then**
9 | | | *Broadcast* (Interest)

10 | **else**
11 | | **if** *(Interest matches FIB entry)* **then**
12 | | | *Forward* (Interest, destId)

13 | | **else**
14 | | | **if** *(Data-prefix in CCT)* **then**
15 | | | | *Forward* (Interest, destId)

16 | | | **else**
17 | | | | **if** *Urban scenario* **then**
18 | | | | | *Forward_To_RSU* (Interest, destId)

19 | | | | **else**
20 | | | | | *Broadcast* (Interest)

---

a hypothesis, that this issue can be mitigated by using some alternative mechanisms such as the mobility prediction and/or by leveraging the overheard packets to extract the neighborhood-related information (see Sect. 3.1), as proposed in this work.

Whenever an intermediate good candidate for relay exists, it will be selected to forward the messages.

Algorithm 3 describes the routing process in place on vehicles and on the RSU. As explained in Sect. 3.2, in urban environments the RSU broadcast beacon messages for content discovery. On response of the beacon message, or on a self initiated content announcement from the content source in rural environment, the content sources send back a special Data (sData) that carries an Prefix Announcement (PA). If a packet holding the prefix announcement is received in a node, a FIB entry is created or updated. As referred earlier, besides the PA, FIB will also include the NMSI which for this case is related to the content source (NMSI-CS). If the received Data packet is unsolicited and does not include a PA, then a data prefix is extracted from this new packet and a FIB entry is created. In this latter case, the NMSI is related to the intermediate node from which the packet was received (NMSI-IN).

A periodic time triggered mobility prediction process takes place in each node. Neighbors are mobile nodes and the model should avoid beacon broadcast whenever possible. Therefore, a Short-Term Mobility Prediction (STMPA) to track and update the current location of a neighbor is used. Additionally, a Long-Term Mobility Prediction (LTMPA) - deployed only on static nodes, example the RSU - is used to track the trajectory of vehicles.

Routes in FIB are periodically updated by: 1) the mobility prediction algorithm; 2) the updates from the RSU periodic beacon broadcast process; and 3) from the control information extracted from all overheard packets, in each node.

Algorithm 3: Routing process

Input   : PA; NMSI-CS; NMSI-IN; DP: *Data-Prefix*;

1 **if** *(New packet received)* **then**
2   **if** *(packet holds a Prefix Announcement)* **then**
3   ⌊ *CreateOrUpdateFIB* (PA, NMSI-CS)
4   **else**
5   ⌊ *CreateOrUpdateFIB* (DP, NMSI-IN)
6   *ExtractNeighborhoodInfo* ()
7   *UpdateListNeighbors* (NMSI-IN)

   // Time triggered mobility prediction
8 **if** *(processing for vehicles)* **then**
9   *UpdateListNeighbors* (NMSI-IN, *STMPA*)
10   *UpdateFIBNext-Hops* (NMSI-IN, *STMPA*)
11 **else if** *(processing for RSU)* **then**
12   *UpdateFIBNext-Hops* (NMSI-CS, *LTMPA*)

---

4   Security Considerations

IP-based networks provide security by creating and securing the point-to-point channel between the hosts. That is, instead of the packets, the communicating channel is secured. NDN, on the other hand, have security built into the network layer. Each content producer includes its signature and other authentication information in each Data packet before sending it through the network. That is, protection and trust are embedded in the Data packet [29]. The consumer receiving the Data verifies and accepts the Data if the signature is authentic. The Data security and integrity in the proposed model relays on this mechanism. Our model allows intermediate nodes to extract the list of cached content of the previous node, from the received Data. When an intermediate node receives a Data, it copies the received Data to extract the aforementioned list, then it includes its own list. It encapsulates the copied Data including the list of cached content in a new Data packet, and then it signs and authenticate the packet before sending it back into the network. By allowing nodes to modify the Data packets in order to include their list of cached content, our model is prone to attacks, where a malicious node can mislead the network by injecting false pair of PA and NMSI, redirecting the network traffic. As mentioned, the solution adopted in this work is to force each node that modifies the received Data packet to sign and authenticate the packet after the inclusion of its own list of cached content, encapsulating the Data from the previous node. We highlight that only the Data sent by content source in response of the RSU periodic broadcast can be modified as described above in this section.

5   Summary and Discussion of Contributions

The model is currently being evaluated as first step, by means of simulation. ndnSIM and Simulation of Urban MObility (SUMO) were selected to be used for simulations. The simulation results are extracted and statistically analyzed, using either MATLAB or R environment. The results are not included in the present paper, and will be presented in future. Our intention here is to present the idea under development.

In summary, the changes proposed to the NDN structure are: a) Inclusion of a *link adaptation layer*: to adapt the NDN architecture from its wired nature to wireless and ad hoc, the base for vehicular communications. This layer is responsible on maintaining the neighborhood list, and to piggyback NMSI to the outgoing packets; b) *the CCT*: to allow to catalog cached content of other nodes; c) *inclusion of nodes ID*: to allow the identification of wireless nodes, which are not well identified by the Face system; d) *the node mobility status information (NMSI)*: included into the NDNLP packet headers, used for mobility tracking; e) *fields included in PIT and FIB*: used in parallel with NMSI and node ID, to forward messages to specific nodes, to avoid the need of flooding. With this proposal we expect an overall improved performance of VANET, at a cost of an increased computational overhead due to the added complexity for the processing of all overheard packets, which is performed to extract neighborhood information and predict the location and the nodes's trajectories.

References

1. Amadeo, M., Campolo, C., Molinaro, A.: Forwarding strategies in named data wireless ad hoc networks. J. Netw. Comput. Appl. **50**(C), 148–158 (2015). https://doi.org/10.1016/j.jnca.2014.06.007
2. Amadeo, M., Molinaro, A., Ruggeri, G.: E-CHANET: routing, forwarding and transport in information-centric multihop wireless networks. Comput. Commun. **36**(7), 792–803 (2013). https://doi.org/10.1016/j.comcom.2013.01.006
3. Angius, F., Gerla, M., Pau, G.: BLOOGO: BLOOm filter based GOssip algorithm for wireless NDN. In: Proceedings of the 1st ACM Workshop on Emerging Name-Oriented Mobile Networking Design - Architecture, Algorithms, and Applications, NoM 2012, pp. 25–30. Association for Computing Machinery, New York (2012). https://doi.org/10.1145/2248361.2248369

4. Coutinho, R., Boukerche, A., Yu, X.: A novel location-based content distribution protocol for vehicular named-data networks. In: 2018 IEEE Symposium on Computers and Communications (ISCC), pp. 01007–01012 (2018). https://doi.org/10.1109/ISCC.2018.8538481

5. Cunha, F., et al.: Data communication in VANETs: protocols, applications and challenges. Ad Hoc Netw. **44**, 90–103 (2016). https://doi.org/10.1016/j.adhoc.2016.02.017

6. Duan, M., Zhang, C., Li, Y., Xu, W., Ji, X., Liu, B.: Neighbor cache explore routing protocol for VANET based on trajectory prediction. In: 2018 IEEE 3rd Advanced Information Technology, Electronic and Automation Control Conference (IAEAC), pp. 771–776 (2018). https://doi.org/10.1109/IAEAC.2018.8577903

7. Grassi, G., Pesavento, D., Pau, G., Vuyyuru, R., Wakikawa, R., Zhang, L.: VANET via named data networking. In: 2014 IEEE Conference on Computer Communications Workshops (INFOCOM WKSHPS), pp. 410–415, April 2014. https://doi.org/10.1109/INFOCOMW.2014.6849267

8. Grassi, G., Pesavento, D., Pau, G., Zhang, L., Fdida, S.: Navigo: interest forwarding by geolocations in vehicular named data networking. In: 2015 IEEE 16th International Symposium on "A World of Wireless, Mobile and Multimedia Networks" (WoWMoM), Los Alamitos, CA, USA, pp. 1–10. IEEE Computer Society, June 2015. https://doi.org/10.1109/WoWMoM.2015.7158165

9. Kalogeiton, E., Braun, T.: Infrastructure-assisted communication for NDN-VANETs. In: 2018 IEEE 19th International Symposium on "A World of Wireless, Mobile and Multimedia Networks" (WoWMoM), pp. 1–10, June 2018. https://doi.org/10.1109/WoWMoM.2018.8449740

10. Kalogeiton, E., Iapello, D., Braun, T.: A geographical aware routing protocol using directional antennas for NDN-VANETs. In: 2019 IEEE 44th Conference on Local Computer Networks (LCN), pp. 133–136, October 2019. https://doi.org/10.1109/LCN44214.2019.8990760

11. Kalogeiton, E., Iapello, D., Braun, T.: Equipping NDN-VANETs with directional antennas for efficient content retrieval. In: 2020 IEEE 17th Annual Consumer Communications Networking Conference (CCNC), pp. 1–8 (2020). https://doi.org/10.1109/CCNC46108.2020.9045198

12. Kalogeiton, E., Kolonko, T., Braun, T.: A multihop and multipath routing protocol using NDN for VANETs. In: 2017 16th Annual Mediterranean Ad Hoc Networking Workshop (Med-Hoc-Net), pp. 1–8, June 2017. https://doi.org/10.1109/MedHocNet.2017.8001640

13. Kalogeiton, E., Kolonko, T., Braun, T.: A topology-oblivious routing protocol for NDN-VANETs. Ann. Telecommun. **73**(9), 577–587 (2018). https://doi.org/10.1007/s12243-018-0661-4

14. Kato, T., Minh, N.Q., Yamamoto, R., Ohzahata, S.: How to implement NDN MANET over ndnSIM simulator. In: 2018 IEEE 4th International Conference on Computer and Communications (ICCC). pp. 451–456, December 2018. https://doi.org/10.1109/CompComm.2018.8780792

15. Khan, J.A., Ghamri-Doudane, Y.: STRIVE: socially-aware three-tier routing in information-centric vehicular environment. In: 2016 IEEE Global Communications Conference (GLOBECOM), pp. 1–7, December 2016. https://doi.org/10.1109/GLOCOM.2016.7842301

16. NFD Development Team: NDN Link Protocol v2 (NDNLPv2), January 2021. https://redmine.named-data.net/projects/nfd/wiki/NDNLPv2

17. Park, C.M., Rehman, R.A., Tran-Dinh, H., Kim, B.S.: Enhanced protocol for wireless content-centric network. In: Computer Science & Information Technology, vol. 6, May 2016. https://doi.org/10.5121/csit.2016.60614

18. Perallos, A., Hernandez-Jayo, U., Onieva, E., Zuazola, I.J.G.: Intelligent Transport Systems: Technologies and Applications. Wiley, Chichester (2015)

19. Pereira, A., Nicolau, M., Costa, A., Macedo, J., Santos, A.: Named data for mobile AdHoc networks. In: Intelligent Environments (2016). https://doi.org/10.3233/978-1-61499-690-3-288

20. Shi, J., Newberry, E., Zhang, B.: On broadcast-based self-learning in named data networking. In: 2017 IFIP Networking Conference (IFIP Networking) and Workshops, pp. 1–9 (2017). https://doi.org/10.23919/IFIPNetworking.2017.8264832

21. Silva, E., Macedo, J., Costa, A.: Systematic literature review on the improvement of VANET by NDN. Technical report, Algorithm Centre - University of Minho, June 2021

22. Wang, L., Afanasyev, A., Kuntz, R., Vuyyuru, R., Wakikawa, R., Zhang, L.: Rapid traffic information dissemination using named data. In: Proceedings of the 1st ACM Workshop on Emerging Name-Oriented Mobile Networking Design - Architecture, Algorithms, and Applications, NoM 2012, pp. 7–12. Association for Computing Machinery, New York (2012). https://doi.org/10.1145/2248361.2248365

23. Xu, W., Ji, X., Zhang, C., Liu, B.: NIHR: name/ID hybrid routing in information-centric VANET. In: 2020 IEEE Wireless Communications and Networking Conference (WCNC), pp. 1–7 (2020). https://doi.org/10.1109/WCNC45663.2020.9120459

24. Yan, Z., Zeadally, S., Park, Y.: A novel vehicular information network architecture based on named data networking (NDN). IEEE Internet Things J. 1(6), 525–532 (2014). https://doi.org/10.1109/JIOT.2014.2354294

25. Yi, C., Abraham, J., Afanasyev, A., Wang, L., Zhang, B., Zhang, L.: On the role of routing in named data networking. In: Proceedings of the 1st ACM Conference on Information-Centric Networking, ACM-ICN 2014, pp. 27–36. Association for Computing Machinery, New York (2014). https://doi.org/10.1145/2660129.2660140

26. Yi, C., Afanasyev, A., Moiseenko, I., Wang, L., Zhang, B., Zhang, L.: A case for stateful forwarding plane. Comput. Commun. 36(7), 779–791 (2013). https://doi.org/10.1016/j.comcom.2013.01.005

27. Yu, Y., Li, X., Gerla, M., Sanadidi, M.Y.: Scalable VANET content routing using hierarchical bloom filters. In: 2013 9th International Wireless Communications and Mobile Computing Conference (IWCMC), pp. 1629–1634 (2013)

28. Yu, Y.T., Li, Y., Ma, X., Shang, W., Sanadidi, M., Gerla, M.: Scalable opportunistic VANET content routing with encounter information. In: 2013 21st IEEE International Conference on Network Protocols (ICNP), pp. 1–6, October 2013. https://doi.org/10.1109/ICNP.2013.6733679

29. Zhang, L., et al.: Named data networking. Comput. Commun. Rev. 44(3), 66–73 (2014). https://doi.org/10.1016/j.cosrev.2016.01.001

A Novel Adaptive Hello Mechanism Based Geographic Routing Protocol for FANETs

Bo Zheng[1]([✉]), Kun Zhuo[1], Hua-Xin Wu[2], and Hengyang Zhang[1]

[1] Information and Navigation Institute, Air Force Engineering University, Xi'an 710077, China
zbkgd@163.com
[2] Radar NCO School, Air Force Early Warning Academy, Wuhan 430019, China

Abstract. In geographic routing protocols for flying Ad hoc networks (FANETs), unmanned aerial vehicles need to maintain real-time positions of their one-hop neighbor nodes to make effective routing decisions. Periodic broadcasting of Hello packets that involve real-time geographic position coordinates of nodes itself is a popular method to maintain neighbor information table. However, the traditional periodic Hello mechanism ignores node mobility, network connectivity and traffic type, thus causes temporary communication blindness (TCB). To address this problem, an adaptive Hello mechanism (AHM) for geographic routing is proposed in this paper. The Hello period of working nodes is calculated according to the real-time relative characteristic values between the node and its upstream node, and the Hello period of idle nodes adopts a fixed value according to the movement characteristics relative to all neighbor nodes. Moreover, the AHM is integrated into the widely-used greedy perimeter stateless routing (GPSR) protocol, and is compared with the original GPSR in simulation. The results show that AHM significantly mitigates the TCB problem and gains a high packet successful transmission rate without producing more routing overhead.

Keywords: Flying Ad hoc network · Geographic routing · Adaptive Hello mechanism · Temporary communication blindness · Successful transmission rate

1 Introduction

Recently, Unmanned Aerial Vehicles (UAVs) with the characteristic of low cost, strong robustness, various applications etc., have become a high-tech with rapid growth, and attracted much attention in both military and civil fields. Especially, the multi-UAV system, which has the advantages of good scalability, high invulnerability and high efficiency, etc., can play an important role in multiple military operations, such as battlefield reconnaissance, border patrolling, communication relay, precision strike, etc. A flexible, dynamic, distributed, and robust communication network for multi-UAV is the basis and premise for task coordination between UAVs. Flying Ad hoc Network (FANET) is the core technology for constructing UAV communication networks [1, 2]. Not relying on prebuilt communication infrastructures, it can transmit multiple kinds of information between UAVs, such as control instruction, situational awareness, and

© ICST Institute for Computer Sciences, Social Informatics and Telecommunications Engineering 2022
Published by Springer Nature Switzerland AG 2022. All Rights Reserved
W. Bao et al. (Eds.): ADHOCNETS 2021/TridentCom 2021, LNICST 428, pp. 33–45, 2022.
https://doi.org/10.1007/978-3-030-98005-4_3

reconnaissance intelligence, etc., through aeronautical wireless channel, thus forming a multi-hop, self-organized, temporary and distributed network. Several key technologies, such as dynamic topology control and routing protocol, etc., are used in FANET to achieve the interconnection of multiple UAVs [3]. It can not only extend the communication coverage, provide high-reliability and high-robustness communication links, but also improve the efficiency of task execution for UAVs.

FANET is a special form of mobile Ad hoc network (MANET), and routing protocol is responsible for discovering one or more paths and delivering packets from source to destination through a multi-hop path [4]. Till now, a large number of routing protocols have been used in FANETs, such as, DSDV, OLSR, DSR, AODV, TORA, and so on [5, 6]. Among these routing protocols, geographic routing protocols have received much attention due to their substantial advantages as compared to topology based routing protocols [7–10]. Geographic routing protocols have been shown to be efficient with accurate position information in static topology networks. However, in situations where nodes are mobile, the local topology rarely remains static. Hence, it is necessary that each node periodically broadcasts its up-dated location information to all of its neighbors. These position update packets are usually referred to as Hello information. In most geographic routing protocols, Hello packets are broadcast periodically for maintaining a neighbor table at each node. Periodic Hello mechanism has several drawbacks: (1) In the mobile scenarios, fixed period Hello mechanism will bring out temporary communication blindness (TCB) problem and will cause massive data packets loss; (2) Reception and processing of Hello packets consumes energy which is wasteful in idle nodes; (3) Hello packets may collide with data packets.

The periodic Hello mechanism for MANETs stems from the Hello protocol in OSPF version 2 and is adopted by most geographic routing protocols. Chakeres et al. in [11] studied Hello protocol in 802.11 ad-hoc networks and suggested that the lifetime for which a neighbor entry should be 2 times the Hello interval for optimal throughput in mobile scenarios. Han et al. in [12] proposed an adaptive Hello scheme to save energy by suppressing unnecessary Hello information. Mahmud et al. in [13] also proposed an energy efficient Hello scheme based on some mission-related information to save energy for FANET routing protocols. Hernandez-Cons et al. in [14] proposed an adaptive Hello mechanism based on the link change rate. Park et al. in [15] proposed a Hello mechanism where the Hello interval is determined by node speed and transmission range.

In this paper, we propose a novel adaptive Hello mechanism (AHM) for geographic routing protocols to mitigate the drawbacks of the periodic Hello mechanism in FANETs. In the AHM, the Hello period of working nodes is calculated according to the real-time relative characteristic values between the node and its upstream node, and the Hello period of idle nodes adopts a fixed value according to the movement characteristics relative to all neighbor nodes. Furthermore, we integrate the AHM into the widely-used greedy perimeter stateless routing protocol (GPSR) [16] to verify its performance.

The rest of paper is organized as follows. In Sect. 2, we briefly describe the TCB problem. A detailed description of the AHM is provided in Sect. 3. The performance of AHM protocol is verified and analyzed through simulation in Sect. 4. Finally, Sect. 5 concludes the paper.

2 Description of TCB

In geographic routing protocols, when a source node needs to send a packet to a destination, it searches its neighbor table for a node that is closest to the destination. However, the selected node is often close to its communication boundary. The communication link between them may easily break down due to the movement of nodes, and the link stability is poor. Meanwhile, the upstream node does not recognize the situation timely that the link is broken. Thus, packets transmitted on the link will be lost. This phenomenon is defined as the TCB problem, and it is caused by high node dynamics, long Hello period and short node transmission range.

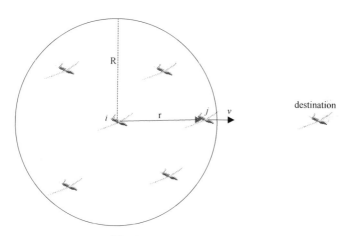

Fig. 1. The TCB problem.

The TCB is shown in Fig. 1. Hello period is assumed to set as 4s in geographic routing protocol. The upstream node i selects node j as the next hop node from its neighbor table at time 0 s, for it is the closest to the destination in its neighbor nodes. However, due to the movement of node i and node j, node j may move out from the transmission range of node i at time 2 s. If node i forwards a packet to node j after time 2 s, node j cannot receive the packet. And it is not recognized by node i at the time of forwarding the packet. In the periodic Hello mechanism, the lifetime of neighbor nodes in neighbor table is often set to be 2 times of the Hello period. Thus, node j will be removed from the neighbor table of node i at time 8s. During this period, TCB will lead to packet loss and affect the performance of the geographic routing protocol seriously.

3 Adaptive Hello Mechanism

3.1 Network Model

In this paper, FANET is modeled as a graph $G(V, E)$, where V is the set of nodes and E is the set of full-duplex, directed communication links. E is changing over time when nodes move. Each node has at least one transmitter and one receiver, and is represented by a unique identifier. Let $N(i)$ denote the set of neighbor nodes of node i. In addition, among the numerous characteristic variables, we assume that the characteristics of FANET are determined by the following factors: location, velocity, direction and transmission range of each UAV. Thus, a set of characteristic variables about any node i is denoted as a_i^t,

$$a_i^t = \left(\left(x_i^t, y_i^t \right), v_i^t, \theta_i^t, R_i \right) \tag{1}$$

Where $\left(x_i^t, y_i^t \right)$, v_i^t, and θ_i^t represents location, velocity and direction of node i at time t respectively, and R_i represents the transmission range of node i.

Node j is a neighbor node of node i, and a_{ij}^t is used to represent characteristic value of node j relative to node i. Hence, a_{ij}^t is the function of relative location, relative velocity and transmission range of node j and node i, namely,

$$a_{ij}^t = \left(\left(x_{ij}^t, y_{ij}^t \right), v_{ij}^t, \theta_{ij}^t, R_i, R_j \right) \tag{2}$$

Where $\left(x_{ij}^t, y_{ij}^t \right) = \left(x_j^t, y_j^t \right) - \left(x_i^t, y_i^t \right)$ represents the relative location vector between node j and node i at time t. v_{ij}^t and θ_{ij}^t represents the relative velocity and the relative direction between node j and node i at time t, respectively.

In this paper, we make the following assumptions:

(1) The transmission range of all nodes is equal. For any $i, j \in \forall (V)$, $R_i = R_j = R$;
(2) Each node i knows its position $\left(x_i^t, y_i^t \right)$, which can be acquired through GPS device or other types of positioning service;
(3) Each node in FANET makes random motion with a velocity valued randomly at $[0, v_{max}]$, and a direction valued randomly at $[0, 2\pi]$, and the velocity and direction are independent of each other. That is

$$v \sim U[0, v_{max}], p(v) = \frac{1}{v_{max}}, v \in [0, v_{max}] \tag{3}$$

$$\theta \sim U[0, 2\pi], p(\theta) = \frac{1}{2\pi}, \theta \in [0, 2\pi] \tag{4}$$

$$p(v, \theta) = p(v)p(\theta) \tag{5}$$

(4) Δt is defined as the Hello period of the Hello mechanism. We assume that in Eq. (3) to Eq. (5), v and θ are constant values in the short time interval Δt.

3.2 Theoretical Derivation of Adaptive Hello Period

According to the above assumptions, node j is a neighbor node of node i and makes movement relative to node i. The departure probability P is defined as the probability that node j moves out of the transmission range of node i after Δt. Intuitively, P is a monotonous increasing function of Δt. One Hello period Δt is corresponding to a certain probability $1 - P$ within which node j will stay in the transmission range of node i. So we can select a certain value of P and correspondingly calculate the value of Δt. If the value of P is smaller, the value of Δt is smaller correspondingly, and the TCB problem will be mitigated. If P is 0, the TCB problem will be eliminated. We select a certain value of P (defined as the threshold P_0 of departure probability) and calculate the variable Hello period Δt as follows.

As shown in Fig. 2, it is easy to know that the characteristic value of node j relative to node i at time t_0 is $a_{ij}^{t_0}$, namely

$$a_{ij}^{t_0} = \left(\left(x_{ij}^{t_0}, y_{ij}^{t_0} \right), v_{ij}^{t_0}, \theta_{ij}^{t_0}, R \right) \tag{6}$$

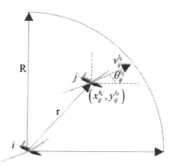

Fig. 2. Characteristic value $a_{ij}^{t_0}$ of node j relative to node i at time t_0.

The   position   of   node j after Δt can   be   expressed   as $\left(x_{ij}^{t_0} + v_{ij}^{t_0} \Delta t \cos \theta_{ij}^{t_0}, y_{ij}^{t_0} + v_{ij}^{t_0} \Delta t \sin \theta_{ij}^{t_0} \right)$.

So the condition that node j moves out from the transmission range of node i can be expressed as

$$\left(x_{ij}^{t_0} + v_{ij}^{t_0} \Delta t \cos \theta_{ij}^{t_0} \right)^2 + \left(y_{ij}^{t_0} + v_{ij}^{t_0} \Delta t \sin \theta_{ij}^{t_0} \right)^2 \geq R^2 \tag{7}$$

It can be derived from Eq. (7) that

$$\Delta t \geq \frac{-\gamma_{ij}^{t_0} + \sqrt{R^2 - \left(r_{ij}^{t_0} \right)^2 + \left(\gamma_{ij}^{t_0} \right)^2}}{v_{ij}^{t_0}} \tag{8}$$

Where

$$\gamma_{ij}^{t_0} = x_{ij}^{t_0} \cos \theta_{ij}^{t_0} + y_{ij}^{t_0} \sin \theta_{ij}^{t_0} \tag{9}$$

$$\left(r_{ij}^{t_0} \right)^2 = \left(x_{ij}^{t_0} \right)^2 + \left(y_{ij}^{t_0} \right)^2 \tag{10}$$

Where $r_{ij}^{t_0}$ represents the distance between node j and node i at time t_0.

From Eq. (8) to (10), Δt is a function of $\left(x_{ij}^{t0}, y_{ij}^{t0}\right)$, v_{ij}^{t0}, and θ_{ij}^{t0}. Given the relative position $\left(x_{ij}^{t0}, y_{ij}^{t0}\right)$ of the two nodes and the distributed density of v_{ij}^{t0} and θ_{ij}^{t0}, and with the derivation of the distributed density $p(\Delta t)$ of Δt, the threshold P_0 can be set. Therefore, it has

$$p(\Delta t) = \int_0^{\Delta t} p(t)dt = P_0 \tag{11}$$

The value of Hello period Δt can be obtained according to Eq. (11). However, it is very difficult to derive the value of Δt by this method, and the following method can be used to replace the above one.

The departure probability $p(\Delta t)$ that node j moves out of the transmission range of node i after Δt can be expressed as

$$p(\Delta t) = \iint_\Omega p(v, \theta)dvd\theta = \iint_\Omega p(v)p(\theta)dvd\theta \tag{12}$$

Where Ω represents the area where node j will appear outside the transmission range of node i.

The area where node j will appear after time Δt is a circle with radius $l = v_{max}^{ij} \cdot \Delta t$, in which v_{max}^{ij} represents the maximal relative velocity between node j and node i. According to the relationship between l, R and r, there are three circumstances, as shown in Fig. 3.

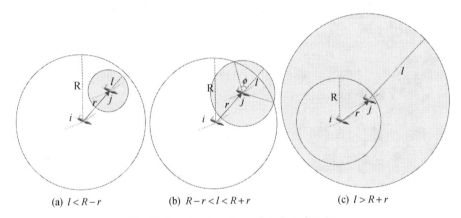

(a) $l < R - r$ (b) $R - r < l < R + r$ (c) $l > R + r$

Fig. 3. Possible locations of node j after Δt.

(1) As shown in Fig. 3(a), if $l < R - r$, it can be obtained that $p(\Delta t) = 0$.
(2) As shown in Fig. 3(b), if $R - r < l < R + r$, the relative velocity v should satisfies that

$$0 \le \frac{R - r}{\Delta t} \le v \le \frac{R + r}{\Delta t} \le v_{max}^{ij} \tag{13}$$

Here, we define $v_- = \max\left(0, \frac{R-r}{\Delta t}\right)$ and $v_+ = \min\left(v_{max}^{ij}, \frac{R+r}{\Delta t}\right)$. Therefore,

$$p(\Delta t) = \int_{v_-}^{v_+} p(v) \int_{-\phi(v)}^{\phi(v)} p(\theta)d\theta dv \tag{14}$$

Where $\phi(v)$ means the maximal direction which node j can move out of the transmission range of node i, and it can be expressed as

$$\phi(v) = \pi - \arccos\left(\frac{(v\Delta t)^2 + r^2 - R^2}{2rv\Delta t}\right) \tag{15}$$

(3) As shown in Fig. 3(c), if $l > R + r$, when v is valued at $\left[\frac{R+r}{\Delta t}, v_{max}^{ij}\right]$, node j can move out of the transmission range of node i with any direction, and it has

$$p(\Delta t) = \int_{\frac{R+r}{\Delta t}}^{v_{max}^{ij}} p(v) \int_{0}^{2\pi} p(\theta)d\theta dv \tag{16}$$

Based on the above analysis, the Hello period Δt can be calculated from Eq. (11). Figure 4 shows the numerical results of departure probability P as a function of time Δt. In Fig. 4, the relative velocity v_{ij} is uniformly distributed on [300, 340] m/s, the transmission radius R is 200 km, and the distance r between two nodes is 180 km and 150 km, respectively. It can be seen that P increases with the increase of Δt, and when the distance between two nodes is longer, the faster P rises with the increase of Δt. When P_0 is 0, Δt will be less than $\frac{R-r}{v_{max}}$. This means that the departure probability P that a node j moves out of the transmission range of node i is 0. In this case, the TCB problem will not occur and packets will not be lost.

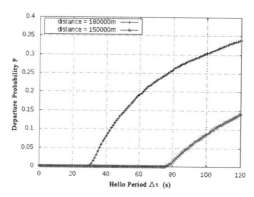

Fig. 4. Departure probability P as a function of time Δt.

In FANETs, if node i have $K = num(N(i))$ neighbor nodes, the Hello period of node i relative to all nodes in $N(i)$ can be derived as Δt_n $(n = 1, 2, 3, \cdots, K)$ using the above method.

3.3   Description of Adaptive Hello Mechanism

The overall flow of the proposed AHM in this paper is shown in Fig. 5. It is mainly composed of three modules: node state differentiation, calculation of Hello period for working nodes, and calculation of Hello period for idle nodes.

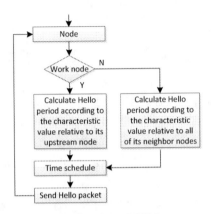

Fig. 5.   Flow of AHM.

The first module differentiates node state. When a small percent of nodes in a large FANET are involved in packet forwarding, channel resource spent by all of its neighbor nodes in maintaining their positions is a huge waste. To address this problem, we divide all nodes into working nodes and idle nodes. Working nodes are packet forwarding nodes, which are participating in packet transmission. The other nodes are idle nodes, which are not participating in packet transmission. However, with the change of tasks or network topology, the state of nodes may change at any time.

The second module is calculation of Hello period for working node. For working nodes, they should send Hello packets timely to its upstream node to provide accurate position for routing decision. Therefore, the Hello period of working nodes should be calculated according to the relative characteristic values between the node and its upstream node using the method described in Part B of Sect. 3. And the Hello period is updated timely according to the changes of their relative motion.

The third module is calculation of Hello period for idle nodes. For an idle node, it should get the characteristic values relative to all of its neighbor nodes firstly, and then calculate the Hello period respectively. Finally, its Hello period Δt is obtained by $\Delta t = \frac{1}{K} \sum_{n=1}^{K} \Delta t_n$. In order to simplify the calculation and save energy, the idle node can adopt a fixed Hello period, which can be set longer than that in GPSR protocol.

4   Simulations

In this paper, we have incorporated the AHM to the traditional GPSR protocol, which is labeled as AGGR. In this section, the effectiveness of AHM will be verified by the comparison of simulations for AGGR and GPSR protocol which adopted the Hello scheme of fixed period (10s). The simulations are conducted in NS-2. The main simulation parameters are set as in Table 1.

Table 1. Simulation parameters.

Parameter	Value	Parameter	Value
Number of nodes	50	Simulation scenario	$500 \times 500 \times 20\ km^3$
Transmission range of nodes	200 km	Simulation time	3600 s
Packet type	CBR 512 bits	Packet rate	10 packets/s
Channel bandwidth	2 Mbit/s	Node velocity	[200,280], [280,360], [360,440], [440,520], [520,600], [600,680] m/s

Instant throughput of GPSR and AGGR protocol under different node velocity is shown in Fig. 6. As can be seen, GPSR protocol using the periodic Hello mechanism causes the TCB problem. With the increase of node velocity, the network dynamics increases, and the packet loss caused by TCB becomes more serious. However, the AGGR protocol using the AHM reduces TCB effectively, and gets a high instant throughput.

Delivery success ratio, control overhead, average throughput and transmission delay of GPSR and AGGR protocol are shown from Fig. 7, 8, 9 and Fig. 10, respectively. As can be seen from Fig. 7, the packet successful transmission rate decreases with the increase of node velocity in the GPSR protocol using periodic Hello mechanism, but it is less affected by the motion of nodes in the AGGR protocol. It indicates that the AGGR protocol has good adaptability to dynamic network topology and can be applied to highly-dynamic FANETs. As shown in Fig. 8, in the GPSR protocol, due to the increase of node velocity, the total number of packets successful transmitted is reduced, while the number of Hello packets is basically unchanged, resulting in an increase of the control overhead. In the AGGR protocol, the Hello period decreases adaptively with the increase of velocity of relative motion between nodes, and the number of Hello packets increases, resulting in an increase of control overhead. But it is still lower than that in GPSR. Figure 9 shows that after adopting the AHM, the neighbor node table is accurately constructed and maintained, which can reflect the changes of local topology, improve the sensitivity to link breakages, and reduce packet loss. Figure 10 shows that due to the accurate construction of neighbor table, the optimal node can be chosen for the next hop, and the transmission delay is also reduced.

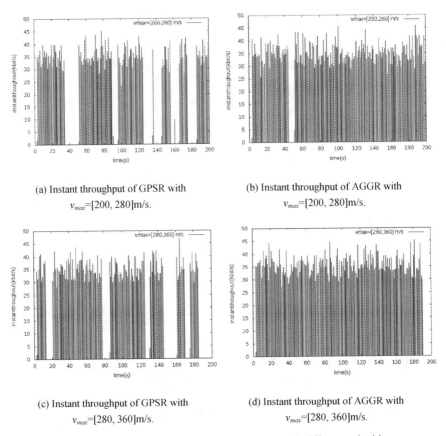

(a) Instant throughput of GPSR with v_{max}=[200, 280]m/s.

(b) Instant throughput of AGGR with v_{max}=[200, 280]m/s.

(c) Instant throughput of GPSR with v_{max}=[280, 360]m/s.

(d) Instant throughput of AGGR with v_{max}=[280, 360]m/s.

Fig. 6. Instant throughput of GPSR and AGGR with different velocities.

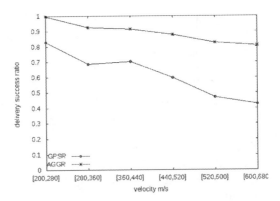

Fig. 7. Delivery success ratio of GPSR and AGGR.

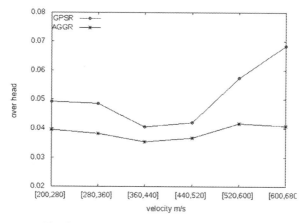

Fig. 8. Control overhead of GPSR and AGGR.

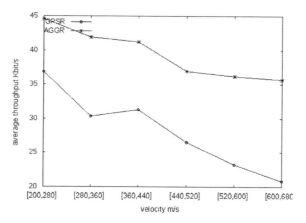

Fig. 9. Average throughput of GPSR and AGGR.

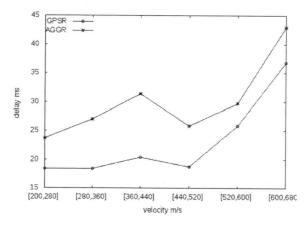

Fig. 10. Transmission delay of GPSR and AGGR.

5   Conclusions

In this paper, in order to address the TCB problem in geographic routing protocols, a novel AHM is proposed for FANETs. The AHM divides all nodes into working nodes and idle nodes, and nodes in different states adopt different methods for the Hello period. It can eliminate the drawbacks of the periodic Hello scheme and gain a high packet successful transmission rate without causing more routing overhead. Simulation results show that it improves the accuracy and real-time performance of the neighbor table, provides a reliable basis for geographic routing protocols, and is scalable and applicable to FANETs.

References

1. Bekmezci, I., Sahingoz, O.K., Temel, S.: Flying ad-hoc networks (FANETs): a survey. Ad Hoc Netw. **11**(3), 1254–1270 (2013)
2. Guillen-Perez, A., Cano, M.-D.: Flying ad hoc networks: a new domain for network communications. Sensors **18**(10), 3571 (2018)
3. Chriki, A., Touati, H., Snoussi, H., et al.: FANET: communication, mobility models and security issues. Comput. Networks **163**, 106877.1–106877.17 (2019)
4. Lakew, D.S., Sa'Ad, U., Dao, N.N., et al.: Routing in flying Ad hoc networks: a comprehensive survey. IEEE Commun. Surv. Tutorials **22**(2), 1071–1120 (2020)
5. Singh, K., Verma, A.K.: Experimental analysis of AODV, DSDV and OLSR routing protocol for flying adhoc networks (FANETs). In: IEEE International Conference on Electrical. Computer and Communication Technologies (ICECCT), pp. 1–4. Coimbatore, India (2015)
6. Vasiliev, D.S., Meitis, D.S., Abilov, A.: Simulation-based comparison of AODV, OLSR and HWMP protocols for flying ad hoc networks. In: Balandin, S., Andreev, S., Koucheryavy, Y. (eds.) NEW2AN 2014. LNCS, vol. 8638, pp. 245–252. Springer, Cham (2014). https://doi.org/10.1007/978-3-319-10353-2_21
7. Bujari, A., Palazzi, C.E., Ronzani, D.: A comparison of stateless position-based packet routing algorithms for FANETs. IEEE Trans. Mob. Comput. **17**(11), 2468–2482 (2018)
8. Gupta, N.K., Yadav, R.S., Nagaria, R.K.: 3D geographical routing protocols in wireless ad hoc and sensor networks: an overview. Wireless Netw. **26**, 2549–2566 (2020)
9. Oubbati, O.S., Lakas, A., Zhou, F., et al.: A survey on position-based routing protocols for flying ad hoc networks (FANETs). Vehic. Commun. **10**, 29–56 (2017)
10. Agrawal, J., Kapoor, M.: A comparative study on geographic-based routing algorithms for flying ad-hoc networks. Concurr. Comput.: Pract. Exper. **33**(16) (2021)
11. Chakeres, I.D., Belding-Royer, E.M.: The utility of Hello messages for determining link connectivity. In: 5th International Symposium on Wireless Personal Multimedia Communications (WPMC). IEEE, Honolulu, Hawaii (2002)
12. Han, S.Y., Lee, D.: An adaptive hello messaging scheme for neighbor discovery in on-demand MANET routing protocols. IEEE Commun. Lett. **17**(5), 1040–1043 (2013)
13. Mahmud, I., Cho, Y.Z.: Adaptive Hello interval in FANET routing protocols for green UAVs. IEEE Access **7**, 63004–63015 (2019)
14. Hemandez-Cons, N., Kasahara, S., Takahashi, Y.: Dynamic hello/timeout timer adjustment in routing protocols for reducing overhead in MANETs. Comput. Commun. **33**(15), 1864–1878 (2010)

15. Park, N.-U., Nam, J.-C., Cho, Y.-Z.: Impact of node speed and transmission range on the hello interval of MANET routing protocols. In: International Conference on Information and Communication Technology Convergence (ICTC), pp. 634–636. IEEE, Jeju, Korea (2016)
16. Karp, B., Kung, H.T.: GPSR: greedy perimeter stateless routing for wireless networks. In: MOBICOM, pp. 243–254. ACM, Boston, MA, USA (2000)

Network Security (ADHOCNETS 2021)

Evaluation of Denial of Service Attacks in Software Defined-Cognitive Radio Networks

Mampuele Lebepe$^{(\boxtimes)}$ (ID) and Mthulisi Velempini (ID)

University of Limpopo, Private Bag X1106, Sovenga 0727, South Africa
mampuele.lebepe@gmail.com, mvelempini@gmail.com

Abstract. Software defined networks (SDN) offer a novel network resource management framework which addresses network resources management challenges. It addresses the spectrum scarcity problem by employing efficient and dynamic spectrum access. Cognitive radio networks (CRN) enables secondary users to coexist with licensed users in non-interfering manner. Unfortunately, SDN is susceptible to security threats. We integrate a SDN and a CRN and evaluate the denial of service (DoS) in the integrated environment. The DoS attack is a threat to SDN based networks. The DoS attack overloads the controller and floods the switch Content Addressable Memory (CAM tables), which degrades the performance of the network. We evaluate the effectiveness of the SDN-Guard and the Jamming Attack in addressing the effects of the DoS.

SDN-Guard is designed to minimize the overloading of the controller, and the flow tables while managing the flow routes dynamically, timeouts of entry rule and to aggregate flow rule entries given the probability of the threat of the flow which is determined by an intrusion detection system (IDS). IDS is used to detect and control the jamming attack. It is a set of procedures and systems that are able to identify intrusions in a system. This study evaluates the effects of DoS attack on software defined cognitive radio networks. The study observed that the SDN-Guard detects the DoS attack earlier and it reduces the average round trip time and the average processing time compared to the Jamming Attack Defender.

Keywords: Software defined networks · Cognitive radio network · Denial of service · Intrusion detection system

1 Introduction

Software Defined Network (SDN) framework addresses several network resources management challenges. The Cognitive Radio Networks (CRN) on the other hand, is designed to address the spectrum scarcity by employing efficient and dynamic spectrum access (DSA). CRN provides secondary users with the ability to coexist with primary users in non-interfering mode. In this study, we integrate the two networks and evaluate the effects of Denial of Service attack (DoS) in the integrated environment - Software defined Cognitive Radio Network (SD-CRN).

© ICST Institute for Computer Sciences, Social Informatics and Telecommunications Engineering 2022
Published by Springer Nature Switzerland AG 2022. All Rights Reserved
W. Bao et al. (Eds.): ADHOCNETS 2021/TridentCom 2021, LNICST 428, pp. 49–62, 2022.
https://doi.org/10.1007/978-3-030-98005-4_4

A DoS is any type of attack which overwhelms a server and prevents it from servicing its clients. DoS is a challenge in the Internet and other forms of networks. This attack is also a challenge in the SD-CRN. It can overload the controller and overwhelms its processing capacity and floods the switch CAM tables and degrade the performance of the network [1]. This result in loss of revenue for online businesses. Reverse proxy is one effective defense mechanics which counters the DoS [2]. However, it requires complementary schemes to improve its effectiveness [2]. More robust approaches are required to mitigate the effects of the DDoS attacks.

A DoS attack can cause the network to be unstable, unusable by sending data in special patterns or by flooding the network with packets. Remote services can be overwhelmed by a stream of packets from attackers or compromised nodes. However, the effects of DoS can be mitigated in SD-CRN.

The study evaluates the effects of DoS attacks in SD-CRN. The DoS is simulated in SD-CRN environment and two countermeasures are evaluated, the Jamming attack Defender and the SDN-Guard. The effectiveness of these countermeasures is evaluated and comparative results are presented. The following metrics are used for comparison purposes: the controller workload, bandwidth of the control plane, Flow table, bandwidth of the network, Average processing time, Round trip time, and Signal strength.

2   Related Work

Given the significance of 5G enabling technologies such as the SD-CRN, there is need to address the security challenges of such technologies. This Section presents related work and evaluates DoS schemes in SD-CRN. These issues are discussed in [1] and [2]. Nonetheless, we are focus on DoS attacks in SD-CRN in this study.

In [3], a scheme is proposed to mitigate DoS in SDN using a Path Randomization technique. The study focussed on minimizing the effects of DoS on flow tables, which can degrade the network switches. The authors used an algorithm to aggregate flows that produced a positive outcome.

In [4], the effects of DoS on network performance is discussed. The study shows how the attack affects parameters such as the bandwidth of the control plane (controller-switch channel) and latency. The impact on the performance of controller was also analysed. Unfortunately, these issues were not solved.

In addition, a scheme was proposed in [5], the FlowRanger which detects and mitigates the effects of DoS. While the FlowRanger is consist of the following three components:

(1) The trust management element which computes a trust value based on its origin for each packet-in message.
(2) The element of the queuing management which stores the message in the priority queue which corresponds to its trust value and
(3) The message scheduling component which uses a weighted Round Robin strategy to process messages.

In [6], a scheme was proposed to protect SDN from the distributed IP filtering DoS attacks. The proposed scheme analyses user behaviour and assigns flow timeouts based on user behaviour. The flows of malicious users were assigned short timeouts while flows of trusted ones were assigned long timeouts. This approach requires malicious traffic entries to be deleted quickly from CAM table's switches. Nevertheless, if the flow length is greater than the fixed timeout, this may result in new packet-in messages being transmitted to the controller. This approach also eliminates malicious traffic, which can pose problems for false-positive flows.

A scheme in [7] leverages SDN's hierarchical strategy and programmability and proposes a self-management scheme involving an ISP and its clients to address DoS. The ISP collects risk data from users to use it in the implementation of a security approach and to update network flow tables. The ISP controller assigns a high priority value if a flow is assumed to be trustworthy. If the authenticity of the flow is in question, the ISP controller assigns a low priority to the flow and manage it through the path assigned to malicious flow. This reduces the effects of the DoS on the network performance by adjusting the load. Unfortunately, it does not address the overloading of the controller and the flooding of the flow tables within the switches.

The available schemes cannot reduce the load of the controller, the round trip time, the switch-to-controller bandwidth, the average processing time, and the network bandwidth usage while detecting the malicious nodes. Table 1 summarises the research gaps in SD-CRN.

Table 1. Analysis of the gaps in the literature

Approach	Objective: Minimizing the effects of the following metrics						
	Controller workload	Control plane bandwidth	Flow table usage	Network bandwidth	Average processing time	Round trip time	Signal strength
SDN-Guard [8]	✓	✓	✓	✓	✓	✓	✓
Flow Ranger Invalid source specified.	✓	✗	✗	✗	✗	✗	✗
IP filtering approach [6]	✓	✓	✓	✓	✗	✗	✓
Jamming attack defender[1]	✓	✓	✓	✓	✓	✓	✓
Self-management scheme [7]	✗	✗	✗	✓	✓	✓	✓

Regarding security requirements in CRN's, the work in [9] stated that the security requirements such as availability, integrity, identification, authentication, confidentiality are essential in CRNs. Availability refers to the ability of primary users (PU) and secondary users (SU) to access the spectrum timeously.

A number of methods for detecting malicious activity using Openflow have been investigated. These methods vary from local network detection of infected hosts by comparing flows [10] to deterministic sampling using Openflow to inspect certain classes of traffic [11]. With available features in Openflow version 1.0, we explored the possibilities of using Openflow to detect the DoS attacks. An ideal DoS solution may consist of the following: the initial detection, sampling techniques, and blocking behaviour.

In [12], the focus was on mitigating the DoS attack on flow tables which result in the degradation of the network switches. In order to address this issue, a path randomization technique and flow aggregation algorithm was proposed. The system performance was evaluated in a simulation environment that showed some positive results.

3   Methodology

DoS is the most common and unavoidable threats to SDN security and all types of networks. The DoS overloads the network and servers by overwhelming them with streams of traffic while starving legitimate users of valuable service [13].In this study, we investigated the best algorithms designed to detect and address the DoS. This Section, generates statistical data through simulations to meet the objectives of this study. Table 2 depicts the simulation environment and Table 3 presents the parameters used.

Table 2. Simulation environment

Computer	HP L425.SCMSDOM.LOCAL
RAM	8,00 GB
CPU	intel®Pentium(D) CPU 2037 @3.19 GHz
OS (operating system)	Microsoft windows

Table 3. Parameters and tools

1 Parameters	2 Tools
3 Network Simulator	4 Matlab
6 Controller	6 Floodlight 1.2
7 Switch Software	8 OpenFlow V 1.3
9 IDS	10 Snort 2.0.6
11 Simulation Area	12 150 m * 150 m

An SDN-Guard is an SDN application that is plugged into an SDN controller and which uses the network traffic ID to analyse the flow and raise an alarm when a malicious traffic is detected. Given the alerts and the current state of the network, appropriate decisions designed to minimize the effects of DoS are made for each flow. It consists of the three following modules (Fig. 1):

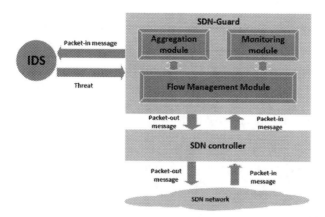

Fig. 1. SDN-Guard layout

The flow management module selects the routing path for each flow and determines the firm timeout of the TCAM entries informed by the risk of flow, to mitigate the effects of the DoS [14].

Rule based aggregation module which aggregates malicious traffic inputs to minimize the number of inputs used in TCAM switches [14].

Monitoring module collects multiple flow, switch and link statistics (e.g. flow, switch TCAM and link bandwidth usages) so that other modules can use them [14].

SDN-Guard communicates with an IDS which analyses packet-in messages and alerts SDN-Guard of the likelihood of flow threats. An IDS can be replaced by a system capable of evaluating accurately the risk of flows like the one used in [15].

To address the DoS on the SD-CRN, the proposed scheme consists of the following:

Threat-Based Routing: To address the effects of DoS on bandwidth usage and queuing delays, SDN-Guard reroutes malicious traffic to the least-used links based on bandwidth requirements and switch ternary content addressable memory (TCAMs). Due to the statistical data collected by the monitoring module, the flow management module has access to the values of these two parameters. A generated path may ensure minimal impact of attack and may not be a shortest path. Malicious traffic must reach the destination where it can theoretically be further analysed by IDS or by a prevention system (which is critical in case of false positive malicious flows). We do not drop malicious traffic to ensure that false positive malicious flows, with higher delays, can reach their destination. The non-malicious flows are routed through the shortest paths to ensure minimum delays [14].

Timeout Management: Depending on the probability of threat, the flow management module set the timeout to each flow. The switch communicates with the controller when the hard timeout expires. The controller has a shorter hard timeout which increases traffic. This does not only increase the bandwidth usage of the switch-to-controller, but it overloads the controller. If the flow is malicious, the SDN-Guard sets high timeout to the flow. The idea is to ensure that the flows do not trigger higher controller to the switch traffic [14].

Malicious Flow Rule Aggregation: Malicious flows are assigned longer hard timeout. These flows are retained for a longer duration. These may overload entries in the flow tables as the number of entries increase in the flow tables. Flow aggregation is considered as a solution to the challenge where the aggregation module aggregates malicious flows in a given switch on the bases of the same source and destination [14].

When a new flows are received by a switch, which cannot be associated with any rule, control is passed to the controller for an appropriate forwarding rule. The packet-in messages are sent to the IDS to analyse their threats. The threat probability is used for routing decision making and setting timeouts for entries in switches' TCAMs. Two cases can be identified:

Table 4. Flow management decisions

Flow type	Threat probability	Timeout	Path	Rule aggregation
Legitimate	Low	Default	Shortest	Optional
Malicious	High	High	Least-utilized links	Mandatory

The Placement of IDS and Traffic Management.
There are two IDS deployment options:

- Under the first option, multiple IDS can be deployed to one switch. Each IDS then analyses the traffic passing through its associated switch.
- In the second option, a single IDS is deployed which analyse all the traffic.

The following are proposed as possible solutions:

(1) optimal IDS placement and traffic mirroring
(2) switch-to-IDS traffic sampling

The two possible solutions are discussed in detail in the sequel:

Optimal IDS Placement and Traffic Mirroring: An optimal location of IDS determines switches which should mirror the flows to minimize the mirrored traffic and the bandwidth required (by minimizing the number of links used by mirrored traffic). The Integer Linear Program (ILP) can be used to model the placement problem of IDS [4].

Let $G = (N, L)$ represent the network where N is the set of switches and L is the set of links connecting to the switches.

We define $p_{n\bar{n}}$ as the cost of the shortest path from switch $n \in N$, which corrresponds to the number of hops between the two switches.

Let $i \in I$ denote a flow in transit in a network. The throughput of the flow i is denoted by f_i.

Define $r_{in} \in \{0, 1\}$ as a boolean variable which equals to 1 if the flow $i \in I$ passes through the switch $n \in \bar{N}$.

The controller has knowledge of the defined variables, a flow i cannot be forwarded from a switch n if it doesn't pass through the switch, hence we have

$$x_{in} \leq r_{in} \quad \forall n \in N \;\; \forall i \in I. \tag{1}$$

We also define the decision variable $x_{in} \in \{0, 1\}$ as a boolean variable that indicates whether the flow i is mirrored from the switch n to the IDS. Each flow i is mirrored only once to the IDS. The following constraint may be met:

$$\sum_{n \in N} x_{in} = 1 \quad \forall n \in I. \tag{2}$$

The cost of mirroring the flows to an IDS $\bar{n} \in N$ corresponds to the amount of mirrored traffic forwarded from the switches to the IDS. This can be calculated as:

$$C_{\bar{n}} = \sum_{i \in I} \sum_{n \in N} x_{in} p_{n\bar{n}} f_i \quad \forall n \in N. \tag{3}$$

Finally, the objective is to find the switch $\bar{n} \in N$ that minimizes the mirriring cost:

$$\min_{\bar{n} \in \bar{N}} C_{\bar{n}} \tag{4}$$

The proposed ILP provides the location of the IDS (ie, $\bar{n}$) and switches which forward the traffic to the IDS (using the decision variable x_{in}). Figure 2 depict the experimental environment.

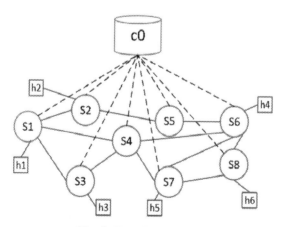

Fig. 2. Experimental setup

Figure 2 shows a topology with eight Openflow switches and six hosts. The controller C0 is connected to switch S5, and data is forwarded through switch S5. The hosts h1, h2, and h3 are malicious nodes in which the server h6 is a DoS target [4].

The experiment begins when normal traffic consisting of TCP flows are sent by all source nodes. In this case, the DoS transmission lasted for 10 min in which the server was flooded with TCP streams. To launch the DoS, TCP traffic was sent using the ping command to generate a streams of traffic designed to flood the target, the server with TCP-SYN, ICMP, and UDP packets from different sources with different IP source addresses. This traffic mimics a DoS originating from different sources [4].

The efficiency of the IDS was evaluated using sampled traffic. The performance was evaluated using packet-processing time when sampling rates were differed. Three types of DoS were generated namely, TCP-SYN, UDP, and ICMP flooding for 30 min. A number of experiments where sampling rates were differed were conducted. A sampling rate of p% depicts that p% of the mirrored traffic is dropped randomly at the switches thereafter it is forwarded to the IDS. The efficiency was determined by the percentage of detected attacks, the number of attacks which were detected successfully in sampled traffic divided by the total number of attacks detected [4].

The second scheme we used is the Jamming Attack Defender.

In jamming attack, the (jammer) attacker maliciously sends or receives data to interfere with genuine users in a session. This situation in turn creates a DoS condition. The jammer may continuously send data packets so that a genuine user may not sense the channel as idle. On the other hand, the legitimate users receive junk packets sent continuously by the jammer. The jammer may overwhelm radio transmission and corrupt the data packets that legitimate users receive. In the worst case, the attacker may jam the dedicated channel used to communicate sensing information among CRs. This attack is called as common control data attack. In addition, if the attacker listens on the control data, the attacker overhears which new channel the CRN is switching to and jams it. These jamming attacks can be done at MAC and physical layers [5].

The attackers have different network attack strategies. The detection of security threats is therefore possible. The attackers may attack both PUs and SUs while in general, SUs are targeted. A number of detection techniques have been introduced in the detection and mitigation of attacks in CRN. The detection technique involves two phases which are the learning phase and the detection phase [5].

In this work, the physical layer attack namely the jamming attack is considered. Jamming attack is detected through the observation of signal strength (SS) and packet delivery ratio (PDR). The collection of information regarding SS and PDR facilitates the detection phase of the IDS to effectively detect the unknown attacks in CRNs. In the learning phase, the normal network behaviour or its performance is observed. In detection phase, the abnormal changes are detected using the non-parametric cumulative sum control chart (cusum) algorithm [5].

During the detection phase, the IDS detects the point of change in CRN operation. In case of a malicious user, the SU is jammed, the SS is measured at the SU is examined. If the SS is high, then its PDR is dropped. The PDR is the ratio of the number of packets received by user to the number of packets sent [3, 16]. To detect the change in the PDR of SU targeted by jamming attacker, the cusum algorithm based on change point detection algorithm is employed. It is assumed under normal conditions that the mean value of the random sequence is negative, it becomes positive if any change is detected.

G_n sequence is obtained as:

$$G_n = \beta - F_n \tag{5}$$

Where β is the average of the minimum (negative peak) values of F_n throughout the profiling period. The increase in the mean G_n value can be lower bounded by $h = (2\beta)$ during a jamming attack. Then, the cusum sequence Y_n is expressed as in Eq. (7) where:

$$q^+ = q \; if \; q > 0; \; otherwise \; q^+ = 0 \tag{6}$$

A large value of Y_n implies an anomaly. The detection threshold θ is computed as follows

$$Y_n = (Y_{n-1} + G_n)^+; \; Y_0 = 0 \tag{7}$$

$$\theta = (m - \beta)t_{des} \tag{8}$$

where t_{des} denotes the desired detection time. It is set to a small value for earliest detection of an anomaly in the CRN. In detection phase, the IDS computes Y_n over a certain period. The value of Yn remains close to zero while the CRN is in normal operation condition. The value of Y_n starts to increase in the presence of a jamming attack. If Yn goes above the pre-determined value of θ, and the SS at the SU is high, an alert is generated indicating a possibility of jamming attack [3, 16]. Figure 3 depict the operations of IDS.

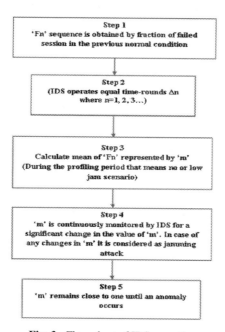

Step 1
'Fn' sequence is obtained by fraction of failed session in the previous normal condition

Step 2
(IDS operates equal time-rounds Δn where n=1, 2, 3...)

Step 3
Calculate mean of 'Fn' represented by 'm' (During the profiling period that means no or low jam scenario)

Step 4
'm' is continuously monitored by IDS for a significant change in the value of 'm'. In case of any changes in 'm' it is considered as jamming attack

Step 5
'm' remains close to one until an anomaly occurs

Fig. 3. Flow chart of IDS operation

The IDS is implemented in MATLAB environment. The presence of a licenced users or SU is recognised using the power spectral density in a particular channel. We assume that IDS operates at equal time bounds (Δn where n = 1, 2, 3...). Then the operation described in Fig. 3 is performed by the SUs or the cognitive users.

4 Results

In this Section, we present and analyse the generated results of the study which are represented graphically. We considered two schemes in this research, SDN-Guard and the jamming attack defender. The set of results of the two schemes are therefore presented.

Figure 4 depict the simulation area. It shows the 10 nodes which are moving within the 150 m * 150 m grid area. In addition, the network also consists of a base station and four attacking nodes. The malicious nodes launch the DoS attack in the network.

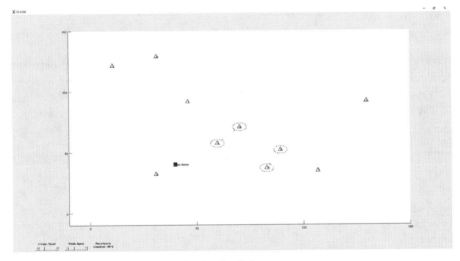

Fig. 4. Simulation area

To evaluate the two schemes and generate comparative results, we considered the following metrics: Average round trip time, Average packet processing time, and Power Spectral density.

Figure 5 presents the average RTT values of the SDN-Guard and the Jamming Attack Defender. The RTT for Jamming Attack Defender is higher than the RTT of the SDN-Guard caused by longer time-outs associated with malicious traffic. This prevent the switches from requesting new flow rules. The requests are also not sent to the controller for flow entry requests. We can see that SDN-Guard is the better scheme because it has lower RTTs.

A Power Spectral Density (PSD) is the measure of signal's power content versus frequency. A PSD characterize broadband random signals. The magnitude of the PSD is normalized by the spectral resolution employed to digitize the signal.

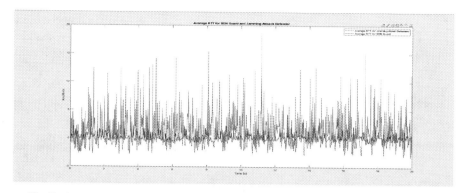

Fig. 5. Average Round-Trip-Time (RTT) for SDN-Guard and Jamming Attack Defender

Figures 6 and 7 present the power density spectrum of one PU available in the slot. The other four user slots are free which means the spectrum is available for SU.

Figure 6 shows the power spectral density of the Jamming Attack Defender. At frequency 0, the magnitude is at 17dB. As the frequency increases to 5 Hz, the magnitude increases to 40dB and it starts decreasing thereafter. The magnitude then remains constant at 15dB as the frequency increases from 25 Hz to 30 Hz.

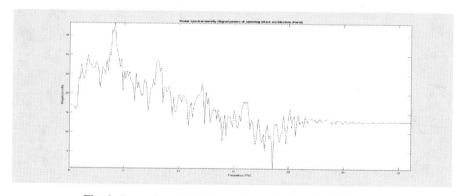

Fig. 6. Power Spectral density of Jamming Attack Architecture

Figure 7 presents the PSD of the SDN-Guard architecture. At frequency 0, the magnitude is at 17 dB. As the frequency increases, the magnitude starts decreasing. This means that the Jamming Attack Defender has a better PSD because it remains constant while the PSD of the SDN-Guard decreases. Therefore, the Jamming Attack Defender has better signal strength than the SDN-Guard.

Sampling reduces the IDS workload which reduces the packet-processing time of the IDS. It relates to amount of time an IDS takes to analyse a packet. It consists of a number of security rules and the IDS workload. Figure 8 depicts average packet processing time for the SDN-Guard in which sampling rates were differed. When sampling is not considered, the average packet-processing time is about 14 s. The sampling rate later

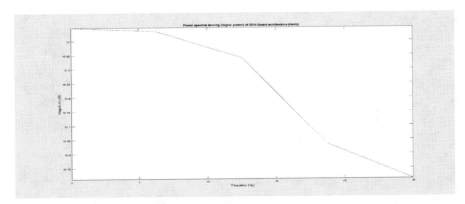

Fig. 7. Power Spectral density of SDN-Guard Architecture

decreased to 10.5 s and thereafter gradually as the sampling rate increases to 80%. Which means that as we increased the size of the sample, the processing time decreased which shows that the SDN-Guard can process large number of packets at a faster rate.

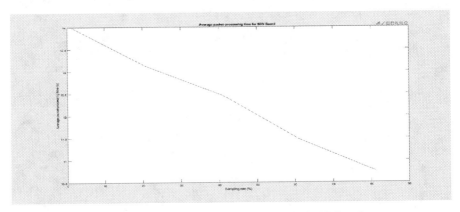

Fig. 8. Average packet processing time for SDN-Guard

Figure 9 shows the average packet processing time of the Jamming Attack Defender where sampling rates were differed. When sampling is not considered, the average packet-processing time is about 23 s. The sampling rate later decreased to 19.5 s as the sampling rate was increased to 80%. We observed that as we increased the number of packets the processing time decreased.

Given the results in Figs. 8 and 9, we can conclude that the sampling rate of 80% reduces the mirrored traffic while the packet-processing time reduces to 50% with IDS accuracy remaining at 100%. We can also conclude that the SDN-Guard reduces the packet processing time efficiently as compared to the Jamming Attack Defender. Which means that the SDN-Guard is superior to the Jamming Attack Defender.

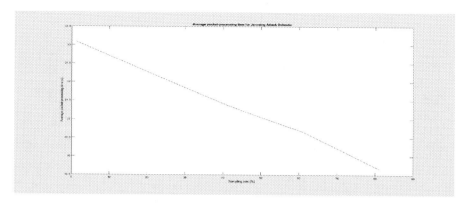

Fig. 9. Average packet processing time for Jamming Attack Defender

5   Conclusion

The study compared SDN-Guard to the Jamming Attack Defender. The objective was to evaluate the performance of the two schemes in order to have an in-depth understating of the two schemes with a view of designing a new scheme best on their best performing attributes of the two schemes. SDN-Guard and Jamming Attack Defender rely on IDS alarms in analysing the network traffic to efficiently protect the SD-CRN.

We also investigated the use of sampling to reduce mirrored traffic. We observed that the SDN-Guard is efficient in reducing the amount of mirrored traffic compared to the Jamming Attack Defender. We also observed that in terms of the source-to-destination RTT, the SDN-Guard takes less time compared to the Jamming Attack.

Lastly, we observed that the Jamming Attack Defender outperforms the Jamming Attack Defender in terms of PSD.

The main objective of the study was to compare the SDN-Guard and the Jamming Attack Defender to find out which scheme detects and mitigates the DoS in SD-CRN efficiently with a view of improving the two schemes. We considered the average round trip time, average packet processing time, and the Power Spectral Density. The results show that the SND-Guard outperforms the Jamming Attack Defender.

References

1. Weiss, A.: A Denial of Service attack can disrupt your organization's web site and network services. Here's how to defend yourself (2012)
2. Manogna, C., Naik, K.: Detection of jamming attack in cognitive radio networks. Int. J. Recent Adv. Eng. Technol. **2014**(6, 7), 2347–2812 (2014)
3. W, Xu, Trappe, W., Zhang, Y., Wood, T.: The Feasibility of Launching and Detecting Jamming Attacks in Wireless Networks. In: Proceedings ACM international symposium on Mobile Ad Hoc (2005)
4. Zhani, M.F., Dridi, L.: A holistic approach to mitigating DoS attacks in SDN networks. Int. J. Network Mgmt. **28**(1), e1996 (2017) (Montreal, QuebecH3C1K3,Canada)
5. Leavline, E.J., Dinesh, M.: Jamming attack detection technique in cognitive radio networks. In: Jamming Attack Detection Technique in Cognitive Radio Networks. India (2015)

6. Park, J., Cho, Z.Z.S.: A feasible method to combat against DDOD attack in SDN. In: International Conference on Information Networking (ICON) (2015)

7. Sahay, R., Blanc, G.: Towards autonomic DDoS mitigation using SDN. In: Network and Distributed System Security (NDSS) Symposium (201)5

8. Dridi, L., Zhani, M.F.: SDN-guard: DoS attacks mitigation in SDN. In: Ecole de Technologie Superieure(ETS). Canada (2008)

9. Hanen, I., Kevin, D., Mustafa, S.: Security challenges in cognitive radio networks. In: Proceedings of the World Cognress on Engineering. London, U.K (2014)

10. Sahay, R., Blanc, G., Zhang, Z., Debar, H.: Towards autonomic DDoS mitigation using software defined networking. In: Networks (2015)

11. Shirali, S.S., Ganjali, Y.: Flexible Sampling Extension for Monitoring and Security Applications in OpenFlow (2011)

12. Bharathi, N.A., Vetriselvi, V., Parthasarathi, R.: Mitigation of DoS in SDN Using Path Randomization. In: Smys, S., Bestak, R., Chen, J.I.-Z., Kotuliak, I. (eds.) International Conference on Computer Networks and Communication Technologies: ICCNCT 2018, pp. 229–239. Springer Singapore, Singapore (2019). https://doi.org/10.1007/978-981-10-8681-6_22

13. Jararweh, A.K.Y.: SD-CRN: software defined cognitive radio network framework. In: IEEE International Conference on Cloud Engineering. Boston, MA, USA (2014)

14. Lobna, D., Mohamed, F.Z.: SDN-Guard: DoS Attacks Mitigation in SDN Networks. Canada (2016)

15. Sahay, R., Blanc, G., Zhang, Z., Debar, H.: Towards autonomic DDoS mitigation using software defined networking. In: Network and Distributed System Security (NDSS) Symposium (2015)

16. Axelsson, S.: Intrusion detection systems: a survey and taxonomy. In: Technical report, Department of Computer Engineering, Chalmers University of Technology. Sweden (2000)

The Evaluation of the Two Detection Algorithms for Distributed Denial of Service Attack

Vukosi Rikhotso[iD] and Mthulisi Velempini[✉][iD]

University of Limpopo, Private Bag X1106, Sovenga 0727, South Africa
kingvuksy@gmail.com, mvelempini@gmail.com

Abstract. The study evaluates two Distributed Denial of Service (DDoS) attacks detection schemes, the Cloud based and the Netplumber. The schemes are evaluated in terms of CPU and memory utilization. The main objective is to identify the better algorithm with a view of enhancing the schemes. The related work on detection algorithms was reviewed. The schemes are evaluated in a Software defined and Cognitive Radio (SD-CRN) Network environment. An early detection and lightweight detection schemes is desirable.

The desirable algorithm detects the attack within the least number of packets. It also consumes less memory and the least amount of CPU time on average. The study uses a statistical approach with the covariance matrix to evaluate the effect of the attack on the SD-CRN controller. SD-CRN introduces a programmable, dynamic, adaptable, manageable and cost-effective network architecture.

DDoS attacks deplete the network bandwidth or exhausts the victim's resources. Researchers have proposed a number of defence mechanisms (such as attack prevention, trackback, reaction, detection, and characterization) in an endeavour to address the effects of the DDoS attacks. Unfortunately, the incidents of the attacks are on the rise. However, the results of this evaluation show that the Netplumber is the promising algorithm.

Keywords: Detection · Distributed Denial of Service · Performance evaluation

1 Introduction

Technological advances in a number of fields have created a cyber-world in which things are done electronically with speed. The advances are increasing complexity and information overload while drastically reducing decision making durations.

Software Defined Networking (SD-CRN) introduces a programmable, dynamic, adaptable, well-managed and cost-effective network architecture. Network administrators have a global view of the network topology and can manage the behavior of the network through abstraction of higher-level functionality by separating the control plane from the data plane. This emerging architecture is dynamic and is able to deal with dynamic applications. Software Defined Networking (SDN) employs an open standard-based and vendor-neutral approach using the Open Flow protocol for the realization of the SD-CRN architecture. Its fundamental feature is to manage the flow of traffic on the

W. Bao et al. (Eds.): ADHOCNETS 2021/TridentCom 2021, LNICST 428, pp. 63–71, 2022.
https://doi.org/10.1007/978-3-030-98005-4_5

network through defining flow table entries. Network administrators can manage easily an SDN network [1].

SDN attempt to build a computer network by separating it into two systems. The first system is the control plane, which provide performance and fault management, and network flow and management of network topology. Controller can process connection request, link management between devices. The second system is a data plane, where switches may rely on the controller to make decisions or can make decisions on their own. The controller can determine connection a path, if the switch request for one from the controller. The controller could do so by using the control protocol. The controller decides whether the flow could be granted [1].

CRN is an adaptive, intelligent radio and network technology that can detect available channels in a wireless spectrum and change transmission parameters to adapt to the spectrum environment. It also enables a number of communication sessions to run concurrently. It's also an intelligent, reconfigurable and dynamic radio technology [2].

2 Related Work

Several studies have been done with the aim of determining the performance of SDN controllers. The work done in [3], provides a comparative study of the SDN controllers, considered a limited number of controllers such as the NOX-MT, Beacon and Maestro. It focused on the performance of controllers. However, these controllers have since been replaced by other controllers such as the POX, Ryu, Floodlight and OpenDaylight which are the most used controllers in the network environment.

The study conducted provided a set of requirements that are the basis of the comparison between the controllers: TLS Support, virtualization, open source, interfaces, GUI, RESTful API, productivity, documentation, modularity, platform support, age, OpenFlow support, and OpenStack Neutron support. The comparison was done using a Multi Criteria Decision Making (MCDM) method named the Analytic Hierarchy Process (AHP) adapted by a monotonic interpolation/extrapolation mechanism which maps the values of the properties to a value in a pre-defined scale. By using the adapted AHP, five controllers (POX, Ryu, Trema, Floodlight, and OpenDaylight) have been compared, and "Ryu" was observed as to be the best controller based on metrics used. However, the assumed scale is subjective and changing the scale would result in a different conclusion. In this study, we compare four schemes using only one controller [4].

In [4], the malicious nodes are detected through the unique identifier of nodes. The algorithm is effective in detecting malicious nodes however; it does not address the effects of the attacks. In [5], the effects of the distributed denial of service attack are examined and proposed some detection techniques that can be implemented in an effort to prevent the DDoS attack.

3 Simulation Environment

This study employed a statistical approach which was used to collect data using mathematical and statistical equations or computational simulations such as discrete event and Matlab simulators. This study depends on network simulations to collect data.

This approach refers to the systematic empirical investigation of social phenomena using statistical, mathematical, or computational techniques. This approach is useful when a study involves the large scale networks such as WiMAX.

This study uses a cluster sampling to sample the nodes of the network. In cluster sampling, the population is divided into groups usually, geographically. These groups are called clusters. The clusters are randomly selected, and each element in the selected cluster is used. In this study, the population of 150 nodes was divided into four clusters. The four scenarios had the following number of nodes: 30, 50, 80,150, for each scenario 30% to 90% of attacking nodes were considered. The packets were sent to the controller randomly using simple random sampling (SRS).

4 Results and Analysis

4.1 The Effect of DDoS Attack on the Controller

The flooding of the controller by the DDoS is one scenario which can directly affect the controller with a stream of packets. Packets that do not have a match in the flow table were sent to the controller for processing. Most DDoS attacks use spoofed source address, which translates into new incoming packets at the switch. When the number of new incoming packets exhaust the bandwidth of the channel and the processing power controller, the attack overwhelms the controller. The DDoS uses a number of compromised distributed streaming nodes designed to overwhelm the target, the controller.

4.2 Controller Usage Without the DDoS Attack

During this experiments, we monitored the bandwidth usage, the consumption of the CPU time of the controller, the response rate and also the memory utilization of the controller. The study also evaluated the usage of the resources on the controller under normal conditions when there is no attack. To ensure that the results are not distorted, all the processes on the machine were disabled, in order to effectively monitor the usage resources of the controller. The bandwidth on the controller was set to 1000 Mbps, the memory of the controller was set to 1.7 GB, and the CPU was set to 1.80 GHz. The study also evaluated the response rate of the controller. The CPU and bandwidth results are show in Figs. 1 and 2 respectively.

Attacking nodes generate large amount of traffic that are forwarded to the controller. The streams of generated traffic degrade the performance of the controller to the extent that it may not be able to provide service to legitimate nodes. When there were 100 nodes in the network, the traffic rate was observed to be 548.88 Mbps. This is a large traffic that cannot be handled by one controller. Increasing the number of nodes is likely to degrades the controller's response time. It also consumes a lot of CPU time while few nodes require less CPU processing time. It also consumes a lot of memory when the number of nodes is increased. When the number of nodes was set to 80, 36% of the memory was utilized while for 100 nodes, 40% of the memory was used as shown in Fig. 1. If the number of nodes were kept increasing, the controller is likely to crush when 100% of the CPU time is utilized. This may also cause some bottlenecks in the connection.

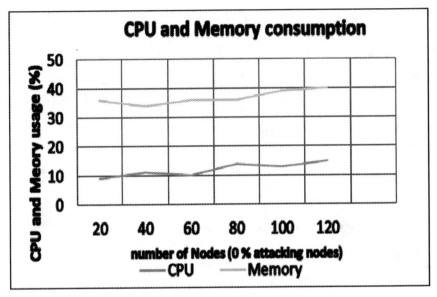

Fig. 1. CPU and Memory usage with 0% of attacking nodes

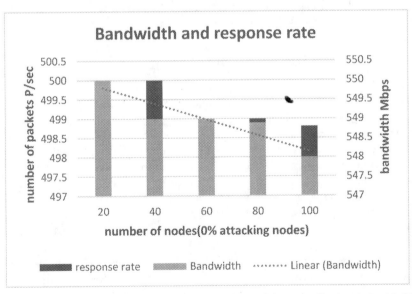

Fig. 2. Bandwidth utilization in Mbps and response rate of the controller in p/sec with 0% of attacking nodes results

4.3   Comparison of DDoS Attack Detection Algorithms

In Fig. 3, we compared the performance of cloud-based and NetPlumber detection algorithms to find out which of the two schemes detects earlier the DDoS attack. Cloud-based scheme detects the DDoS attack within the first 650 packets received by the controller in the network with 20 nodes. The number of received packets decreased for all the detection schemes as the number of nodes in the network increased as shown in Fig. 3.

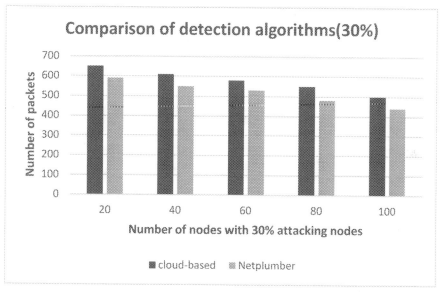

Fig. 3. Comparison of two DDoS attack detection algorithms with 30% of the attacking node

Figure 3 also presents the performance of the algorithms as the number of nodes were increased in the network. This increased the amount of traffic in the network. Suppose that if a specific node can produce 100 packets per millisecond, when the number of nodes in the network is 100. Therefore, if there are 40 malicious nodes in the network, 700 packets per millisecond would be generated. In this case, the NetPlumber detection scheme outperformed the cloud-based algorithm. It detected the DDoS attack within the first 590 packets.

In Fig. 4, we present the results of the scenario populated with 60% of malicious nodes. The results show a change in the detection rate.

The results in Fig. 4 show that NetPlumber and cloud based schemes were still performing better compared to a scenario with 30% attacking nodes. They were able to detect the attack within the least number of packets received compared to when the scenario with 30% attacking nodes. However, the NetPlumber detection scheme performed better than the cloud-based algorithm. The experiment was run three times to verify the results. We observed that as the number of nodes in the network increased, the detection rate improved. The NetPlumber detection algorithm managed to detect the attack within the first 435 received packets in a network scenario with 100 nodes and

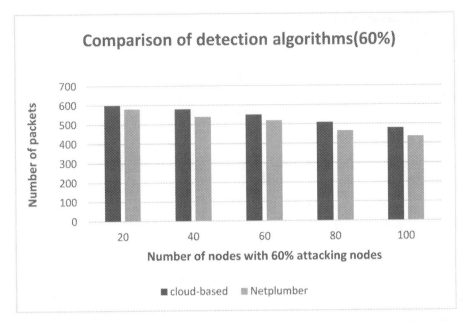

Fig. 4. Comparison of two DDoS attack detection algorithms with 60% of the attacking nodes

60 malicious nodes, which produced 2000 stream of packets per millisecond worth of traffic.

Figure 5 depicts the results of the third scenario. The NetPlumber detection algorithm was observed as the better performing algorithm.

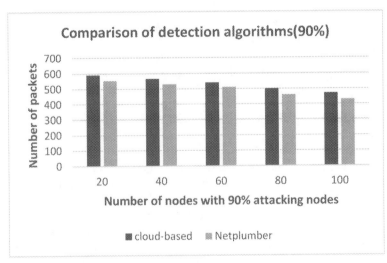

Fig. 5. Comparison of two DDoS attack detection algorithms with 90% of the attacking nodes

A fast detecting scheme that is also lightweight in terms of CPU and memory usage is desirable. The cloud-based at some point performed better than NetPlumber detection algorithm, however it consumed a higher percentage of the CPU and memory of the controller as compared to the NetPlumber algorithm. The NetPlumber consumed less memory and CPU time. However, it takes less time and fewer packets to detect the attack as compared to cloud-based algorithm. Figure 6 depicts the memory utilization results.

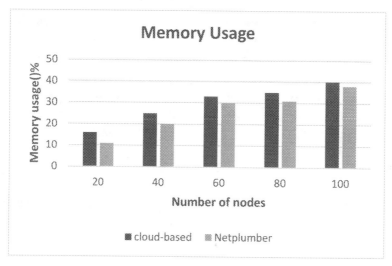

Fig. 6. Memory usage for experiments

The results presented in Fig. 6 shows that NetPlumber detection algorithm is the best performing scheme in terms of the CPU consumption. It consumed 26% of the memory while cloud-based consumed 30% on average. The cloud-based is also poor in the detection of the DoS attack. Figure 7 presents the CPU utilization results.

Figure 7 presents the results of the CPU usage of the two algorithms. The NetPlumber detection algorithm achieved the better performance as compared to the cloud based algorithm. It consumed the least amount of CPU time. It consumed 47% on average the controller's CPU time. Cloud based detection algorithm is the worst performing scheme, which consumed the most processing power of the controller, which is 48.2% on average.

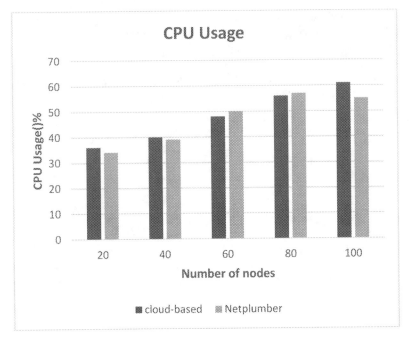

Fig. 7. CPU usage for experiments

5 Conclusion

In our study we investigated two algorithms designed to detect the DDoS attack. The results show that the Netplumber is a lightweight and early detection algorithm which can detect high traffic rate of DDoS attack. We also observed that the controller can withstand the attack for few seconds when the number of malicious packets is less than 300Mbps. Network scenarios with many controllers may be considered in the future.

References

1. Bany Salameh, H., Krunz, M.: Channel access protocols for multihop opportunistic networks: challenges and recent developments. In: IEEE Network-Special Issue on Networking over Multi-hop Cognitive Networks, July 2017
2. Stevenson, C., Chouinard, G., Lei, Z., Wendong, H., Shellhammer, S., Caldwell, W.: IEEE 802.22: the first cognitive radio wireless regional area network standard. IEEE Commun. Magaz. **47**(1), 130–138 (2009). https://doi.org/10.1109/MCOM.2009.4752688
3. Marx, S.E., Luck, J.D., Hoy, R.M., Pitla, S.K., Darr, M.J., Blankenship, E.: Validation of machine CAN bus J1939 fuel rate accuracy using Ne-braska Tractor Test Laboratory fuel rate data. Comput. Electron. Agric. **118**, 179–185 (2015)
4. Bera, S., Misra, S., Vasilakos, A.V.: Software-defined networking for Internet of Things: a survey. IEEE Internet Things J. **4**(6), 1994–2008 (2017)
5. wiki. MATLAB (2017). https://en.wikipedia.org/wiki/MATLAB. Accessed 27 Feb 2017
6. Shin, S., Gu, G.: Attacking Software-Defined Networks: A First Feasibility Study (2013)

7. Feamste, N., Hyojoo, K.: Improving Network Management with Software Defined Networking (2013)
8. Mousavi, S.M., St-Hilaire, M.: Early detection of DDoS attacks against SDN controller. In: International Conference on Computing, Networking and Communications, Communications and Information Security Symposium (2015)
9. Mousavi, S.M., St-Hilaire, M.: Early detection of DDoS attacks against SDN controller. In: International Conference on Computing, Networking and Communications, Communications and Information Security Symposium (2017)
10. Giotis, K., Androulidakis, G., Maglaris, V.: Leveraging SDN for efficient anomaly detection and mitigation on legacy networks. In: Third European Workshop on Software-Defined Network (2014)
11. Kokila, R., Selvi, T., Govindaraja, K.: DDoS detection and analysis in SDN-based environment using support vector machine classifier. In: Sixth International Conference on Advanced Computing (ICoAC) (2014)
12. Khurshid, A., Zou, X., Zhou, W., Caesar, M., Godfrey, P.: VeriFlow: Verifying Network-wide Invariants in Real Time (2013)
13. Kazemian, P., Chang, M., Zeng, H., Varghese, G., McKeown, N., Whyte, S.: Real Time Network Policy Checking Using Header Space (2013)
14. Dhawan, M., Poddar, R., Mahajan, K., Mann, V.: SPHINX: Detecting Security Attacks in Software-Defined Networks (2015)
15. Gkounis, D., Kotronis, V., Dimitropoulos, X.: Towards Defeating the Crossfire Attack using SDN (2013)
16. Krishnan, R., Durrani, M., Phaal, P.: Real-time SDN Analytics for DDoS mitigation (2014)
17. Anderson, C.J., et al.: NetKAT: Semantic foundations for networks. InPOPL (2014)
18. Bailis, P., Andkingsbury, K.: The Network is reliable. Queue **12**(7), 20:20–20:32 (2014)
19. Beckett, R., Zou, X.K., Zhang, S., Malik, S., Rexford, J., Andwalker, D.: An assertion language for debugging SDN applications. In: HotSDN (2014)
20. Radware. DefenseFlow: The SDN Application that Programs Networks for DoS Security. Network Applications in Software Defined Networking (SDN) (2017)
21. Morales, L., Murillo, A., Rueda, S.: Extending the floodlight controller. In: 2015 IEEE 14th International Symposium on Network Computing and Applications (2015)
22. Floodlight. Floodlight Project. http://www.projectfloodlight.org/floodlight/. Accessed 15 July 2016
23. Bhuyan, M., Kashyap, H., Bhattacharyya, D., Kalita, J.: Detecting Distributed Denial of Service Attacks: Methods, Tools and Future Directions (2017)
24. Nhu-Ngoc, D., Junho, P., Minho, P., Sungrae, C.: A Feasible Method to combat against DDoS Attack in SDN Network
25. Aggarwal, A., Gupta, A.: Survey on data mining and IP traceback technique in DDoS attack. Int. J. Eng. Comput. Sci. **4**(6), 12595–12598 (2015). ISSN:2319-7242

Investigating the Effectiveness of Spectrum Sensing Data Falsification Attacks Defense Mechanisms in Cognitive Radio Ad Hoc Networks

Sekgoari Mapunya[✉], Bokang Makgolane, and Mthulisi Velempini

Department of Computer Science, University of Limpopo, Polokwane, South Africa
{sekgoari.mapunya,mthulisi.velempini}@ul.ac.za

Abstract. Cognitive Radio Networks (CRN) was proposed to improve the utilization of wireless spectrum resources. However, it is susceptible to various security attacks like any other wireless network. CRN technology allows secondary users (SU) to opportunistically utilize the idle spectrum while avoiding interfering with primary users (PU). Spectrum sensing is a key characteristic of this technology and it is the main enabling functionality in facilitating the utilization of free channels by PUs and SUs. Unfortunately, malicious users can interfere with either the PUs or SUs. Spectrum Sensing Data Falsification (SSDF) attack is one of the major attacks in CRN which result in incorrect wrong spectrum access decisions being made which result in interference. There is therefore a need to investigate this attack and design robust SSDF mitigation schemes. In this study, we investigate different approaches to prevent or mitigate SSDF attack and evaluate comparative results of two best mitigation schemes in literature and make recommendations for future research. Three metrics were used for evaluation. These are: missed detection, success and false alarm probabilities which were used to evaluate the performance of the schemes. It is shown though MATLAB simulation results that extreme studentized cooperative consensus spectrum sensing performs better compared to the reputation-based and majority ruling scheme.

Keywords: Spectrum Sensing Data Falsification · Cognitive Radio Ad hoc Network

1 Introduction

The advancement in wireless technology resulted in spectrum congestion due to ever increasing demand for the wireless spectrum [1]. Joseph Mitola proposed cognitive radio network (CRN) as a solution to the problem of spectrum congestions [2]. This is achieved by allowing Unlicensed users/secondary users (SUs) to opportunistically utilize the licensed spectrum band. The Federal Communications Commission (FCC) in 2008 [3] followed by the office of communication in 2010 [4] made a decision to avail the licensed spectrum to unlicensed users. The SUs scan the radio environment to check for the

W. Bao et al. (Eds.): ADHOCNETS 2021/TridentCom 2021, LNICST 428, pp. 72–80, 2022.
https://doi.org/10.1007/978-3-030-98005-4_6

availability of the spectrum bands and utilize them opportunistically. They are expected to vacate them when the signals of the Primary User (PU) are detected. SUs cooperate in using the idle spectrum. Therefore, security is a critical aspect of this technology. Hence, in this paper we focus on Spectrum Sensing Data Falsification (SSDF) also known as the byzantine attack. The attack impacts negatively on the success of CRN since it interferes with spectrum sensing phase which is significant for spectrum access decision making. This attack shares false spectrum occupancy data with its neighbours which results in incorrect spectrum access decisions being made.

The study investigated different types of SSDF attacks, which can be categorized according to their signatures [5]. Greedy SSDF attack is an attacker which reports that a spectrum is occupied by PU yet it's not. This result in an attacker monopolizing a specific band by deceiving other legitimate nodes in assuming that the spectrum is occupied. Malicious SSDF attack is where the attacker's main objective is to cause disruption on the network. A malicious user may send the wrong sensing results to the Fusion Centre (FC) or other nodes. This causes other nodes to assume that there exists a PU which is active in the spectrum when it is not, or it may cause the other nodes to assume that there is no PU occupying the spectrum when the spectrum is not idle. This causes the legitimate users to vacate the spectrum band in the first case and causes interference to the PU in the second case.

Furthermore, the paper compered two best schemes in literature designed to mitigate the SSDF attack. The evaluated schemes are the Reputation-based and Majority ruling scheme [6] and Extreme Studentized Cooperative Consensus Spectrum Sensing (ESCCSS) scheme [7]. The schemes utilize energy detection, which means that the received energy is a proportion of a specific part of the spectrum. The detector compares the computed energy to a threshold value to decide when the channel is free [8].

The rest of this paper is organized as follows: The related work is presented in Section 2. In Section 3, we describe the schemes to be analysed. We present the methodology in Section 4. The comparative results are presented in Section 5. Finally, we conclude and recommend future research direction in Section 6.

2   Related Work

There are a number of studies which sought to address SSDF attack in literature and this section reviews some related works.

The authors in [9] developed a scheme called the Conjugate Prior-Based Detection scheme (CoPD) to mitigate the SSDF attacks in a cognitive radio environment. The scheme isolates false sensing reports generated by Malicious Users (MUs), so that SUs can correctly detect the activities of PUs. The scheme handles the sensing reports from SUs as random variables, then considers the probability density of the random variables through a method known as the Conjugate-Prior. The CoPD can also isolate false sensing reports received from any misbehaving SU. When a sensing report is considered to be false, the sensing report is not included in the final decision making. Therefore, when SUs are clustered, the scheme was not able to achieve the best performance in mitigating the SSDF attacks on the spectrum.

The authors in [10] proposed a Detection Bio-inspired consensus Cooperative sensing scheme. The scheme counters SSDF attacks in a distributed manner. When there is a lack of central entity in an infrastructure-less CRN, users sense the spectrum band and report their local energy data to their neighbors. From the reports gathered from all the users, each user then uses a selection-criteria to isolate reports that are likely to be from attackers. SUs exclude MUs by calculating the mean value of energy. Each node then compares its value with the ones from the neighboring nodes. The node with the most deviation is then regarded as an attacker and the remaining nodes' reports are considered in final decision making. This scheme is based on the assumption that two neighboring nodes can exchange consistently trustworthy data hence, the topology of the network stays unchanged during a given period however, in reality, Cognitive Radio Ad-Hoc Network (CRAHN) topology is dynamic and characterized with frequent topological changes.

In [11], authors proposed a Trust-aware consensus Distributed Cooperative Spectrum Sensing (DCSS) scheme to counteract SSDF attacks. The scheme requires every node to update the trust score of its neighboring nodes. The score serves as an indication of how much a node can be trusted and whether its local decision can be included in the global decision. Thus, they are able to detect the untrustworthiness of a neighbor and isolate its reports from the aggregation of reports in the next update, which helps in achieving better sensing results. This can minimize the number of attacks on a CRAHN environment. The results of the simulation show that the scheme performs well only with one attacker, which means that if attackers are more than one, the performance is degraded.

3   Evaluated Schemes

This Section presents the details of the reputation-based majority ruling and ESCCSS schemes. The two schemes were selected primarily because according to the literature, they are best performing schemes.

Reputation Based and Majority Ruling Scheme

Users sense the spectrum, share their observations and isolate MUs which are known as outliers using the reputation-based system to achieve a well-informed decision. After outliers have been excluded, the Threshold Value (TV) of 60% is used, where if a given SU behaviour exceeds it, then it is classified as an outlier which result in its reports being excluded from the final decision-making process.

The scheme penalizes outliers by incrementing their current reputation value (CRV) so that they reach the TV and risk being excluded from the CRAHN. SUs with a good reputation, will have its CRV unchanged. If malicious SUs stops misbehaving, its reputation can be restored by decrementing it by 1. This is shown in Algorithm 1.

Algorithm 1		
Step 1	:	$if\ s_i(t) < \gamma\ then$
Step 2	:	$d_i(t) = 0$
Step 3	:	$else$
Step 4	:	$d_i(t) = 1$
Step 5	:	$if\ s_i(t) \notin outlier\ then$
Step 6	:	$if\ d_i(t) == g_m(t)\ then$
Step 7	:	$r_{m_i} = r_{mi} + 0.1$
Step 8	:	$else$
Step 9	:	$if\ d_i(t) \neq g_m(t)\ then$
Step 12	:	$r_{mi} = r_{mi} - 1$

Where, m is the device-id of the assessor device.

i is the device-id of the neighbouring device.

$d_i(t)$ is the status of the primary user.

$s_i(t)$ is the value of the report from the neighbouring device i.

$g_m(t)$ is the final decision at device m.

r_{mi} is the current reputation of device i at device m

TV is the threshold value

ESCCSS Scheme

The ESCCSS scheme addresses the impact that might be caused by the greedy attacker (always yes) and the malicious attacker (always no) by isolating altered data from the final decision of the sensing user which is interested in spectrum occupancy. It uses consensus algorithm which enables users to share and arrive at a global decision without the use of a base station or fusion centre.

Each cognitive radio computes $Xi(n)$ as the average of all the observations at each time step j after data has been shared and malicious data have been isolated and consensus algorithm has been executed. The final decision about the spectrum occupancy is done using the following equation:

$$Xi(n) = \frac{1}{N}\sum_{j=1}^{N} Yj(n) \tag{1}$$

Where N is the maximum time step at which each SU observes and records energy value, n and i is the node index. The computed average is compared to TV in order to make a final decision.

$$Decision = \begin{cases} 1; & Xi(n) > \beta \\ 0; & otherwise \end{cases} \tag{2}$$

If the average is greater than the threshold then the spectrum is said to be in use denoted by 1, otherwise the spectrum is said to be vacant and SUs can make use of the available spectrum. The scheme is described in Algorithm 2.

Algorithm 2

Step 1	:	Sort the received energy values $Y1, ... YN$ of N SUs at time k in ascending order. Let this sorted value be denoted by $X1, ... XN$
Step 2	:	Estimate the number of outliers/malicious users U
Step 3	:	Compute the mean $\bar{x}$ and s standard deviation of the received energy values $Y1, ... YN$
Step 4	:	Compute $\mathcal{R}j = \max i \left\{ \dfrac{\lvert xi - \bar{x} \rvert}{s} \right\}, j = 1, 2, ... U$
Step 5	:	After computing $\mathcal{R}j$, Put xi aside that has maximized $\lvert xi - \bar{x} \rvert$
Step 6	:	Repeat step 1 to step 5 with estimated outliers been removed, up until j= U
Step 7	:	Declare isolated $xi's$ as suspicious data and they are excluded from participating when consensus algorithm is run.

ESCCSS is activated after suspicious data is disregarded from the final decision making. Consensus algorithm is applied by the nodes so that they have the same global view of the network. Thereafter, the average of the consensus value is compared to TV to determine whether the spectrum is available or not.

4   Simulation Model

MATLAB simulation tool installed in Windows 10 operating system was used to simulate the two schemes. The network size was kept constant throughout simulations with 25 nodes. We set the population size of MUs to the following scenarios: 10%, 15% and to 25% of the total nodes in the network. The simulation parameters are listed in Table 1.

Table 1. Simulation parameters.

Parameter	Settings
Simulation time	200 s
Environment	CRAHN
Sus	25
Grid size	1000 m * 1000 m
Propagation model	Tworay ground
Fusion time	.5 s
Mus	10%, 15%, 25%
Sensing type	Energy detection

Table 1 presents simulation parameters which where considered in the simulation of the two mitigation schemes. Energy detection was the sensing type chosen by the authors because the simulated schemes where designed using the same sensing type. The simulated time was set to 200 s.

For the purpose of this research, spectrum sensing is done cooperatively, which implies that SUs sense the spectrum band and then share their observations with neighboring nodes prior to making a final decision about whether the spectrum is occupied or not. Both schemes utilized cooperative spectrum sensing, and are also affected by noise uncertainty, fading and shadowing [12].

5   Results

To evaluate the performance of the schemes effectively, we used different types of metrics. These are false alarm probability, success probability, and missed detection probability. The schemes were simulated in a CRAHN environment in a network with 25 nodes. In each scenario, we considered different percentages of MUs which were: 10%, 15% and 25% to have an in deep analysis of how the schemes perform under different network conditions. The missed detection Probability results are presented in Fig. 1.

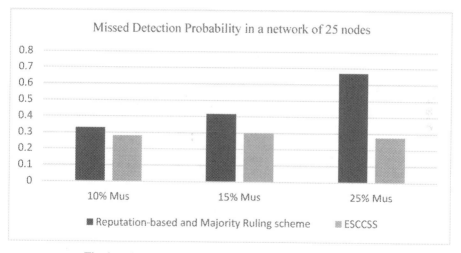

Fig. 1. Missed detection probability in a network of 25 nodes.

Figure 1 shows that in a network with 25 nodes were the reputation-based and majority ruling scheme was used, the missed detection probability is slightly higher compared to ESCCSS when there is 10% of MUs in the network. However, as the number of MUs increased in the network, the missed detection probability of the ESCCSS decreased while the reputation-based and majority ruling scheme increased.

Figure 2 depicts the success probability results. The success probability indicates the ratio of the scheme's accuracy in sensing the SSDF attacks and MUs in a CRAHN and then mitigate the attacks by disregarding the falsified reports and use results non-malicious users. The results presented are from different network scenarios consisting of different number of nodes.

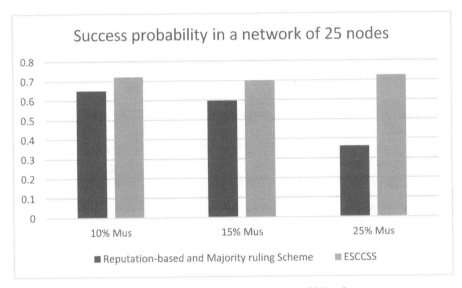

Fig. 2. Success probability in a network of 25 nodes.

In the simulation results of a network containing 25 nodes, we observed that when we have a small percentage of MUs (10%) in the network or even a high percentage (25%), the reputation-based and majority ruling scheme's performance was poor compared to ESCCSS. However, as the number of MUs increased, the success probability of the reputation-based and majority ruling scheme decreased, meaning that the scheme fails to detect accurately the SSDF attacks in CRAHN compared to ESCCSS.

The false alarm probability results are depicted in Fig. 3. We observed that as the number of MUs increased, the probability of false alarm of reputation-based and majority ruling scheme increased which shows that the scheme was not able to handle even a small percentage of MUs in the network.

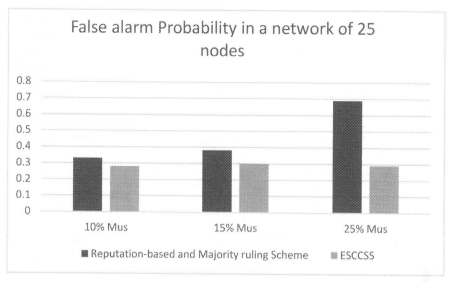

Fig. 3. False alarm probability in a network of 25 nodes

6   Conclusion

This work evaluated two types of SSDF attacks, which are the MU attack and the greedy SSDF attack. We presented comparative results of the two schemes designed to mitigate the SSDF attack. We compared the performance of the schemes with regard to the probability of missed detection, success probability and probability of false alarm.

The simulation results showed that the ESCCSS scheme is a better performing scheme in mitigating the SSDF attacks in CRAHN. Furthermore research may be conducted to evaluate the efficiency of the ESCCSS scheme in a CRAHN environment with different number of nodes and different network conditions such as cooperative or non-cooperative nodes may be considered.

7   Future Work

There is a need to develop a scheme that detects MUs earlier than ESCSS. Hence, during the simulation it was observed that both schemes starts detecting MUs after 100 s of running the simulation. We propose the use of advanced machine learning techniques in addressing the effects of this attack. The scheme may be evaluated using both a testbed and simulation techniques.

References

1. Cordeiro, C., Challapali, K., Birru, D.: IEEE 802.22: the first worldwide wireless standard based on cognitive radios. In: First IEEE International Symposium on New Frontiers in Dynamic Spectrum Access Networks, 2005. DySPAN 2005, pp. 328–337. IEEE (2005)

2. Mitola, J.: Cognitive radio for flexible mobile multimedia communications. In: 1999 IEEE International Workshop on Mobile Multimedia Communications (MoMuC 1999) (Cat. No. 99EX384), pp. 3–10. IEEE (1999)
3. Commission, F.C.: In the Matter of Unlicensed Operation in the TV Broadcast Bands and Additional Spectrum for Unlicensed Devices Below 900 MHz and in the 3 GHz band. Second Report and Order and Memorandum Opinion and Order FCC 08-260. Washington, D.C. (2008)
4. https://stakeholders.ofcom.org.uk/binaries/consultations/cog-nitive/statement/statement.pdf
5. Fragkiadakis, A.G., Tragos, E.Z., Askoxylakis, I.G.: A survey on security threats and detection techniques in cognitive radio networks. IEEE Commun. Surv. Tutorials 15, 428–445 (2012)
6. Ngomane, I., Velempini, M., Dlamini, V.: Detection and mitigation of the spectrum sensing data falsification attack in cognitive radio Ad Hoc networks. In: 2018 Conference on Information Communications Technology and Society (ICTAS). Durban, South Africa (2018)
7. Mapunya, S., Velempini, M.: The design of byzantine attack mitigation scheme in cognitive radio ad-hoc networks. In: 2018 International Conference on Intelligent and Innovative Computing Applications (ICONIC), pp. 1–4. IEEE (2018)
8. Rawat, A.S., Anand, P., Chen, H., Varshney, P.K.: Collaborative spectrum sensing in the presence of Byzantine attacks in cognitive radio networks. IEEE Trans. Signal Process. 59, 774–786 (2010)
9. Chen, C., Song, M., Xin, C.: CoPD: a conjugate prior based detection scheme to countermeasure spectrum sensing data falsification attacks in cognitive radio networks. Wireless Netw. 20(8), 2521–2528 (2014). https://doi.org/10.1007/s11276-014-0758-2
10. Chen, R., Park, J.-M., Reed, J.H.: Defense against primary user emulation attacks in cognitive radio networks. IEEE J. Sel. Areas Commun. 26, 25–37 (2008)
11. Limbasiya, T., Das, D., Yadav, R.N.: A Reputation-based trust management model in multi-hop cognitive radio networks. In: Sa, P.K., Bakshi, S., Hatzilygeroudis, I.K., Sahoo, M.N. (eds.) Recent Findings in Intelligent Computing Techniques: Proceedings of the 5th ICACNI 2017, Volume 2, pp. 183–192. Springer Singapore, Singapore (2018). https://doi.org/10.1007/978-981-10-8636-6_20
12. Akyildiz, I.F., Lo, B.F., Balakrishnan, R.: Cooperative spectrum sensing in cognitive radio networks: a survey. Phys. Commun. 4(1), 40–62 (2011)

Active Attack that Exploits Biometric Similarity Difference and Basic Countermeasures

Pin Lyu[1] , Wandong Cai[1], and Yao Wang[2(✉)]

[1] Northwestern Polytechnical University, Xi'an 710129, China
lvpin@mail.nwpu.edu.cn, caiwd@nwpu.edu.cn
[2] Xidian University, Xi'an 710126, China
wangyao@xidian.edu.cn

Abstract. As one of the most popular IoT (Internet of Things) devices, smartphone stores sensitive personal information. As a result, authentication on smartphones attracts widespread attention in recent years. Sensor-based authentication methods have achieved excellent results due to their feasibility and high efficiency. However, the current work lacks comprehensive security verification, undetected potential vulnerabilities are likely to be leveraged to launch attacks on these authentication approaches. We propose a novel attack to evaluate the reliability and robustness of the existing authentication methods. The basic idea behind our strategy is that the system has its authentication error; we elaborately analyze the false-negative samples to summarize its vulnerable properties and leverage such vulnerabilities to design our attack. The experiment result proves the feasibility of our attack and also demonstrates the drawbacks of the existing approaches. In addition, we propose a corresponding protect approach to defend against this attack, of which the scheme has the self-learning ability to update according to the newly detected attacks. Compared with authentications using multiple sensors, we only adopt a single accelerometer to achieve an EER of 5.3%, showing the convenience and effectiveness of our system.

Keywords: Gait authentication · Wearable sensors · Impersonation attack

1 Introduction

Biometric authentication combines computer and optical, acoustic, biosensor, and biostatistical principles using the human body's inherent physiological characteristics (e.g., fingerprints, faces, and irises) and behavioral features (e.g., handwriting, voice, and gait) to identify individuals. It provides both convenience and security for mobile device users, leading to biometric authentication

Supported by the National Natural Science Foundation of China (Grant No. 62002278).

W. Bao et al. (Eds.): ADHOCNETS 2021/TridentCom 2021, LNICST 428, pp. 81–95, 2022.
https://doi.org/10.1007/978-3-030-98005-4_7

being the most prevalent authentication method. With the development of IoT devices, there are more and more built-in sensors in smartphones, including many biometric sensors. Users can use smartphones to implement more authentication schemes, these methods can be authenticated without the user's knowledge and added to the security systems to determine the legitimate users. One of the actual implementations is gait recognition, which has matured in recent years to become a low-cost and reliable method for authenticating users [1,2].

Although biometric-based authentication systems can balance security and usability, they also face many security threats. Playback attacks and imitation attacks are more efficient and less disruptive to the system in terms of complexity and efficiency of implementation [3]. They affect the authentication process and difficult for the system to detect. In contrast, in the scenario of an imitation attack, the attacker has the same status as the victim when facing authentication systems. The available resources and knowledge about victims can directly affect the complexity of an attack on a biometric system. However, unlike other biometric features, the various data related to gait can be collected in public. In addition, applications [4–9] based on biometric uniqueness are increasing, so it is essential to ensure the robustness [2,4,10–12] of the authentication system.

We designed an attack plan, training 20 participants with similar physical conditions using the same gait, and conducted training lasting four months. This work complements the part about the failure to complete the zero-effort and minimum-effort attacks in mimic attacks [1]. Then, we used the existing gait recognition scheme as a target system and analyzed the results to study the reasons behind underperformance.

We propose a new algorithm by studying feature loss, long-time training, and muscle memory. We use the direction of force lost in calculating the acceleration value to calculate the similarity. This process does not require the use of new sensors or equipment. The experimental results show that our method performs better than the multi-device multi-sensor solution. Furthermore, it is stable in multiple scenes.

2   Related Work

Human gait refers to a manner of walking, stepping, or running [13]. Kinetic studies and clinical studies on gait systems began in the 1950s. Gait is universal uniqueness [14], and according to that, we can extract gait features during walking, and after classification and recognition, they can finally achieve the purpose of authentication or recognition.

2.1   Attack Models of Behavioral Biometric Traits

An attack on a biometric system challenges the uniqueness of a person's behavioral biometric traits. A.K. Jain divided the attacks that can compromise the security provided by the system into two basic types:

Zero-Effort or Passive Attacks. The identification system uses biometric features to distinguish people. When there is a fundamental similarity between the attacker and victim's features, it will cause a false match (FM).

Adversary or Active Attacks. An attacker actively impersonates a legitimate user through knowledge about the victim and the biometric system. The attacker can spoof the identity system by using digital or physical artifacts with the victim's characteristics.

2.2 Gait Recognition for Authentication

In 2005, Ailisto et al. [15] published their research on using a WS-based approach for gait analysis. It is the first work in this area to our knowledge. After that, researchers used many kinds of motion sensors [16–18] for collecting the motion of specific body parts. Studies by Gafurov [19] show that different human limb movements have different degrees of uniqueness and universality. Nowadays, smartphones have many built-in sensors, such as accelerometers, gyroscopes, and magnetometers. Gait analysis based on dedicated wearable sensors made it possible to use the smartphones' built-in sensors for authentication. Since2009, smartphone-based gait authentication has become a hot research area, and many researchers have made significant contributions [1,20–24]. With the popularization of devices such as smartwatches and sports bracelets in recent years, authentication schemes that combine multiple devices have gradually emerged [2,4].

2.3 Impersonation Attacks

Although human gait is unique, the detection system is often not perfect, so many researchers are keen to design various imitation attacks to break through the existing authentication system.

In Stang's work [25], 13 students volunteered to contribute to his experiment. During the imitation process, the attackers did not see the victims' gaits, but only a simple description displayed on a big screen. The drawback in Stang's work is the experimental environments, too few data points can hardly form a curve, sample rate as low as 30, and 5 s is too short of making the gait from start to natural.

Gafurov et al.'s experiment [26] divided the attackers into two parts: the "friendly" scenario and the "hostile" scenario. In the former scenario, participants walked naturally in their styles, while participants tried to imitate their partners in the latter scenario. A dedicated sensor was attached to the belt around the right hip. Gafurov et al.'s results indicated that the chances of accepting impostors employing a minimal effort, mimicking the "hostile" scenario, is not higher than the chances of impostors succeeding in the "friendly" scenario.

Based on the work of predecessors, Mjalaand et al. [27] divided their experiment into three scenarios: friendly, short-term hostile, and long-term hostile. In the friendly scenario, they selected one victim and six attackers from participants. The selected victims had visible gait characteristics that made the imitation process more accessible, and the victim's gait is steady to suffer psychological and outside influence. The attackers who were close in height to the victims were selected. This research using belt attachment. Muaaz [1] pointed out that watching a video or looking at a walking data chart obscures many details of the target.

In Muaaz's study [1], the chosen five attackers were acting students trained as mime artists, specializing in mimicking body motions and body language. Like previous studies [26,27], in 29% of impersonation attempts, attackers lost regularity while mimicking the victim.

Rajesh Kumar et al. [28] and Babins Shrestha et al. [2] used digital treadmills to train attackers. Although the attacker has a sample of the victim's gait pattern in this attack, the attacker does not imitate it. They use a treadmill to restrict the attacker's gait features, such as speed, step length, stride length, and match the features extracted from the victim's walking pattern.

In summary, there are already excellent solutions in the scenario of zero-effort attack, and the scenario of active attack requires us to focus. So when designing a gait authentication system, the following criteria must be considered:

1. Robust: The system needs to resist the attacker's mimic attacks and passive attacks in different scenarios.
2. Fast: Based on ensuring precision and recall rate, perform faster authentication.
3. Lightweight: Based on ensuring accuracy, minimize resource consumption, including memory consumption and power consumption due to calculation.

3 Design and Implementation of Attack

The rationale of biometric systems is using the uniqueness of physiological features to resist attacks. However, in the actual scenario, if the features cannot distinguish between the attacker and the legitimate user, the attacker will be authorized. For a lightweight system, the attacker can not pass authentication is the essential requirement; the victim's performance can be much better than the "Same" evaluation.

3.1 Our Motivation

Our attack mode inspired by Cauchy sequence (Eq. 1) in math: A sequence $\{x_i\}$ of elements in a metric space $\{X, d\}$ such that for any $\varepsilon > 0$ there is a number N such that:

$$d\left(x_n, x_m\right) < \varepsilon \qquad \forall m, n \geq N \tag{1}$$

In a successful impersonation attack of the gait authentication system, the attacker's performance can get the "Same" evaluation of the system. Since the legal user's performance is on the "Same" side, at least two different people will get the system's "Legal" evaluation in a successful attack. That leads to our attack: in the evaluation function of an authentication system, make the performance of at least two users as similar as possible and get the "Legal" evaluation. Base on the theory above, we suppose to use one action specification to train the participants and then detect whether the system can separate each other.

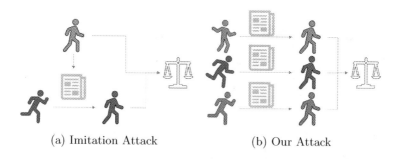

(a) Imitation Attack   (b) Our Attack

Fig. 1. Imitation attack and our attack

As shown in Fig. 1, we do not use the imitation method of Fig. 1a but use Fig. 1b to implement our attack. We use the same action method to train all participants and then use their gait after training to make comparisons. Increased FAR or incorrect authorization will indicate the effectiveness of our attack. Our attack scheme has performed well on some systems, and we will discuss this result in later chapters. Besides, the training method designed in this way can well avoid the "wolves" (better imitators) and "sheep" (more likely to be imitated) problem [29] among the participants. Using uniform movement specifications and participants' are similar in size, which made "sheep" cannot exist. Furthermore, the participants' training time is long enough, and they formed muscle memory of the gait; in this situation, the advantages of "wolf" are also no longer apparent.

3.2   Participant Demographics

We invite 20 young men who will participate in the selection of honor guards to join our research. Before being invited, they had at least three months of military training and four months of Goose-step training which experience allowed them to persevere in our training program. Since the selection qualifications include body values, which provides great convenience for our research, the values of our participates are similar: all participants were male and of similar age, height, weight.

3.3   Training Instructions

Before participating in our research, the participants have gone through quite a long goose-step training. We combined the goose-step with the gait of ordinary people to design our walk style.

We train the participants of this gait for one hour a day for three months. Participants are required to walk every day in this style. In addition to daily individual training, they also train together every Sunday. Besides, we asked participants to walk in a queue when meeting other participants in daily life. The primary purpose of this training method is to build muscle memory of the training gait to avoid the problems of improvisation and irregular in the previous studies [1].

3.4   Performance of Our Attack on Previous Method

To examine the effectiveness of the attack we designed, we implement Muaaz's method [1] as the evaluation standards.

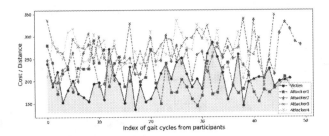

Fig. 2. Our attack on the existing system.

Figure 2 shows our attack effects in the existing scenario. The horizontal axis is the gait period arranged in chronological order, and the vertical axis is the distance between the gait and the template. The polyline represents the DTW distance (or cost) between the participants and the victim's gait template. The blue one is the evaluation of the victim; the other four polylines represent the best four attackers' performance. The smaller the distance, the higher the similarity with the victim. It can be seen from Fig. 2 that it is difficult to find a value as a threshold to distinguishing attackers and the victim.

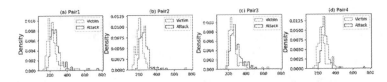

Fig. 3. Distribution of the best four attacker-victim pairs when using acceleration values to calculate DTW distance.

Figure 3 shows the distributions of DTW distance of the four attacker-victim pairs in all attempts. In the figure, the horizontal axis represents the DTW distance of the participant's gait and the template, and the vertical axis represents the distribution density. From the figure, we observe that the attackers' data are similar to the victims'.

Obviously, after a training period, the previous gait recognition system based on acceleration values did not distinguish between attackers and a victim by using a threshold; in other words, our attack can confuse the system to produce misjudgment.

3.5 Reasons Behind Underperformance

According to the performance of our attack, we need to study the reasons behind the result.

Muscle Memory. All the participants in our study formed muscle memory of the gait through long-term training. Thus all the participants can avoid the problems of improvisation and irregularity found in previous work [1]. We can see the results from Fig. 2 and Fig. 3, which show that participants have stable performance. Furthermore, the result shows that the gait we designed has become participants' own.

Detailed Instructions. The gait details used in training are all quantified, and the training process includes single training and collective training, which avoids mutual compromise during joint training [30, 31].

Feature Loss. The raw data obtained from the accelerometer is the acceleration in three directions of the mobile phone are three vectors $(a_x(t), a_y(t), a_z(t))$. In calculating the acceleration value (see Eq. 2), lost the characteristic of the direction, and finally, only a scalar $(A(t))$, acceleration value, is remained. Therefore, it will be vulnerable when only relying on one feature to deal with our attacks.

$$A(t) = \sqrt{a_x^2(t) + a_y^2(t) + a_z^2(t)} \tag{2}$$

4 Our Authentication Approach

In this section, we introduce our system and its components and algorithm.

4.1 Approach Overview

Our goal is that the system can authorize attackers who have been trained together with legitimate users for a long time under the same instruction. In addition, we also need to minimize the use of resources while meeting the essential authentication functions. After many attempts, we use the changing of the force in walking as the feature of our study. Thus we use the data collected by the accelerometer to construct an authentication scheme.

We first preprocess the obtained raw data and then divide it into gait cycles. After aligning the coordinate system, we calculate the distance between the current user's gait from the victim's template, and we use spherical radian as the distance unit in the calculation. Finally, using the evaluation system to decide whether to authorize the current user.

4.2   Data Preprocessing

The primary function of data preprocessing is to convert the raw data into usable gait cycles.

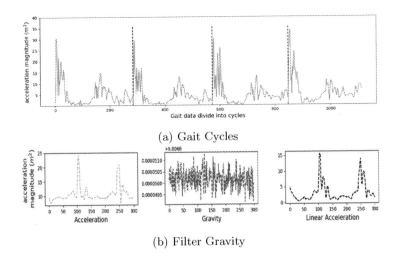

(a) Gait Cycles

(b) Filter Gravity

Fig. 4. Data preprocessing

Walking Data Extraction. Since the start time of the gait data record is earlier than the start time of the walk, and the end time is later than the end time of the walk, it is necessary to remove the non-walking phase data. In our study, we used 250 sample points as a sliding window. When the value of acceleration exceeds the threshold (the default value is 16) for five consecutive windows, it indicates that these windows are in the walking phase.

S-G Filter. Raw data contains random noise, and we used S-G [32] filters (as in (3)) to filter out significant portions of the high-frequency content and noise and minimize the error while maintaining waveform and height. As shown in formula 3, $X \cdot \left(X^T \cdot X\right)^{-1} \cdot X^T$ is the convolution coefficient, Y is the observation value, and Y' is the smoothing result.

$$Y' = X \cdot \left(X^T \cdot X\right)^{-1} \cdot X^T \cdot Y \tag{3}$$

Cycle Extraction. We took 200 consecutive sample points from the middle of the data as a sliding window and then slid back in steps of 1 to get a series of data sets containing 200 sample points. The sums of the Euclidean distances of each point set and the corresponding point in the first window were calculated, finally yielding a distance sequence. The distance between the local minimums is the length of the cycle, and then the number of sample points per cycle is averaged.

After finding the length of one cycle, we began to divide the data set into separate cycles. We used 1.5 times the cycle length of the interval to detect the local minimum, When obtain a minimum value, starting from the index of that point, we created a new interval (length of 1.5 times the cycle length) forward. We searched the local minimum from the vicinity of a cycle length position within this interval. The use of 1.5 times the period as the interval length is due to the uncertainty of the gait. Although there is always a deviation in the interval length of each step, the deviation will not be too large (see Fig. 4a).

Gravity Separation. During walking, the direction of gravity relative to the smartphone's coordinate is constantly changing. Since the value is too significant (approximately $9.8 \, \text{m/s}^2$) to ignore, we need to eliminate the contribution of the force of gravity. From the built-in filter in Android, we can obtain linear acceleration through the function $Sensor.TYPE\_ACCELEROMETER$.

Abnormal Cycles Removal. Occasionally, some accidental situations caused data anomalies during walking, and we needed to remove the abnormal cycles. We used DTW (dynamic time warping) to determine the degree of dispersion of the cycles and cross-compare the DTW distances between different cycles. We removed cycle pairs that had a significant deviation from the distance.

4.3   Coordinate Aligning

In order to assess whether the direction of the force can be used as a feature to identify the movement of the people's gait, we made a simple comparison. Figure 5 show the differences of direction in a gait cycle between victims alone and victims with attackers. From this, we can see that based on the victim's gait template (red triangle and orange line), the attacker's performance (see Fig. 5b) is more chaotic than the victim (see Fig. 5a). Therefore, we believe that we can use the force direction as an essential feature for identity verification.

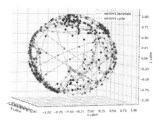 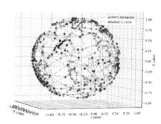

(a) Comparison of the two gait cycles of the victim

(b) Comparison of the gait cycle of victim and attacker

Fig. 5. Differences in the direction of acceleration

According to the distribution characteristics of Fig. 5, we need to rotate the coordinate system of the gait data obtained in the certification process to make it conform to the coordinate system of the template.

Direction Extraction
Acceleration is a vector with magnitude (or length) and direction. We determined the magnitude $A(t)$ from (2) in Sect. 4.2. Therefore, we can obtain the direction on the three axes:

$$d_x = \frac{a_x}{A(t)}, \quad d_y = \frac{a_y}{A(t)}, \quad d_z = \frac{a_z}{A(t)} \tag{4}$$

Using (4), the acceleration can be changed into a unit vector with length 1. Applying this method to the gait data, we will get a sequence of ordered point sets distributed over a unit sphere. Each point represents the direction of acceleration, that is, the direction of the force at that time.

Distance Between Cycles
The shortest path between two points on a sphere, also known as an orthodrome, is a segment of a Great-Circle. The spherical distance can be measured using arc length, which is the angle between two points in polar coordinates. We can use the inner vector product to calculate the angle:

$$\cos(\theta) = \frac{\vec{a} \cdot \vec{b}}{|\vec{a}| \, |\vec{b}|} \tag{5}$$

In (5), the lengths of vectors are 1, so the distance between the two points is:

$$dist(a, b) = \theta = \arccos\left(\vec{a} \cdot \vec{b}\right) \tag{6}$$

In addition, according to our statistical results, the angle between two adjacent points is between 0 and 0.5π, because based on our sampling rate, no one can swing his or her leg more than $90°$ in such a short time.

$$D(i, j) = dist(i, j) + min \begin{cases} D(i-1, j) \\ D(i, j-1) \\ D(i-1, j-1) \end{cases} \tag{7}$$

We used the formula (as in (7)) to calculate the distance between cycles. The calculation is using in the template creation phase and the authentication phase. A shorter distance means more similar to the template. If the distance is below a certain level, we will decide on the success of the authentication.

Finally, we cross-compare the cycles and calculate the distance. We use the KNN (k-Nearest Neighbor) algorithm to determine which cycles to submit for the system. If it is in the registration phase, the submitted cycles using as legal user's template; the distance will be saved for the authentication function to get the threshold. If it is in the verification phase, the system using it to calculate the distance. We will drop it for the cycles that the distance is far from the current template (the default distance is 450).

Coordinate System Alignment
Before comparison, we need to align the coordinate system of the new data with the template. We will reposition the phone before the data collection each time, causing the offset in the position and the twist of the orientation.

In $p = [0, \mathbf{p}]$, we can represent a three-dimensional vector as a pure quaternion. In $q = \left[\cos\frac{1}{2}\theta, \sin\frac{1}{2}\theta\hat{\mathbf{v}}\right]$, we use a rotation quaternion to represent the rotation, where $\hat{v}$ represents the axis of rotation and θ represents the angle of rotation around $\hat{v}$. Finally, using (8), we can get the vector p' after vector p is rotated by the quaternion q.

$$p' = qpq^{-1} \tag{8}$$

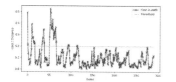 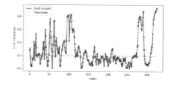

(a) Distribution of distance of victim's two cycles

(b) Distribution of distance of victim and attacker

Fig. 6. Differences in the distribution of cycles

According to Fig. 6, for different participants, the distance in a cycle in the middle part is significantly shorter than the remaining part (most of the points is less than o.2). Therefore, we use that part to calculate the quaternion, then use the entire cycle to get the distance.

Using the Lagrange multiplier to calculating the shortest distance, we can obtain the quaternion required to rotate the coordinate system. The quaternion represents the rotation and then applies to other data cycles. At last, we are using the rotated cycles to calculate the similarity.

4.4 Similarity Comparison

As mentioned in Sect. 4.3, we measure the distance between the current user's live template and the saved template. When the distance is below the threshold, return the confidence score (the maximum value is 100%). If the confidence score exceeds 50%, we consider the current user (and the user in the template) to be "Same."

5   Performance and Discussion

Our experiment uses two OPPO-R9s, two MI8s, and one MI8 SE as devices to collect gait data; twenty participants (mentioned in Sect. 3.2). We installed the app on the devices and then saved the calculation results and the original data separately and recorded the timestamps for future research. When collecting data, participants place the smartphone in the front right pocket of the trousers. Moreover, participants must walk for at least 1 min in the trained gait. The detection error tradeoff (DET) curve, which represents the performance based on our approach (given in Sect. 4)'s false match rate (FMR) and false non-match rate (FNMR) errors. Finally, we achieved an EER of 5.3%.

5.1   Performance of Our Approach

Since the attacker does not need to imitate a specific victim in our scheme, we can select the best-performing attacker-victim pair for evaluation. Figure 7 shows the confidence scores of the best-performing attacker-victim pairs for authentication.

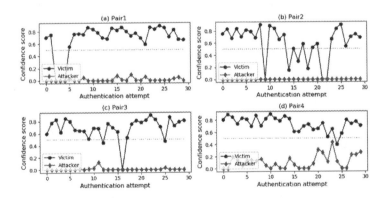

Fig. 7. Best-performing attacker-victim pairs.

Figure 7 shows the confidence scores of the best-performing attacker-victim pairs for authentication. The results show that no attacks were successful; that is to say, our scheme can resist our attacks. However, in the 6% scenario, the victim did not pass the verification of his template. We checked the timestamp and found that most of this event occurred at the end of the walk, and the confidence scores of the victims would fluctuate greatly. When we extended the walking time, the appearance of this phenomenon was delayed. One possible reason is that when the walk is nearing the end, the participants' attention will shift to other aspects, such as waiting for a stop signal or preparing to take out the device, thus losing the stability of their gaits. At this stage, the real-time scores of the victim and the attacker also cause large fluctuations.

In addition, we analyzed the original data sequence and found that 1.7% of attacks were successful in the best-performing victim-attacker pair. The peak of confidence reached 54.1%, but this data was abandoned during the data preprocessing (Sect. 4.3) and failed to enter the authentication phase.

5.2 Performance Under Different Gait

As mentioned in Sect. 3.2, we recruited 20 participants. We collected three different gait data from them (gait of their own, our trained style, and the goose style). We collected ten sets of data for each participant's gait and finally divided them into about 1200 samples (for each gait). We use 10-fold cross-validation to measure the performance of participants. Compared with the previous multi-sensor authentication system using random forest, our results have similar precision and recall rates.

Table 1. Result of our approach

	FNR	FPR	Recall	Precision	F1-score
Goose step	0.093	0.092	0.907	0.907	0.907
Training style	0.077	0.082	0.918	0.922	0.920
Own style	0.054	0.053	0.945	0.946	0.945

6 Conclusion

Research in the field of mobile-based biometrics is continuing. In our work, we propose and implement a novel attack scheme to evaluate the reliability of the gait recognition scheme. We designed and implemented an Android application to record the user's exercise data. Although a human can not imitate other's gait, we have proved that it is possible to successfully attack specific gait verification systems. Based on that, we propose a new gait authentication scheme to defend against this attack and to upgrade our application. In the attack scenario, we achieved an EER of 5.3%. Moreover, it achieved the same precision and recall rate as the verification scheme [2] using multiple devices and machine learning algorithms. Although the data used in the attack scenario only contains a few topics, the results of this study complement previous work [1] and prove that high-intensity training can increase the attacker's chances of passing the verification system. We believe that there is a decline in similarity in training to imitate (the attacker loses the regularity of his pace while imitating the victim). After that, it rises (muscle memory formed as the gait becomes natural).

In future work, we want to solve some related problems. We want to infer some physical information of the phone holder based on the acceleration data. Moreover, we want to know how long it takes to learn and adapt to a new gait to pass specific gait verification systems. We can study these issues as information security topics.

References

1. Muaaz, M., Mayrhofer, R.: Smartphone-based gait recognition: from authentication to imitation. IEEE Trans. Mobile Comput. **16**(11), 3209–3221 (2017). https://doi.org/10.1109/TMC.2017.2686855, http://ieeexplore.ieee.org/document/7885511/

2. Shrestha, B., Mohamed, M., Saxena, N.: Zemfa: zero-effort multi-factor authentication based on multi-modal gait biometrics. In: 2019 17th International Conference on Privacy, Security and Trust (PST), pp. 1–10 (2019)

3. Ratha, N.K., Connell, J.H., Bolle, R.M.: An analysis of minutiae matching strength. In: Bigun, J., Smeraldi, F. (eds.) AVBPA 2001. LNCS, vol. 2091, pp. 223–228. Springer, Heidelberg (2001). https://doi.org/10.1007/3-540-45344-X_32

4. Brüsch, A., Nguyen, N., Schürmann, D., Sigg, S., Wolf, L.: Security properties of gait for mobile device pairing. IEEE Trans. Mobile Comput. **19**(3), 697–710 (2020). https://doi.org/10.1109/TMC.2019.2897933

5. Revadigar, G., Javali, C., Xu, W., Vasilakos, A.V., Hu, W., Jha, S.: Accelerometer and fuzzy vault-based secure group key generation and sharing protocol for smart wearables. IEEE Trans. Inf. Forensics Secur. **12**(10), 2467–2482 (2017). https://doi.org/10.1109/TIFS.2017.2708690

6. Nandakumar, K., Jain, A.K., Pankanti, S.: Fingerprint-based fuzzy vault: implementation and performance. IEEE Trans. Inf. Forensics Secur. **2**(4), 744–757 (2007). https://doi.org/10.1109/TIFS.2007.908165

7. Nandakumar, K., Jain, A.K.: Multibiometric template security using fuzzy vault. In: 2008 IEEE Second International Conference on Biometrics: Theory, Applications and Systems, pp. 1–6, September 2008. https://doi.org/10.1109/BTAS.2008.4699352

8. Zhang, Z., Wang, H., Vasilakos, A.V., Fang, H.: ECG-cryptography and authentication in body area networks. IEEE Trans. Inf. Technol. Biomed. **16**(6), 1070–1078 (2012). https://doi.org/10.1109/TITB.2012.2206115

9. Venkatasubramanian, K.K., Banerjee, A., Gupta, S.K.S.: PSKA usable and secure key agreement scheme for body area networks. IEEE Trans. Inf. Technol. Biomed. **14**(1), 60–68 (2010). https://doi.org/10.1109/TITB.2009.2037617

10. Hoang, T., Choi, D.: Secure and privacy enhanced gait authentication on smart phone. Sci. World J. **2014** (2014)

11. Mjaaland, B.B.: Gait mimicking: attack resistance testing of gait authentication systems. Master's thesis, Institutt for telematikk (2009)

12. Liu, L.-F., Jia, W., Zhu, Y.-H.: Survey of gait recognition. In: Huang, D.-S., Jo, K.-H., Lee, H.-H., Kang, H.-J., Bevilacqua, V. (eds.) ICIC 2009. LNCS (LNAI), vol. 5755, pp. 652–659. Springer, Heidelberg (2009). https://doi.org/10.1007/978-3-642-04020-7_70

13. Dictionary.com: Gait — define gait at dictionary.com. https://www.dictionary.com/browse/gait. Accessed 1 Oct 2018

14. Murray, M.P.: Gait as a total pattern of movement: including a bibliography on gait. Am. J. Phys. Med. Rehabil. **46**(1), 290–333 (1967)

15. Ailisto, H.J., Lindholm, M., Mantyjarvi, J., Vildjiounaite, E., Makela, S.M.: Identifying people from gait pattern with accelerometers. In: Biometric Technology for Human Identification II. vol. 5779, pp. 7–15. International Society for Optics and Photonics (2005)

16. Jin, R., Shi, L., Zeng, K., Pande, A., Mohapatra, P.: Magpairing: pairing smartphones in close proximity using magnetometers. IEEE Trans. Inf. Forensics Secur. **11**(6), 1306–1320 (2015)

17. Morris, S.J.: A shoe-integrated sensor system for wireless gait analysis and real-time therapeutic feedback. Ph.D. thesis, Massachusetts Institute of Technology (2004)
18. Huang, B., Chen, M., Huang, P., Xu, Y.: Gait modeling for human identification. In: Proceedings 2007 IEEE International Conference on Robotics and Automation, pp. 4833–4838, April 2007. https://doi.org/10.1109/ROBOT.2007.364224
19. Gafurov, D.: A survey of biometric gait recognition: approaches, security and challenges. In: Annual Norwegian Computer Science Conference, pp. 19–21 (2007)
20. Heinz, E.A., Kunze, K.S., Sulistyo, S., Junker, H., Lukowicz, P., Tröster, G.: Experimental evaluation of variations in primary features used for accelerometric context recognition. In: Aarts, E., Collier, R.W., van Loenen, E., de Ruyter, B. (eds.) EUSAI 2003. LNCS, vol. 2875, pp. 252–263. Springer, Heidelberg (2003). https://doi.org/10.1007/978-3-540-39863-9_19
21. Sprager, S., Zazula, D.: A cumulant-based method for gait identification using accelerometer data with principal component analysis and support vector machine. WSEAS Trans. Signal Process. 5(11), 369–378 (2009)
22. Kwapisz, J.R., Weiss, G.M., Moore, S.A.: Cell phone-based biometric identification. In: 2010 Fourth IEEE International Conference on Biometrics: Theory Applications and Systems (BTAS), pp. 1–7. IEEE (2010)
23. Nickel, C.: Accelerometer-based biometric gait recognition for authentication on smartphones. Ph.D. thesis, Technische Universität (2012)
24. Zhong, Y., Deng, Y., Meltzner, G.: Pace independent mobile gait biometrics. In: 2015 IEEE 7th International Conference on Biometrics Theory, Applications and Systems (BTAS), pp. 1–8. IEEE (2015)
25. Stang, Ø.: Gait analysis: is it easy to learn to walk like someone else? Master's thesis (2007)
26. Gafurov, D., Snekkenes, E., Bours, P.: Spoof attacks on gait authentication system. IEEE Trans. Inf. Forensics Secur. 2(3), 491–502 (2007). https://doi.org/10.1109/TIFS.2007.902030
27. Mjaaland, B.B., Bours, P., Gligoroski, D.: Walk the walk: attacking gait biometrics by imitation. In: Burmester, M., Tsudik, G., Magliveras, S., Ilić, I. (eds.) ISC 2010. LNCS, vol. 6531, pp. 361–380. Springer, Heidelberg (2011). https://doi.org/10.1007/978-3-642-18178-8_31
28. Kumar, R., Phoha, V.V., Jain, A.: Treadmill attack on gait-based authentication systems. In: 2015 IEEE 7th International Conference on Biometrics Theory, Applications and Systems (BTAS), pp. 1–7 (2015)
29. Mjaaland, B.B.: The plateau: imitation attack resistance of gait biometrics. In: IFIP Working Conference on Policies and Research in Identity Management. pp. 100–112. Springer, Berlin (2010). https://doi.org/10.1007/978-3-642-37282-7
30. Fernandez-Lopez, P., Sanchez-Casanova, J., Liu-Jimenez, J., Morcillo-Marin, C.: Influence of walking in groups in gait recognition. In: 2017 International Carnahan Conference on Security Technology (ICCST), pp. 1–6, October 2017. https://doi.org/10.1109/CCST.2017.8167842
31. Fernandez-Lopez, P., Kiyokawa, K., Wu, Y., Liu-Jimenez, J.: Influence of walking speed and smartphone position on gait recognition. In: 2018 International Carnahan Conference on Security Technology (ICCST), pp. 1–5 (2018). https://doi.org/10.1109/CCST.2018.8585427
32. Anwary, A.R., Yu, H., Vassallo, M.: Optimal foot location for placing wearable IMU sensors and automatic feature extraction for gait analysis. IEEE Sens. J. 18(6), 2555–2567 (2018). https://doi.org/10.1109/JSEN.2017.2786587

Network Protocols (ADHOCNETS 2021)

LEACH-S Enhancement to Ensure WSN Stability

Mahamadi Boulou$^{(\boxtimes)}$, Tiguiane Yélémou, Sy Ibrahim Ouattara,
and Bakary Hermane Magloire Sanou

University Nazi BONI, Bobo-Dioulasso, Burkina Faso
mamadiboulou@gmail.com

Abstract. Due to miniaturization of sensor nodes and the ease and low cost of deployment, the use of Wireless Sensor Networks (WSN) has grown rapidly. Several fields are concerned, including environmental monitoring, e-health, precision agriculture, and smart home. These sensor nodes have limited resources, especially energy resource. An efficient management of this resource is necessary for the effectiveness of these networks. Several energy management solutions have been proposed in the literature, including clustering. In this paper, we propose a new approach based on the LEACH-S protocol called Balance Member's Nodes in LEACH-S (BMN-LEACH-S). This approach allows, first to balance the number of member nodes between the different clusters. For this purpose, a fuzzy logic system using as basic metrics the number of nodes in the cluster and the RSSI with the cluster head are used during the construction of the network topology. Second, it allows to allocate a quantum of energy to each Cluster Head (CH) after which the CH gives up its role to another node. This CH selection is done in turn. BMN-LEACH-S reduces instability of WSN due to the frequent change of CHs and increases network lifetime as a result of balancing nodes between clusters.

Keywords: Balance nodes · Energy consumption · LEACH · Fuzzy system · WSN instability

1 Introduction

A sensor network is a set of nodes deployed in a study environment to collect and transmit data to a sink. These sensor nodes are applied in many domains such as smart homes, precision agriculture, e-health to automate and facilitate information gathering and monitoring tasks. These sensor nodes generally run on batteries and their deployment environment often does not allow them to be recharged. Therefore, once a node runs out of energy, it becomes unusable. This has a direct impact on the life of the network. Facing this problem, researchers are working on all layers of the OSI model to propose solutions that optimize energy consumption in these sensor nodes. One of the best known techniques at the network layer is clustering routing. The LEACH protocol and several of its variants are part of this routing approach. LEACH-S [1] is an enhancement to

W. Bao et al. (Eds.): ADHOCNETS 2021/TridentCom 2021, LNICST 428, pp. 99–113, 2022.
https://doi.org/10.1007/978-3-030-98005-4_8

LEACH [2] that eliminates the cluster rebuild cycles that consume energy in the network. However, in LEACH-S to elect a new cluster head, the outgoing Cluster Head (CH) compares the residual energy to the average residual energy of the cluster to make a decision. This could lead to instability in the network because the residual energy of the CH quickly falls below the average. This leads to a frequent change of CHs, causing instabilities in the network. Also, in LEACH-S after the initial cycle, clusters are formed. A node remains in the same cluster indefinitely. As a result, the nodes acting as CHs in clusters with more nodes than average deplete faster than others. This cause instability in the cluster due to the rapid change of CHs. To provide a solution to these problems, we proposed a new approach called Balance Member Nodes in LEACH-S (BMN-LEACH-S). This approach consists of balancing different nodes between clusters when building the network. This balancing is done based on a fuzzy logic system using the parameters number of nodes in the cluster and Received Signal Strength Indication (RSSI). Also, BMN-LEACH-S solves the problem of fast CH changes in LEACH-S by assigning a quantum of energy to each CH instead of relying on the average energy of the cluster. At the end of this quantum, the CH could be replaced by another node chosen among nodes not yet elected as CH. The main contributions of our research are:

- Saving energy by avoiding to CH the computation and exploitation of the average residual energy of the cluster.
- Reducing the size of the control message by removing the field used to collect the residual energy of the nodes. This helps to reduce the routing overhead and thus reduce the energy consumption of the nodes.
- Reduced network instability due to frequent CH changes.
- Better traffic distribution and thus better distribution of the CHs' energy consumption. This improves the network lifetime.

The rest of this paper is organized as follows. In Sect. 2, we present related work. Our proposed solution, BMN-LEACH-S, is described in detail and we conduct an analytical performance evaluation of our approach compared to LEACH-S in Sect. 3. We conclude in Sect. 4.

2   Related Work

Please Wireless sensor nodes are very often manufactured with non-rechargeable batteries. These nodes therefore have limited energy autonomy. A sensor network does not work well when some of the nodes run out of energy. Energy conservation and the lifetime aspect of the sensor network are important challenges in the wireless sensor network environment. To address these challenges, many routing techniques have been proposed including those based on clustering.

LEACH protocol [2] is the one cluster-based communication protocol following a hierarchical routing approach. LEACH uses random rotation of clusters to evenly distribute the energy load among network nodes. LEACH improves energy management through a load balancing and data aggregation.

PEGASIS [3] is an improvement of the LEACH protocol. However, unlike LEACH which is based on a cluster formation, the main idea of PEGASIS is that each node receives and transmits to its close neighbours and takes the lead role for transmission to the base station. To achieve these energy conservation goals, PEGASIS performs data fusion at every node except the end nodes of the chain. To do this, a distance threshold is set between neighbours to be a leader. This approach allows the energy load to be distributed equally among the sensor nodes in the network. PEGASIS saves energy compared to LEACH.

In a network of sensor nodes, instead of each node sensing information and sending it to the sink individually, HEED protocol [4] proposes a distributed clustering scheme so that a cluster node head takes care of the transmission to the sink. The HEED protocol, has the task of circulating the server role between all the nodes of the cluster for balance maintenance between the residual energy of all the nodes constituting the cluster. This will increase the lifetime of the network.

LEACH-B [5] is an improvement of LEACH that takes into account the residual energy at the sensor nodes. Thus after the first selection of the cluster head according to the LEACH protocol, a second selection is introduced to modify the number of cluster heads taking into account the residual energy of the nodes. This allows a balanced distribution of clusters in the network. LEACH-B, by favouring nodes with a good energy level in the selection of cluster heads, provides a longer network lifetime compared to LEACH.

To solve the long-range problem between cluster heads and the sink in LEACH, Kaur et al. [6] propose a technique of electing a master node near the sink called Master Cluster Head. The latter will be responsible for aggregating and transmitting data from the different cluster heads to the base station. In sensor networks, most of the energy is consumed during the long distance transmission. The advantage is therefore the reduction of the communication between the cluster heads and the receiving node.

In LEACH, the residual energy and the distance between the base station and the sensor node are not considered in the process of electing the cluster head nodes. The energy efficient cross layer-LEACH model for a wireless sensor network is proposed in [7]. It addresses the problem of collecting correlated sensor data from a sink node in a WSN. CL-LEACH maximizes the network lifetime by considering the routing layer, physical layer and link access to the MAC layer. In addition, the residual energy and the distance between the node and the base station are taken into account for cluster head selection. The energy consumed during data transmission between the cluster head and the base station is directly proportional to the distance between them. After the routing mechanism, the CL-MAC model is processed by taking the threshold value, the remaining energy and the node as input. Initially, the position of the node is updated and the neighbouring node with a distance of one hop is estimated. In addition, it checks whether the node is in the neighbour list or not. If it is, then it checks if the remaining energy is greater than the threshold value. If the condition is met, then the relay node is selected. Once the node is equal to the destination, then the data will be processed and stop at the relay station.

In order to reduce the energy consumption of the sensor nodes, authors proposed a super cluster head [8] (CH) to collect data from the CHs to send to the receiving node. Moreover, these super CHs use fuzzy temporal rules to perform optimal routing. The first cluster head is responsible for data collection and has low mobility. The super CH is static in nature and performs all types of routing and monitoring activities towards the other CHs.

3   Our Solution: BMN-LEACH-S

To cope with the rapid change of CH and its corollaries, we propose a new approach called BMN-LEACH-S. This solution, on the one hand, proposes a technique for balancing the number of cluster member nodes based on a fuzzy logic system exploiting the basic metrics: number of nodes already managed by the CH and the RSSI of the target node with the CH. On the other hand, it proposes a simple and efficient technique to change the CH of a cluster based on the determination of an energy quantum to be used up by each CH before it hands over to another node (new CH). These new mechanisms contribute to balancing traffic load among different CHs and thus reduce the instability of some clusters and increase the lifetime of the network.

Our BMN-LEACH-S algorithm runs in cycles, and each cycle consists of two phases: the configuration phase and the stable phase. The configuration phase of the initial cycle consists of cluster head election process and the cluster choice process by nodes based on a fuzzy system metrics. For the other cycles, the selection of a new CH is performed by the outgoing CH.

3.1   CH Election Process in the Initial Round

As in LEACH-S, in BMN-LEACH-S, the initial cycle begins with a setup phase where each sensor node decides whether or not to act as a CH for that particular round. This decision for a sensor node to act as CH is based on the value of the number (between 0 and 1) randomly selected. A node becomes a cluster head for this first round if this number is below a predefined threshold. It then broadcasts a control message announcing its CH status. Unlike LEACH-S, in our approach, the CH announcement messages include the number of nodes already in the cluster.

3.2   Node Membership Process in a Cluster

When a node that is not a CH receives an announcement message from a CH, it sends its membership request message to the CH. In the case where this node receives an announcement message from several CHs, it calculates the cost associated with each CH using the fuzzy system. The fuzzy system takes as parameters RSSI and the number of member nodes contained in the CH cluster. The process of calculating the cost of the CH by our fuzzy system is presented in Appendix 1. The node will choose the cluster whose CH has the best cost. After that, it sends a membership message to the concerned CH. This message contains its identity information.

3.3   Cluster Heads Change Process

The cluster head function is played in turn. Unlike LEACH-S which averages the cluster energies and compares them with its residual energy, in our new approach, to solve the instability problem in clusters, we define a quantum of energy that the CH node must exhaust before giving up its place to another node. To do this, the outgoing CH node informs the new CH of the list of nodes that have already been elected and also the list of nodes not yet elected. Thus, the cluster head will choose a node from the list of not-yet-elected nodes as its successor and add its identity to the list of already-elected nodes before handing over its role. When all the nodes rotate as cluster head, i.e., when a CH has no more nodes in the not-yet-elected list, then the already-elected list is automatically copied to the not-yet-elected list, then the elected list is emptied, and the process starts again. Thus, member nodes will no longer need to inform the CH of their energy status, thus avoiding burdening the control packet. The approach also helps to avoid the operations of calculating the average of the residual energies of the different nodes of the cluster and its comparison with the CH.

Analytical evaluation of the solution
To highlight the relevance of the proposed solution, we conduct an analytical study. This study consists in describing and comparing the operating process of LEACH-S and BMN-LEACH-S. To do so, we first describe the environment of our study. Then, we present the results of the analytical experimentation. Finally, we analyse and interpret the results from the study.

3.4   Estimation Context

We consider two identical 17-nodes networks, one running with the LEACH-S protocol and the other with the BMN-LEACH-S. We observe the process of these two networks in different communication rounds (T0T1T2…T16). We assume that during a communication round, a member node consumes 0.5 Energy Units (EU) to communicate with its CH and the latter also uses 0.5 EU for the processing of each received message. Therefore, to process messages from N nodes, the CH needs N*0.5UE. A CH chooses a replacement when it exhausts an amount of energy equal to $C = 4UE$. In the experimental phase, the 17 nodes formed 3 clusters named cluster I, cluster J and cluster K. Each node has 20 UE as its initial energy.

3.5   Experimental Results

Experimentation with LEACH-S
In LEACH-S after the initial phase, the network formed 3 clusters I, J and K. These clusters I, J and K contain respectively 9, 7 and 3 nodes. NI1, NJ1 and NK1 are the cluster heads of cluster I, J and K respectively.

In round T1, we have the topology shown in Fig. 1. The cluster head is in blue and the other nodes in green. The links symbolize the direction of the communication.

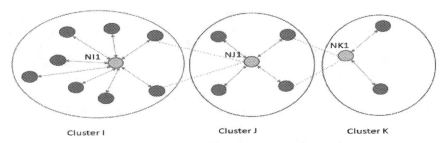

Cluster I   Cluster J   Cluster K

Fig. 1. State of the network at tower T1

The following table shows the energy status of the network nodes after the T1 round (Table 1).

Table 1. Energy status of the network after the T1 round on LEACH-S

Node	Cluster I									Cluster J					Cluster K		
Node	NI1	NI2	NI3	NI4	NI5	NI6	NI7	NI8	NI9	NJ1	NJ2	NJ3	NJ4	NJ5	NK1	NK2	NK3
E,	16	19.5	19.5	19.5	19.5	19.5	19.5	19.5	19.5	18	19.5	19.5	19.5	19.5	19	19.5	19.5
Stat	INSTABILITY									STABLE					STABLE		

Nodes periodically send data from their environments to the CH. A round corresponds to the event of sending data to the CH, i.e., a period. We repeat the experiment until round T16 and collect the information to count the number of instabilities on the network. We call INSTABILITY the change of CH. This change generates a specific broadcast of control messages to announce the new CH. We assume that the energy consumed by an ordinary (non-CH) node receiving a packet from a neighbouring node is negligible. A non-CH node destroys this packet at the network access layer.

Table 2 Summarizes the information from rounds T1 to T16.

INSTABILITY Experimentation with BMN-LEACH-S

In BMN-LEACH-S, thanks to our member node balancing process, we end up this time with 7 nodes in cluster I, 5 in cluster J and 5 in cluster k. The CHs for these clusters I, J and K are respectively, NI1, NJ1 and NK1. As a reminder, in BMN-LEACH-S membership in a cluster is a function of the cost that the non-CH node has with the CH. Each node chooses the CH with which it has the highest cost. This cost is computed with our fuzzy logic system presented in Appendix 1.

Table 2. Summarizes the information from rounds T1 to T16 on LEACH-S

Cluster	LEACH-S																
	I									J					K		
Nodes	NI1	NI2	NI3	NI4	NI5	NI6	NI7	NI8	NI9	NJ1	NJ2	NJ3	NJ4	NJ5	NK1	NK2	NK3
T0	20	20	20	20	20	20	20	20	20	20	20	20	20	20	20	20	20
T1	16	19.5	19.5	19.5	19.5	19.5	19.5	19.5	19.5	18	19.5	19.5	19.5	19.5	19	19.5	19.5
Stat	INSTABILITY									STABLE					STABLE		
T2	15.5	15.5	19	19	19	19	19	19	19	16	19	19	19	19	18	19	19
Stat	INSTABILITY									INSTABILITY					STABLE		
T3	15	15	15	18.5	18.5	18.5	18.5	18.5	18.5	15.5	17	18.5	18.5	18.5	17	18.5	18.5
Stat	INSTABILITY									STABLE					STABLE		
T4	14.5	14.5	14.5	14.5	18	18	18	18	18	15	15	18	18	18	16	18	18
Stat	INSTABILITY									INSTABILITY					INSTABILITY		
T5	14	14	14	14	14	17.5	17.5	17.5	17.5	14.5	14.5	16	17.5	17.5	15.5	17	17.5
Stat	INSTABILITY									STABLE					STABLE		
T6	13.5	13.5	13.5	13.5	13.5	13.5	17	17	17	14	14	14	17	17	15	16	17
Stat	INSTABILITE									INSTABILITY					STABLE		
T7	13	13	13	13	13	13	13	16.5	16.5	13.5	13.5	13.5	15	16.5	14.5	15	16.5
Stat	INSTABILITY									STABLE					STABLE		
T8	12.5	12.5	12.5	12.5	12.5	12.5	12.5	12.5	16	13	13	13	13	16	14	14	16
Stat	INSTABILITY									INSTABILITY					INSTABILITY		
T9	12	12	12	12	12	12	12	12	12	12.5	12.5	12.5	12.5	14	13.5	13.5	15
Stat	INSTABILITY									STABLE					STABLE		
T10	11.5	11.5	11.5	11.5	11.5	11.5	11.5	11.5	08	12	12	12	12	12	13	13	14
Stat	INSTABILITY									INSTABILITY					STABLE		
T11	11	11	11	11	11	11	11	07.5	07.5	11.5	11.5	11.5	11.5	10	12.5	12.5	13
Stat	INSTABILITY									STABLE					STABLE		
T12	10.5	10.5	10.5	10.5	10.5	10	07	07	07	11	11	11	11	08	12	12	12
Stat	INSTABILITY									INSTABILITY					INSTABILITY		
T13	10	10	10	10	10	06.5	06.5	06.5	06.5	10.5	10.5	10.5	09	07.5	11.5	11.5	11
Stat	INSTABILITY									STABLE					STABLE		
T14	09.5	09.5	09.5	09	06	06	06	06	06	10	10	10	07	07	11	11	10
Stat	INSTABILITY									INSTABILITY					STABLE		
T15	09	09	09	05.5	05.5	05.5	05.5	05.5	05.5	09.5	09.5	08	06.5	06.5	10.5	10.5	09
Stat	INSTABILITY									STABLE					STABLE		
T16	08.5	08.5	05	05	05	05	05	05	05	09	09	06	06	06	10	10	08
Stat	INSTABILITY									INSTABILITY					INSTABILITY		

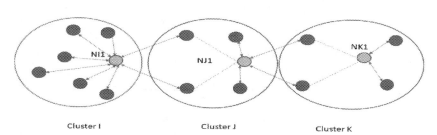

Cluster I   Cluster J   Cluster K

Fig. 2. Fuzzy-based CH selection of nodes in the respective clusters

In round T1, we have (Table 3):

Table 3. Energy status of the network after the T1 round BMN-LEACH-S

	Cluster I							Cluster J					Cluster K				
Nodes	NI1	NI2	NI3	NI4	NI5	NI6	NI7	NJ1	NJ2	NJ3	NJ4	NJ5	NK1	NK2	NK3	NK4	NK5
E		19.5	19.5	19.5	19.5	19.5	19.5	18	19.5	19.5	19.5	19.5	18	19.5	19.5	19.5	19.5
Stat	STABLE							STABLE					STABLE				

We repeat the experiment until round T16 and collect the information to count the number of instabilities on the network. Table 4 summarizes information from rounds T1 to T16.

Table 4. Information from the network running on BMN-LEACH-S

	BMN-LEACH-S																
Cluster	I							J					K				
Nodes	NI1	NI2	NI3	NI4	NI5	NI6	NI7	NJ1	NJ2	NJ3	NJ4	NJ5	NK1	NK2	NK3	NK4	NK5
T0	20	20	20	20	20	20	20	20	20	20	20	20	20	20	20	20	20
T1	17	19.5	19.5	19.5	19.5	19.5	19.5	18	19.5	19.5	19.5	19.5	18	19.5	19.5	19.5	19.5
Stat	STABLE							STABLE					STABLE				
T2	14	19	19	19	19	19	19	16	19	19	19	19	16	19	19	19	19
Stat	INSTABILITY							INSTABILITY					INSTABILITY				
T3	13.5	16	18.5	18.5	18.5	18.5	18.5	15.5	17	18.5	18.5	18.5	15.5	17	18.5	18.5	18.5
Stat	STABLE							STABLE					STABLE				
T4	13	13	18	18	18	18	18	15	15	18	18	18	15	15	18	18	18
Stat	INSTABILITY							INSTABILITY					INSTABILITY				
T5	12.5	12.5	15	17.5	17.5	17.5	17.5	14.5	14.5	16	17.5	17.5	14.5	14.5	16	17.5	17.5
Stat	STABLE							STABLE					STABLE				
T6	12	12	12	17	17	17	17	14	14	14	17	17	14	14	14	17	17
Stat	INSTABILITY							INSTABILITÉ					INSTABILITÉ				
T7	11.5	11.5	11.5	14	16.5	16.5	16.5	13.5	13.5	13.5	15	16.5	13.5	13.5	13.5	15	16.5
Stat	STABLE							STABLE					STABLE				
T8	11	11	11	11	16	16	16	13	13	13	13	16	13	13	13	13	16
Stat	INSTABILITY							INSTABILITY					INSTABILITÉ				
T9	10.5	10.5	10.5	10.5	13	15.5	15.5	12.5	12.5	12.5	12.5	14	12.5	12.5	12.5	12.5	14
Stat	STABLE							STABLE					STABLE				
T10	10	10	10	10	10	15	15	12	12	12	12	12	12	12	12	12	12
Stat	INSTABILITY							INSTABILITY					INSTABILITY				
T11	09.5	09.5	09.5	09.5	09.5	12	14.5	11.5	11.5	11.5	11.5	10	11.5	11.5	11.5	11.5	10
Stat	STABLE							STABLE					STABLE				
T12	09	09	09	09	09	09	14	11	11	11	11	08	11	11	11	11	08
Stat	INSTABILITY							INSTABILITY					INSTABILITY				
T13	08.5	08.5	08.5	08.5	08.5	08.5	11	10.5	10.5	10.5	09	07.5	10.5	10.5	10.5	09	07.5
Stat	STABLE							STABLE					STABLE				
T14	08	08	08	08	08	[illegible]	08	10	10	10	07	07	10	10	10	07	07
Stat	INSTABILITY							INSTABILITY					INSTABILITY				
T15	07.5	07.5	07.5	07.5	07.5	05	07.5	09.5	09.5	08	06.5	06.5	09.5	09.5	08	06.5	06.5
Stat	STABLE							STABLE					STABLE				
T16	07	07	07	07	07	02	07	09	09	06	06	06	09	09	06	06	06
Stat	INSTABILITY							INSTABILITY					INSTABILITY				

From the analytical study we conducted, during the 16 rounds, according to Tables 2 and 4, we notice that the total number of instability cases in LEACH-S for the whole network is 28 against 24 in BMN-LEACH-S.

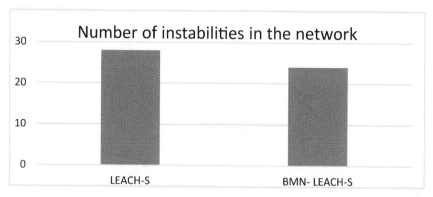

Fig. 3. Number of instability in the network

Looking in detail the number of instabilities per cluster, we notice that in LEACH-S, for clusters I, J and K, we have respectively 16, 8 and 4 cases of instabilities. In the network running with BMN-LEACH-S, with this experiment, we have the same number (8) of instabilities for each of the three clusters I, J, K (see Table 2 and Table 4).

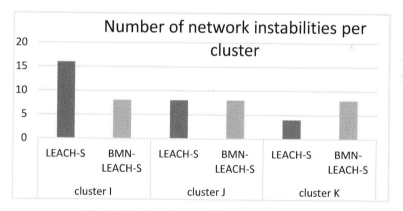

Fig. 4. Number of network instability per cluster

3.6 Analysis and Interpretation

The results of the experiments show that in all the networks, with the LEACH-S protocol we observe 28 instabilities against 24 for BMN-LEACH-S (see Fig. 3.). The use of LEACH produces more instabilities than the use of BMN-LEACH-S. If we analyse the results by cluster, the imbalance is more visible. In cluster I, we see that the CH was changed 16 times with LEACH-S versus 8 for BMN-LEACH-S (see Fig. 4.).

Knowing that each CH change induces special control message broadcast for new CH announcement, we can deduce that BMN-LEACH-S improves the routing load compared to LEACH-S. This leads to the reduction of the overall network energy consumption. BMN-LEACH-S also improved packet loss rate due to topology changes or network overload and average packet transmission delay.

With these experiments, the CH was changed 8 times for each cluster driven by BMN-LEACH-S. We can say that BMN-LEACH balances the traffic load between the different CHs. This increases the lifetime of the network.

4 Conclusion

In this paper, we proposed a new clustering-based routing solution called BMN-LEACH-S. This method is an improvement of the LEACH-S protocol to decrease the instability of some clusters due to frequent CH changes. Also, it solves the problem of unequal distribution of member nodes between clusters. To do this, BMN-LEACH-S allocates a quantum of energy to each cluster head. When the CH exhausts the quantum of energy, it appoints a replacement among the nodes not yet elected. Also, it implements a function based on a fuzzy logic system using the parameters number of nodes in the cluster and the RSSI to estimate the cost of a CH. Each node uses this cost to make its choice of CH. This allows more equitable distribution of nodes in the different clusters. An analytical evaluation of our solution shows that it reduces network instabilities compared to LEACH-S. This improves the lifetime of the network. This performance should be confirmed by extensive simulation and tesbed.

Appendix 1 : The Fuzzy Function for Costing

Our fuzzy node balancing solution works in three steps. The fuzzification of the analog values (number of nodes and RSSI), the inference system and the defuzzification.

The Fuzzification Phase
In this phase, we translate the analog input parameters (RSSI signal strength and number of nodes in the cluster) into discrete values between 0 and 1. The first parameter is the number of nodes in the cluster. Since our goal is to balance the size of the clusters, it is necessary to take into account the number of nodes (NN) owning each cluster so that the cluster with more nodes has less chance to receive a new node. Also, the second parameter is the signal strength (RSSI) between the node and the CH. We considered the signal strength so that the cluster with a good communication link has a higher chance of receiving the node.

To do this, we use a membership function to translate these analog values. It should be noted that there are several types of membership function, namely the triangular membership function, the sinusoidal function, etc. But we have chosen the triangular membership function. Also, we choose the same linguistic variables to delimit our fuzzy sets (Very low, low, medium, high, Very high) for both parameters.

For example, if a node has the choice between two clusters named I and J. The number of nodes in cluster I is 8 and its RSSI is 70 and the number of nodes in cluster J is 3 and its RSSI is 50.

Cluster I (NN = 8; RSSI = 70) Cluster J (NN = 3; RSSI = 50)

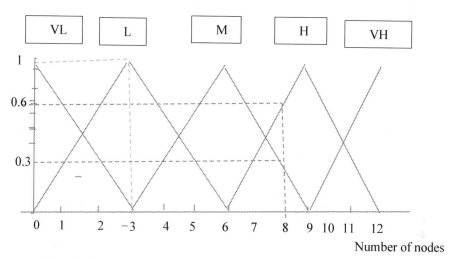

fuzzification process of number of nodes related to CH I and J

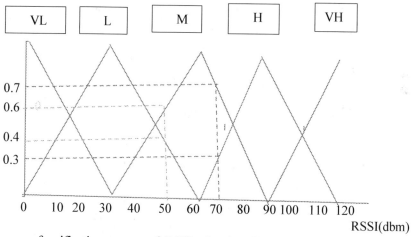

fuzzification process of RSSI related to CH I and J

After fuzzification, cluster I has as fuzzy values (NN(0.66 high; 0.34 medium) RSSI(0.3 High; 0.7 medium)). cluster J has as fuzzy values(NN(1 low) RSSI(0.4 low; 0.6 medium))

The Inference System
Once the different parameters have been translated into "fuzzy language", the inference aims at building decision rules and finding for each of them the rule of belonging of the

conclusion. The construction of these rules, mainly based on "AND", is mathematically translated in the following form.

Rule i	Description (**Ri**)	Output rule (Cluster choice level)
1	NN (very low) AND RSSI (very low)	Medium
2	NN (very low) AND RSSI (low)	Medium
3	NN (very low) AND RSSI (medium)	High
4	NN (very low) AND RSSI (high)	Very high
5	NN (very low) AND RSSI (very high)	Very high
6	NN (low) AND RSSI (very low)	Medium
7	NN (low) AND RSSI (low)	Medium
8	NN (low) AND RSSI (medium)	High
9	NN (low) AND RSSI (high)	Very High
10	NN (low) AND RSSI (very high)	Very High
11	NN (medium) AND RSSI (very low)	Low
12	NN (medium) AND RSSI (low)	Low
13	NN (medium) AND RSSI (medium)	Medium
14	NN (medium) AND RSSI (high)	Medium
15	NN (medium) AND RSSI (very high)	Medium
16	NN (high) AND RSSI (very low)	Very low
17	NN (high) AND RSSI (low)	Low
18	NN (high) AND RSSI (medium)	Low
19	NN (high) AND RSSI (high)	Medium
20	NN (high) AND RSSI (very high)	Medium
21	NN (very high) AND RSSI (very low)	Very Low
22	NN (very high) AND RSSI (low)	Very Low
23	NN (very high) AND RSSI (medium)	Low
24	NN (very high) AND RSSI (high)	Low
25	NN (very high) AND RSSI (very high)	Low

After the establishment of the rule base, We use the truth values associated with the clusters to activate the rules using Zadeh operators.

Cluster I

Rule	Value	Result
NN (high) AND RSSI (medium))	Min (0.66; 07)	0.66 low
NN (high) ET RSSI (high))	Min (0.66; 0.3)	0.3 medium
NN (medium) ET RSSI (medium))	Min (0.34; 0.6)	0.34 medium
NN (medium) ET RSSI (high))	Min (0.34; 0.4)	0.34 medium

Cluster J

Rule	Value	Result
NN (low) ET RSSI (low))	Min (1; 0.4)	0.4 medium
NN (low) ET RSSI (medium))	Min (1; 0.6)	0.6 high

Aggregating the Results
This step of the inference consists in grouping all the rules. This aggregation is therefore done on the basis of logical "Or", which translates into "Max".
   Aggregation of the CHI values of Cluster I

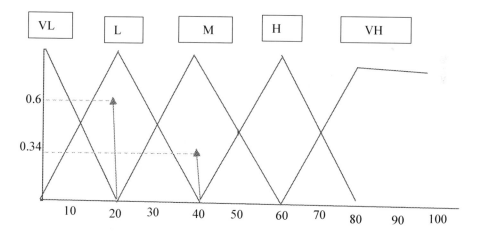

Aggregation of CHJ values of Cluster J

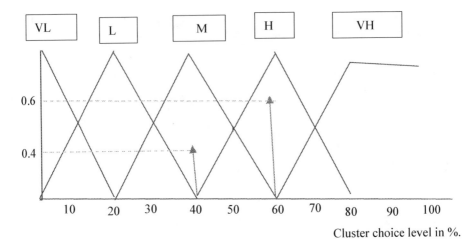

Cluster choice level in %.

Defuzzification

Defuzzification consists in transforming the fuzzy output subset into a non-fuzzy value called the cluster head cost. A node wanting to integrate into a cluster will choose the cluster whose CH offers a better cost. To compute the cost, we will use the weighted average method which consists of averaging the maximums of the output values.

$$CG= \frac{\sum_{i=0}^{n} \mu_A(K_i).(K_i)}{\sum_{I=0}^{n} \mu_A(K_i)}$$

$$Cost\ (CHI) = \frac{30*0.66+ 60*0.34}{0.66+ 0.34} =40.2$$

$$Cost\ (CHJ)= \frac{40*0.4+ 60*0.6}{0.6+ 0.4} = 52$$

So the node will choose cluster J because it is the CHJ that offers a better cost.

References

1. Bendjeddou, A., Laoufi, H., Boudiit, S.: LEACH-S: Low Energy Adaptive Clustering Hierarchy for Sensor Network (2018). https://doi.org/10.1109/ISNCC.2018.8531049
2. Wendi, H., Anantha, R.C., Hari, B.: Energy-efficient communication protocol for wireless microsensor networks. In: Proceedings of the 33rd Annual Hawaii International Conference on System Sciences (2000). https://doi.org/10.1007/s00440-002-0224-4

3. Lindsey, S., Raghavendra, C.S.: PEGASIS: power-efficient gathering in sensor information systems. IEEE Aerosp. Conf. Proc. **3**, 1125–1130 (2002). https://doi.org/10.1109/AERO.2002. 1035242
4. Ossama, Y., Sonia, F.: 'HEED: a hybrid, energy-efficient, distributed clustering approach for ad hoc sensor networks.' IEEE Trans. Mob. Comput. (2004). https://doi.org/10.1109/TMC. 2006.141
5. Mu, T., Tang, M.: LEACH-B: an improved LEACH protocol for wireless sensor network. In: 6th International Conference on Wireless Communications Networking and Mobile Computing. WiCOM 2010, pp. 2–5 (2010). https://doi.org/10.1109/WICOM.2010.5601113
6. Kaur, K., Deepika, S.: Improvement in LEACH protocol by electing master cluster heads to enhance the network lifetime in WSN. Int. J. Sci. Eng. Appl. **2**(5), 110–114 (2013)
7. Marappan, P., Rodrigues, P.: An energy efficient routing protocol for correlated data using CL-LEACH in WSN. Wireless Netw. **22**(4), 1415–1423 (2015). https://doi.org/10.1007/s11 276-015-1063-4
8. Selvi, M., Logambigai, R., Ganapathy, S., Ramesh, L.S., Nehemiah, H.K., Arputharaj, K.: Fuzzy temporal approach for energy efficient routing in WSN. In: ACM International Conference Proceeding Series, vol. 25–26 (2016). https://doi.org/10.1145/2980258.2982109

M-ODD: A Standard Protocol for Reporting MANET Related Models, Simulations, and Findings

Izabela Savić[✉], Marshall Asch, Keefer Rourke, Fatemeh Safari, Patrick Houlding, Jeremie Fraeys de Veubeke, Jason Ernst, and Daniel Gillis

University of Guelph, Guelph, ON, Canada
{savici,masch,krourke,safarif,phouldin,jfraeysd,dgillis}@uoguelph.ca,
ernstjason1@gmail.com

Abstract. There has been a steady increase in the number of research publications in the Mobile ad hoc Network (MANET) domain over the last two decades. However, several studies have indicated that the credibility of MANET simulation publications may be in question because numerous publications lack vital information (e.g., simulation tools, variables, parameters used) and statistical rigor. This has led to issues of repeatability and reproducibility of previous work and calls into question the validity of the simulation results which are difficult or impossible to verify. To address this, we propose a modified Overview, Design Concepts, and Details (ODD) protocol, based on the work of Grimm et al., as a standard documentation protocol for MANET simulation studies. The MANET ODD (M-ODD) protocol will promote credibility within the domain of study by increasing repeatability, reproducibility, and statistical rigor.

Keywords: MANET · Mobile ad hoc · Ad hoc networks · Standardization · Simulation · Scientific communication · Documentation protocol

1 Introduction

Mobile ad hoc Networks (MANETs) provide a means of communication between mobile users without the need for fixed infrastructure (e.g., wireless internet access points). Interest in MANETs has grown over the years as its applications have become more widespread and evident. Such applications are providing communication in disaster relief, providing wireless connectivity in suburban environments, as well as providing communication in military situations [1,2]. However, multiple surveys of MANET simulation papers have found the credibility of MANET research to be severely compromised. It has been observed that there is a "lack of reliability of MANET simulation-based studies" by Kurkowski et al. [3] and that less than 15% of MobiHoc papers published between 2000 and 2005 are repeatable [3]. An analysis of MANET simulation papers published from the

© ICST Institute for Computer Sciences, Social Informatics and Telecommunications Engineering 2022
Published by Springer Nature Switzerland AG 2022. All Rights Reserved
W. Bao et al. (Eds.): ADHOCNETS 2021/TridentCom 2021, LNICST 428, pp. 114–129, 2022.
https://doi.org/10.1007/978-3-030-98005-4_9

Institute of Electrical and Electronics Engineers (IEEE) and the Association for Computing Machinery (ACM) between 2010 and 2017 held comparable results. It indicated that only 26% of papers were completely repeatable, and that there were design flaws, unrealistic assumptions, lack of reproducibility, and statistically invalid results in a large majority of published papers [4]. The reason most studies were found to lack reproducibility was that they were missing key information, such as the simulator used, type of simulation used, value of initial variables, number of simulations run, and Pseudo Random Number Generator (PRNG) information [3,4]. The lack of reproducibility reduces author credibility and hinders further academic progress within the field since the stable and reliable groundwork that new researchers depend on to conduct their experiments and develop new methods is unverifiable, unreliable, or lacking in rigor. Instead, researchers must focus their efforts on correcting, verifying, or reinvestigating domain knowledge before further advancements can be made. Ultimately this reduces the credibility and trustworthiness of domain results.

These challenges are not unique to MANET simulation-based research. In fact, simulation-based research involving agent-based and individual-based models once shared similar issues: the research was difficult to replicate, difficult to understand, and was often described verbally rather than with equations, tables, figures, etc. [5]. These issues prompted Grimm et al. (2006) to create a standard documentation protocol for describing these models called the Overview, Design Concepts, and Details (ODD) protocol. The original ODD protocol included three main sections: Overview, Design Concepts, and Details. The Overview and Details sections were each further divided into three subsections. The Overview included subsections of 1) Purpose, 2) State Variables and Scales, and 3) Process Overview and Scheduling. Subsections of Initialization, Input, and Sub-models made up the details section. The protocol was updated in 2010 and again in 2020 [6,7] to include a wider set of design concepts (e.g., adaptation, learning, prediction, sensing) [6], and to include example documents (e.g., TRACE documents, Nested ODD) to improve clarity, replication, and structural realism [7].

In this paper, we propose a modified version of Grimm et al.'s ODD documentation protocol, to provide a standard documentation protocol for future MANET simulation studies. Specifically, we propose the addition of two subsections to the details section that are necessary for reproducibility: System Requirements, and Software Overview. These two subsections will allow researchers to reproduce documented simulations accurately by ensuring they have the correct tools (e.g., simulation tools, computer setups, etc.) to do so. As such, the proposed MANET ODD (M-ODD), will provide a protocol for researchers to improve the reproducibility, consistency, and statistical soundness of their studies. Ultimately, M-ODD will improve the credibility of MANET simulation research.

We begin with a summary discussion of the common pitfalls in MANET simulation studies that have been identified in previous reviews, particularly those that hinder replicability and verifiability in Sect. 2. Following this, we present the subsections of the proposed M-ODD protocol in Sect. 3. In Sect. 4 we evaluate a series of MANET papers against the proposed M-ODD protocol (co-authored by one of the authors of this work) and provide specific examples that could improve the work. This is not to suggest that the findings are invalid, but that improvements in documentation could be helpful to ensure reproducibility of the work. Discussion and conclusions are provided in Sect. 5.

2   Common Pitfalls in MANET Research

In this section, we summarize some of the findings of two review papers of the MANET research domain. This is necessary to contextualize the proposed M-ODD framework.

2.1   Simulation Identification

Identifying the simulator used in a MANET simulation study is a key factor in determining a study's validity and reproducibility. It is vital that researchers identify and list the simulator used in their paper. Of 114 simulation papers surveyed in [3], roughly 30% failed to identify the simulator used and 27% used a custom simulation tool. Similarly, fewer than 40% of the simulation studies reviewed in [4] reported the simulation tool and version used. Neglecting to specify the simulation tool and version, or failure to provide access to the custom simulation tool compromises the repeatability and reproducibility of the simulation.

2.2   Input Parameters

Clearly identifying the input parameters used in a MANET simulation study is a crucial factor in determining a study's reproducibility. It was found that 10% of MANET simulation study papers surveyed in [4] did not report any parameters used in the simulation, and only 32% provided partial information. Of the papers surveyed in [3], 43% did not state the number of nodes used or the transmission range, 55% did not state the simulation duration, 64% did not state the number of simulation runs, and 47% did not state the size of the simulation area. The lack of incomplete parameters given (along with the lack of identifying simulation tools) rendered 53% of papers reviewed in [4] non-reproducible. It is important to list the input parameters, as the default parameters are not always appropriate for the purpose of the study. This may cause a researcher attempting to reproduce the simulation to choose incorrect parameters or assume that the default parameters are correct, making it impossible to reproduce (and verify) simulation results. See Fig. 1 for example.

parameter	symbol	value(s)
Number of nodes	n	127, 2110, 37777, 108360
Node speed	v	(0,10) m/s
Node pause time	p_t	(0,20) s
simulation length	T	4h
world area		5km x 5km
routing protocol		DSDV
messages sizes		512 bytes
number of iterations per setup		30
Radio model		802.11b, $2.4GHz$
propagation delay model		constant speed delay
propagation loss model		log distance loss
loss exponent		3
loss reference loss		$41.7dB$
antenna Rx gain		0 dB
antenna Tx gain		0 dB

Fig. 1. An example list of parameters from a proposed simulation study in [8].

2.3 Mobility and Propagation Models

The mobility models used in a MANET simulation study are important for the verification of the study. This is because different mobility models result in different movement characteristics of nodes [9,10]. It allows other researchers to verify the validity of the study and the information presented. For example, using a freeway mobility model to represent node mobility of students walking on campus would be an inappropriate choice. In [4], Only 5% of studies provided complete information on the mobility and propagation models used, while 47% did not mention the mobility model used and 69% did not report the radio propagation model used. Additionally, in [3], 42% did not mention the type of mobility tool used, while approximately 57% did not state the type of mobility model used. For the correct conclusions to be drawn in MANET research, it is imperative that a peer reviewer be able to verify the validity of a MANET study, and to do so a researcher needs to provide complete information regarding the mobility model and propagation model used. It is also equally important that the appropriate mobility model is chosen, as using the incorrect mobility model renders the simulation and its findings irrelevant.

2.4 Statistical Validity

Statistical analysis is necessary to ensure the validity of findings of any simulation-based paper. MANET simulation studies are not exempt from this. Regardless, of the papers reviewed in [4], 84% did not report the seed value,

61% did not report the number of simulations run, and 66% did not report confidence intervals. Further, 64% of papers in [3] failed to indicate how many simulations were conducted. This is problematic as observations from a single simulation run should never be used for conclusive or generalizable results; single simulation runs fail to account for the stochastic nature of a simulation [3]. It is also important to identify sources of bias (removing or mitigating bias where possible) for a study to be statistically sound and generalizable. However, over 90% of studies in [3] may have suffered from initialization bias - the influence of initialization settings on study results. The presence of this bias may result in "contamination" of the conclusions determined by the study. To avoid this bias, researchers often delay gathering data from a simulation for a given period, called the "warm up" period [11]. Overall, less than 6% of the simulation studies reviewed in [3] and [4] were statistically sound. Statistical validity is essential to the credibility of a simulation paper. Thus, it is important to provide all required statistical information, as "lack of statistical information puts the validity of the paper in doubt" [4].

2.5 File Accessibility and Sharing

The lack of file accessibility and sharing impedes MANET research. It hinders the ability of researchers to reproduce a given simulation, which in turn makes the validity of a simulation extremely difficult to determine. Of the hundreds of MANET simulation papers available, it is impossible to expect a reader to be able to perfectly reproduce a simulation study with only a (partial) list of variables, functions, processes, equations, and the simulator details. Not being able to access simulation code and data sets creates a barrier for researchers trying to reimplement an algorithm. It leaves researchers and peer reviewers with no way to verify that the simulation was properly coded or configured, that the data used in the simulation was feasible, or that a replicated simulation is accurate. Despite this, not a single paper reviewed by [3] provided statements about code or dataset availability. This makes it so that new researchers cannot reproduce any studies [3], hindering further research and advances in the space. Thus, MANET simulation code, configuration files, and data sets should be publicly available, or described in sufficient detail to facilitate reproducibility.

3   M-ODD Protocol

The purpose of the M-ODD protocol is to provide a structure and guideline for future MANET simulation studies that ensures all information required to verify the validity of the study is present. The M-ODD protocol can be broken into three main sections with nine subsections (compared to the original seven subsections). We retain the three main sections of Overview, Details, and Design Concepts [5]. The Overview section remains unchanged with three subsections: Purpose, State Variables and Scales, and Process Overview and Scheduling. The purpose of the Overview section is to provide the reader with a skeleton of the program implemented for simulations [5]. We follow the outline of the design concepts section, which discusses related general concepts, the design of the model, model objectives, and collection of observations [7]. We also propose two additional subsections (System Requirements and Software Overview) to the Details section to ensure that researchers know which materials are required to reproduce the simulation study. As such, the Details section is now composed of Initialization, Input, System Requirements, Software Overview, and Sub-models subsections. The details section aims to provide the reader with enough information to "re-implement the model and run the baseline simulations" [5].

3.1   The O of M-ODD: Overview

Purpose. The Purpose subsection is used to justify the model chosen, and to list the goals of the model [5]. Due to the nature of MANET studies, it is important that all models and algorithms be listed in the Purpose subsection, along with a short and concise justification of the chosen model or algorithm, and what the researcher hopes to achieve with the use of the model or algorithm. For example: if one uses a random waypoint mobility model with a quality-of-service algorithm, there should be a brief description of the model and algorithm, appropriate references, and justification and expectations of both items. This is typically provided in the introduction of the paper [5].

State Variables and Scales. The State Variables and Scales subsection is used to list all the state variables needed for the simulation study. State variables or low-level variables are variables that cannot be derived from other variables. Such variables should include the number of nodes, transmission range, movement speed, pseudo random number generator seed, and more. The unit of measurement should be provided for variables that require them. State variables should be presented in a table along with a brief description of the variable (see table 3 in [5] for an example). Scales can be presented in a separate table with the scale name. Network topology can also be described. A list of all messages and functions should be provided (for examples, see [12,13]). Due to the considerable number of variables needed to conduct a MANET simulation, it may be challenging to list all variables in a table in a conference or journal paper. We suggest that variables most integral to the study be published in a table in the body of the paper, with a complete list of simulation variables provided in supplementary materials or publicly available.

Process Overview and Scheduling. The Process Overview and Scheduling Subsection should provide the user with a "skeleton" of the functions and algorithms used in the simulation. Each process (including the order in which they are executed) and the effects of the process (including the order in which variables are updated) should be described for the reader [5]. If there are many processes used for the model, a table with all the processes listed should be provided [5]. See section V of [13], or [14,15] for several good examples of this. In particular, [13] describes the algorithms included in each function and the order in which the processes occur. To improve readability and understanding, the use of flow charts, sequence diagrams, class diagrams, and other UML diagrams are highly encouraged.

3.2   The First D of M-ODD: Design Concepts

Description of general design concepts begins with the inclusion of the basic principles and objectives of a simulation. General concepts, theories, hypotheses, and modelling approaches related to the simulation design are included here, as well as a description of how they relate to the simulation's execution [7]. The scope of the system and applications of the simulation should be discussed, as well as its objectives, how the objectives will be measured, and potential thresholds to determine if a simulation has achieved its objectives [7]. The simulation design should also be clearly stated.

In the case of MANET simulation studies, it is particularly important to address the following two questions as part of the simulation design: 1) how are things grouped, and 2) how are data collected from the simulation for testing, understanding, and analysis? [5]. In the former case, this question should be used to provide details about how a cluster is grouped, how a network partition is grouped, and so on (see [16] for a detailed discussion describing how a node is grouped into a network partition). In the latter case, details regarding the method of collecting data across all simulation runs are required. For example, if the first 400 seconds of data were ignored in a 2000-second-long simulation, justification and reasoning should be provided. If simulations were completed under different scenarios (e.g., using a different number of nodes, transmission range, grid size, etc.) then each scenario should be described, including purpose and justification for inclusion in the study. Researchers may also want to include a description of the traffic model here. Which nodes are sources and sinks? How many of each, how often are they generating packets? Of what size? Is the payload constant, or variable? Is it using TCP, UDP, QUIC, or something else? What is the network stack model? Is it using a TCP/IP stack? Is it using 802.11 WLAN? Something custom? Has any of it been modified? If so, are those algorithms provided?

Here we also discuss the results and analysis of the study, specifically addressing whether the observed outcomes matched expected outcomes. For clarity, observations should be provided in accessible tables or figures (including the unit of measurement when needed). Figures should be labelled and drawn to support accessibility and understanding. Any other additional visual materials used to support the analysis of simulation results can be included in the observation subsection.

3.3   The Second D of ODD: Details

Initialization. The Initialization subsection is similar to the State Variables and Scales subsection from the Overview section. However, rather than listing a brief description of each state variable, we now provide a table with a list of all the state variables and their values. If the values change per simulation, then it is recommended to include multiple tables or a multi-column table with the values for each simulation run. The initialization table and the state variables table can be viewed as one table shown in [5]. Just as mentioned in the State Variables subsection, the units of measurement must be included with the values of the variables that require them. As a MANET simulation typically has hundreds of variables, it is unreasonable to expect all variables to be listed in the paper given space constraints. A reference to a publicly available table with all variables and their values should be provided in the paper or in supplemental materials. The initialization table must include: the transmission range, the transmission range type (e.g., asymmetrical), number of nodes, PRNG seed, number of simulations run (for each simulation type), data generation variables, how nodes are placed, the length of time the simulation is run. If there are additional factors that may alter the communication range of a node (e.g., constructive, or destructive interference), they should be listed as additional notes relating to the initialization table.

Input. The Input subsection follows a similar format to the Initialization subsection. Specifically, a table describing all simulation input variables and their values across each simulation is required. If the number of input variables is large (relative to publication guidelines), a reference to a publicly available input file should be available. It is incredibly important that all input variables are provided and correctly recorded, as the simulation output is a direct reflection of the dynamically input variables [5].

System Requirements. The System Requirements subsection provides the tools that a researcher will need to replicate output from a MANET simulation. For transparency, a list of system requirements should be provided. The list should consist of CPU specifications, the operating system and version, the kernel version, the storage space needed to run the simulation and host all the files and programs needed for the simulation, along with any additional requirements needed to run the simulation (for example, see Fig. 2).

Software Overview. The Software Overview subsection is an essential subsection of the M-ODD protocol, as there is no way to reproduce a simulation if the tools used to program and run the simulation are unknown to a researcher. To facilitate reproducibility, the simulation software and version should be documented, along with any additional simulation software modules used. Animator software and version, code language and version, data types, variable settings, and encryption standards also need to be documented in the paper. In addition, if a finite state machine is used, the name of the machine, along with the appropriate state diagram and transition table should be included. All configuration and scenario files and code should be made publicly available and referenced

Item	Version
CPU	Ryzen7 2700x
GPU	ROG Strix 2080ti-OC
Operating system	Fedora 31
Kernel version	5.8.18-100
NS3 version	3.32
Netanim	3.108
Python	3.7.9

Fig. 2. Example system requirements list [8].

in the paper. If a custom simulation tool was used, the simulation tool should also be made publicly available for download and referenced in the paper (or described in sufficient detail to support replication). See [17] for example. It is also recommended to reference a Docker image or an executable that is runnable on most machines. For example, the simulation study described in Fig. 2 indicates it was implemented using a Fedora 33 operating system, with kernel version 5.12.8-200, using simulation tool NS3 version 3.32.

Sub-models. The Sub-models subsection provides the reader with an in depth understanding of the processes listed in the "Process Overview and Scales" sections in [5]. There are two approaches that can be taken to the Sub-models subsection, which depends entirely on the space limitation of the paper. The reader should be provided with enough detail to thoroughly understand and re-implement the model to complete the simulation themselves. The first option, if limited in space, is to supply a mathematical "skeleton" of the model [5]. The skeleton version should consist of a list of the equations, parameters and rules used in the model. Each equation and rule should have a brief explanation, while parameters should have a slightly more in-depth explanation. If the list of equations is too long, a complete list should be referenced and publicly available to the reader.

Our second option is to provide a full model description. The full model description is a more detailed version of the skeleton version. This means that the choice of equations and parameters should be fully explained and justified. All assumptions made must also be explained and justified. When completing a full model description, you want to answer questions such as: "What specific assumptions are underlying the equations and rules? How were parameter values chosen? How were sub-models tested and calibrated?" [5]. We can see a brief list of the parameters used in the model in Fig. 1. To improve upon this table, we could include a brief explanation of the parameter. It would also be helpful to provide a list of equations used for the calculations of any parameters or values. In addition, when providing a full model description, we will be following the

"Inclusion of rationale" guide provided by Grimm et al. (Section 4.3, [6]). This includes providing clarity and credibility to the readers by answering "why was this model chosen?" [6].

4   Application of the M-ODD Protocol

In this section, we begin with a review and ranking of a series of research publications by Ernst and Brown [17–23]. Each paper is reviewed and ranked based on the presence (+1 point) or absence (no points) of information required by the M-ODD protocol. Each paper can achieve a total of 35 points: 6 points from the Overview section; 2 points from the Design Concepts section; and 27 points from the Details section. Points are achieved by including information such as initialization of variables, system requirements, design concepts, and any other information suggested in the M-ODD outline. Following this, we describe the work of [17] through the lens of the M-ODD protocol and in comparison to [18–23]. We chose to apply the M-ODD protocol to [17] as it was neither the highest nor lowest ranked paper, but still performed well in comparison to [18–23].

4.1   Ranking

Each paper [17–23] was reviewed and scored using a simple presence/absence scoring system (see Table 1). The total score is a weighted average of the scores achieved in the Overview, Design Concepts, and Details sections of the M-ODD protocol. A score of 0% indicates that the article did not satisfy any of the M-ODD requirements, and we assert would be difficult to reproduce. A score of 100% indicates that an article satisfied all the M-ODD requirements, and by extension should be reproducible.

The lowest scoring paper [18] achieved a score of 16%. This score was due to the lack of inclusion of purpose, state variables, initialization variables, software overview, system requirements, input, and grouping information (to name a few). The paper provided insufficient information to allow a researcher to easily reproduce or verify it. The same can be said for [20] which scored only slightly higher at 19%. On the opposite end of the spectrum, [23] scored 61%. This paper satisfied all the requirements of the Overview section, Design Concepts section, and half the requirements of the Details section. The unsatisfied requirements of the Details section come from initialization values not being specified (i.e., transmission range, pseudo random number generator seed, etc.), as well as lack of information regarding system requirements.

The remaining papers have scores that range between 30% and 40%. The variation is due to the amount of detail provided in the papers that sufficiently describe the initialization variables, system requirements, and software overview. None of the surveyed papers provided information describing the system requirements, the pseudo random number generator seed, or the transmission range. Very few of them described the simulation tool(s) used, the number of nodes, the number of simulations run, or the length of the simulation.

Table 1. M-ODD protocol performance scores of [17–23]

Article	Article total score	Overview score	Design concepts score	Details score
[17]	40%	75%	100%	28%
[18]	16%	25%	50%	11%
[19]	37%	75%	100%	24%
[20]	19%	8%	50%	15%
[21]	27%	33%	100%	20%
[22]	30%	42%	100%	24%
[23]	61%	100%	100%	50%
Average	33%	51%	86%	25%

4.2   Application of the M-ODD Protocol

In this section, we further explore Ernst and Brown's research in [17]. Their study aimed to improve the performance of multi-hop wireless networks as peripheral nodes would often suffer from poor performance due to starvation. They analyzed the performance of multi-hop wireless networks using the mixed-bias technique, TS mixed-bias technique, as well as the evolutionary mixed-bias technique. Here we provide a detailed discussion of the scores this paper achieved in reference to the requirements of the M-ODD protocol.

Overview. As indicated in Table 1, [17] achieved a score of 75% for the Overview section of the M-ODD protocol. This score was achieved because the paper clearly described its purpose and because it described the necessary details required of the Process Overview and Scheduling subsection. However, it failed to describe the state variables and scales that are needed to improve the reproducibility of the work.

Purpose. The paper describes that the purpose of the use of mixed-bias scheduling is to "improve the performance of peripheral nodes in multi-hop networks," and "give more resources to nodes closer to gateways to improve their ability to handle their own traffic and peripheral traffic" [17]. This information is clearly included in the introduction and excerpt of the paper. Further, the paper describes how mixed-bias scheduling was chosen as "mixed-bias has a lower likelihood of starvation compared to max-min, and proportional fairness may not contain a strong enough bias to support nodes which are multiple hops away from the gateway" [17]. Overall, [17] fulfilled the Purpose requirements, as it justified the scheduling algorithm chosen, as well as its main goal in the introduction.

State Variables and Scales. In the case of state variables, not much information is provided. While the paper indicates that the number of routers used in the simulation is 100, the number of clients is not known. Further, the pseudo random number generator seed is not provided, neither is the transmission range of the nodes. In terms of the State Variables and Scales subsections, [17] performs extremely poorly.

Process Overview and Scheduling All information needed in the Process Overview and Scheduling subsection can be found in section 3 of [17]. In section 3, a handful of algorithms are provided to the reader, as well as a detailed explanation of the purpose and function of each algorithm. This provides the reader with a clear understanding of the "flow" of the program, along with its purpose.

Design Concepts. Ernst and Brown's research in [17] received a Design Concepts score of 100%. For grouping, the paper describes that nodes on the network were grouped into one of three types: gateway, router, client. We also note that all observational figures and graphs were labelled properly, and that the data was color coded depending on the algorithm used for readability. All graphs were followed by a paragraph discussing the results of the simulations. All the requirements for the Design Concepts section were clearly satisfied by the information provided in [17].

Details. Ernst and Brown's research in [17] received a sub-par score for the Details section of the ODD protocol (28%). The score was the result of failing to satisfy most of the subsections of the M-ODD protocol.

Initialization. The initialization subsection performs well compared to other papers surveyed in this study, as the transmission type, number of nodes, and placement of nodes are discussed. However, the transmission range, pseudo random number generator seed, number of simulations run, length of time a simulation is run, as well as any data generation variables were not listed. Initialization variables can be found in Table 2. Additional information such as the number of nodes, the number of points that generate the nodes, and maximum delay time were also not included. These are all variables that are referenced in [17], but whose values are not defined. In addition, there is no reference to, or mention of, a file or additional table which holds all the initialization variables. Due to the considerable number of variables and unprovided values, [17] does not satisfy the requirement of the Initialization subsection.

Input. There is no mention of whether any values were input into the simulation, and no table or additional file is referenced.

System Requirements. The System Requirements subsection remains unsatisfied. There is no information regarding the CPU used, OS version and kernel, or storage space required. However, the paper does provide some information describing the finite state machine used (in the form of a state table and transition table).

Table 2. Initialization values described in [17]

Parameter	Value
Size of network	100 (10×10 routers)
α	0.5
β_1	2
β_2	5
Transmission type	IEEE 802.11
Inter-arrival rate	0.01
Node distribution	Uniformly distributed

Software Overview. There is some improvement in the Software Overview subsection, as we can note the simulation tool used is ns-3.13. However, information such as if any additional modules are required, the data types, variable settings, animator software version, and encryption standards are not mentioned. There is also no executable referenced. Some of the requirements of the Software Overview section are satisfied, but overall [17] performs poorly here.

Sub-models. Various mathematical formulas and calculations are provided, along with an explanation of the variables, and purpose of the formula. Any assumptions made are stated in the paper, along with a justification for the assumptions made. Most parameters are listed and explained, however, they are not provided in a table and the reader is forced to search through various sections of [17] to gather all the parameters. For that reason, we have created a list of parameters that can be viewed in Table 3 that would improve the readability and ease of reproducibility.

Table 3. Parameters of [17]

Parameter	Value
α Controls mix between strong and weak bias	$0 \leq \alpha \leq 1$
β How strongly to bias against a characteristic?	N/A
c characteristic one wishes to bias proportionally against	N/A
Q_{max} Limit of the maximum number of states a machine is allowed to process in an evolutionary process.	N/A
TABUMOVE Number of iterations before a new move is attempted on the network.	N/A
TABURESET How long before a reset back to the current known best solution	N/A

5   Conclusions

Creating reproducible and credible work should be a top priority for researchers. Yet, there are and continue to be shortcomings in published MANET research that hinders reproducibility. As noted by previous reviews, a majority of Mobi-Hoc papers published between 2000 and 2005, and IEEE and ACM papers published between 2010 and 2017 are not reproducible. The aim of the M-ODD protocol is to provide researchers with a standard format for publicizing MANET simulation research papers. This will in turn ensure that a simulation paper is reproducible, statistically sound, and credible. Improving the reproducibility of MANET simulation papers will allow peer reviewers to be able to verify the validity of the results presented, and provide a stable stepping stone for future researchers to be able to expand upon existing research and conduct the simulations presented with greater ease.

Further, the M-ODD protocol should allow researchers to achieve the green, blue, or red Artifact Available badge (see [24]) for their simulations. The green artefact signifies that any artefacts are available in a permanent archival repository while a red artifact signifies that "a reviewer has verified that the artefact is documented, complete, consistent and exercisable" [24]. Lastly, the blue artefact means that an independent reviewer has successfully reproduced the study and obtained the results of the paper [24].

In the 4-year span between the publication of [5] and [6], Grimm et al.'s ODD protocol was included in over 50 publications. This is a result we hope to see in Mobile ad hoc Network Simulation publications with the presentation of the M-ODD protocol in this document. With the achievement of such a result, and a continuous increase of papers published using the protocol, the reproducibility of MANET simulation papers should improve over the years.

Acknowledgements. The Dish With One Spoon Wampum speaks to our collective responsibility to steward and sustain the environment in which we live and work, so that all peoples, present and future, may benefit from the sustenance it provides. As we continue to strengthen our relationships with and continue to learn from our Indigenous neighbours, we recognize the partnerships and knowledge that have guided the learning and research conducted as part of this work. We acknowledge that the University of Guelph resides in the ancestral and treaty lands of several Indigenous peoples, including the Attawandaron people and the Mississaugas of the Credit, and we recognize and honour our Anishinaabe, Haudenosaunee, and Métis neighbours. We acknowledge that the work presented here occurred on their traditional lands so that we might work to build lasting partnerships that respect, honour, and value the culture, traditions, and wisdom of those who have lived here since time immemorial.

This research was funded in part by Mitacs, and the Work Integrated Learning Digital Subsidy offered through the Internet Communications and Technology Council of Canada via the Government of Canada's Student Work Placement Program.

References

1. Jadhav, S.S., Kulkarni, A.V., Menon, R.: Mobile ad-hoc network (MANET) for disaster management. In: 11th International Conference on Wireless and Optical Communications Networks (WOCN), pp. 1–5. IEEE, September 2014
2. Raja, L., Baboo, S.S.: An overview of MANET: applications, attacks and challenges. IJCSMC **3**(1), 408–417 (2014)
3. Kurkowski, S., Camp, T., Colagrosso, M.: MANET simulation studies: the incredibles. ACM Mob. Comput. Commun. Rev. **9**, 50–61 (2005)
4. Latif, Z., Sharif, K., Alvi, M.K., Li, F.: Simulation standardization: current state and cross-platform system for network simulators. In: Zhu, L., Zhong, S. (eds.) MSN 2017. CCIS, vol. 747, pp. 497–508. Springer, Singapore (2018). https://doi.org/10.1007/978-981-10-8890-2_38
5. Grimm, V., et al.: A standard protocol for describing individual-based and agent based models. Ecol. Modell. **198**, 115–126 (2006)
6. Grimm, V., Berger, U., DeAngelis, D.L., Polhill, J.G., Giske, J., Railsback, S.F.: The ODD protocol: a review and first update. Ecol. Modell. **221**(23), 2760–2768 (2010)
7. Grimm, V., et al.: The ODD protocol for describing agent-based models and other simulation models: a second update to improve clarity, replication and structural realism. JASSS **23**(2) (2020)
8. Asch, M., Lin, X., Gillis, D.: Replicability and Efficacy of the 'Replication in Highly Partitioned Mobile ad hoc Networks' Data Replication Scheme (2022, unpublished)
9. Gorawski, M., Grochla, K.: Review of mobility models for performance evaluation of wireless networks. In: Gruca, D.A., Czachórski, T., Kozielski, S. (eds.) Man-Machine Interactions 3. AISC, vol. 242, pp. 567–577. Springer, Cham (2014). https://doi.org/10.1007/978-3-319-02309-0_62
10. Asch, M., Seymour, P.F., Ernst, J., Gillis, D.: Incorporation of node mobility in data replication schemes in mobile ad hoc networks. In: 10th Annual Information Technology, Electronics and Mobile Communication Conference (IEMCON), pp. 230–236. IEEE, October 2019
11. Schruben, J.W.: Detecting initialization bias in simulation output. Oper. Res. **30**(3), 569–590 (1982)
12. Yu, J., Chong, P.H.J.: An efficient clustering scheme for large and dense mobile ad hoc networks (MANETs). Comput. Commun. **30**, 5–16 (2006)
13. El-Bazzal, Z., Kadoch, M., Agba, B., Haidar, M., Gagnon, F.: A quality of service driven approach for clustering in mobile ad hoc networks based on matrics adaptation: looking beyond clustering. J. Commun. Softw. Syst. **4**(4), 254–265 (2008)
14. Runkler, T.: Wasp swarm optimization of the c-means clustering model. Int. J. Intell. Syst. **23**(3), 269–285 (2008)
15. Shahzad, W., Khan, F.A., Siddiqui, A.B.: Weighted clustering using comprehensive learning particle swarm optimization for mobile ad hoc networks. Int. J. Future Gener. Commun. Netw. **3**(1), 342–349 (2010)
16. Asakura, K., Kato, H., Watanabe, T.: An efficient broadcast method based on hexagonal tessellation for mobile ad-hoc networks. In: Proceedings of the 12th International Conference on Ubiquitous Information Management and Communication, pp. 1–5. IEEE, January 2018
17. Ernst, J.B., Brown, J.A.: Performance evaluation of mixed-bias scheduling schemes for wireless mesh networks. IJSSC **3**(1), 22–34 (2013)

18. Ernst, J.B., Denko, M.K.: The design and evaluation of fair scheduling in wireless mesh networks. J. Comput. Syst. Sci. **77**(4), 654–664 (2011)
19. Ernst, J.B., Nkwe, T.: Adaptive mixed bias resource allocation for wireless mesh networks. In: International Conference on Broadband, Wireless Computing, Communication and Applications, pp. 622–626. IEEE, November 2010
20. Ernst, J.B., Denko, M.K.: Fair scheduling with multiple gateways in wireless mesh networks. In: International Conference on Advanced Information Networking and Applications, pp. 106–112. IEEE, May 2009
21. Ernst, J.B., Brown, J.A.: Co-existence of evolutionary mixed-bias scheduling with quiescence and 802.11 DCF for wireless mesh networks. In: 26th International Conference on Advanced Information Networking and Application Workshops, pp. 678–683. IEEE, March 2012
22. Ernst, J.B., Brown, J.A.: An online evolutionary programming method for parameters of wireless networks. In: International Conference on Broadband and Wireless Computing, Communication and Applications, pp. 515–520. IEEE, October 2011
23. Ernst, J.B., Kremer, S.C., Rodrigues, J.J.P.C.: A wi-fi simulation model which supports channel scanning across multiple non-overlapping channels in NS3. In: 28th International Conference on Advanced Information Networking and Applications, pp. 268–275. IEEE, May 2014
24. Steuwer, M.: Artefact Review and Badging: Improving Confidence in our Experimental Results. ACM Future of Computing Academy, Updated, 14 November 2018. https://acm-fca.org/2018/11/14/artefactreview/. Accessed 15 Dec 2020

Frame Design for Adaptability in Long-Range Underwater Communication

Michel Barbeau[1]([⊠])(iD), Stéphane Blouin[2](iD), and Ahmad Traboulsi[1](iD)

[1] Carleton University, Ottawa, ON, Canada
barbeau@scs.carleton.ca
[2] Defence R&D Canada, Atlantic Research Centre, Dartmouth, NS, Canada

Abstract. The problem addressed in this paper is adaptable long range underwater acoustic communications. We use low frequency underwater acoustic waves that have potential for long range communications. Underwater propagation conditions can vary considerably. We define protocol elements for adaptable underwater communications. They comprise six frame formats with a wide range of robustness with respect to the underwater communication conditions. We vary the interval of symbols of 4-tone Frequency-Shift Keying modulation from one format to another. This has the effect of increasing the SNR. Hence, the ability to operate in less favorable conditions. The performance of our design is evaluated through simulation.

Keywords: Underwater communications · Weak signal communications · Arctic · Software-defined communications

1 Introduction

The underwater environment is a relatively new data communication challenge. The need for underwater communication is related to applications such as monitoring and surveillance of coastal waters [21], submarine activity sensors [22], autonomous undersea vehicles [10], underwater robots [7] and submerged airplane locator beacons [29].

In this paper, we focus on low frequency acoustic communications [11,16]. We aim at long-range underwater acoustic communications that are robust to environmental changes. They are critical for wide-area surveillance systems developed for the Canadian Arctic [12]. Recent studies [13] tend to demonstrate that underwater communications in high frequencies ranges can reach up to 10-to-20 km with reasonable power levels. In contrast to high frequencies, Stojanovic has

This work was supported by the Public Works and Government Services Canada under Contract No. W7707-216847/001/HAL through the Defence Research and Development Canada.

W. Bao et al. (Eds.): ADHOCNETS 2021/TridentCom 2021, LNICST 428, pp. 130–143, 2022.
https://doi.org/10.1007/978-3-030-98005-4_10

pointed out that attenuation is lower in low frequencies [26]. The potential for very-long distance transmissions in low frequencies has been established [15].

In our research, we focus on the acoustic 200 Hz to 2 kHz frequency band for long-rang underwater communications. We also acknowledge that the narrow half-power bandwidth, associated with low underwater acoustic frequencies and long distances, limits applications to low data rates. In Refs. [1–4, 8, 18, 19], we describe the design of a physical and frame layer protocol for long range under-water communications. In a recent companion paper, we have been able to show that we can achieve source-receiver separation distances well above 30 km in the Canadian Arctic environment [9]. The goal of the research presented in this paper is to improve the robustness of our communication system. We aim to achieve much larger source-receiver separation distances (in the order of 100-to-500 km) and introduce adaptability to environmental changes (such as variations in the nature or magnitude of noise, ice presence, and sound speed profile). The intention is to realize a design that can achieve long-range communications in the Canadian Arctic environment, in all seasons.

In this paper, we define six frame formats with increasing degree of robust-ness. Our strategy is to increase robustness by augmenting the Signal-to-Noise Ratio (SNR), in particular the energy contained in every 4-tone Frequency-Shift Keying (4-FSK) symbol. The performance of the six frame formats is char-acterized through simulation. Building on these six frame formats, we define adaptability protocols to variable underwater propagation conditions.

Related work is reviewed in Sect. 2. The underwater communication system design is reviewed in Sect. 3. The design of the receiver is outlined in Sect. 4. Its Matlab™ implementation is discussed in Sect. 5. Performance evaluation results are presented in Sect. 6. The adaptability protocols are specified in Sect. 7. Section 8 concludes the paper.

2   Related Work

Song et al. emphasized that one of the key underwater communication issues is adaptability to changing propagation conditions [25]. Most of the adaptability techniques rely on the use of feedback returned by the receiver to the source to dynamically adapt transmission parameters, such as modulation or Forward Error Correction (FEC) [5, 6, 24, 28].

In this paper, we adapt the SNR to the propagation conditions. The SNR is defined as the following equation:

$$SNR = \frac{P}{N} = \frac{E_b R}{B N_0} \tag{1}$$

This equation tells that the SNR is equal to the ratio of the signal power (P) over the channel noise power (N). In turn, the signal power is equal to the product of the energy per bit (E_b) times the data rate (R). While the channel noise power is equal to the product of the channel bandwidth (B) times the noise power spectral density (N_0). It is a well-established fact that augmenting the SNR increases the robustness of communications [23]. Indeed, higher SNR does achieve better Bit Error Rate (BER) and Frame Error Rate (FER). To increase the SNR, we can either augment the values of the numerators E_b or R or lower the values of the denominators B or N_0. The noise power spectral density is function of the environment. The transmission power, hence the quantity E_b, can be cranked up at the expense of energy consumption. The transmission power is constrained by the capabilities of the equipment. The bandwidth can be narrowed. We do use a very narrow bandwidth signal already (4.4 Hz). In this paper, we make the choice of lengthening the time interval of symbols to improve robustness of underwater communications. The data rate R is reduced. For a given power level P, there is more energy in every bit (E_b). The bit SNR (E_b/N_0) is augmented, proportionally to the reduction of R.

Table 1. Frame formats of the six communication modes.

Mode	T (sec.)	F (sec.)	R (bps)	Efficiency	k	Samples/ symbol	FFT bin width (Hz)
1 min	0.34	55.30	0.90	0.21	1	128	1.46
2 min	0.68	110.59	0.45	0.10	2	256	0.73
4 min	1.37	221.18	0.23	0.05	4	512	0.37
8 min	2.73	442.37	0.11	0.03	8	1024	0.18
16 min	5.46	884.74	0.06	0.01	16	2048	0.09
20 min	6.83	1105.92	0.05	0.01	20	2560	0.07

3   Communication System Design

To support various underwater communication propagation conditions, we define six different modes of communications. Every mode has a corresponding frame format. Table 1 shows key design parameters for every format.

The formats have common and specific parameters. For all modes, every frame comprises 162 channel symbols that encode 50 data bits. Convolutional FEC of the data bits yields 162 code bits. Every code bit is paired with a synchronization bit. Each pair makes a channel symbol. The 4-FSK complex modulation envelope frequencies are -2.2, -0.73, 0.73 and 2.2 Hz, corresponding to the channel symbols 11, 10, 01 and 00. The signal bandwidth is 4.4 Hz. Every mode has a specific symbol time interval (T) and, consequently a specific frame interval (F), the second and third columns in Table 1. The value of the third column results from the product of the number of symbols (162) time the symbol time interval. For each frame format, the fourth column shows the achieved effective data rate (the ratio $50/F$). Defining the bandwidth efficiency as the ratio effective data rate over bandwidth, (the ratio $R/4.4$), the fifth column shows the bandwidth efficiency for every mode.

In previous papers, we described several aspects of our communication system design. [1–4, 8, 18, 19]. In the sequel, we focus on the aspects that are new and required for the support of the six frame formats. We also briefly summarize the mechanisms that have been described in our previous papers.

3.1   Physical Layer: 4-FSK

We use 4-FSK modulation, a specific kind of Multiple Frequency-Shift Keying (MFSK). Orthogonality of MFSK symbols is guaranteed when the frequency separation between symbols Δf is equal to the ratio $k/(2T)$, for a positive integer k (see Ref. [20], P. 110). As a function of the supported mode, the sixth column of Table 1 shows the value of the positive integer k. The resulting frequency separation between symbols and signal bandwidth are the same for all modes, i.e., 1.46 and 4.4 Hz. Despite the fact that six different frame formats are defined, solely on type of modulation needs to be supported. This simplifies the implementation.

4   Receiver Design

The receiver uses a common sampling rate for all supported modes, 375 samples per second. It means, that 187 Hz of signal bandwidth is simultaneously processed. The receiver searches for frames in a frequency domain representation of the signal bandwidth. This achieves an auto tune capability that can deal with frequency drifts due to Doppler effects and source-receiver miss frequency alignments.

4.1   Frequency Domain Representation

The seventh column of Table 1 shows the number of samples per symbol for every mode. The receiver constructs a frequency domain representation of the signal bandwidth using the Fast Fourier Transform (FFT). Every FFT spans the duration of two symbols. The eight column of Table 1 provides for every mode the FFT bin width (Hertz). The bin width is calculated dividing the sample rate by two times the number of samples per symbol.

Using the frequency-domain representation, candidate frequencies are identified as the presence of local Signal-to-Noise Ratio (SNR) peaks and correlation with the bit synchronization pattern. To find the peaks, the smoothed average magnitude level at each frequency bin is calculated. The magnitude is smoothed taking, for each frequency, the sum of the magnitudes of signals within the signal bandwidth (4.4 Hz). The frequency domain representation is normalized with respect to the noise level. The smoothed representation of the spectrum yields candidate frequencies, that is, signal peaks with potential frames. Candidate frequencies are examined to evaluate correlation with the 162-bit synchronization pattern. There is correlation when there is consistently energy peaks at signal positions corresponding to synchronization bits. When a correlation with the bit pattern is confirmed, candidate frequencies are analyzed deeper. Following that second frequency-domain analysis, relevant parameters are obtained that include the estimated time shift (relative to the sample window start) and SNR. The next step resolves time delays and demodulate the signals at the candidate frequencies.

4.2   Soft Symbol Calculation

We use Fano sequential decoding of convolutional codes [14,17]. It is sub-optimal, but it can process codes with long coding sequences, 32 bits in our case. Fano sequential decoding requires the calculation of soft symbols. We explain how we calculate soft symbols. Let $x_0, x_1, \ldots, x_{n-1}$ represent the discrete complex samples of channel data. In 4-FSK, at every symbol position there are four possible symbol values. For every of the four 4-FSK possibilities, the power of the signal at every position is calculated. Over a symbol interval of length T, signal samples x_t correlated with the waveform values $e^{-j2\pi ft}$ are added together to obtain the total signal magnitude at every symbol frequency, $i = 0, \ldots, 161$ and $f = -2.2, -0.73, 0.73, 2.2$:

$$
P_{i,f} = \left| \sum_{t=iT+\tau}^{(i+1)T+\tau-1} x_t \cdot e^{-j2\pi ft} \right|
$$

This calculation of cumulative power is represented in the diagram of Fig. 1.

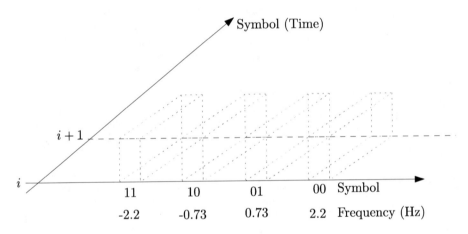

Fig. 1. At symbol position i, cumulative power for every of the four 4-FSK possible symbols (red-dotted line delimited). (Color figure online)

The corresponding channel symbols, in binary, are also shown, $00, 01, 10$ and 11. Every box, delimited by red dotted lines, represents a frequency-symbol-amplitude space where sample values x_t for symbol i are correlated with waveform values $e^{-j2\pi ft}$ and summed up resulting into a magnitude denoted as $P_{i,f}$. For every channel symbol, note that the most significant bit is the data bit while the least significant bit is the synchronization bit.

For every symbol index i, soft symbol σ_i is calculated, according to the value of synchronization bit at position s_i:

$$
\sigma_i = s_i \cdot (P_{i,2.2} - P_{i,-0.73}) + \neg s_i \cdot (P_{i,0.73} - P_{i,-2.2}) \tag{2}
$$

When the synchronization bit (s_i) is one, the term $P_{i,2.2} - P_{i,-0.73}$ represents the difference of power at the symbol corresponding to data bit one versus the power at the symbol corresponding to data bit zero. The term $P_{i,0.73} - P_{i,-2.2}$ does the same when the synchronization bit at position i is a zero. A positive σ_i value proportionally indicates that the symbol at position i is a one, whereas a value of σ_i in the negative indicates proportionally, in the negative direction, that it is a zero. A near-zero σ_i corresponds to an ambiguous symbol.

The soft symbol σ_i is mapped to a normalized score z_i. Let SD denote the standard deviation of the 162 soft symbols. The score z_i expresses soft symbol σ_i in scaled units of standard deviation SD, that is:

$$z_i = 50\frac{\sigma_i}{SD} \tag{3}$$

The multiplicand 50 is the scaling factor. When the standard deviation SD is null, the score z_i is equal to the product $50\sigma_i$. Finally, every score is mapped in the $[1, 256]$ interval, adding value 129 to each of them. Figure 2 shows the scores obtained in non-noisy conditions (standard deviation is 265.55). Binary value zero is scored 79, while binary value one is scored value 179. Figure 3 shows the scores obtained in noisy conditions, with a 2.5 kHz SNR of -27 dB (standard deviation 30.02). The lowest values represent the most definite binary zeros, while the highest values represent the most definite binary ones. Finally, every score z_i is mapped to a quality metrics q_i. Figure 4 shows the quality metrics versus the scores. Small scores correspond to good quality zeros or poor quality ones, while it is the opposite for high scores. While the search is conducted for mapping channel symbols to data bits, quality symbols are tried first. When the decoding fails, alternative decoding with lower quality symbols is attempted.

5   Matlab Implementation

Using the Matlab™ app designer, the Oceanus application has been developed. It supports all communication modes explained in this paper. Using the interface, the user has the option of choosing one of the available six frame formats (Table 1). The interface comprises two panels, see Fig. 5. The first panel is for the transmitter. It contains the option of typing hexadecimal data or generating random frames. The user also has the option of choosing the output device and carrier frequency. Moreover, quiet time, sampling rate and the type of output file are options the user can pick. The transmitter enables the user to either play signals directly to output devices or to save to files, giving the option to replay signals with many of the available audio applications. For simulation purposes, the user can add white noise to signals and generate signals with different SNRs. Oceanus also supports generating a probe signal. The probe signal can be used for adaptability. The user can choose frequency, sampling frequency, and file type in case the user chose to save the signal. The probe signal consists of six frames each in a different mode. Starting with mode 1 up to mode 6. The second panel is dedicated to the receiver. The user can click start the receiving state. The

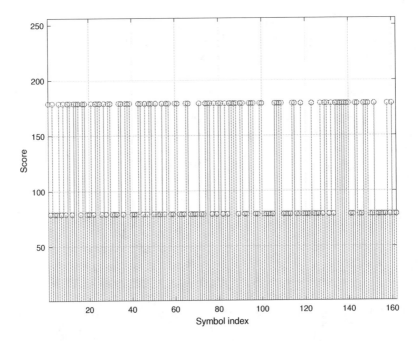

Fig. 2. Non-noisy symbol scores.

application starts listening for frames through the chosen input device. The user may choose the carrier and sampling frequencies. Oceanus provides the option of decoding in real-time from an input device or from files, in various audio formats (WAV, FLAC, OGG or MP4). Moreover, the receiver also supports adaptability. In the receiver panel, the start probe mode button would make the receiver start listening and try decoding the received signal using all the six modes in order to find the best mode. The code of the application is available online [27].

6   Performance Evaluation Through Simulation

Figure 6 shows the FER versus SNR obtained through simulation for every frame format described in Table 1. Every data point is the average of 10 trials. For this simulation, the reference bandwidth is 6 kHz. A frame is considered error-free when it is transmitted and received with no bit error. When a frame contains one or more errors, the whole frame is in error. To obtain the target SNRs, white Gaussian noise is added to the signals. Every frame format exhibits a waterfall behavior, that is, an abrupt transition from a 100% to a null FER. This is a well-known phenomenon associated with convolutional coding. From the *one minute* to the *20 min* formats, there is increase in robustness, that is, the ability to equally perform with a three dB drop SNR, from one format to another. Simulation results confirm the expected relative performance from one format to another. The symbol interval time, energy and SNR, in linear form

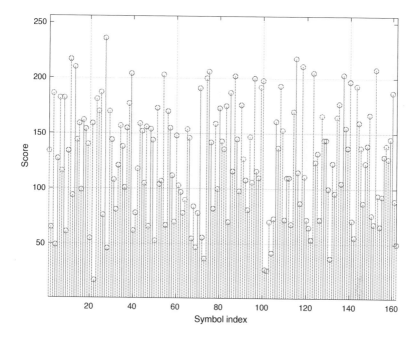

Fig. 3. Noisy symbol scores.

are consistently multiplied by two from one format to the other. From the two minutes to the 20 min mode, the crest of the waterfall is shifted -10 dB, which is consistent with the fact that symbols contain 10 times more energy.

7 Adaptability

In this section, we discuss adaptability to propagation conditions leveraging the six frame formats defined in Sect. 3. Three two-way handshake protocols are outlined to select between two peers, an Initiator and a Responder, a frame format suitable to the propagation conditions. The goal is to select the less robust frame format that can be supported, since it is also the most efficient. Feedback based, the protocols are half duplex, full duplex or parallel.

7.1 Half Duplex Feedback Protocol

Figure 7 illustrates the first protocol, where half-duplex communications are assumed. There is an Initiator and a Responder. The Initiator starts the execution of the protocol by sending a sequence of six frames. The frames are in the *one* to the *20 min* modes. That is from the less robust, but most efficient, to the most robust, but least efficient. The goal is to determine the most efficient format that can be supported by the propagation conditions. After each frame transmission, the Initiator remains silent for a duration corresponding to the

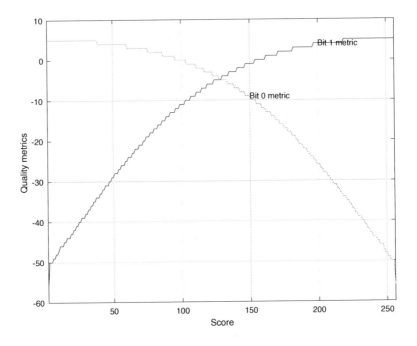

Fig. 4. Mapping of score to quality metrics.

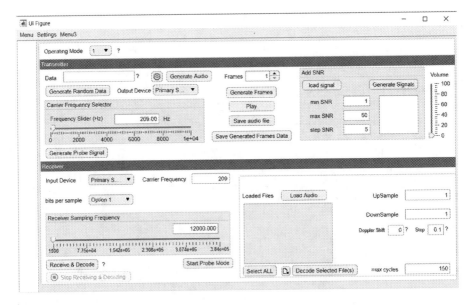

Fig. 5. Oceanus user interface.

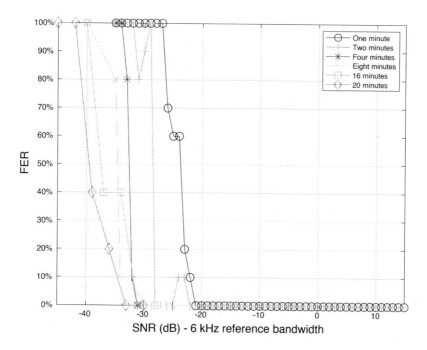

Fig. 6. FER vs. SNR.

frame time interval. It listens. In Fig. 7, at time t_1 the Initiator completes the transmission of the frame in the four minutes mode. The frame is received with success. The Responder confirms by sending a frame in the same format. From time t_2, both the Initiator and Responder continue the conversation in the *two minutes* modes. For the sake of simplicity, Fig. 7 makes abstraction of processing time and propagation delays. Symmetric propagation conditions are assumed. The Initiator and Responder can periodically repeat the handshake to update the choice of frame format to changing propagation conditions.

7.2   Full Duplex Feedback Protocol

Figure 8 illustrates the second feedback protocol, where the six supported frame formats are sent sequentially by the Initiator, one after the other from time t_0. Transmission completion is expected after a time corresponding to the sum of the time intervals all six modes. Slightly after time t_1, the Responder receives with success the frame in the *four minutes* mode. It acknowledges with a frame in the same mode. Starting from time t_2, the Initiator-Responder conversation can carry on in the *four minutes* mode.

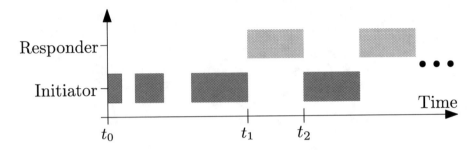

Fig. 7. Half duplex feedback protocol.

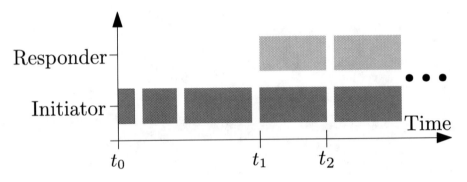

Fig. 8. Full duplex feedback protocol.

7.3   Parallel Feedback Protocol

Figure 9 depicts a third feedback protocol. At time t_0, the Initiator sends the six frame formats in parallel. Slightly after time t_1, the Responder receives with success the frame in the *four minutes* mode. It acknowledges with a frame in the same mode, reaching the Initiator at time t_2. The sequel of the Initiator-Responder conversation can carry on in the *four minutes* mode, full duplex. This feedback scheme is possible only when the Initiator and Responder have the capacity to send and receive frames in parallel.

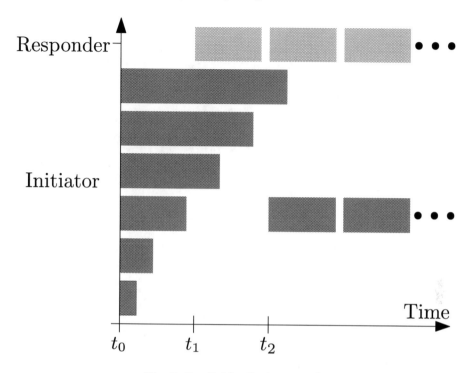

Fig. 9. Parallel feedback protocol.

8   Conclusion

We have introduced the design of six frame formats for underwater acoustic communications. The design addresses physical and link layer issues. The design has been implemented and evaluated through simulation in the Matlab™ environment. Simulation results confirm a robustness increase from one format to the other. This is due to the fact that the symbol interval is doubled from format-to-format. It has proportionally the same effect on the bit SNR, for a given transmission power level. The six formats can be used for adaptable underwater acoustic communications. We have described three adaptability protocols, that can be chosen according to available acoustic communication resources. Note that the system design does not require dynamic memory allocation anywhere. Hence, the amount of required hardware resources is predictable, in particular memory. The system design can easily be implemented on resource constrained devices.

References

1. Ahmad, A.M., Barbeau, M., Garcia-Alfaro, J., Kassem, J., Kranakis, E.: Tuning the demodulation frequency based on a normalized trajectory model for mobile underwater acoustic communications. Trans. Emerg. Telecommun. Technol. **30**(12), e3712 (2019)
2. Ahmad, A.M., Barbeau, M., Garcia-Alfaro, J., Kassem, J., Kranakis, E., Porretta, S.: Doppler effect in the acoustic ultra low frequency band for wireless underwater networks. Mob. Netw. Appl. **23**(5), 1282–1292 (2018)
3. Ahmad, A.-M., Barbeau, M., Garcia-Alfaro, J., Kassem, J., Kranakis, E., Porretta, S.: Doppler effect in the underwater acoustic ultra low frequency band. In: Zhou, Y., Kunz, T. (eds.) Ad Hoc Networks. LNICST, vol. 223, pp. 3–12. Springer, Cham (2018). https://doi.org/10.1007/978-3-319-74439-1_1
4. Ahmad, A.-M., Barbeau, M., Garcia-Alfaro, J., Kassem, J., Kranakis, E., Porretta, S.: Low frequency mobile communications in underwater networks. In: Montavont, N., Papadopoulos, G.Z. (eds.) ADHOC-NOW 2018. LNCS, vol. 11104, pp. 239–251. Springer, Cham (2018). https://doi.org/10.1007/978-3-030-00247-3_22
5. Ahmed, R., Stojanovic, M.: Joint power and rate control for packet coding over fading channels. IEEE J. Oceanic Eng. **42**(3), 697–710 (2016)
6. Anjangi, P., Chitre, M.: Model-based data-driven learning algorithm for tuning an underwater acoustic link. In: 2018 Fourth Underwater Communications and Networking Conference (UComms), pp. 1–5. IEEE (2018)
7. Antonelli, G.: Underwater Robots. Springer Tracts in Advanced Robotics, vol. 96. Springer, Cham (2014). https://doi.org/10.1007/978-3-319-02877-4
8. Barbeau, M.: Weak signal underwater communications in the ultra low frequency band. In: Proceedings of the GNU Radio Conference, vol. 2, p. 8 (2017)
9. Barbeau, M., Blouin, S., Traboulsi, A.: Performance of an underwater communication system in a sea trial done in the Canadian Arctic. In: 2021 IEEE International Mediterranean Conference on Communications and Networking (MeditCom), pp. 448–453. IEEE (2021)
10. Button, R.W., Kamp, J., Curtin, T.B., Dryden, J.: A survey of missions for unmanned undersea vehicles. RAND National Defense Research Institute (2009)
11. Decarpigny, J., Hamonic, B., Wilson, O.: The design of low frequency underwater acoustic projectors: present status and future trends. IEEE J. Oceanic Eng. **16**(1), 107–122 (1991)
12. Defence Research and Development Canada: All Domain Situational Awareness (ADSA). Goverment of Canada, November 2016. https://www.canada.ca/content/dam/drdc-rddc/documents/en/adsa-program.pdf. Accessed 05 Mar 2021
13. Dol, H.S., Casari, P., van der Zwan, T., Otnes, R.: Software-defined underwater acoustic modems: historical review and the nilus approach. IEEE J. Oceanic Eng. **42**(3), 722–737 (2017)
14. Fano, R.: A heuristic discussion of probabilistic decoding. IEEE Trans. Inf. Theory **9**(2), 64–74 (1963)
15. Freitag, L., Partan, J., Koski, P., Singh, S.: Long range acoustic communications and navigation in the arctic. In: OCEANS 2015 - MTS/IEEE Washington, pp. 1–5, October 2015
16. Hixson, E.: A low-frequency underwater sound source for seismic exploration. J. Acoust. Soc. Am. **126**(4), 2234 (2009)
17. Jiang, Y.: A Practical Guide to Error-Control Coding Using Matlab. Artech House, Norwood (2010)

18. Kassem, J., Barbeau, M., Ahmad, A.M., Garcia-Alfaro, J.: GNU Radio blocks for long-lasting frames in mobile underwater acoustic communications. In: French GNU Radio Days, Lyon, France (2018). https://gnuradio-fr-18.sciencesconf.org/211038/document. Accessed 25 Feb 2019

19. Kassem, J., Barbeau, M., Ahmad, A.M., Garcia-Alfaro, J.: The implementation of GNU radio blocks for decoding long-lasting frames in mobile underwater acoustic communications. In: The Technical Proceedings of the 8th Annual GNU Radio Conference, Henderson, NV (2018). https://pubs.gnuradio.org/index.php/grcon/article/view/50. Accessed 25 Feb 2019

20. Massoud Salehi, P., Proakis, J.: Digital Communications. McGraw-Hill Education, New York (2007)

21. Otnes, R., Voldhaug, J.E., Haavik, S.: On communication requirements in underwater surveillance networks. In: OCEANS 2008-MTS/IEEE Kobe Techno-Ocean, pp. 1–7. IEEE (2008)

22. Otnes, R., et al.: Underwater Acoustic Networking Techniques. Springer, Heidelberg (2012). https://doi.org/10.1007/978-3-642-25224-2

23. Proakis, J., Salehi, M.: Digital Communication, 5th edn. McGrah-Hill Higher Education, New York (2008)

24. Radosevic, A., Ahmed, R., Duman, T.M., Proakis, J.G., Stojanovic, M.: Adaptive OFDM modulation for underwater acoustic communications: design considerations and experimental results. IEEE J. Oceanic Eng. **39**(2), 357–370 (2013)

25. Song, A., Stojanovic, M., Chitre, M.: Editorial underwater acoustic communications: where we stand and what is next? IEEE J. Oceanic Eng. **44**(1), 1–6 (2019)

26. Stojanovic, M.: On the relationship between capacity and distance in an underwater acoustic communication channel. SIGMOBILE Mob. Comput. Commun. Rev. **11**(4), 34–43 (2007)

27. Traboulsi, A., Barbeau, M.: Oceanus (2021). https://github.com/ahmadtraboulsi/oceanus

28. Wan, L., et al.: Adaptive modulation and coding for underwater acoustic OFDM. IEEE J. Oceanic Eng. **40**(2), 327–336 (2014)

29. Wikipedia: Underwater locator beacon (2018). https://en.wikipedia.org/wiki/Underwater_locator_beacon

Adaptive Data Rate Based Congestion Control in Vehicular Ad Hoc Networks (VANET)

Srihari Jayachandran and Arunita Jaekel[✉]

University of Windsor, Windsor, ON N9B 3P4, Canada
{jayacha1,arunita}@uwindsor.ca

Abstract. Vehicular Ad Hoc Networks (VANET) supporting Vehicle-to-Vehicle (V2V) and Vehicle-to-Infrastructure (V2I) communication can increase the efficiency and safety of the road transportation systems. V2V communication uses wireless technology and in scenarios with high vehicle densities, the communication channel faces congestion, negatively impacting the reliability of the safety applications. To address this, various decentralized congestion control techniques have been proposed to effectively lower the channel load, by controlling different transmission parameters like message rate, data rate and transmission power. In this paper, we propose a novel data rate control algorithm to control the network congestion based on the Channel Busy Ratio (CBR). Simulation results demonstrate that the proposed approach outperforms existing data rate based algorithms, in terms of both packet reception and overall channel load.

Keywords: VANET · Congestion control · Vehicular communication · V2V · Basic safety message (BSM) · Intelligent Transportation System (ITS)

1 Introduction

Traffic accidents can occur due to various factors, such as hazardous road conditions, driving under the influence of alcohol/drugs, driver skill level, and speeding that could cause loss of property and lives [1]. Vehicular Ad-Hoc Networks (VANET) [2], a subset of Mobile Ad-Hoc Networks (MANET) [3], forms an integral part of an Intelligent Transportation Systems (ITS) [4] aimed at improving vehicle and road safety. Generally, VANETs are composed of high-speed mobile communication nodes, i.e., vehicles traveling at high velocities, as well as infrastructure nodes, such as roadside units (RSUs). Typical VANET characteristics include rapid changes in topology, high density of nodes in the network, and no energy restrictions [2,5]. Participating nodes (vehicles) in a VANET use wireless

Supported by Natural Sciences and Engineering Research Council of Canada (NSERC)

W. Bao et al. (Eds.): ADHOCNETS 2021/TridentCom 2021, LNICST 428, pp. 144–157, 2022.
https://doi.org/10.1007/978-3-030-98005-4_11

technology to directly communicate with each other. This type of direct communication between different nodes is known as vehicle-to-vehicle (V2V) communication [5], and will be main focus of this paper. In addition to V2V, VANET also supports vehicle-to-infrastructure (V2I) and infrastructure-to-infrastructure (I2I) communications.

VANET applications are categorized into service and safety applications [6]. Safety applications include forward collision warning, curve speed warning, pre-crash awareness, left turn to assist, emergency brake lights, lane change warning, etc. Service applications include route guidance and traffic optimization, infotainment applications such as internet connectivity, media, payment services such as E-toll collection, etc. Many safety applications rely on periodic beacons sent by each vehicle, containing its status information. These periodic messages are referred to as *Basic Safety Messages* (BSMs) in the U.S. [7] and *Cooperative Awareness Messages* (CAMs) in Europe [8] and contain important information, including a vehicle's current position, speed, acceleration, heading etc. These messages are sent through the channels allocated in the DSRC/WAVE system [9], and processed using the On-Board Units (OBUs) that are placed inside each vehicle.

In the United States, the FCC has allocated 75 MHz spectrum in the 5.9GHz band for Dedicated Short Range Communication (DSRC) [10]. This spectrum is divided into seven 10 MHz channels with associated guard bands, from which channel 172 is assigned for exchange of safety messages [11]. A 6 Mbps data rate for BSM transmissions has been widely adopted for many VANET simulations [10,12,13], and also used in some standardization activities [14]. Other data rates have also been considered in some papers, e.g., in [15–17] 3 Mbps is used due to its low SINR requirement. Each vehicle typically transmits 10 beacons per second, which can cause heavy channel load as vehicle density increases. Channel congestion occurs when the load is high enough that the nodes start competing to acquire access to the channel [18]. It has been shown that when the channel load exceeds 40% of the channel capacity, packet collisions and packet delays grow rapidly [19]. Therefore, appropriate congestion control algorithms should be implemented to avoid channel congestion and ensure the proper delivery of messages.

Most VANET congestion control techniques either reduce the BSM transmission rate or transmission power, or a combination of both, to reduce channel load. However, these can have a significant impact on the level of awareness of surrounding vehicles. In recent years, a number of papers have investigated adjusting the BSM transmission *data* rate (i.e. bitrate) to control congestion. For the remainder of the paper, we will use the terms *data rate* and *bitrate* interchangeably. When lower data rates are chosen, packet transmissions take longer, but the signal strength is high, reducing the chance of corrupted or lost packets. On the other hand, when higher data rates are chosen, packet transmissions are faster, reducing channel congestion, but signal strength is also reduced. Therefore, it is important to choose a suitable data rate for each BSM transmission that can balance the need for lower channel congestion and error-free packet reception.

In this paper, we propose a new approach that dynamically selects an appropriate data rate for each BSM transmission, based on the current *channel busy ratio* (CBR). Unlike existing algorithms that typically increment the bitrate only one level at a time, regardless of how high the CBR is, the proposed algorithm directly estimates the appropriate bitrate to use based on the current CBR value. This allows the channel congestion to converge to the desired level much faster, leading to lower packet loss and improved packet delivery ratio. Similarly, when current CBR is below the desired threshold, the proposed algorithm calculates the appropriate bitrate and starts transmitting directly using this bitrate, rather than moving through intermediate levels. Our simulation results indicate that the proposed approach is able to outperform existing data rate based algorithms in terms of both successful packet delivery rate and overall channel congestion.

The remainder of the paper is organized as follows. In Sect. 2, we provide an overview of existing VANET congestion control approaches. In Sect. 3, we present our proposed congestion control approach. We discuss our simulation results in Sect. 4 and present our conclusions and some directions for future work in Sect. 5.

2   Background Review

In VANET, the safety messages are of two types: periodic and event-driven messages. Event-driven messages are sent whenever certain events like traffic accidents or road hazards are detected. On the other hand, Basic Safety Messages (BSMs), are sent periodically by each vehicle in the network, regardless of traffic conditions. This means that as the vehicle density increases, the total number of BSMs being transmitted also increases correspondingly. It has been shown that even with relatively simple traffic scenarios, the bandwidth of the allocated channel can quickly become depleted, leading to channel congestion [19]. In this section, we will first briefly review some of the important congestion control techniques that use message rate and power control. Then, we will focus on how the transmission data rate can be used for congestion control, as well as some hybrid approaches.

2.1   Message Rate Based Approaches

The default BSM transmission rate is 10 Hz, i.e., each vehicle normally transmits ten BSMs per second. Message-rate based approaches adapt the rate at which the messages are generated per second. As congestion increases, the message rate is reduced accordingly. The main limitation of these approaches is that reducing the message rate also reduces awareness and can affect vehicle safety, as most safety applications rely on up-to-date information from neighboring vehicles. Some well-known congestion control algorithms using message rate control are discussed below.

In [13], the authors proposed a new scheme called Linear Message Rate Control algorithm (LIMERIC) that used linear feedback to adapt the message rate. The vehicles in a specific region sensed the channel load and adapted their message rates to meet the required predefined CBR. In [20], the authors proposed a new congestion control strategy called Periodically Updated Load Sensitive Adaptive Rate Control (PULSAR), where CBR was measured at the end of a fixed time interval and compared against the target value. When the measured value was higher than the target value, the transmission rate was decreased. This approach handled the channel congestion by maintaining the CBR below the predefined target value. In [15] the transmission rate was a function of both channel load (LIMERIC component) and vehicle dynamics (Suspected Tracking Error (STE) component). The LIMERIC component executed the LIMERIC algorithm and computed a periodic message rate based on the channel load. This message rate was used to schedule the next packet after every transmission. Meanwhile, STE component determined a time when the channel is expected to reach a threshold, and ensured that the packet is sent no later than that time. In [21] the authors proposed a method that extended the LIMERIC algorithm to control the total channel load according to a predefined target value. In [22], the vehicles transmit their packets by varying the beacon rates. The cars request their neighboring vehicles whether to increase/decrease the Beacon Transmission Rate (BTR). The BTR adjustment requests, which depend on the channel condition, are sent by attaching them to the beacons that are broadcast by each vehicle. In [23], the beacon messages were scheduled according to the priorities and transmission power. Messages were dequeued automatically according to the priority queue model. In [24], the congestion control scheme adapts the message rate according to the local vehicle density.

2.2 Power Control Based Approaches

Transmission power determines how far a message can travel and get delivered successfully. The goal of power control is to adapt the transmission range based on the level of channel congestion. A low-power transmission means that only nearby vehicles can see the BSMs. This reduces awareness, but also lowers channel congestion.

In [25], the vehicles adjusted their transmission power according to their speed. This approach was able to reduce the beacon error rate and channel busy time. In [26], the vehicles made their packet transmissions using different transmission power levels, based on the surrounding vehicle density. When the vehicle density was high, low transmission power was used. During moderate conditions, medium transmission power was used and high transmission power was used when the vehicle density was low. In [27], the authors proposed a method called Distributed Fair Transmit Power Adjustment for VANET (D-FPAV) to achieve congestion control by adjusting the transmission power based on the application-layer traffic and number of vehicles in the surrounding. In [28], all vehicles in the network transmitted beacon messages with an initial transmission power. Then a forecasted value of congestion was calculated and if it was less than a given threshold, then all cars increased their transmission power; otherwise, all the vehicles decreased their transmission power. In [29], the authors proposed to increase the awareness quality. Random transmission power was selected for each packet transmission and each vehicle controlled its power selection by using Complementary Cumulative Distribution Function (CCDF) because of its strong correlation with awareness quality.

2.3   Data Rate Based Approaches

The most commonly used data rate for BSM transmissions is 6 Mbps [12]. However, it is possible to use other bitrates and DSRC has specified 8 possible rates that can be used: (3, 4.5, 6, 9, 12, 18, 24, and 27 Mbps). Data rate-based approaches adapt the bitrate used for BSM transmissions and this approach is gaining more attention in recent years [12].

In [30], the vehicles adapted their data rate based on the network's channel load, which was calculated in terms of the channel busy ratio. Only the data rates between 3 and 12 Mbps were considered to avoid flooding. Four states were assigned depending on the channel load: relaxed state, active state 1, active state 2, and restrictive state. Each state had a different data rate for the vehicles to transmit the packets. In [31], the algorithm increased the data rate levels to reduce the CBR of the network. The transition from one state to another was done based on CBR measurements for every T seconds, where the states corresponded to the levels of congestion. The algorithm increased the level if the CBR was higher than the mean threshold $C1$, and maintained same level when the CBR was lower than the mean threshold $C1$ and greater than $Cmin$. In [32], packet count Pc was used together with the CBR measurements to adjust the data rate. The data rate D was adjusted depending on the packet count Pc measured for every second.

2.4   Hybrid Approaches

Instead of using a single parameter to control congestion, a number of recent approaches have proposed using a combination of different parameters, e.g. power and message rate, to effectively reduce channel load. Some interesting hybrid approaches that use multiple control parameters are discussed in this section.

In [33], two different transmission power levels were maintained, where each vehicle sent a certain percentage of BSMs with high power and the rest with low power. This technique was combined with LIMERIC to further reduce congestion. This approach had a lower Beacon Error Rate (BER) compared to other approaches. In [34], the authors proposed a new mechanism called Combined Power and Rate Control (CPRC), which made the rate and power adjustments in a single loop rather than a two-phase approach. CPRC exhibited cooperative behavior by increasing the transmission rate of the nodes involved in a potentially dangerous situation and reducing the transmission power of the other nodes. This approach prevented the channel load from exceeding a predefined threshold value. In [29], the authors proposed a new congestion control strategy called Random Transmission Power Control (RTPC) to reduce the channel load. RTPC was combined with TRC (Transmit Rate Control), and the sending rate was increased until the target load was reached. In [32], the authors proposed a combined data rate and message rate congestion control scheme. Beacon frequency was kept above the required minimum value by reducing the message rate. During high traffic densities, the data rate was increased to provide more channel capacity. This approach performed better in reducing the channel busy time.

3   Proposed Approach

The amount of time it takes to transmit a packet of a given size depends on the bitrate used for transmission. Using a higher bitrate reduces transmission time (and hence channel congestion) but also reduces the signal strength and the distance the signal can travel.

In the proposed approach, each vehicle participating in the network estimates the channel load based on its measured *channel busy ratio* or CBR value. The CBR value measured by a vehicle represents the percentage of time the channel was sensed as "busy" by its OBU over a given interval. The overall motive of our congestion control algorithm is to maintain the CBR between two specified thresholds (*cbrhigh*) and (*cbrlow*), by adjusting the data rate of the transmitted BSMs. Thus, when there is very little traffic, the transmission bitrate is reduced, making the packets visible even to distant vehicles. On the other hand, when congestion is high, a higher bitrate is used that results in faster packet transmission, but potentially increasing the beacon error rate for distant vehicles.

The *data rate control algorithm* (DRCA) shown in Algorithm 1 is used to determine the bitrate that will be used to transmit each BSM. Each vehicle runs this algorithm each time it is ready to send the next BSM. The transmission data rate is calculated based on the most recent CBR value measured by the vehicle, which is given as an input to the proposed DRCA scheme.

During initialization, the high CBR (*cbrhigh*) and low CBR (*cbrlow*) thresholds are set and a list (*B*) of allowed bitrate values is also specified. Based on the current standards, the available bitrates that we have used are: 3 Mbps, 6 Mbps, 9 Mbps, 12 Mbps, 18 Mbps and 24 Mbps. So, we set B = [3, 6, 9, 12, 18, 24]. The previous bitrate is specified using the parameter *level*, which is used as an index for the list *B*, to determine bitrate being used. For example, if *level* = 1 then the corresponding bitrate is $B[1] = 6$ Mbps. Finally, the parameter *maxlevel* corresponds the highest possible index value for the list *B* and is given by $maxlevel = len(B) - 1$.

After initialization, depending on the above parameters and current measured CBR value (*cbr*), Algorithm 1 executes and changes (if necessary) the bitrate for sending the next BSM. This same process is executed for the next BSM and so on. Each vehicle runs this process in its OBU, independently of the other vehicles. This means that it is a decentralized congestion control process, which does not require coordination with other vehicles.

Steps 2 to 11 are executed when the current CBR (cbr) goes below the low CBR threshold ($cbrlow$). Step 1 checks if the current CBR (cbr) is below the threshold ($cbrlow$). If the condition is satisfied, then steps 2–11 are used to determine if a lower bitrate can be used. Steps 2 and 3 are used to assign the previous BSM bitrate as the new value. This will be used only if a lower bitrate cannot be found. Steps 4–10 are used to iterate through each potential bitrate value from bitrate from $B[0]$ to $B[level]$ to see if it can be used, i.e. the condition in step 5 is satisfied. Step 5 checks whether the expected CBR, when using the new bitrate $B[i]$ falls below 95% of the high CBR threshold ($highcbr$). If so, the corresponding value of i is used to determine the bitrate to use (step 7), the loop is terminated (step 8) and these updated values of $newlevel$ and $bitrate$ (steps 6 and 7) are returned. This means that the *lowest* possible bitrate that satisfies the condition in step 5 is selected as the new bitrate.

Algorithm 1. Data Rate Control Algorithm

Input: List of bitrate values (B), index indicating which bitrate in B is currently being used ($level$), high ($cbrhigh$) and low ($cbrlow$) CBR threshold values, and current CBR (cbr)

Output: Updated bitrate values and newlevel

1: **if** $cbr < cbrlow$ **then**
2:      $newlevel = level$
3:      $bitrate = B[newlevel]$
4:      **for** $i \in (0, level)$ **do**
5:          **if** $cbr * (B[level]/B[i]) < 0.95 * cbrhigh$ **then**
6:              $newlevel = i$
7:              $bitrate = B[i]$
8:              break
9:          **end if**
10:     **end for**
11: **end if**
12: **if** $cbr > cbrhigh$ **then**
13:     $newlevel = maxlevel$
14:     $bitrate = B[newlevel]$
15:     **for** $i \in (level + 1, maxlevel)$ **do**
16:         **if** $cbr * (B[level]/B[i]) < 0.95 * cbrhigh$ **then**
17:             $newlevel = i$
18:             $bitrate = B[newlevel]$
19:             break
20:         **end if**
21:     **end for**
22: **end if**
23: **if** $cbrlow \leq cbr \leq cbrhigh$ **then**
24:     $newlevel = level$
25:     $bitrate = B[newlevel]$
26: **end if**

Steps 13 to 22 are executed when the current CBR (*cbr*) is higher than the threshold (*cbrhigh*). This means that the channel is getting congested and a higher bitrate must be used. Step 12 checks if the current CBR (*cbr*) is below the threshold (*cbrhigh*). If the condition is satisfied, then steps 13–22 are used to determine if a suitable higher bitrate for BSM transmission. Steps 13 and 14 are used to assign the highest possible bitrate as the new value. This will be used only if even the highest bitrate does not satisfy the condition in step 16. Steps 15–21 are used to iterate through each potential bitrate value from bitrate from next higher bitrate $B[level + 1]$ to the highest bitrate $B[maxlevel]$ to see if it can be used, i.e. the condition in step 16 is satisfied. Step 16 is similar to step 5 and checks whether the expected CBR, when using the new bitrate $B[i]$ falls below 95% of the high CBR threshold (*highcbr*). If so, the corresponding value of i is used to determine the bitrate to use (step 18), the loop is terminated (step 19) and these updated values of *newlevel* and *bitrate* (steps 17 and 18) are returned. This means that the *lowest* possible bitrate that satisfies the condition in step 16 is selected as the new bitrate.

Steps 24 to 26 are executed when the CBR (*cbr*) falls between high (*cbrhigh*) and low CBR (*cbrlow*) thresholds, i.e. the condition in step 23 is satisfied. This means that the CBR is within the proper range and no bitrate variation is required since the channel load is already balanced. So, the *level* which is already in use will be assigned as the *newlevel* by step 24. Step 25 assigns the $B[newlevel]$ as the next *bitrate* for the packet transmission.

4   Results and Analysis

4.1   Simulation Setup

Testing the effectiveness of congestion control algorithms for VANET becomes difficult in real-world situations due to the costs incurred, required equipment, resources, and safety concerns. Therefore, we have used a simulation environment to evaluate our proposed approach. We used Simulation of Urban Mobility (SUMO) [35] as the traffic simulator and Objective Modular Network Testbed (OMNET++) [36] as our network simulator.

For our traffic model, we considered a 1000 m long four-lane highway composed of two lanes in either direction. There was a total of 80 vehicles in the simulation, each with a maximum speed of 50 km/h. The simulation was run for 120 s. To generate different levels of channel load, we used different combinations of BSM packet sizes and beacon intervals, as indicated below:

- LOW load: Packet size = 256 Bytes and Beacon interval = 0.1 s.
- MEDIUM load: Packet size = 256 Bytes and Beacon interval = 0.01 s.
- HIGH load: Packet size = 1024 Bytes and Beacon interval = 0.01 s.

4.2   Comparison with Constant Bitrate Transmissions

In this section, we compare the performance of the proposed DRCA approach, which dynamically adapts the data rate, with using a constant bitrate for different bitrate values, viz., 3 Mbps, 6 Mbps, 12 Mbps, 18 Mbps, and 24 Mbps.

The performance is analyzed based on the total number of BSMs successfully received by the vehicles and the average CBR of the network.

Comparison of Received BSMs

Figure 1 shows the total amount of packets received with different bitrates (i.e., constant bitrates) and the DRCA approach. From the graph, we can see that using 3 Mbps performed better in low congestion scenarios and 24 Mbps performed best for medium to high congestion scenarios, in terms of the total amount of packets received. The proposed DRCA achieved the highest received BSMs (same as with 3 Mbps) for low load, and was very closed to the best results for medium and high loads. The above results indicate the advantages of using an adaptive congestion control technique, such as DRCA, since channel load can vary widely over time.

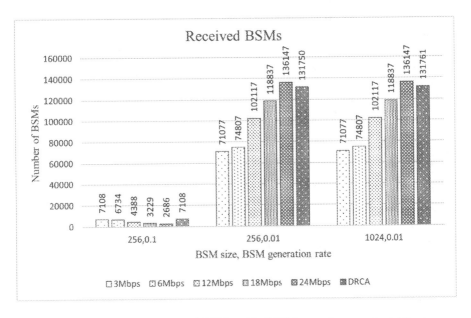

Fig. 1. Comparison of received BSMs with DRCA vs using constant bitrates

Comparison of CBR Values

In this section, we are comparing the average CBR the network had when simulated with the constant bitrates and the DRCA approach. Figure 2 shows the average CBR over the entire duration of the simulation, when using DRCA as well as different constant bitrates. It can be seen that DRCA approach was successful in maintaining a lower average CBR, close to the minimum value possible, for medium and high loads when compared with the constant bitrates. For low channel loads, lowering the CBR is not really necessary so DRCA tries to achieve better packet reception (as shown in Fig. 1) at the cost of higher CBR.

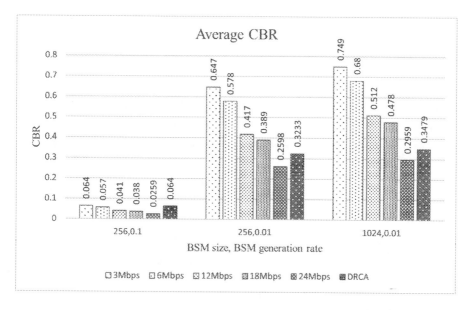

Fig. 2. Comparison of CBR with DRCA vs using constant bitrates

4.3   Comparison with Existing Congestion Control Techniques

The results from the previous section demonstrated the advantages of adapting bitrates according to the current congestion in the network. In this section, we compare the proposed DRCA approach with 2 other existing data rate control approaches: Data Rate- Decentralized Congestion Control(DR-DCC) [31] and Transmission Data Rate Control (TDRC) [30]. The proposed DRCA approach was run with two different high (*cbrhigh*) and low (*cbrlow*) thresholds. For DRCA1, we set *cbrhigh* = 0.5 and *cbrlow* = 0.3, while for DRCA2 we used *cbrhigh* = 0.4 and *cbrlow* = 0.2.

Comparison of Received BSMs

Figure 3 compares the total number of BSMs received under different channel loads, using DRCA, DR-DCC and TDRC. Under low loads, the performance of all 3 approaches were very similar. For medium and high loads, both DRCA1 and DRCA2 outperformed the other techniques. In particular, DRCA2 was able to achieve a significantly higher number of successfully received packets.

Comparison of CBR Values

Figure 4 shows the average CBR for the 3 techniques, under different channel loads. Under low load, all techniques report very low values of CBR, with TDRC having the lowest value. For medium to high loads, both DRCA1 and DRCA2 were able to significantly reduce the average CBR value compared to the other 2 approaches. Finally, we note that DRCA2 achieved the lowest overall CBR, showing that it can effectively reduce channel congestion, while improving packet delivery ratio.

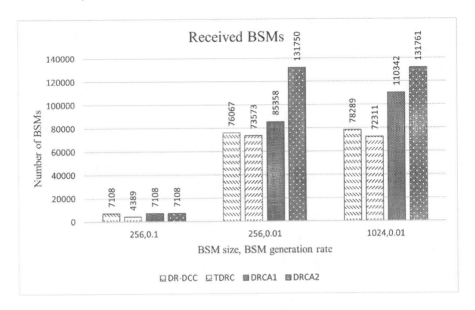

Fig. 3. Comparison of received BSMs with DRCA vs existing approaches

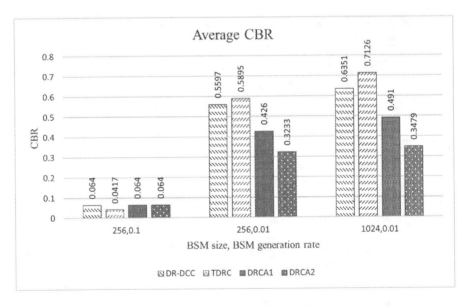

Fig. 4. Comparison of CBR with DRCA vs existing approaches

5   Conclusion and Future Work

In this paper, we have proposed and analyzed a new approach for dynamically adapting the bitrates used for BSM transmission, based on the level of congestion in the network. The proposed *data rate control algorithm* (DRCA) was able to significantly improve packet reception and control channel congestion, compared to both constant bitrates and existing data rate control approaches. For future work, we are extending the proposed approach to automatically select appropriate threshold values for CBR, based on current traffic conditions. It will also be interesting to combine DRCA with power-control techniques to further reduce congestion.

References

1. National Highway Traffic Safety Administration: Vehicle-to-Vehicle Communications: Readiness of V2V Technology for Application, August 2014
2. Zeadally, S., Hunt, R., Chen, Y.S., Irwin, A., Hassan, A.: Vehicular ad hoc networks (VANETS): status, results, and challenges. Telecommun. Syst. **50**(4), 217–241 (2012)
3. Jha, R.K., Limkar, S.V., Dalal, D.U.: A performance comparison of routing protocols (DSR and TORA) for security issue in MANET (mobile ad hoc networks). IJCA Special Issue MANETs, **2**, 78–83 (2010)
4. Calabuig, J., Monserrat, J.F., Gozalvez, D., Klemp, O.: Safety on the roads: LTE alternatives for sending ITS messages. IEEE Veh. Technol. Mag. **9**(4), 61–70 (2014)
5. Nassar, L., Jundi, A., Golestan, K., Sattar, F., Karray, F., Kamel, M., Boumaiza, S.: Vehicular Ad-hoc Networks (VANETs): Capabilities, Challenges in Context-Aware Processing and Communication Gateway. In: Kamel, M., Karray, F., Hagras, H. (eds.) AIS 2012. LNCS (LNAI), pp. 42–49. Springer, Heidelberg (2012). https://doi.org/10.1007/978-3-642-31368-4_6
6. Hartenstein, H., Laberteaux, K. (eds.): VANET: Vehicular Applications and Inter-Networking Technologies, vol. 1. Wiley, Hoboken (2009)
7. SAE J2735: Dedicated Short Range Communications (DSRC) Message Set Dictionary; Society of Automotive Engineers, DSRC Committee: Warrendale, PA, USA (2009)
8. ETSI (2013) ETSI EN 302 637-2 (V1.3.0)-Intelligent Transport Systems (ITS); Vehicular Communications; Basic Set of Applications; Part 2: Specification of Cooperative Awareness Basic Service; Vehicular Communications (2013). https://www.etsi.org/deliver/etsi_en/302600_302699/30263702/01.03.02_60/en_30263702v010302p.pdf. Accessed 10 May 2019
9. Liu, Y., Dion, F., Biswas, S.: Dedicated short-range wireless communications for intelligent transportation system applications: state of the art. Transp. Res. Rec. **1910**(1), 29–37 (2005)
10. Kenney, J.B.: Dedicated short-range communications (DSRC) standards in the United States. Proc. IEEE **99**(7), 1162–1182 (2011)
11. Amendment of the Commission's Rules Regarding Dedicated Short-Range Communication Services in the 5.850-5.925 GHz Band (5.9 GHz Band); Technical Report; U.S. Federal Communications Commission: Washington, DC, USA (2006)
12. Liu, X., Jaekel, A.: Congestion control in V2V safety communication: problem, analysis, approaches. Electronics **8**(5), 540 (2019)

13. Bansal, G., Kenney, J.B., Rohrs, C.E.: LIMERIC: a linear adaptive message rate algorithm for DSRC congestion control. IEEE Trans. Veh. Technol. **62**(9), 4182–4197 (2013)
14. ETSI. Intelligent Transport Systems (ITS); European Profile Standard on the Physical and Medium Access Layer of 5 GHz ITS (2009). https://www.etsi.org/deliver/etsi_es/202600_202699/202663/01.01.00_50/es_202663v010100m.pdf. Accessed 20 Dec 2018
15. Bansal, G., Lu, H., Kenney, J.B., Poellabauer, C.: EMBARC: error model based adaptive rate control for vehicle-to-vehicle communications. In: Proceeding of the Tenth ACM International Workshop on Vehicular Inter-Networking, Systems, and Applications, pp. 41–50, June 2013
16. Huang, C.L., Fallah, Y.P., Sengupta, R., Krishnan, H.: Intervehicle transmission rate control for cooperative active safety system. IEEE Trans. Intell. Transp. Syst. **12**, 645–658 (2011)
17. Torrent-Moreno, M., Mittag, J., Santi, P., Hartenstein, H.: Vehicle-to-vehicle communication: fair transmit power control for safety-critical information. IEEE Trans. Veh. Technol. **58**, 3684–3703 (2009)
18. Taherkhani, N.: Congestion control in vehicular ad hoc networks. Doctoral dissertation, Ecole Polytechnique, Montreal (Canada) (2015)
19. Weinfeld, A.: Methods to reduce DSRC channel congestion and improve V2V communication reliability. In: Proceedings of the 17th ITS World Congress, Busan, Korea, 25–29 October 2010 (2010)
20. Tielert, T., Jiang, D., Chen, Q., Delgrossi, L., Hartenstein, H.: Design methodology and evaluation of rate adaptation based congestion control for vehicle safety communications. In: 2011 IEEE Vehicular Networking Conference (VNC), pp. 116–123. IEEE, November 2011
21. Bansal, G., Kenney, J.B.: Achieving weighted-fairnessin message rate-based congestion control for DSRC systems. In: 2013 IEEE 5th International Symposium on Wireless Vehicular Communications (WiVeC), pp. 1–5. IEEE, June 2013
22. Kim, G., Lee, S., Park, H., Kim, D.: A request based adaptive beacon rate control scheme for vehicular ad-hoc networks. In: 2016 Eighth International Conference on Ubiquitous and Future Networks (ICUFN), pp. 67–69. IEEE, July 2016
23. Sharma, S., Chahal, M., Harit, S.: Transmission rate-based congestion control in vehicular ad hoc networks. In: 2019 Amity International Conference on Artificial Intelligence (AICAI), pp. 303–307. IEEE, February 2019
24. Chaabouni, N., Hafid, A., Sahu, P.K.: A collision-based beacon rate adaptation scheme (CBA) for VANETs. In: 2013 IEEE International Conference on Advanced Networks and Telecommunications Systems (ANTS), pp. 1–6. IEEE, December 2013
25. Facchina, C., Jaekel, A.: Speed based distributed congestion control scheme for vehicular networks. In: 10th IEEE ISCC MoCS Workshop (MoCS 2020), July 2020
26. Akinlade, O., Saini, I., Liu, X., Jaekel, A.: Traffic density based distributed congestion control strategy for vehicular communication. In: IEEE International Conference on Distributed Computing in Sensor Systems (DCOSS 2019) Santorini Island, Greece, 29–31 May 2019 (2019)
27. Torrent-Moreno, M., Santi, P., Hartenstein, H.: Distributed fair transmit power adjustment for vehicular ad hoc networks. In: 2006 3rd Annual IEEE Communications Society on Sensor and Ad Hoc Communications and Networks, vol. 2, pp. 479–488. IEEE, September 2006

28. Mo, Y., Yu, D., Song, J., Zheng, K., Guo, Y.: A beacon transmission power control algorithm based on wireless channel load forecasting in VANETs. PLoS ONE **10**(11), e0142775 (2015)

29. Kloiber, B., Härri, J., Strang, T.: Dice the tx power-improving awareness quality in vanets by random transmit power selection. In: 2012 IEEE Vehicular Networking Conference (VNC), pp. 56–63. IEEE, November 2012

30. Patil, A., Deeksha, M., Shekar, N., Shet, V., Kulkarni, M.: Transmit data rate control based decentralized congestion control mechanism for VANETs. In: 2019 International Conference on Data Science and Communication (IconDSC), pp. 1–5. IEEE, March 2019

31. Math, C.B., Ozgur, A., de Groot, S.H., Li, H.: Data rate based congestion control in V2V communication for traffic safety applications. In: 2015 IEEE Symposium on Communications and Vehicular Technology in the Benelux (SCVT), pp. 1–6. IEEE, November 2015

32. Math, C.B., Li, H., de Groot, S.H., Niemegeers, I.: Fair decentralized data-rate congestion control for V2V communications. In: 2017 24th International Conference on Telecommunications (ICT), pp. 1–7. IEEE, May 2017

33. Willis, J.T., Jaekel, A., Saini, I.: Decentralized congestion control algorithm for vehicular networks using oscillating transmission power. In: WTS 2017, Chicago, USA, 26–28 April 2017 (2017)

34. Baldessari, R., Scanferla, D., Le, L., Zhang, W., Festag, A.: Joining forces for vanets: a combined transmit power and rate control algorithm. In: 6th International Workshop on Intelligent Transportation (WIT), March 2010

35. https://www.eclipse.org/sumo/

36. https://omnetpp.org/

Network Applications (ADHOCNETS 2021)

Analyzing Aggregate User Behavior on a Large Multi-platform Content Distribution Service

Raushan Raj[1], Adita Kulkarni[2(✉)], Anand Seetharam[1], Arti Ramesh[1], and Antonio A. de A. Rocha[3]

[1] SUNY Binghamton, Binghamton, USA
{rraushal,aseethar,artir}@binghamton.edu
[2] SUNY Brockport, Brockport, USA
akulkarni@brockport.edu
[3] Fluminense Federal University, Niteroi, Brazil
arocha@ic.uff.br

Abstract. In recent years, Video on Demand (VoD) streaming has increased exponentially as a result of reduced streaming costs and higher bandwidth. For retention of consumers, it is crucial for content providers to understand the behavior of their users and continuously improve performance. In this paper, we analyze the user behavior on *Globo.com*, the largest content distribution service in Brazil. We consider 1.4 billion logs spanning a period of four weeks from October 25, 2020 to November 21, 2020. We analyze the user request patterns and the trends in server's response time. We explore metrics such as protocol, status code, cache hits, user agent, content category popularity and geographical distribution of users. We finally investigate the video popularity distribution and trends in size of content downloaded. We observe that the highest number of requests occur between 8 pm and 11 pm. We observe that 57% of requests are served over HTTPS, while significant portion (43%) are still served over HTTP. Our analysis also reveals that nearly 97% of requests result in a cache hit. Additionally, we observe that the video popularity distribution is skewed and follows a power law with 10% of the videos accounting for 87% of the requests.

1 Introduction

Video streaming has become extremely popular in recent years and video traffic is expected to account for more than 70% of the total Internet traffic in the upcoming years [7]. Video on Demand (VoD) streaming services such as Netflix, Amazon, Hulu, YouTube and Globo continue to see a huge increase in consumers globally. These content providers generate large amounts of revenue via user subscriptions and advertisements [16], which necessitate good quality of experience for user retention. With the advancements in video streaming such as live video streaming, Ultra High Definition (UHD) or 4K videos, and Augmented Reality/Virtual Reality (AR/VR) video streaming, the user expectations for uninterrupted and high quality video service continue to increase.

© ICST Institute for Computer Sciences, Social Informatics and Telecommunications Engineering 2022
Published by Springer Nature Switzerland AG 2022. All Rights Reserved
W. Bao et al. (Eds.): ADHOCNETS 2021/TridentCom 2021, LNICST 428, pp. 161–172, 2022.
https://doi.org/10.1007/978-3-030-98005-4_12

To effectively manage the exponentially growing content and consumer population as well as to provide high user quality of service while keeping costs to a minimum, it is critical to investigate user behavior on a large content distribution service. To this end, in this paper, we partner with *Globo.com* [2], the largest content distribution service in Brazil (also ranked 1st in Latin America) to analyze and investigate user behavior on its platform. *Globo* is a Brazilian television network that provides online content via *Globo.com*. According to data released by one of *Globo*'s directors [1], they witnessed an increase of 89% in the number of subscribers to *Globoplay*, one of the component of *Globo.com*, in 2020 as compared to 2019. They now stream around 100 million hours of content every month. The main content categories on *Globo.com* are news, sports, entertainment, technology and food.

We collect and analyze around 1.4 billion user requests made to *Globo.com* between October 25, 2020 and November 21, 2020 at server side. We begin our analysis by studying the user request patterns and the time taken by the server to respond to user requests. We then investigate important network-related metrics such as the protocol used, status code, cache hits, user agent, content category popularity and geographical distribution of users. We conclude our study by examining the video popularity distribution and the trends in the size of the content downloaded by users.

Our main findings are summarized as follows:

– By analyzing the traces, we observe that the highest number of requests to *Globo.com* occur at night between 8 pm and 11 pm and the least number of requests occur between 3 am and 8 am. Though expected, this finding is important as it informs the content provider how to provision for peak load. We also observe that the time needed for the server to serve the requests, is the lowest between 3 am and 8 am. Interestingly, we observe that the time required to serve requests is not significantly impacted by the peak load when compared to the rest of the day. We also observe that the request load is least on Saturday followed by Friday. A possible reason is that people socialize more on the weekend with the result that they spend less time on the Internet and *Globo.com*.

– We investigate the performance impact of different network parameters and interestingly, observe that though majority of the requests are served over HTTPS, a sizable portion of requests are still served over HTTP (43%). For improved security, we believe that more requests will transfer over to HTTPS in future. We also observe that roughly 95% of HTTP(S) requests are satisfied with 200 OK message. We also find that most requests (96.5%) result in cache hit at the server, which indicates that the Globo CDNs are caching content effectively.

– Our analysis also reveals that the most popular web browser and operating systems used by the users to watch videos on *Globo.com* are Chrome and Android, respectively. We also find that majority of the videos watched are related to movies or web series (*Globoplay* component of *Globo.com*). Additionally, we observe that 99.93% requests to *Globo.com* occur from Brazil and the majority of the traffic (around 81%) is generated from the five states Ceará, Bahia, Pernambuco, Paraíba and Maranhão. The request distribution within the country can be attributed to the fact that the CDN we collect the data from is located in the northeast of Brazil.

– We explore the video popularity distribution on *Globo.com* and discover that the distribution is skewed and follows the power law where top 10% of videos account for 87% of the total requests while the remaining 90% videos account for just 13% of the requests. A possible reason for this is people share with others when they find some videos to be good and once they watch a certain kind of videos, the recommendation algorithm recommends similar videos to users making less number of content more popular [20].

Our exploration provides characterization of user activity on *Globo.com*, and facilitates improving the platform's service and designing streaming algorithms to enhance the user quality of service.

2   Related Work

In this section, we discuss the existing literature on user behavior analysis on video streaming services.

Research in [3,14,17,18] explores user behavior analysis for live video streaming. Two of them analyze the transmission sessions also considering data from *Globo.com*'s server logs. In [18], authors characterize the behavior of mobile users when watching large popular live events in Brazil. In [17], the same authors extend the previous analysis, using data mining techniques, to extract key factors of popular live streaming sessions to understand what factors may impact the quality of the users' experience using mobile devices. [3] analyze QoE and its impact on user engagement for large-scale live video streaming. Liu *et al.* study personalized 360° live video streaming on two commercial platforms, YouTube and Facebook in [14].

[11–13] focuses on analyzing behavior of mobile users towards VoD consumption. [12] characterizes the geographical patterns of a large-scale commercial mobile VoD system, by measuring uniformity and intensity of geographic interests on videos. Authors in [11] analyze users' behavior, video popularity patterns, impact of the connection type and the type of mobile device used using data from a mobile VoD system. In [13], authors analyze viewing behavior of users with respect to three factors—viewing time, user population, and user locality on PPTV (an Internet video provider in China) logs.

Work in [5,6,8] presents user engagement and performance characterization of video streaming services. Authors in [6] analyze the significance of factors such as service quality metrics, network quality metrics, video content and viewer demography in determining viewer engagement and propose personalized models for predicting individual viewer's engagement. In [5] authors characterize use watching time distributions of 1000 most popular videos on PPLive, a commercial Internet VoD system in China. Ghasemi *et al.* present performance characterization of Yahoo's video streaming service in [8].

[9,10,15,19] focuses on analyzing the Quality of Experience (QoE) in video streams. [10] studies the relationships between Quality of Service (QoS) and QoE in a session-based Over-The-Top (OTT) video service through a data-driven machine learning approach. Authors explore the use of outlier analysis and clustering as tools for interpreting QoE data of an OTT Video Service in [9]. Authors propose a machine learning based approach to monitor QoE metrics for encrypted video traffic and present results on YouTube videos in [15]. [19] subjectively assesses QoE during the entire life cycle of video sessions.

3   Data and Problem Statement

3.1   Data

In this section, we provide an overview of our VoD streaming dataset obtained from *Globo.com*. *Globo* is the largest television network in Brazil that also offers content over the Internet via its online platform *Globo.com* [2]. For delivering content to its user, the company uses an architecture of multiple Content Delivery Networks (CDNs), located at different cities in Brazil, comprising of multiple servers that cache the most popular content in order to reduce the latency in serving requests to the end users. In this work, we analyze the data collected at one specific CDN, in the northeast of Brazil (state of Ceará). This state (and CDN) is strategically located close to submarine cables connecting Brazil to North America, Europe and Africa. Besides this CDN, *Globo* uses at least others six CDNs to serve data over the Internet.

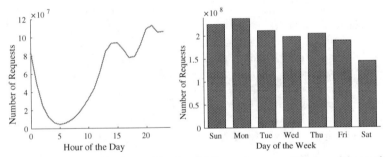

(a) Requests grouped by hour of the day (b) Requests grouped by day of the week

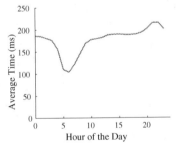

(c) Response time grouped by hour of the day

Fig. 1. Trends in requests sent to *Globo.com* (hourly and weekly basis) and server's response time (hourly basis)

Globo.com architecture also uses NGINX web service solution on its HTTP servers. NGINX controls the streaming video service via different HTTP streaming protocols, such as HLS, DASH, MSS, Smoothstreaming, among others. Each NGINX records user session information in log files and sends it to a central repository. We partner with *Globo* guaranteeing access to us to this data repository. Thus, we collect approximately 1.4 billion VoD logs from the service for the analysis presented in this work. Logs contain information of the video requested by a user and server's response to it. As the log is collected at the server, all our analysis is presented from the server's perspective. The logs span four weeks from October 25, 2020 to November 21, 2020. Each log consists of the following fields:

- **Timestamp:** It consists of the date and time when the request was served. The date is logged in YYYY-MM-DD format and the time is logged in HH-MM-SS format.
- **IP address:** It consists of the IP address from where the request was sent.
- **Country Code:** It consists of the postal abbreviation code of the country from where the request occurred.
- **Status Code:** It includes a three-digit numeric code which decides how the user agent (defined in the last point) handles the response.
- **Cache Hit/Miss:** If the requested content is present in the server's cache, it is logged as a hit. If not, it's a miss and the content is retrieved from the backend server.
- **Payload:** It includes the size of the content in bytes that is returned to the user.
- **Response Time:** It consists of time in milliseconds which determines the time elapsed between when the user sent the request and when the request was served. It comprises the time for either finding the video in the server's cache or retrieving it from the backend server and returning it to the user.
- **Video Identification:** This field contains the details of the content requested. It includes the video id, video name and the protocol used.
- **Uniform Resource Locator (URL):** This field contains the web address of the content requested by the user.
- **User-Agent:** It includes the information of the software that renders the web content to the user. This software agent is usually the web browser, media player or a plug in.

3.2   Problem Statement

In this paper we adopt a data-driven approach to analyze the underlying patterns in the *Globo.com* dataset to discern key insights related to user trends (e.g., request rate), network performance metrics (e.g., cache hit rate) and video popularity distributions. Our investigation provides a superior understanding of user interactions on *Globo.com*, a unique multi-platform content distribution service and lays the foundation for improving the platform's service and designing streaming algorithms that enhance the user quality of service.

4   Results

In this section, we first analyze the users' request patterns and the server's response to them. We then investigate important metrics such as protocol, status code, cache hits, user agent, category popularity and the geographical distribution of users. We then evaluate the video popularity distribution and the trends in the content size returned to the users.

4.1   Trends in User Requests

We study the trends in the requests occurring at the server on an hourly and weekly basis. Figure 1a shows the total number of requests occurring at a particular hour of the day during the month. Here, 0 denotes 12 am and 23 denotes 11 pm. We observe that highest number of requests occur at night between 8 pm and 11 pm, after which the number of users accessing the service starts decreasing and the number of requests experience a dip early morning between 3 am and 8 am. This trend is quite natural and corresponds to sleeping patterns of humans. Figure 1b shows the total number of requests occurring at a specific day of the week during the month. We see that highest requests occur on Monday whereas the lowest number of requests occur on Saturday followed by Friday. This is because people prefer spending their weekend nights, in particular Friday night and Saturday night, going out rather than staying at home and watching TV. Analyzing user request patterns is important as it informs the content provider how to provision for peak load.

4.2   Trends in Response Time

Response time is the elapsed time between the user requesting a content and the request getting served. It also includes the time taken by the server to search the content in its cache and if not found, fetch it from the back end server. Response time is an important metric to analyze in web surfing and video streaming as low response times, especially while video streaming, could ruin the user experience. Investigating response time is important to improve user engagement and attract more users to use the service. As around 97% requests result in a cache hit at the server (see Sect. 4.3), Fig. 1c shows the average response time of these requests on an hourly basis. We observe that the average time needed to return contents to the users is between 100 ms and 220 ms. We also observe that the average response time is the lowest between 3 am and 8 am. The reason behind this is as we observed in the previous section (Fig. 1a), the server experiences a low number of requests early morning enabling it to serve the requests faster. Interestingly, we observe that the time required to serve requests is not significantly impacted by the peak load when compared to the rest of the day.

4.3   Key Metrics

Protocol. VoD services deliver videos to clients over Hypertext Transfer Protocol (HTTP). Hypertext Transfer Protocol Secure (HTTPS) is an extension of HTTP where

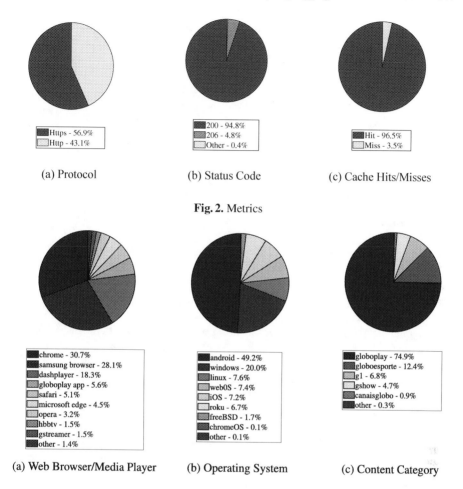

(a) Protocol   (b) Status Code   (c) Cache Hits/Misses

Fig. 2. Metrics

(a) **Web Browser/Media Player**   (b) **Operating System**   (c) **Content Category**

Fig. 3. Web browser/media layer, operating system and content category popularity pie charts

the communication protocol is encrypted using Transport Layer Security (TLS). This provides confidentiality, i.e., no one on the network is aware of what the user is watching, and integrity, i.e., no one can alter the video stream. We investigate the protocol used to send requests. Figure 3b shows the percentage of HTTP and HTTPS requests. Interestingly, we observe that around 57% requests are sent over HTTPS whereas a significant percentage of users (43%) still stream videos over HTTP.

Status Code. The first line of the HTTP response, called the status line, includes a numeric status code and a textual reason phrase. The way content is retrieved and rendered on web page depends mainly on the status code and thus is an important metric to analyze. Figure 3c shows the percentage of different status codes returned for all the requests. We observe that 94.8% requests are successful and have the status code 200 OK, 4.8% requests are returned only part of the requested resource as they have the status code 206 Partial Content, while remaining 0.4% requests have 4XX and 5XX class status codes which indicate errors occurring at client and server respectively.

Cache Hits/Misses. If the content requested by the user is present in the server cache, it is denoted as a hit. Else, it is a miss and the content needs to be retrieved from the backend server. To reduce the total delay experienced by users getting their requests served, it is important that majority requests incur a cache hit at the server. Figure 3a shows the percentage of requests incurring a hit or a miss. We see that 96.5% requests result in a hit whereas just 3.5% result in a miss, which demonstrates that the *Globo* CDN is able to effectively serve user requests. Further investigation into the 3.5% miss requests can help them understand the reason behind a miss and design approaches to transform such requests into hits.

User Agent. A user agent is a software that retrieves and renders web content to the end users. The *user-agent* string in the HTTP request header enables to identify web browsers and media players which act as the user agents for the clients. This information is crucial to the video streaming platforms to provide quality service. From the total logs considered, 31.5% of the requests do not contain information about the user agent. We analyze the remaining 68.5% logs to obtain the most widely used web browser/media player to watch videos and the operating system on which the browser/player runs. Figure 3a shows the most popular web browsers/media players. We observe that about 31% requests occur from Chrome browser, followed by 28% requests from the default browser on Samsung devices and around 18% requests from Dash-player. Other browsers and media players such as Globoplay App, Safari, Microsoft Edge, Opera, etc. constitute comparatively smaller percentage of requests. Figure 3b shows the percentage of requests from different operating systems (OS). We see that Android is the most popular OS with 49% requests, followed by Windows, Linux, WebOS, iOS, Roku TV OS and FreeBSD, respectively. Other operating systems have minimal requests. This denotes that the majority of the consumers are mobile users.

Category Popularity. *Globo.com* offers content in mostly seven different categories—*g1 (journalism), ge (sports), gshow (entertainment), globoplay (TV, web series, and movies), tech (technology), cartola fc (soccer),* and *receitas (recipes).* In this subsection, we identify which categories on *Globo.com* are most popular. About 50% of the logs do not contain valid content category information. Thus, we only consider the remaining 50% logs to determine category popularity. Figure 3c shows the pie chart for percentage of requests received for different content categories. We observe that *globoplay (TV, web series, and movies)* is the most popular among users as it incurs the highest percentage of requests, followed by *globoesporte (sports), g1 (news),* and *gshow (entertainment),* respectively. Rest of the content receives only around 1.2% of the total requests.

Geographical Distribution of Users. Prior research shows that the geographic location of users, especially mobile users, has a significant impact on video popularity [12]. Investigating the geographical distribution enables content providers to better understand regional popularity and plan their service accordingly. We learn from our data that 99.93% requests to *Globo.com* come from Brazil and the remaining 0.07% come from the rest of the world. Figure 4 shows the distribution of user requests in different states of Brazil. As mentioned in Sect. 3, we collect data from the CDN from the state

Fig. 4. Map of Brazil showing distribution of requests. The five states Ceará, Bahia, Pernambuco, Paraíba and Maranhão contribute majority of the traffic.

of Ceará located in the northeast of Brazil. Therefore, it is understandable that the top five states contributing majority traffic to *Globo.com* in our dataset are Ceará, Bahia, Pernambuco, Paraíba and Maranhão with 41%, 13%, 11%, 7.6% and 7.6% requests, respectively as user requests are generally routed to the geographically closest located CDN. The remaining states contribute significantly less amount of traffic.

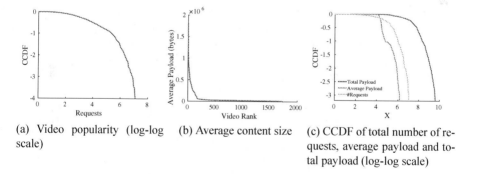

(a) Video popularity (log-log scale)

(b) Average content size

(c) CCDF of total number of requests, average payload and total payload (log-log scale)

Fig. 5. Video popularity and average content size

4.4   Discussion on Video Popularity Distribution and Content Download Size

We investigate the video popularity distribution on *Globo.com*. Figure 5 shows the complementary cumulative distribution function (CCDF) of the video requests. We observe from the data that top 10% videos account for 87% of total requests. The content popularity distribution is skewed and follows the power law. Existing research also indicates that power law is widely prevalent in the real world content popularity distribution [4]. *Globo.com* can leverage these top 10% videos by caching them closer to the end user to reduce latency. Our analysis can also be used to optimize their caching policies and improve the deployment of CDNs. Video popularity also has an important role in video recommendation [20] and therefore, our analysis lays the groundwork to design smarter recommendation algorithms based on the knowledge of popularity changes.

We next analyze the size of the content downloaded from the server. We investigate the total bytes downloaded per video as well as the average bytes downloaded per video considering all user sessions. We obtain a user session as follows—we get the first and the last request received for a video and the user session is the time interval between them. We have two assumptions while considering a user session—i) if two consecutive requests for a video do not occur within a five minute span, we treat them as different sessions. ii) a session cannot be longer than three hours. Both these assumptions are valid because the data that we are investigating is only for VoD and not for live stream videos. So, if a request for the next chunk for the same video does not occur within five minutes, it is highly likely that a user has stopped watching the video. Also, majority of the movies or documentaries are less than three hours. We consider all the sessions for every video requested and get an average of the data (in bytes) returned by the server. Figure 5b shows the average data downloaded for all the videos. We observe that the average size of the data returned for the top 9% videos is greater than 100 MB and up to 1.8 GB. The average size of the content downloaded for all other videos is less than 100 MB.

Figure 5c shows the complementary cumulative distribution function (CCDF) of total number of requests, average bytes and total bytes downloaded per video. We observe that the popularity of the video is correlated to the total bytes downloaded for that video, i.e., videos with higher number of requests have higher number of total bytes downloaded. When we obtain average bytes downloaded considering different user sessions, this does not hold true since the user sessions vary for every video.

5   Conclusion

In this paper, we analyzed users' behavior on *Globo.com*, the largest content distribution service in Brazil. We considered user requests made to *Globo.com* over a period of four weeks and investigated the user request patterns and trends in the server's response times. We examined metrics such as protocol, status code, cache hits/misses, user agent, content category popularity and geographical distribution of users. We finally studied the video popularity distribution and size of content downloaded. The findings from this paper can be used by *Globo.com* to make their service more efficient.

References

1. Deadline.com. https://deadline.com/2021/01/how-brazilian-tv-giant-globo-is-planning-to-compete-with-netflix-amazon-in-the-streaming-war-1234676055
2. Globo.com. https://www.globo.com
3. Ahmed, A., Shafiq, Z., Bedi, H., Khakpour, A.: Suffering from buffering? Detecting QoE impairments in live video streams. In: 2017 IEEE 25th International Conference on Network Protocols (ICNP), pp. 1–10. IEEE (2017)
4. Cha, M., Kwak, H., Rodriguez, P., Ahn, Y.Y., Moon, S.: Analyzing the video popularity characteristics of large-scale user generated content systems. IEEE/ACM Trans. Netw. 17(5), 1357–1370 (2009)
5. Chen, Y., Liu, Y., Zhang, B., Zhu, W.: On distribution of user movie watching time in a large-scale video streaming system. In: 2014 IEEE International Conference on Communications (ICC), pp. 1825–1830 (2014). https://doi.org/10.1109/ICC.2014.6883588
6. Chen, Y., Chen, Q., Zhang, F., Zhang, Q., Wu, K., Huang, R., Zhou, L.: Understanding viewer engagement of video service in wi-fi network. Comput. Netw. 91, 101–116 (2015)
7. Forecast, G.: Cisco visual networking index: global mobile data traffic forecast update, 2017–2022. Update 2017, 2022 (2019)
8. Ghasemi, M., Kanuparthy, P., Mansy, A., Benson, T., Rexford, J.: Performance characterization of a commercial video streaming service. In: Proceedings of the 2016 Internet Measurement Conference, IMC 2016, p. 499–511. Association for Computing Machinery, New York (2016). https://doi.org/10.1145/2987443.2987481
9. Li, W., Spachos, P., Chignell, M., Leon-Garcia, A., Jiang, J., Zucherman, L.: Capturing user behavior in subjective quality assessment of OTT video service. In: 2016 IEEE Global Communications Conference (GLOBECOM), pp. 1–6. IEEE (2016)
10. Li, W., Spachos, P., Chignell, M., Leon-Garcia, A., Zucherman, L., Jiang, J.: A quantitative relationship between application performance metrics and quality of experience for over-the-top video. Comput. Netw. 142, 194–207 (2018)
11. Li, Z., et al.: Watching videos from everywhere: a study of the PPTV mobile VoD system. In: Proceedings of the 2012 Internet Measurement Conference, pp. 185–198 (2012)
12. Li, Z., Xie, G., Lin, J., Jin, Y., Kaafar, M.A., Salamatian, K.: On the geographic patterns of a large-scale mobile video-on-demand system. In: IEEE INFOCOM 2014 - IEEE Conference on Computer Communications, pp. 397–405 (2014). https://doi.org/10.1109/INFOCOM.2014.6847962
13. Lin, J., Li, Z., Xie, G., Sun, Y., Salamatian, K., Wang, W.: Mobile video popularity distributions and the potential of peer-assisted video delivery. IEEE Commun. Mag. 51(11), 120–126 (2013). https://doi.org/10.1109/MCOM.2013.6658663
14. Liu, X., Han, B., Qian, F., Varvello, M.: Lime: understanding commercial 360° live video streaming services. In: Proceedings of the 10th ACM Multimedia Systems Conference, MMSys 2019, pp. 154–164. Association for Computing Machinery, New York (2019). https://doi.org/10.1145/3304109.3306220,https://doi.org/10.1145/3304109.3306220
15. Mazhar, M.H., Shafiq, Z.: Real-time video quality of experience monitoring for HTTPS and QUIC. In: IEEE INFOCOM 2018-IEEE Conference on Computer Communications, pp. 1331–1339. IEEE (2018)
16. Research, D.T.: Global OTT TV and Video Forecasts (2020)
17. Correa da Silva, D.V., Velloso, P.B., Rocha, A.A.d.A.: Using data mining techniques to extract key factors in mobile live streaming. In: 2019 IEEE Symposium on Computers and Communications (ISCC), pp. 1–6 (2019). https://doi.org/10.1109/ISCC47284.2019.8969600
18. da Silva, D.V.C., Domingues, G.d.M.B., Velloso, P.B., Antonio, A.D.A.: Analysis of mobile-live-users of a large CDN. In: 2018 IEEE Symposium on Computers and Communications (ISCC), pp. 00946–00951. IEEE (2018)

19. Spachos, P., et al.: Subjective QoE assessment on video service: laboratory controllable approach. In: 2017 IEEE 18th International Symposium on a World of Wireless, Mobile and Multimedia Networks (WoWMoM), pp. 1–9 (2017). https://doi.org/10.1109/WoWMoM.2017.7974323
20. Zhou, R., Khemmarat, S., Gao, L.: The impact of youtube recommendation system on video views. In: Proceedings of the 10th ACM SIGCOMM Conference on Internet measurement, pp. 404–410 (2010)

An AI-Based Transmission Power-Control Certificate Omission in Vehicular Ad-Hoc Networks

Emmanuel Charleson Dapaah[(✉)], Parisa Memarmoshrefi, and Dieter Hogrefe

Institute of Computer Science, University of Göttingen, Göttingen, Germany
e.dapaah@stud.uni-goettingen.de,
memarmoshrefi@cs.uni-goettingen.de,
hogrefe@informatik.uni-goettingen.de

Abstract. Fundamental to achieving cooperative awareness amongst vehicles is the periodic dissemination of beacons. However, ensuring the secure dissemination of these beacons has over the years become an issue of importance as these beacons often than not contain some level of safety-critical information which are susceptible to attack. Consequently, researchers have proposed in the literature the use of digital certificates issued by a trusted authority as means of ensuring beacon authenticity and the use of a digital signature as a means of ensuring beacon integrity. Nonetheless, this security method is characterized by an increase in communication overhead caused by the increase in the beacon payload size. To address this issue, some researchers have in recent years proposed approaches like the Neighbor-based Certificate Omission (NbCO) and Transmission Power-control Certificate Omission (TPCO) strategy that uses a certificate omission technique to control channel congestion. Upon evaluation, these strategies have proved to be promising as they focus on tuning the beacon payload size which has a direct impact on the communication channel load and hence reducing channel congestion. Despite the benefits of these strategies, they face the general issue of how to maintain a steady and minimized number of Cryptographic Packet Loss (CPL) and Network Packet Loss (NPL) even as the traffic congestion situation in a vehicular environment increases (*i.e.: CPL are beacons dropped because they are unverifiable due to the absence of a corresponding certificate and NPL are the beacons dropped over the network due to congestion*).

Therefore, we propose in this work an Artificial Intelligence-based Transmission Power-Control Certificate Omission (AI-TPCO) scheme which allows vehicles to demonstrate an efficient control over communication channel load by intelligently tuning their transmission power using fuzzy logic and also reactively adapting their beacon size using NbCO strategy. Our obtained simulation results prove that our proposed AI-TPCO scheme is able to attain a steady and minimized number of CPL and NPL even as the traffic congestion situation in a vehicular environment increases and as such maximizing cooperative awareness amongst vehicles.

Keywords: VANET · Security · Certificate omission · Congestion · Fuzzy logic

W. Bao et al. (Eds.): ADHOCNETS 2021/TridentCom 2021, LNICST 428, pp. 173–187, 2022.
https://doi.org/10.1007/978-3-030-98005-4_13

1 Introduction

In the early 1800s, the world of mobility observed a paradigm shift which was termed as the "Horseless carriage" [1] and this paradigm shift spearheaded the transitioning of mobility by animals (horses) to mobility by vehicles. Many years on, vehicles have become a significant part of our everyday life and as such, the number of vehicles on our roads has increased significantly. According to the US Car Ownership Statistics report in 2021 [2], about 91.3% of households in the US is reported to own at least one vehicle. Hence, as the rate of vehicle ownership in our world today increases at a study pace, the issue of road accidents and traffic congestion has become even more alarming. To curb these issues, the world is currently observing another paradigm shift in mobility called "Autonomous Vehicles" [3] which will be steered by some technologies like Vehicle to Vehicle (V2V) communication.

V2V communication is characterized by the periodic broadcast of beacons among vehicles on the road to enable them to take proactive safety decisions like slowing down in time when approaching a construction site or an accident scene. Often than not, these periodic beacons contain some level of safety critical information which requires that we authenticate the message itself as well as its source. And to do so, some researchers have proposed the use of a digital certificate issued by a trusted certificate authority.

Despite the benefits of the proposed security mechanism, it raises the issue of high communication overhead as it causes the size of the beacon payload to increase by over 200 bytes [5] and consequently leading to a congestion in the communication channel when vehicle density is high. To combat this issue, researchers have proposed in the literature several congestion control algorithms. Peculiar to our interest in this work is the beacon size control strategies (certificate omission schemes) proposed in the literature [6–9]. The general idea of these certificate omission schemes is to adapt the beacon payload size whenever the communication channel is observed to be congested by omitting the digital certificate attached to the beacons. However, these strategies are faced with the issue of how to significantly minimize and maintain a steady packet loss (NPL and CPL) even as traffic congestion in the vehicular environment increases.

In this paper, we tackle the aforementioned issue by proposing an Artificial Intelligence-based Transmission Power-Control Certificate Omission (AI-TPCO) scheme which is a Beacon Size Control (BSC) strategy supplemented with an intelligent Transmission Power Control (TPC) strategy. In this work, we perform an intelligent adaptation of vehicle transmission power by using an Artificial Intelligence (AI) algorithm like fuzzy logic and an NbCO [7] strategy to tune beacon size in order to effectively control channel congestion.

The structure of the paper is as follows: Sect. 2 presents a literature review of some closely related works. Section 3 covers a detailed explanation of the features and working procedure of our proposed AI-TPCO scheme. Section 4 covers the simulation configuration and implementation. Section 5 presents the performance evaluation of our proposed AI-TPCO scheme against the Periodic Omission of Certificates (POoC) and NbCO schemes. Section 6 covers the conclusion of this work.

2   Related Work

In this section, we review some closely related works.

2.1   Certificate Omission Schemes

Periodic Omission of Certificates (POoC); as the name implies, a POoC [6] strategy operates by attaching a certificate to beacons only on periodic bases. Thus, if a vehicle is expected to send 'n' number of beacons within a second, the POoC strategy will require that a certificate affixed to only the 'nth' beacon and omit the certificate from the remaining 'n-1' beacons it broadcast. Upon evaluation, the performance of this scheme is noticed to be context dependent as CPL increases under situations where vehicle mobility is high and beacon transmission frequency is low and as such compromising vehicle cooperative awareness.

Neighbor-based Certificate Omission (NbCO); in VANETs, vehicles are made aware of other neighboring vehicles through the reception of periodic beacons. And a vehicle upon identifying a new neighbor, records the details of this new neighbor into a neighboring table for reference purposes. Employing the neighboring table concept, the NbCO [7] strategy controls channel congestion by attaching a certificate to a beacon only when it observes an update in its neighboring table. Upon evaluation, the scheme produced promising results as it was able to reduce packet loss. However, its performance was also demonstrated to be context-dependent as it reduced NPL significantly only in situations where vehicle mobility is low and also reduced CPL significantly only in circumstances where vehicles mobility is high. From this, we observe that the NbCO strategy is unable to attain a fair balance between CPL and NPL as its performance conditions are contradictory.

Congestion-based Certificate Omission (CbCO); the Congestion-based Certificate Omission (CbCO) scheme was proposed by [8] to control channel congestion based on the observed Channel Busy Ratio (CBR). As such, the CbCO scheme upon sensing the communication to be free attaches a certificate to all beacons transmitted so as to reduce CPL and when it senses the communication channel to be congested, it omits certificates from subsequent beacons in an aggressive manner by using a POoC strategy. Upon evaluation, the CbCO scheme proved promising as it was able to reduce the total number of packets that were lost (NPL + CPL) within the simulation time. However, when we consider the individual packets that were lost (NPL and CPL) we observe that its performance is no better than previously proposed schemes.

Transmission Power-control Certificate Omission (TPCO); a TPCO strategy was proposed by [9] to maximize cooperative awareness amongst vehicles by minimizing CPL and NPL. The scheme merged the NbCO strategy and a Distributed Transmission Power Control (D-TPC) strategy to efficiently manage channel congestion. And as such, the NbCO strategy was used as a proactive means of preventing channel congestion whereas the D-TPC strategy was used as a reactive means to help vehicles cooperatively reduce channel congestion upon receiving a distress signal. Although this scheme was able to significantly reduce the number of incurred NPL through its reactive congestion control strategy, it was unable to significantly reduce the number of incurred CPL when evaluated against the NbCO strategy since the performance margin between them can be considered negligible.

We consider it worth mentioning that to the best of our knowledge, these were the only works we found in the literature regarding certificate omission strategies.

2.2 Transmission Power Control (TPC) Schemes

As discussed in previous sections, researchers have proposed in the literature many congestion control approaches, an example being the TPC approach. Generally, this kind of approach controls channel congestion by tuning vehicle transmission power in situations where the contention for channel acquisition is high.

A Distributed Fair Power Adjustments for Vehicular environment (D-FPAV) was suggested in the work [10] to maintain the load of the communication channel beneath a predefined value to avoid packet collision in situations where vehicle density is high. In so doing, the transmission power of vehicles is dynamically adjusted upon receiving information on the status of its neighbouring vehicles indicating that the channel load is high. Chang et al. [11] in their work proposed a D-TPC approach to manage channel congestion, without sacrificing cooperative awareness among vehicles. In his approach, vehicles within communication range cooperatively adjust their transmission power upon sensing the channel to be congested or receiving a distress signal from neighbouring vehicles. In [12] the author proposed a Vehicle Density-Based Power Control (VDBPC) strategy that takes in to account the density state of vehicles in the network. In this work, vehicle density was classified into three states (sparse, moderate and dense) and based on the estimated density state, a vehicle adjusts its transmission within the range of high, medium and low transmission power respectively. However, this strategy may be considered as inefficient as the density of vehicles based on which transmission power is adjusted is randomly assumed.

3 AI-Based Transmission Power-Control Certificate Omission Scheme

In this work, we propose an AI-TPCO scheme to address the aforementioned drawbacks of previously proposed certificate omission schemes. As such, our proposed scheme aims at attaining a well-balanced and minimized number of packet loss (CPL and NPL) even as the traffic congestion situation increases in a vehicular environment and consequently maximizing the level of cooperative awareness attained amongst vehicles. To demonstrate an efficient control over channel load, we designed our AI-TPCO scheme to intelligently tune beacon transmission power using fuzzy logic and reactively adapt beacon size using an NbCO scheme. We also proposed as part of our transmission power control approach, a cooperative adaptation of beacon transmission power to enable the fast convergence of channel load to a reasonable value that is below the predefined channel load threshold. In this section, we will discuss in detail how our proposed scheme works.

3.1 Beacon Size Control (BSC) Approach

As was elaborated in previous sections, the security mechanism adopted in the state-of-the-art for secured beaconing significantly increases the beacon payload size which in turn induces an increase in channel load when vehicle density is high. For this reason, we propose that beacon payload size is reactively adapted through the adoption of an NbCO strategy which is triggered based on the estimated channel load. Thus, when a vehicle estimates the channel load to be high, it aggressively adapts its beacon size by attaching a certificate to beacons only upon observing an update in its neighboring table (i.e.: a new neighbor is found). On the other hand, if the vehicle observes the channel load as low, it will switch to a No omission strategy where it attaches a certificate to every beacon it broadcasts. This will as a result prevent the occurrence of CPL when the communication channel is free whereas the NbCO strategy will significantly reduce NPL when the communication channel load is high. In this work, the NbCO strategy is invoked when the channel is observed to be in a Restrictive state and the No Omission strategy is invoked when otherwise.

$$Estimated\_CL = N * \left(beacon\_rate * M_{length}\right) \qquad (1)$$

We measured the load of the communication channel using the formula in Eq. (1), with Estimated_CL representing a vehicles estimation of the current load of the communication channel, N representing the total number of neighboring vehicles, beacon_rate representing the total number of beacons a vehicle transmits per second and M_{length} representing the size of the beacon payload. We define in Table 1 the pseudo-code for our proposed beacon size control approach.

Table 1. Beacon size control approach (certificate omission strategy)

Data:	Estimated channel load
Output:	Beacon size control
1:	**If** *Estimated_CL* < 40% **then**
2:	Attach certificate to all beacons (No Omission strategy)
3:	Wait time 'ΔT'
4:	**Else**
5:	**If** *New_neighbor* == True **then**
6:	Attach a certificate to the next beacon
7:	Wait time 'ΔT'
8:	**Else**
9:	Omit certificate from beacons
10:	Wait time 'ΔT'
11:	**endIf**

3.2 Transmission Power Control Approach

As a reactive beacon size control approach is generally not efficient enough to combat congestion, we also suggest the proactive and reactive adaptation of beacon transmission power to minimize channel congestion probability which will, in turn, have a positive impact on the number of incurred NPL and CPL. In so doing, we employed the use of fuzzy logic as a decision-making system to enable vehicles adapt transmission power independently and cooperatively. In this section, we will discuss in more detail how our modelled fuzzy logic decision-making system functions.

Independent Adaptation of Transmission Power

In our proposed scheme, we modelled a Single Input, Single Output (SISO) fuzzy logic system which accepts a single crisp value as input and produces a single crisp value as an output. A fuzzy logic decision-making system is divided in to various stages and the first of these stages is the initialization stage where we initialize our input and output parameters with their corresponding linguistic variables and membership functions. In this work, we chose estimated channel load as our input parameter and beacon transmission power as our output parameter. The terms Relaxed, Active and Restrictive are defined as our input linguistic variables and we defined the range for our input variable in accordance to [13] as illustrated in Table 2. Also, the terms Low, Medium and High are defined as our output linguistic variables (ranging from 0 to 20 mW). Figure 1 and Fig. 2 illustrates our input and output membership functions respectively. The remaining stages of our fuzzy logic decision making system is elaborated below:

Table 2. Mapping of channel state to channel load threshold

State	Estimated channel load
Relaxed	<15%
Active	15% to 40%
Restrictive	>40%

Factors Calculation: Generally, an estimation of channel load is the measure of the amount of load occupying the communication channel at any given point in time and as such, it is an efficient means of detecting the congestion probability of the communication channel. Hence, we considered the estimation of channel load as our crisp input. We used Eq. (1) as our channel load estimation formula. Also, in measuring the degree of membership to a linguistic variable from the membership functions, we used both the triangular and trapezoidal membership functions [14].

Fuzzification: at this stage, the input value (crisp value) is converted into a fuzzy input set using the corresponding membership function. Hence, each vehicle uses the input membership function (as defined in Fig. 1) to calculate the degree to which their estimated channel load belongs to the input linguistic variables (Relaxed, Active or Restrictive). This membership degree then becomes our fuzzy input set.

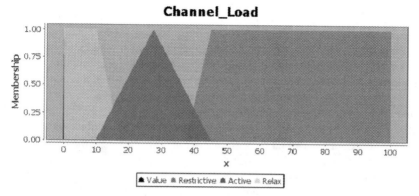

Fig. 1. Membership function for fuzzy logic input parameter (Estimated Channel Load)

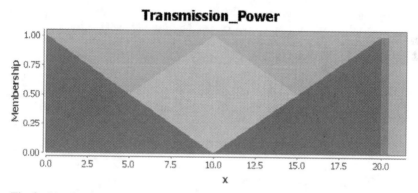

Fig. 2. Membership function for fuzzy logic output parameter (Transmission Power)

Table 3. Fuzzy rule base

	Estimated channel load	Transmission power
Rule 1	Relaxed	High
Rule 2	Active	Medium
Rule 3	Restrictive	Low

Fuzzy Interference Engine: constitutes a list of IF/THEN rules (as specified in Table 3) which forms the decision making brain of the fuzzy system. Here, each vehicle uses the fuzzy rule base to determine to which of the output linguistic variable its fuzzy input value belongs and its corresponding membership degree. As such, a fuzzy output set is generated using the Mamdani fuzzy interference method [15].

Defuzzification: in the defuzzification stage, a crisp output value is generated using the membership function defined for the output parameter (depicted in Fig. 2) and a corresponding degree of membership of the fuzzy output set. In this thesis, we employed the Mean Of Maxima (MOM) method [16] to defuzzify the fuzzy output set. The generated crisp output value then serves as the beacon transmission power of a vehicle.

Cooperative Adaptation of Transmission Power

In addition to the independent adaptation of transmission power by vehicles, we also propose the cooperative adaptation of transmission power (using same fuzzy logic system) upon a vehicle receiving a distress signal from a neighboring vehicle. Thus, when a vehicle estimates its channel load to be high, it generates a distress signal (containing information of the observed channel state) and also piggybacks in to it, its observed number of neighboring vehicles. The distress signal is then broadcast to all neighboring vehicles as a means of informing them of its current state and also soliciting their cooperative support. Therefore, if a vehicle should receive a distress signal, it extracts the piggybacked information (number of neighboring vehicles) and using this information, it estimates the corresponding channel load. Upon estimating the channel load (generated from the piggybacked information), the value is fed into the fuzzy system as input to generate the appropriate transmission power with which it can cooperatively assist in relieving the observed channel condition. Hence, allowing for the effective control of channel load to maximize cooperative awareness amongst the vehicles. Table 4 and Table 5 illustrates the pseudocodes for our proposed transmission power control approach (independent and cooperative transmission power adaptation).

Table 4. Algorithm I: Transmission power control strategy (sending vehicle)

Data:	beacon_rate, M_{length} and N
Output:	Change in channel state, adapted transmission power
1:	Estimate channel load (N = observed no. of neighbors)
2:	If *Estimated_CL* > 15% then
3:	Set channel state = Active or Restrictive
4:	Broadcast 'Distress signal'
5:	Generate transmission power (using fuzzy logic)
6:	Wait time 'ΔT'
7:	Else
8:	Set channel state = Relaxed
9:	Generate transmission power (using fuzzy logic)
10:	Wait time 'ΔT'
11:	endIf

Table 5. Algorithm II: Transmission power control strategy (receiving vehicle)

Data:	Distress signal, beacon_rate and M_{length}
Output:	Adapted transmission power
1:	**If** *Distress signal* == True **then**
2:	Estimate channel load (N = no. of neighbors piggybacked in distress signal)
3:	Generate corresponding transmission power (using fuzzy logic)
4:	Wait time 'ΔT'
5:	**Else**
6:	**Go to** Algorithm I
7:	**endIf**

4 Simulation Configuration and Implementation

As our network simulator, we employed the use of OMNET++ which is an object-oriented modular discrete event network simulation framework that enables the modelling of communication in both wired and wireless networks.

As traffic simulator, we use SUMO is a portable open-source road traffic simulation software that was designed by the Institute of Transportation at the German Aerospace centre to support the simulation of large road networks. In this work, we used SUMO to generate two traffic scenarios. First of which is a 4-way signalized junction as illustrated in Fig. 3 and we imported a real roadmap of Erlangen from Open Street Map as our second traffic scenario as illustrated in Fig. 4. To achieve a dense traffic condition to test the robustness of our proposed scheme, we simulated the communication between 100 to 400 vehicles in each traffic scenario.

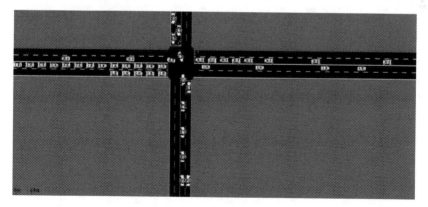

Fig. 3. A 4-way signalized junction

Fig. 4. Erlangen map

Also, we employed the Veins simulation framework which is an open-source VANETs simulation program used to simulate Inter-Vehicular Communication (IVC) by running in parallel the OMNET++ simulator and SUMO simulator. In this work, we extended the Application layer of the Veins framework to model our certificate omission strategy and we also extended the MAC layer of the Veins framework to implement our fuzzy logic based transmission power control strategy.

In Table 6, we present a summary of the network and traffic parameter configurations of our simulation and it is worth mentioning that some of these parameters were configured in conformity with the work of Schoch et al. in [8].

Table 6. Overview of simulation parameters

Parameter	Value	Source location
Number of vehicles	100, 200, 300, 400 vehicles	*.rou.xml
Field size	90 km × 40 km	Omnetpp.ini
Beacon frequency	10 Hz	Omnetpp.ini
Payload size	50 Bytes	Omnetpp.ini
ECC key type	Nistp256, compressed	Omnetpp.ini
Certificate size	125 Bytes	Omnetpp.ini
Signature size	56 Bytes	Omnetpp.ini
MAC	802.11p, 3 Mbit/s	Omnetpp.ini
Max transmission power	20 mW	Omnetpp.ini
Simulation time (sec)	150, 250, 350, 450 s	Omnetpp.ini
Simulation runs	10	Omnetpp.ini

5 Performance Evaluation

In evaluating our proposed AI-TPCO schemes, we performed a comparison between our obtained simulation results and the results obtained from the NbCO and POoC schemes which we considered as the baseline for our comparison. Below are the evaluation metrics we used in our comparison:

- Percentage of CPL: this criterion shows the percentage of CPL incurred during the simulation time. Thereby giving a clear indication of the level of cooperative awareness achieved.
- Percentage of NPL: this metric measures the percentage of NPL incurred during the entire simulation time and as such gives us an estimate of the network performance. As well as the level of cooperative awareness achieved.

Figure 5 and Fig. 6 show the evaluation results in the 4-way signalized junction scenario, whereas Fig. 7 and Fig. 8 show the evaluation results in the Erlangen map scenario.

From Fig. 5, we noticed that when the vehicle population is 100, the POoC, NbCO and AI-TPCO schemes incurred an NPL percentage of 16.06, 8.28 and 12.26 respectively. Here, we observe that our AI-TPCO scheme performed slightly poor as it incurred 3.98 of NPL more than the NbCO strategy. This we believe is a result of the No Omission strategy we perform when channel load is observed to be below a defined threshold. However, as the number of vehicles begins to increase from 100 to 400, the simulation results show that our AI-TPCO strategy outperforms both the POoC and NbCO strategies. When the number of vehicles is 400, we see that our AI-TPCO scheme incurs an NPL percentage of 19.49 which is approximately two times lower than that of the NbCO scheme and approximately three times lower than that of the POoC scheme. Implying that our AI-TPCO scheme can reduce NPL drastically even as channel load or vehicle population increases. We, therefore, attribute this efficient channel control performance demonstrated by our AI-TPCO scheme to the proactive and reactive strategies we adopted in our scheme.

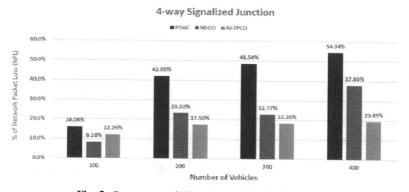

Fig. 5. Percentage of NPL (4-way signalized junction)

Figure 6, depicts the variations in CPL with vehicle population for each congestion control strategy. We compared the percentage of CPL incurred in POoC, NbCO and AI-TPCO schemes as we gradually increase the vehicle population from 100 to 400. The simulation results prove that our proposed AI-TPCO scheme is more efficient at decreasing CPL as it recorded a CPL percentage of 1.85, 2.74, 2.72 and 2.67 (as vehicles increases from 100 to 400 respectively) which is approximately three times lower than that of POoC and NbCO. Hence, making our AI-TPCO scheme the first certificate omission scheme to significantly outperform the NbCO scheme at reducing CPL.

However, when vehicle population is 200 we observe that our proposed AI-TPCO scheme and the POoC scheme incurred its highest CPL and this is because of the indirect impact NPL has on CPL. Thus, depending on the kind of beacon (with certificate or without certificate) that is dropped during a NPL, there may be an effect on CPL. Hence, we deduce that majority of the beacons that were dropped in NPL when vehicle population is 200 were possibly beacons with certificates attached and as such affecting the incurred number of CPL in these schemes when vehicle population is 200.

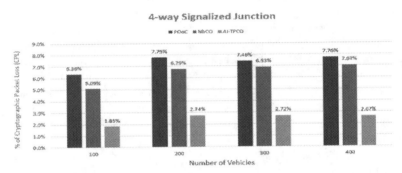

Fig. 6. Percentage of CPL (4-way signalized junction)

In the Erlangen scenario, our proposed AI-TPCO strategy is evaluated using the same evaluation metrics as was used in the highway scenario. Figure 7 and Fig. 8 illustrates the results obtained from this scenario. From Fig. 7, we observe that as the vehicle population increases, the percentage of NPL continues to increase across all the omission strategies under study. For instance, using POoC, NbCO and AI-TPCO, the percentage of NPL are 22.63, 23.45 and 9.59 respectively when the population of the vehicles is 200. And 49.76, 37.08 and 11.99 respectively when the population of vehicles is 300. From the given example, the difference between the two results is 27.13, 13.63 and 2.4 respectively. With this difference, we deduce that our proposed scheme better improves network performance as it can suppress NPL significantly even as the vehicle population increases.

When vehicle population is 300 we observe that all the schemes incurred their highest NPL and this we attribute to the random assignment of routes to vehicles. Thus, in our simulation routes were randomly assigned to the vehicles on the map and as such, the routes vehicles take when their population is 100 is different from the routes the vehicles will take on the same map when their population is 200. Hence, we deduced that due to this random assignment of routes, vehicles experienced higher clustering when their population was 300 which consequently increased traffic congestion and as a resulting affecting the number of NPL incurred.

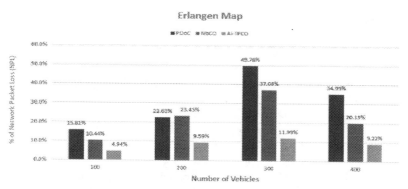

Fig. 7. Percentage of NPL (Erlangen Map)

The results in Fig. 8 show that our AI-TPCO scheme was able to outperform the POoC and NbCO schemes significantly by a performance margin of 4.83 and 3.35 respectively when the vehicle population is 100. And this performance margin is seen to be maintained even as the vehicle population increases from 100 to 400. Hence, comparing the results obtained from the 4-way signalized junction and the Erlangen map scenarios, it is clear that our proposed scheme is consistent at maintaining its performance (of decreasing CPL) regardless of the traffic scenario underuse. Once again, when vehicle population is 300 we observe that the POoC scheme and the NbCO scheme incurred its highest CPL and as we previously explained, we attribute this to the indirect impact NPL has on CPL.

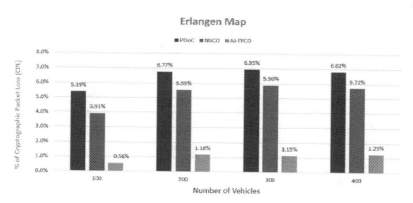

Fig. 8. Percentage of CPL (Erlangen Map)

Comparing results obtained from both traffic scenarios (4-way signalized junction and Erlangen map) we can conclude that our proposed AI-TPCO scheme significantly outperforms the other strategies as it is able to demonstrate effective control over the communication channel even as the vehicle population increases. Thereby maximizing cooperative awareness amongst vehicles.

6   Conclusion

In this paper, we addressed the drawbacks of existing certificate omission strategies and as such we investigated how to significantly decrease CPL and NPL incurred. And we did this with the ultimate aim of maximizing cooperative awareness amongst vehicles even as traffic congestion increases in the vehicular environment. In so doing, we proposed an AI-TPCO scheme that combines the strengths of both a TPC and BSC strategy to effectively control channel congestion in VANETs. To detect congestion, the proposed scheme estimates channel load and uses the TPC and BSC strategy to respectively control channel congestion proactively and reactively. The TPC approach of our proposed scheme controls congestion by tuning the transmission power of vehicles independently or cooperatively using fuzzy logic, whereas the BSC approach of our scheme controls congestion by tuning the beacon size using a No omission or NbCO strategy.

The obtained simulation results justify our claims that the proposed AI-TPCO scheme can incur a significantly low and balanced number of NPL and CPL even as the traffic congestion increases. Thereby justifying consequently that the scheme can maximize cooperative awareness amongst vehicles and also exhibit an effective mastery over the communication channel in both traffic scenarios used.

In conclusion, we have demonstrated through our work that when a beacon size control strategy is supplemented with an intelligent transmission power control strategy, the strategy gains mastery over the communication channel and as such maximizes vehicle cooperative awareness.

References

1. Williams, J.: Horseless Carriages: Road Vehicles. The Electric Century, pp. 136–146 (2017)
2. Peterson, B.: Car Ownership Statistics (2021 Report). ValuePenguin (2021). https://www.val uepenguin.com/auto-insurance/car-ownership-statistics. Accessed 7 Sept 2021
3. Litman, T.: Autonomous vehicle implementation predictions: implications for transport planning. Trid.trb.org (2021). https://trid.trb.org/view/1678741. Accessed 7 Sept 2021
4. Liu, X., Jaekel, A.: Congestion control in V2V safety communication: problem, analysis. Appr. Electr. **8**(5), 1–24 (2019)
5. Feiri, M., Petit, J., Kargl, F.: Evaluation of congestion-based certificate omission in VANETs. In: 2012 IEEE Vehicular Networking Conference (VNC), pp. 101–108 (2012)
6. Calandriello, G., Papadimitratos, P., Hubaux, J., Lioy, A.: On the performance of secure vehicular communication systems. IEEE Trans. Depend. Secur. Comput. **8**(6), 898–912 (2011)
7. Feiri, M., Petit, J., Kargl, F.: Congestion-based certificate omission in VANETs. In: Proceedings of the ninth ACM International Workshop on Vehicular Inter-Networking, Systems, And Applications - VANET 2012, pp. 135–138 (2012)
8. Schoch, E., Kargl, F.: On the efficiency of secure beaconing in VANETs. In: Proceedings of the third ACM Conference on Wireless Network Security - WiSec 2010, pp. 111–116 (2012)
9. Dapaah, E., Memarmoshrefi, P., Hogrefe, D.: Transmission power-control certificate omission in vehicular ad hoc networks. In: Ad Hoc Networks, pp. 164–176 (2021)

10. Torrent-Moreno, M., Santi, P., Hartenstein, H.: Distributed fair transmit power adjustment for vehicular ad hoc networks. In: 2006 3rd Annual IEEE Communications Society on Sensor and Ad Hoc Communications and Networks (2006)
11. Chang, H., Song, Y., Kim, H., Jung, H.: Distributed transmission power control for communication congestion control and awareness enhancement in VANETs. PLoS ONE 13(9), 1–25 (2018)
12. Akinlade, O.: Adaptive transmission power with vehicle density for congestion control. Scholarship at UWindsor (2021). https://scholar.uwindsor.ca/etd/7420/?utm_source=scholar.uwindsor.ca/etd/7420&utm_medium=PDF&utm_campaign=PDFCoverPages. Accessed 7 Sept 2021
13. Anon, n.d. https://www.etsi.org/deliver/etsi_ts/102600_102699/102687/01.01.01_60/ts_102687v010101p.pdf. Accessed 7 Sept 2021
14. eMathTeacher, n.d. Mamdani's fuzzy inference method - Membership functions. http://www.dma.fi.upm.es/recursos/aplicaciones/logica_borrosa/web/fuzzy_inferencia/funpert_en.htm. Accessed 7 Sept 2021
15. Mamdani Fuzzy Model (n.d.). http://researchhubs.com/post/engineering/fuzzy-system/mamdani-fuzzy-model.html. Accessed 7 Sept 2021
16. Coursehero.com. (n.d.) Chapter 5 Defuzzification Methods.pdf-Chapter 5 Defuzzification Methods Fuzzy rule based systems evaluate linguistic if-then rules using fuzzification|Course Hero. https://www.coursehero.com/file/52969005/Chapter-5-Defuzzification-Methodspdf/. Accessed 7 Sept 2021

Dynamic Ephemeral and Session Key Generation Protocol for Next Generation Smart Grids

Vincent Omollo Nyangaresi[1]([✉]), Zaid Ameen Abduljabbar[2,3],
Mustafa A. Al Sibahee[4,5], Enas Wahab Abood[6], and Iman Qays Abduljaleel[7]

[1] Faculty of Biological & Physical Sciences, Tom Mboya University College, Homabay, Kenya
vnyangaresi@tmuc.ac.ke

[2] Department of Computer Science, College of Education for Pure Sciences, University of Basrah, Basrah, Iraq
zaid.ameen@uobasrah.edu.iq

[3] Huazhong University of Science and Technology, Shenzhen Institute, Shenzhen, China

[4] College of Big Data and Internet, Shenzhen Technology University, Shenzhen 518118, China
mustafa@sztu.edu.cn

[5] Computer Technology Engineering Department, Iraq University College, Basrah, Iraq

[6] Department of Mathematics, College of Science, University of Basrah, Basrah, Iraq
enas.abood@uobasrah.edu.iq

[7] Department of Computer Science, College of Computer Science and Information Technology, University of Basrah, Basrah, Iraq
iman.abduljaleel@uobasrah.edu.iq

Abstract. Smart grid networks offer two-way communication between the smart meters and the utility service providers (USPs). This enables the USPs to analyze real-time data emanating from the consumers and offer dynamic adjustments to the power generation and transmission. However, the periodical transmission of consumption reports from the smart meters towards the USPs over public channels exposes the exchanged messages to attacks such as eavesdropping, modification and bogus injections. Consequently, the power adjustments executed may not be occasioned by consumer requirements but by malicious entities within the smart grid network. To curb this, numerous schemes have been presented in literature. However, majority of these protocols are either susceptible to attacks or are inefficient. In this paper, a dynamic ephemeral and session key generation protocol is presented. The security analysis shows that if offers entity anonymity, mutual authentication, forward key secrecy and untraceability. In addition, it is shown to be resilient against typical smart grid attacks such as offline password guessing, denial of service (DoS), packet replays, privileged insider, man-in-the-middle (MitM), impersonation and physical capture. In terms of performance, it has the least execution times and bandwidth requirements among other related protocols.

Keywords: Attacks · Authentication · Privacy · Protocols · Security · Smart grids · Smart meters

© ICST Institute for Computer Sciences, Social Informatics and Telecommunications Engineering 2022
Published by Springer Nature Switzerland AG 2022. All Rights Reserved
W. Bao et al. (Eds.): ADHOCNETS 2021/TridentCom 2021, LNICST 428, pp. 188–204, 2022.
https://doi.org/10.1007/978-3-030-98005-4_14

1   Introduction

The Smart Grid (SG) is envisioned as the next-generation intelligent network that introduces efficiency in the delivery, management and integration of renewable and green energy technologies [1]. The SG basically provides a two-way information and energy exchange between the smart meter (SM) and the utility service provider (USP) [2]. A typical SG consists of control centers, communication modules and smart devices such as smart meters. In the SG networks, the SMs monitor power consumptions and stability of the supplied power [3]. In essence, the SM utilizes the two-way communication channel between the consumer and the USP to manage, exchange and control energy delivery and consumption at the customer premises [4]. Despite the offered convenience, the SMs raise security and privacy issues regarding the transmission of energy consumptions reports over the public networks [4, 5].

As explained in [6], the SG is one of the many application domains of Internet of Things (IoT) that utilizes the Internet Protocol (IP) for the exchange of information between the USP and the SMs. Through the bi-directional communication procedures, energy efficiency is realized [7] through dynamic adjustments to the power transmitted. Compared with the conventional power grids, SGs offer enhanced efficiency, reliability and sustainability [8]. However, many security issues such as Distributed Denial of Service (DDoS) lurk in the SG networks targeting the SMs and other SG components. In addition, other attacks inherent in conventional public channels [9] are also possible in SG networks.

In most application domains, the SMs are installed outside in an open environment within a home. This exposes the SMs to numerous attacks, including physical capture [4, 10] which may facilitate side-channel attacks through power analysis. According to [6], the communication module that interlinks different components introduces security vulnerabilities into the SG as a result of increased complexity and increased surfaces from where attacks can be launched against the electrical power system. As such, although the SG facilitates automated measurement and visualization of power consumptions, spoofing attacks are common in this environment [11]. The requirement that SMs transmit periodical consumption reports to the USP implies increased chances of eavesdropping. Such packet leakages may compromise consumer privacy [12] and may be deployed to infer the conditions of home occupancy from captured power consumption reports.

The USP normally analyzes the received consumption reports from the SMs and adjust power transmission appropriately [13]. In so doing, the USP is able to balance peak and off-peak power consumptions [14]. However, attackers may capture and modify the exchanged reports, leading to erroneous adjustments at the USP [2]. As pointed out in [13], demand response management is critical for reliable and efficient power management in SG environment. This requires frequent data exchanges between the SMs and USP. However, this serves to increase chances of the transmitted data being compromised over insecure channels [13]. On the other hand, packet interceptions, modification and eavesdropping have been identified in [15] as being serious threats in SG networks.

The decentralized nature of the SGs, with their massive components and complex connections have been identified in [16] as being the sources of security, trust and privacy issues in this environment. As such, new techniques and protocols are required to deal with this scenario. Authentication is the first step towards SG network security, which is followed by agreement on some session keys to protect the exchanged packets [4, 17, 18]. The assurance of data privacy, mutual authentication, key establishment, anonymity, untraceability, and unlinkability is critical in SGs. However, the provisioning of these security features at low computation costs is still a challenge [19]. As pointed out in [20], there is need for robust authentication protocols to offer support for secure and private exchange of information among legitimate entities in SGs. The major contributions of this paper include the following:

- Transient security tokens are deployed to dynamically generate the session keys to protect the exchanged power consumption reports.
- All SG network entities communicate using their pseudonyms to uphold their anonymity and untraceability during the authentication and key agreement phase.
- Security analysis is executed to show that the proposed protocol offers superior security features compared with other related schemes.
- Performance evaluation is carried out to show that this protocol provides strong security at the lowest execution times and bandwidth requirements compared with other related protocols.

The rest of this paper is organized as follows: Sect. 2 presents related work while Sect. 3 gives an illustration of the system model adopted in this paper. On the other hand, Sect. 4 presents and discusses the comparative analysis, while Sect. 5 concludes the paper and gives future work.

2   Related Work

Many SG network authentication and key agreement protocols have been presented in literature. For instance, a public and private key based scheme for SMs is presented in [21]. However, this protocol is inefficient due to the intensive computations that must be executed [22, 23]. A SG message authentication technique is introduced in [24], but which is susceptible to DDoS and fails to offer trustworthy mutual authentication [25]. On the other hand, an identity-based encryption protocol is developed in [26]. Although this approach offers mutual authentication and SM anonymity, it cannot assure session key security. In addition, identity-based protocols cannot offer device privacy due to the requirement that the identities be exchanged during mutual authentication [27]. Using elliptic curve cryptography (ECC), a key agreement and authentication (AKA) protocol is presented in [28]. However, this scheme has high communication overheads [7] and is generally complicated.

A blockchain based AKA protocol is introduced in [29] to offer anonymous authentication in SGs. However, the deployed central authority may present some single point of failure [7]. In addition, the blockchain technology employed here has high space and computational complexities [30]. On the other hand, the AKA protocol developed in [31] is still vulnerable to traceability and impersonation attacks. Based on the public key infrastructure (PKI), a lightweight message authentication technique is presented in [32]. However, this protocol has high execution time for the deployed private keys and signatures [23]. In addition, PKI may lead to unnecessarily heavy storage and signaling complexities among the authenticating entities [33]. Authors in [34] have developed a bilinear maps based protocol, but the deployed bilinear maps render it computationally intensive [30]. In addition, the USP may fail to detect any malicious SM messages [19].

An ECC based lightweight AKA protocol is presented in [35] for clients and SG substations authentication. However, this scheme does not offer perfect key secrecy [36]. To provide protection against outsider and insider attacks in SG, an attribute based security protocol is introduced in [17]. However, the communication and storage costs of this scheme are too high for the computation, transmission and energy limited smart gas meter. On the other hand, the scheme presented in [3] is susceptible to impersonation and ephemeral secret leakage attacks [37]. The PKI based one-way authentication scheme developed in [38] prevented DoS, but has high computation and communication complexities [4]. The SG AKA protocol presented in [39] is unable to offer authentication between two SG entities [40]. On the other hand, the privacy-preserving technique in [41] achieves high privacy but provides only one –way authentication. To secure demand response, an ECC based protocol is developed in [42]. However, this scheme has scalability issues and is devoid of initial verification at the USP side which may lead to malicious requests being processed at the USP.

An identity-based AKA scheme is developed in [23] for SG networks, which was shown to be resilient against impersonation, replay and MitM attacks. However, this protocol is still vulnerable to identity spoofing attacks due to the transmission of SM identity in plain-text [43]. Moreover, the protocols presented in [21, 26, 31, 32] and [44] offer mutual authentication in SG networks at the expense of high computation overheads. On the other hand, authors in [45] have proposed an anonymous authentication protocol for smart grids. However, the scheme in [45] does not consider offline password guessing, privileged insider, physical capture and DoS attacks.

3   System Model

The network entities involved in the proposed protocol include the registration authority (RA), utility service provider (USP), gateway node (GWN) and the smart meter (SM) as shown in Fig. 1.

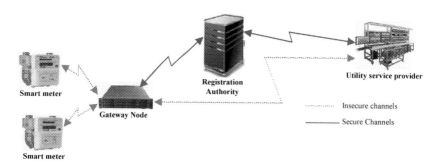

Fig. 1. Network model

As shown in Fig. 1, the smart meters directly communicate with the gateway node, which in turn directly communicated with the registration authority. Similarly, the utility service provider directly communicates with the registration authority. Here, the smart meters measure and submit periodic energy consumption reports to the USP. On the other hand, the USP adjusts power transmission and generation based on the received reports. The registration authority provides the security tokens and parameters needed for the secure transmission and reception of packets over the public channels. As shown in Fig. 1, the communication between the GWN and RA is through secured channels, similar to the connection between RA and USP. However, the communication between SMs and GWN, as well as between USP and GWN is through insecure public channels. Table 1 presents the symbols used in this paper together with their brief descriptions.

Table 1. Symbols

Symbol	Description
RA	Registration authority
USP	Utility service provider
SM	Smart meter
SK_S	SM's secret key
SK_U	USP's secret key
SM_{ID}	SM's identity
PD_{SM}	SM's pseudonym
PID_{USP}	USP's pseudo-identity
PID_S	SM's pseudo-identity
TT_S	SM's transient token
T_{SM}	SM's timestamp during registration
T_{USP}	USP's timestamp during registration
PD_{USP}	USP's pseudonym
ψL	USP's login parameters
$\mathbb{H}$	Master symmetric key for RA and GWN
T_i	Timestamps during AKA
$h(.)$	One-way hashing operation
ΔT	Maximum transmission delays
$Å$	Session key between SM and USP
$\|$	Concatenation operation
$\oplus$	XOR operation

In terms of the execution procedures, the proposed protocol is composed of two major phases, which include registration, followed by authentication and key agreement. The detailed description of these phases is given in the sub-sections below.

3.1 Registration Phase

In this phase, the RA derives master key $\mathbb{H}$, and registers the smart meters and gateway nodes before their actual deployment in the field. To accomplish this, step1 to 5 are utilized.

Step 1: The RA generates shared key SKS and smart meter identity SMID . It then derives the smart meter's pseudonym $PDSM = h(SMID\|SKS)$. Next, using prior computed security parameters and the smart meter's current timestamp TSM, the RA derives the smart meter's transient token $TTs = h(SMID\|SKS\|TSM)$ and additional security parameter $\acute{Z}1 = h(PDSM\|SKS)$. Afterwards, RA sends $\{PDS, TTS, \acute{Z}1\}$ to the smart meter and gateway node (GWN) through a secure channel.

Step 2: For the utility service provider (USP) to send and receive messages to and from the smart meter, registration at the RA is necessary. This begins by having the USP randomly choose its pseudonym PDUSP and send registration request RegReq together with PDUSP to the RA over some secure channels.

Step 3: Upon receiving Reg_{Req}, RA generates secret key SK_U followed by the derivation of the USP's pseudo-identity $PID_{USP} = h(PD_{USP}\|SK_U)$. Next, the RA computes USP's transient token $TT_U = h(PD_{USP}\|SK_U\|T_{USP})$. This is followed by the random selection of secret number S that it uses to derive $K_1 = h(PD_{USP}\|S)$ and $SK_U^* = h(SK_U\|K_1)$. Afterwards, RA sends registration response Reg_{Res} $\{PID_{USP}, TT_U, K_1, h(.), SK_U^*\}$ to the USP through some secure channels.

Step 4: The SM generates nonce $n3$ and determines current time stamp $T5$ that are used to derive the following parameters:

$$\bar{R}=h(\Psi\|M), \; P=h(PD_{USP}\|L)\oplus M$$
$$Q=h(PID_{USP}\|\bar{R}\|L\|K_1\|TT_U)$$
$$K_2=K_1\oplus h(PD_{USP}\|M)$$
$$PID_{USP}^*=PID_{USP}\oplus h(M\|\Psi)$$
$$TT_U^*= TT_U\oplus h(PD_{USP}\|\Psi)$$
$$SK_U^{**}= SK_U^*\oplus h(PD_{USP}\|M\|\Psi\|L)$$

It then buffers $\{PID_{USP}\,^*, TT_U\,^*, K_2, P, SK_U\,^{**}, Q, h(.)\}$ in its memory.

Step 5: Upon successful registration, RA computes $\acute{Z}2 = h(PIDUSP\|SKU)$, $\acute{Z}3 = h(PIDS\|SKS)$ and $\acute{Z}4 = h(SKU\|K1)$ before constructing $Msg1 = E\mathbb{H}(PDUSP, PIDUSP, TTU, \acute{Z}2)$ and sending it to the GWN. Here, shared key $\mathbb{H}$ is utilized to decrypt Msg1 to yield its contents which are then stored in the GWN's database. As such, this database now contains $\{PDUSP, PIDUSP, TTU, PIDS, TTS, \acute{Z}2, \acute{Z}3, \acute{Z}4\}$ for subsequent authentication and key agreement. Figure 2 shows the message flows during the registration phase.

As shown in Fig. 2, four messages are exchanged during the registration phase. The RA generates and transmits a number of security parameters to both the USP and GWN. In addition, the GWN and USP perform some decryption and independent derivations of other security tokens to be used for subsequent authentication and key agreement phase.

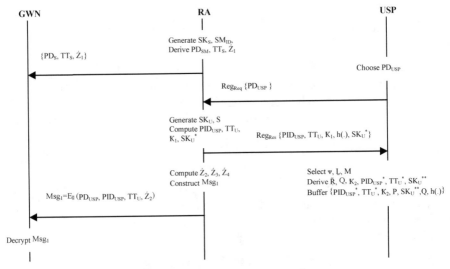

Fig. 2. Registration phase message flows

3.2 Authentication and Key Agreement

This phase is triggered whenever the USP wants to access some data from the remote SM. To accomplish this, the following steps are executed:

Step 1: Using PDUSP, ψ and $\underset{\rightarrow}{L}$, the USP derives the following:

$$M = P \oplus h(PD_{USP}\|\Psi)$$
$$\dot{K}_1 = K_2 \oplus h(PD_{USP}\|M)$$
$$PID_{USP} = PID_{USP}^* \oplus h(M\|\Psi)$$
$$TT_U = TT_U^* \oplus h(PD_{USP}\|\underset{\rightarrow}{L}) \text{ and } \bar{R} = h(\Psi\|M)$$
$$Q^* = h(PID_{USP}\|\bar{R}\|\underset{\rightarrow}{L}\|\dot{K}_1\|TT_U)$$

It then checks whether $Q^* = Q$ and if it is not, authentication is terminated. However, if this check is successful, the USP generates nonce $\eta 1$ and determines the current timestamp $\underset{\sim}{T}1$. This is followed by the derivation of the following security parameters:

$$SK_U^{**} = SK_U^* \oplus h(PD_{USP}\|M\|\Psi\|\underset{\rightarrow}{L})$$
$$Auth_{M1} = PID_{USP} \oplus h(SK_U^{**}\|\underset{\sim}{T}_1)$$
$$Auth_{M2} = PID_S \oplus h(TT_U\|PD_{USP}\|\underset{\sim}{T}_1)$$
$$Auth_{M3} = h(PID_{USP}\|TT_U\|\underset{\sim}{T}_1) \oplus \eta_1$$
$$Auth_{M4} = h(PD_{USP}\|PID_S\|TT_U\|\eta_1\|\underset{\sim}{T}_1)$$

Finally, it composes $Msg_2 = \{Auth_{M1}, Auth_{M2}, Auth_{M3}, Auth_{M4}, \underset{\sim}{T}_1\}$ and sends it to GWN over insecure channels.

Step 2: On receiving Msg_2 from the USP, the GWN determines current timestamp T_2 before checking whether $|T_2 - T_1| \leq \Delta T$, and if this is not the case, the authentication is terminated. However, if this verification is successful, the GWN derives $PID_{USP} = Auth_{M3} \oplus h(h(SK_U \| K_1 \| T_1))$. Next, it retrieves PD_{USP} and TT_U corresponding to the derived PID_{USP} from its database. This is followed by the derivation of nonce $\eta_1 = Auth_{M3} \oplus h(PID_{USP} \| TT_U \| T_1)$ and $Auth_{M5} = h(PD_{USP} \| PID_S \| TT_U \| \eta_1 \| T1)$ before verifying that $Auth_{M5} = Auth_{M4}$. If this validation is unsuccessful, the session is terminated, otherwise the GWN generates nonce η_2 and determines the current timestamp T_3. Next, it derives the following security tokens:

$$Auth_{M6} = h(TT_S \| PID_S) \oplus \eta_2$$
$$Auth_{M7} = h(PID_{USP} \| TT_U \| \eta_1) \oplus h(TT_S \| T_3)$$
$$Auth_{M8} = h(PID_S \| TT_S \| h(PID_S \| SK_S) \| \eta_2 \| T_3)$$

Finally, it composes $Msg3 = \{AuthM6, AuthM7, AuthM8, T3\}$ and transmits it to the SM over insecure channels.

Step 3: Upon receiving $Msg3$ from GWN, the SM determines current timestamp $T4$ and checks whether $|T4 - T3| \leq \Delta T$. If this is not the case, the session is terminated. However, if this condition is true, the SM re-computes the following security tokens:

$$\eta_2 = Auth_{M6} \oplus h(TT_S \| PID_S)$$
$$h(PID_{USP} \| TT_U \| \eta_1) = Auth_{M7} \oplus h(TT_S \| T_3)$$
$$Auth_{M9} = h(PID_S \| TT_S \| h(PID_S \| SK_S) \| \eta_2 \| T_3)$$

It then confirms whether $AuthM9 = AuthM8$, and if this condition is false, authentication session is terminated, otherwise the GWN is successfully authenticated by the SM.

Step 4: The SM generates nonce η_3 and determines current time stamp $T5$ that are used to derive the following parameters:

$$Auth_{M10} = h(h(PID_{USP} \| TT_U \| \eta_1) \| T_5) \oplus \eta_3$$
$$Auth_{M11} = h(h(PID_{USP} \| TT_U \| \eta_1) \| PID_S \| T_5) \oplus h(h(PID_S \| SK_S) \| T_5)$$
$$\mathring{A} = h(h(h(PID_S \| SK_S) \| T_5) \| h(PID_{USP} \| TT_U \| \eta_1) \| PID_S \| \eta_3 \| T_5)$$
$$Auth_{M12} = h(\mathring{A} \| T_5)$$

Thereafter, it constructs $Msg4 = \{Auth_{M10}, Auth_{M11}, Auth_{M12}, T_5\}$ before transmitting it to the USP through some public channels.

Step 5: Upon receiving $Msg4$, the USP determines current timestamp T_6 and checks whether $|T_6 - T_5| \leq \Delta T$, and if this is false, the session is terminated. However, if this condition is true, the USP derives the following security parameters:

$$\eta_3 = Auth_{M10} \oplus h(h(PID_{USP}\|TT_U\|\eta_1)\|T_5)$$
$$h(h(PID_S\|SK_S)\|T_5 = Auth_{M11} \oplus h(h(PID_{USP}\|TT_U\|\eta_1)\|PID_S\|T_5)$$
$$\mathring{A}^* = h(h(h(PID_S\|SK_S)\|T_5)\|h(PID_{USP}\|TT_U\|\eta_1)\|PID_S\|\eta_3\|T_5)$$
$$Auth_{M13} = h(\mathring{A}^*\|T_5)$$

This is followed by the confirmation of whether $Auth_{M13} = Auth_{M12}$ and if this is not the case, the authentication is terminated, otherwise the SM is authenticated by the USP. As such, the computed session key $\mathring{A}^*$ derived at the USP is valid and both the USP and SM set $\mathring{A}^* = \mathring{A}$ as the shared session key to protect the exchanged packets. Figure 3 shows the message flows during the authentication and key agreement phase.

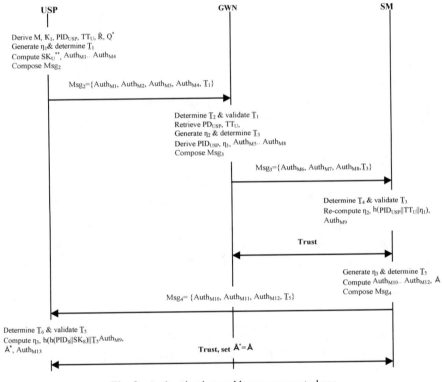

Fig. 3. Authentication and key agreement phase

Based on Fig. 3, a total of three messages are exchanged during the authentication and key agreement phase. It is also evident that each of the network entity independently computes a number of ephemeral security parameters that are then deployed to verify the received messages before some trust levels can be established among all the communicating entities.

4 Results and Discussion

In this section, the security and privacy features provided by the proposed protocol are analyzed as elaborated in Sect. 4.1. In addition, the performance evaluation in terms of execution time and bandwidth requirements is provided in Sect. 4.2 below.

4.1 Security Evaluation

To show the robustness of the proposed protocol against some of the typical smart grid attacks, the following eight

Theorem 1: DoS Attacks are Sufficiently Prevented in the Proposed Protocol.

Proof: During the authentication and key agreement procedures, the USP security parameters PD_{USP}, ψ and $\underset{\rightarrow}{L}$ are verified through the confirmation of whether $Q^* = Q$. As such, the authentication request message $Msg_2 = \{Auth_{M1}, Auth_{M2}, Auth_{M3}, Auth_{M4}\}$ is transmitted towards the GWN upon successful local authentication. Devoid of this successful local verification, authentication request cannot be sent over to the GWN. The incorporation of timestamps and random nonces renders the computed authentication parameters stochastic and hence cannot be easily determined by an adversary for possible session hijacking and hence DoS for the legitimate entities.

Theorem 2: Anonymity and Untraceability are Upheld in the Proposed Protocol.

Proof: In the proposed protocol, timestamps T_1, T_2, T_3, T_4, T_5 and T_6 are deployed in all exchanged messages Msg_2, Msg_3 and Msg_4. The same also applies to random nonces η_1, η_2 and η_3 during the authentication and key agreement. Consequently, all the exchanged messages are session specific and hence an adversary is unable to trace the GWN or the SM during the communication process. In addition, pseudo-identities PID_{USP} and PID_S are components of the exchanged messages Msg_2, Msg_3 and Msg_4. Since both PID_{USP} and PID_S are protected by a one-way hashing operation, they cannot be reversed to decipher their contents. This is due to the collision-resistance feature of the one-way hashing operation.

Theorem 3: The Proposed Protocol is Resilient Against Replay Attacks.

Proof: In the proposed protocol, timestamps are incorporated in the exchanged messages Msg_2, Msg_3 and Msg_4 during authentication and key agreement procedures. Upon receipt of each of these messages, freshness checks are executed using the timestamps in these messages as well as the permissible transmission delay ΔT. Consequently, an attacker is unable to intercept, modify and forward the transmitted messages due to the little transmission delays permitted.

Theorem 4: The Proposed Protocol Preserves Forward Key Secrecy.

Proof: Suppose that an adversary has intercepted exchanged messages Msg_2, Msg_3 and Msg_4 during the authentication and key agreement phase. Since $\mathring{A} = h(h(h(PID_S\|SK_S)\|T_5)\|h(PID_{USP}\|TT_U\|\eta_1)\|PID_S\|\eta_3\|T_5)$, the security of the session key is dependent on long term keys PID_{USP}, PID_S, TT_U, SK_S and ephemerals η_1 and η_3. If an attacker eavesdrops timestamps T_1 and T_5, followed by secrets η_1 and η_3, still the session key $\mathring{A}$ cannot be derived. This is because it requires long terms secrets PID_{USP}, PID_S, TT_U and SK_S. Conversely, without knowledge of short term secrets η_1 and η_3, the session key $\mathring{A}$ cannot be computed. As such, an adversary can only derive $\mathring{A}$ when both short term and long terms secrets are known, which is cumbersome.

Theorem 5: Man-in-the-Middle Attacks Are Thwarted in the Proposed Protocol.

Proof: In this attack, it is assumed that an attacker has eavesdropped $Msg_2 = \{Auth_{M1}$, $Auth_{M2}, Auth_{M3}, Auth_{M4}, T_1\}$. Thereafter, an attempt is made to alter this message and replay it later on. Here:

$$Auth_{M1}=PID_{USP}\oplus h(SK_U^{**}\|T_1)$$
$$Auth_{M2}=PID_S\oplus h(TT_U\|PD_{USP}\|T_1)$$
$$Auth_{M3}=h(PID_{USP}\|TT_U\|T_1)\oplus\eta_1$$
$$Auth_{M4}=h(PD_{USP}\|PID_S\|TT_U\|\eta_1\|T_1)$$

To carry out this modification, an adversary generates nonce η_1^* and timestamp T_1^*, then computes $Auth_{M1}^* = PID_{USP} \oplus h(SK_U^{**}\|T_1^*)$ to substitute in Msg_2. However, devoid of long terms secrets PID_{USP}, PD_{USP}, and SK_U^{**}, the attacker is unable to derive valid message Msg_2 nor can other messages exchanged during the authentication and key agreement process be derived.

Theorem 6: The Proposed Protocol is Resilient Against Impersonation Attacks.

Proof: Suppose that an attacker masquerading as USP attempts to establish an authentication session with the GWN. To construct a valid authentication message $Msg_2^* = \{Auth_{M1}^*, Auth_{M2}^*, Auth_{M3}^*, Auth_{M4}^*, T_1^*\}$ for this impersonation, the adversary needs to generate current timestamp T_1^A and nonce η_A. However, without valid security parameters PID_{USP}, PID_S and SK_U, it is infeasible to compute TT_U, $Auth_{M1}^*$, $Auth_{M2}^*$, $Auth_{M3}^*$ and $Auth_{M4}^*$. As such, an attacker is unable to generate valid Msg_2^* and hence this attack flops.

Let us assume that the adversary is interested in masquerading as GWN by generating current timestamp T_3^*, nonces η_1^* and η_2^*. Thereafter, an attempt is made to transmit message $Msg_3^* = \{Auth_{M6}, Auth_{M7}, Auth_{M8}, T_3^*\}$ to the SM. However, devoid of valid PID_{USP}, PID_S and SK_S, it is impossible to derive $Auth_{M6}^*$, $Auth_{M7}^*$ and $Auth_{M8}^*$ and hence is unable to generate valid Msg_3^*. Suppose that an attacker generates timestamp T_5^*, and nonces η_1^* and η_3^*. Thereafter, an attempt is made to construct and send bogus message $Msg_4^* = \{Auth_{M10}^*, Auth_{M11}^*, Auth_{M12}^*, T_5^*\}$ to the USP. However, without valid PID_{USP}, PID_S and SK_S, it is impossible to derive $Auth_{M10}^*$, $Auth_{M11}^*$ and $Auth_{M12}^*$, and hence this attack fails.

Theorem 7: *The Proposed Protocol is Robust Against Physical Capture Attacks.*

Proof: The assumption made here is that an adversary has captured the smart meter and has obtained secrets {PD_S, TT_S, $h(PD_S\|SK_S$) from the SM's memory. However, in the proposed protocol, security parameters {PD_S, TT_S, $h(PD_S\|SK_S$) are assigned by the RA and hence are quite distinct for each SM in the smart grid network. As such, the physical capture of one SM only yields the session key deployed between the SM and the USP. Consequently, the session keys established between other SMs and the USP cannot be obtained by the attacker, and hence their security is still intact.

Theorem 8: *Offline Password Guessing and Privileged Insider Attacks are Thwarted in the Proposed Protocol.*

Proof: Suppose that some privileged insider intercepts {PD_{USP}} sent from the USP towards the RA during the registration phase. It is also assumed that this privileged insider has utilized power analysis to retrieve security set {PID_{USP}^*, TT_U^*, K_2, P, SK_U^{**}, Q, $h(.)$} from memory. Thereafter, an attempt is made to derive $M = P\oplus h(PD_{USP}\|\psi)$. However, without knowledge of security token ψ, this computation fails since it cannot be determined from the captured memory parameters. Similarly, without M, security parameters PD_S and $\bar{R} = h(\psi\|M)$ cannot be computed. Table 2 presents the security robustness comparisons of the proposed protocol with other related schemes.

Table 2 Attack model comparisons

Attack model	[23]	[35]	[4]	[45]	Proposed
Offline password guessing	–	–	–	–	√
Privileged insider	–	–	–	–	√
Physical capture	–	–	–	–	√
Impersonation	√	√	√	√	√
MitM	√	√	√	√	√
Forward key secrecy	√	√	√	√	√
Replay	√	√	√	√	√
Anonymity	x	x	√	√	√
Untraceability	x	x	–	√	√
DoS	–	–	–	–	√
Mutual authentication	√	√	√	√	√

Legend
√ Effective
x Ineffective
– Not considered

It is evident from Table 2 that the proposed protocol offers the highest number of security features compared with the other related schemes.

4.2 Performance Analysis

In this sub-section, the proposed protocol is evaluated in terms of the number of bytes exchanged during the authentication and key agreement phase. In addition, the execution time for the various cryptographic operations is also provided as discussed below.

Bandwidth Requirements: During the authentication and key agreement phase, messages $Msg_2 = \{Auth_{M1}, Auth_{M2}, Auth_{M3}, Auth_{M4}, T_1\}$, $Msg_3 = \{Auth_{M6}, Auth_{M7}, Auth_{M8}, T_3\}$ and $Msg_4 = \{Auth_{M10}, Auth_{M11}, Auth_{M12}, T_5\}$ are exchanged. Using the values in [45] and [46], the outputs of the various cryptographic operations are given in Table 3 below.

Table 3. Cryptographic output sizes

Operation	Output size (bytes)
EC point addition	40
EC point multiplication	40
HMAC	20
SHA 1	16
AES-128 encryption	16
AES-128 decryption	16
Identity	20
Timestamp	4
Random nonce	16

As shown in Table 3, elliptic curve (EC) point encryption and decryption outputs are 40 bytes long while the Hash-based Message Authentication Code (HMAC) output is 20 bytes. On the other hand, random nonce, one-way hashing, advanced encryption standard (AES) encryption and decryption are 16 bytes each. In addition, timestamp and device identity are 4 bytes and 20 bytes long respectively. Based on these values, the bandwidth requirement of the proposed protocol is computed as follows:

$Msg_2 = \{Auth_{M1} = Auth_{M2} = Auth_{M3} = Auth_{M4} = 16, T_1 = 4\} = 68$ bytes.
$Msg_3 = \{Auth_{M6} = Auth_{M7} = Auth_{M8} = 16, T_3 = 4\} = 52$ bytes.
$Msg_4 = \{Auth_{M10} = Auth_{M1} = Auth_{M12} = 16, T_5 = 4\} = 52$ bytes

Consequently, the total bandwidth requirement in the proposed protocol is 172 bytes. On the other hand, the schemes in [4, 23, 35, 45] have bandwidth requirements of 248 bytes, 298 bytes, 254 bytes and 204 bytes respectively, as shown in Fig. 4.

It is evident from Fig. 4 that the authentication protocol in [35] has the highest bandwidth requirements while the proposed protocol has the least bandwidth requirements. As such, this protocol is the most applicable in a smart grid environment where most devices are energy constrained.

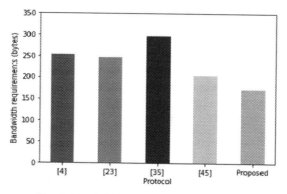

Fig. 4. Bandwidth requirements comparisons

Table 4. Execution times comparisons

Scheme	Execution time (ms)
[45]	0.347
[4]	17.306
[35]	15.965
[23]	15.693
Proposed	0.05678

Execution Time: In a typical authentication scheme, one-way hashing T_H, symmetric encryption T_E, symmetric decryption T_D, elliptic curve point multiplication T_{EM}, elliptic curve point addition T_{EA} and Hash-based Message Authentication Code T_{HMAC} are some of the cryptographic operations carried out. In the proposed protocol, 17 one-way hashing operations are executed on the USP side while 8 hashing operations are executed on the gateway node. On the other hand, 9 hashing operations are carried out on the smart meter side. As such, the total computation overhead is 34 hashing operations. Using the values in [45], T_H, T_E, T_D and T_{EM} operations consume 0.00167 ms, 0.0225 ms, 0.042 ms and 7.5045 ms respectively. As such, the total execution time in the proposed protocol is 0.05678 ms as shown in Table 4.

The scheme in [23] requires $7T_H$ and $5T_{EM}$ operations while the protocol in [35] needs $5T_H$, $5T_{EM}$ and $1T_{EA}$ operations. On the other hand, the scheme in [4] requires $7T_H$, $2T_E$, $2T_D$, $5T_{EM}$ and $4T_{HMAC}$ operations, while the protocol in [45] needs $16T_H$, $2T_D$ and $2T_E$ operations. This explains their high executions times compared with the proposed protocol. Since the proposed protocol has the least execution times, it does not overwhelm the processors and hence is the most ideal for SG devices that are characterized by limited computational power.

5 Conclusion and Future Work

Majority of the conventional smart grid security schemes have been noted to be based on public key infrastructure, blockchain, elliptic curve cryptography and bilinear pairing operations. However, inefficiency and susceptibility to numerous attacks are some of the shortcomings of these security solutions. Owing to the criticality of strong authentication, information privacy, key establishment, untraceability, anonymity and unlinkability, a novel security protocol is presented in this paper. It is shown that this protocol offers these security features at the least execution times and bandwidth requirements. In addition, it is demonstrated to be resilient against smart grid attack vectors such as offline password guessing, denial of service, packet replays, privileged insider, man-in-the-middle, impersonation and physical capture. Consequently, this protocol is ideal for deployment in smart gas meters as well as in other smart grid devices with limited computation, transmission and energy. Future work in this domain lies in the formal verification of the security features provided by this protocol.

References

1. Mollah, M.B., et al.: Blockchain for future smart grid: A comprehensive survey. IEEE Internet Things J. **8**(1), 18–43 (2020)
2. Nyangaresi, V.O., Mohammad, Z.: Privacy preservation protocol for smart grid networks. In: 2021 International Telecommunications Conference (ITC-Egypt), pp. 1–4, IEEE (2021)
3. Mahmood, K., et al.: Pairing based anonymous and secure key agreement protocol for smart grid edge computing infrastructure. Futur. Gener. Comput. Syst. **88**, 491–500 (2018)
4. Kumar, P., Gurtov, A., Sain, M., Martin, A., Ha, P.: Lightweight authentication and key agreement for smart metering in smart energy networks. IEEE Trans. Smart Grid **10**, 4349–4359 (2018)
5. Nyangaresi, V.O., Alsamhi, S.H.: Towards secure traffic signaling in smart grids. In: 2021 3rd Global Power, Energy and Communication Conference (GPECOM), pp. 196–201 (2021)
6. Sureshkumar, V., Anandhi, S., Amin, R., Selvarajan, N., Madhumathi, R.: Design of robust mutual authentication and key establishment security protocol for cloud-enabled smart grid communication. IEEE Syst. J. **15**(3), 3565–3572 (2020)
7. Wang, W., Huang, H., Zhang, L., Su, C.: Secure and efficient mutual authentication protocol for smart grid under blockchain. Peer-to-Peer Netw. Appl. **14**(5), 2681–2693 (2020). https://doi.org/10.1007/s12083-020-01020-2
8. Saxena, N., Choi, B.J.: Integrated distributed authentication protocol for smart grid communications. IEEE Syst. J. **12**(3), 2545–2556 (2018)
9. Nyangaresi, V.O. Ogundoyin, S.O.: Certificate based authentication scheme for smart homes. In: 2021 3rd Global Power, Energy and Communication Conference (GPECOM), pp. 202–207 (2021)
10. Nyangaresi, V.O.: ECC based authentication scheme for smart homes. In: 2021 International Symposium ELMAR, pp. 5–10. IEEE (2021)
11. Liu, S., et al.: Model-free data authentication for cyber security in power systems. IEEE Trans. Smart Grid **11**(5), 4565–4568 (2020)
12. Nyangaresi, V.O., Rodrigues, A.J., Abeka, S.O.: Efficient group authentication protocol for secure 5g enabled vehicular communications. In: 2020 16th International Computer Engineering Conference (ICENCO), pp. 25–30. IEEE (2020)

13. Chaudhry, S.A., Alhakami, H., Baz, A., Al-Turjman, F.: Securing demand response management: a certificate-based access control in smart grid edge computing infrastructure. IEEE Access **8**, 101235–101243 (2020)
14. Guan, Z., Zhang, Y., Zhu, L., Wu, L., Yu, S.: Effect: an efficient flexible privacy-preserving data aggregation scheme with authentication in smart grid. Sci. China Inf. Sci. **62**(3), 32103 (2019)
15. Gupta, R., Tanwar, S., Al-Turjman, F., Italiya, P., Nauman, A., Kim, S.W.: Smart contract privacy protection using AI in cyber-physical systems: tools, techniques and challenges. IEEE Access **8**, 24746–24772 (2020)
16. Ghosal, A., Conti, M.: Key management systems for smart grid advanced metering infrastructure: a survey. IEEE Commun. Surv. Tutor. **21**(3), 2831–2848 (2019)
17. Saxena, N., Choi, B.J., Lu, R.: Authentication and authorization scheme for various user roles and devices in smart grid. IEEE Trans. Inf. Forensics Secur. **11**(5), 907–921 (2016)
18. Nyangaresi, V.O.: Lightweight key agreement and authentication protocol for smart homes. In: 2021 IEEE AFRICON, pp. IEEE (2021)
19. Braeken, A., Kumar, P., Martin, A.: Efficient and provably secure key agreement for modern smart metering communications. Energies **11**(10), 26–62 (2018)
20. Ghani, A., Mansoor, K., Mehmood, S., Chaudhry, S.A., Rahman, A.U., Najmus Saqib, M.: Security and key management in IoT-based wireless sensor networks: an authentication protocol using symmetric key. Int. J. Commun. Syst. **32**(16), e4139 (2019)
21. Nicanfar, H., Jokar, P., Beznosov, K., Leung, V.: Efficient authentication and key management mechanisms for smart grid communications. IEEE Syst. J. **8**(2), 629–640 (2014)
22. Saxena, N., Choi, B.J.: State of the art authentication, access control, and secure integration in smart grid. Energies **8**(10), 11883–11915 (2015)
23. Mohammadali, A., Haghighi, M., Tadayon, M., Nodooshan, A.: A novel identity-based key establishment method for advanced metering infrastructure in smart grid. IEEE Trans. Smart Grid **9**(4), 2834–2842 (2018)
24. Li, X., Wu, F., Kumari, S., Xu, L., Sangaiah, A.K., Choo, K.K.R.: A provably secure and anonymous message authentication scheme for smart grids. J. Parallel. Distrib. Comput. **132**, 242–249 (2019)
25. Wu, L., Wang, J., Zeadally, S., He, D.: Anonymous and efficient message authentication scheme for smart grid. Secur. Commun. Netw. **2019**, 1–13 (2019)
26. Tsai, J., Lo, N.: Secure anonymous key distribution scheme for smart grid. IEEE Trans. Smart Grid **7**(2), 906–914 (2016)
27. Nyangaresi, V.O., Rodrigues, A.J., Taha, N.K.: Mutual authentication protocol for secure vanet data exchanges. In: Perakovic, D., Knapcikova, L. (eds.) FABULOUS 2021. LNIC-SSITE, vol. 382, pp. 58–76. Springer, Cham (2021). https://doi.org/10.1007/978-3-030-784 59-1_5
28. Garg, S., Kaur, K., Kaddoum, G., Rodrigues, J.J.P.C., Guizani, M.: Secure and lightweight authentication scheme for smart metering infrastructure in smart grid. IEEE Trans. Industr. Inf. **16**(5), 3548–3557 (2019)
29. Wang, J., Wu, L., Choo, K.K.R., He, D.: Blockchain-based anonymous authentication with key management for smart grid edge computing infrastructure. IEEE Trans. Industr. Inf. **16**(3), 1984–1992 (2019)
30. Nyangaresi, V.O., Rodrigues, A.J., Abeka, S.O.: Neuro-fuzzy based handover authentication protocol for Ultra Dense 5G networks. In: 2020 2nd Global Power, Energy and Communication Conference (GPECOM), pp. 339–344. IEEE (2020)
31. Odelu, V., Kumar Das, A., Wazid, M., Conti, M.: Provably secure authenticated key agreement scheme for smart grid. IEEE Trans. Smart Grid **9**(3), 1900–1910 (2018)

32. Mahmood, K., Chaudhry, S.A., Naqvi, H., Shon, T., Ahmad, H.F.: A lightweight message authentication scheme for smart grid communications in power sector. Comput. Electr. Eng. **52**, 114–124 (2016)

33. Nyangaresi, V.O.: Hardware assisted protocol for attacks prevention in ad hoc networks. In: Miraz, M.H., Southall, G., Ali, M., Ware, A., Soomro, S. (eds.) iCETiC 2021. LNICSSITE, vol. 395, pp. 3–20. Springer, Cham (2021). https://doi.org/10.1007/978-3-030-90016-8_1

34. Chen, Y., Martínez, J., Castillejo, P., López, L.: An anonymous authentication and key establish scheme for smart grid: FAuth. Energies **10**(9), 1–23 (2017)

35. Mahmood, K., Chaudhry, S.A., Naqvi, H., Kumari, S., Li, X., Sangaiah, A.K.: An elliptic curve cryptography based lightweight authentication scheme for smart grid communication. Futur. Gener. Comput. Syst. **81**, 557–565 (2018)

36. Abbasinezhad-Mood, D., Nikooghadam, M.: Design and hardware implementation of a security-enhanced elliptic curve cryptography based lightweight authentication scheme for smart grid communications. Futur. Gener. Comput. Syst. **84**, 47–57 (2018)

37. Liang, X.-C., Wu, T.-Y., Lee, Y.-Q., Chen, C.-M., Yeh, J.-H.: Cryptanalysis of a pairing-based anonymous key agreement scheme for smart grid. In: Pan, J.-S., Li, J., Tsai, P.-W., Jain, L.C. (eds.) Advances in Intelligent Information Hiding and Multimedia Signal Processing. SIST, vol. 156, pp. 125–131. Springer, Singapore (2020). https://doi.org/10.1007/978-981-13-9714-1_14

38. He, D., Chan, S.C., Zhang, Y., Guizani, M., Chen, C., Bu, J.: An enhanced public key infrastructure to secure smart grid wireless communication networks. Netw. IEEE **28**(1), 10–16 (2014)

39. Challa, S., et al.: Design and analysis of authenticated key agreement scheme in cloud-assisted cyber-physical systems. Futur. Gener. Comput. Syst. **108**, 1267–1286 (2018)

40. Chaudhry, S.A., Shon, T., Al-Turjman, F., Alsharif, M.H.: Correcting design flaws: an improved and cloud assisted key agreement scheme in cyber physical systems. Comput. Commun. **153**, 527–537 (2020)

41. Chim, T.W., Yiu, S.M., Li, V.K., Hui, L.K., Zhong, J.: PRGA: Privacy-preserving recording & gateway-assisted authentication of power usage information for smart grid. IEEE Trans. Dependable Secure Comput. **12**(1), 85–97 (2015)

42. Kumar, N., Aujla, G.S., Das, A.K., Conti, M.: Eccauth: a secure authentication protocol for demand response management in a smart grid system. In: IEEE Trans. Ind. Inform.**15**, 6572–6582 (2019)

43. Mahmood, K., Arshad, J., Chaudhry, S.A., Kumari, S.: An enhanced anonymous identity-based key agreement protocol for smart grid advanced metering infrastructure. Int. J. Commun. Syst. **32**(16), e4137 (2019)

44. He, D., Wang, H., Khurram Khan, M., Wang, L.: Lightweight anonymous key distribution scheme for smart grid using elliptic curve cryptography. IET Commun. **10**(14), 1795–1802 (2016)

45. Zhang, L., Zhao, L., Yin, S., Chi, C.H., Liu, R., Zhang, Y.: A lightweight authentication scheme with privacy protection for smart grid communications. Futur. Gener. Comput. Syst. **100**, 770–778 (2019)

46. Wazid, M., Das, A.K., Bhat, V., Vasilakos, A.V.: LAM-CIoT: lightweight authentication mechanism in cloud-based IoT environment. J. Netw. Comput. Appl. **150**, 102496 (2020)

A Blockchain-Based Data-Sharing Scheme for Inter-vehicular Safety Applications

Doug Lundquist[(✉)]

University of Illinois at Chicago, Chicago, USA
dlundq1@uic.edu

Abstract. Vehicular safety applications could save lives by sharing data not available from line-of-sight sensors but they also require trust among a set of mutually distrustful vehicles. We present a scheme for sharing validated vehicular trajectory data via vehicle-to-vehicle communication to help reduce traffic collisions. It does not require any centralized control or roadside infrastructure to function. Instead, vehicles share and validate data directly among each other. Our scheme combines a distributed blockchain model to create a permanent set of validated trajectory data. Vehicles join one or more consortium blockchains shared among nearby vehicles. Within each blockchain, vehicles share data between others nearby through a fully decentralized controlled flooding protocol. As blockchain and vehicular networks are prone to scalability concerns, we have designed our scheme specifically to address them. It limits the number of vehicles participating in each blockchain, bounds how widely trajectory data are shared, and organizes and merges redundant data to reduce total network traffic. We also discuss several future directions for assessing the relative performance profiles of specific blockchain and networking implementations.

Keywords: V2V applications · Blockchain · Vehicular safety

1 Introduction

Widespread adoption of inter-vehicular safety applications (IVSAs) could save thousands of lives lost to traffic collisions every year [1] using vehicle-mounted mobile devices to share information among nearby vehicles. Although vehicles can use their own line-of-sight sensors to detect and evaluate dangers, many vehicular collisions occur specifically because the colliding vehicles cannot see each other. A common example is one car with the right-of-way entering an intersection while another, concealed behind a large truck, runs a red light and crosses its path (Fig. 1). Such collisions could be prevented by vehicles sharing their real-time trajectories by wireless communication with others nearby.

For IVSAs, accurate and secure information is vital. Malfunctioning sensors could create and distribute bad data. Likewise, malicious participants might deliberately alter IVSA data to provoke vehicular collisions. Many mechanisms to track reputation and

W. Bao et al. (Eds.): ADHOCNETS 2021/TridentCom 2021, LNICST 428, pp. 205–213, 2022.
https://doi.org/10.1007/978-3-030-98005-4_15

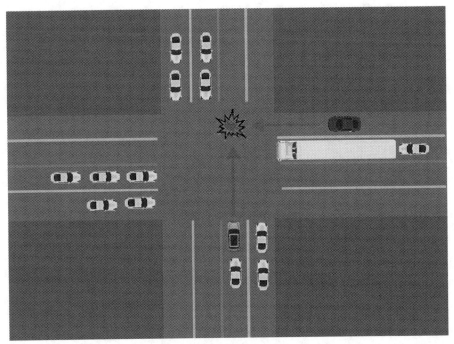

Fig. 1. Traffic collision at an intersection: the blue vehicle has the right-of-way but does not see the red vehicle entering the intersection. (Color figure online)

discourage good behavior have been proposed - [2] provides a good survey - but the recent development of blockchain technology offers novel solutions to the challenges of trust. In blockchain databases, batches of new data are confirmed by mutual agreement. Rather than guaranteeing good behavior, blockchain creates trust between participants because any improperly updated data would be easily detected. This offers a strong defense against isolated malicious participants - vehicles will get the correct information from other, non-malicious sources.

This paper proposes a peer-to-peer data management framework for blockchain-based IVSAs without infrastructure or a stable set of vehicles known to be trustworthy. All secure blockchain models require that either certain users are trusted or the blockchain is shared by a large user group to prevent its takeover by malicious actors. In IVSAs without infrastructure, however, participation of trusted vehicles would be difficult to guarantee. Thus, we focus on blockchain models with distributed ownership. A distributed blockchain - shared by users with equal standing - requires a fairly numerous and continuous population of users to provide data security.

Although the raw number of participants is readily obtained in IVSAs, group membership must still be managed. For example, a group of nearby vehicles belonging to a blockchain would periodically lose members over time due to divergent or completed travel paths. In fact, it is entirely possible that an IVSA could use a hybrid blockchain model. For example, it could combine private and public elements or proof-of-stake intermittently supported by proof-of-work. Likewise, vehicles could simultaneously belong to multiple groups to help ensure a continuous data flow. In this paper, we are therefore agnostic about the specific blockchain implementation and how it manages group membership.

The core of our framework is managing data flows within the vehicular network. Our goal is to ensure fast delivery of useful application data, e.g., the trajectories of nearby vehicles. In large-scale IVSAs, delivering every vehicle's data to every other vehicle is undesirable, as the heavy network traffic would delay delivery of immediately useful data. In large-scale systems, propagation limits must either be enforced or else arise organically and unpredictably when network traffic injections exceed the actual delivery capacity. We propose adopting the Self-Balancing Supply/Demand (SBSD) protocols [3], which dynamically bound data propagation according to metrics of the data's age, popularity, and distance from the source.

The rest of this paper is structured as follows. Section 2 discusses a selection of relevant research. Section 3 briefly covers the basics of blockchain and the SBSD model. Section 4 describes how our scheme will operate, in particular the mechanics of generating, processing, and sharing data. We conclude in Sect. 5 with a summary of our proposal and offer a few future directions for our research.

2   Related Research

Useful vehicle-to-vehicle (V2V) communication technologies exist but have not been widely implemented. Basic questions, like the selection and usage of wireless communication standards and security policies, have not been fully unresolved. Ongoing debates involving automakers, technology developers, and government agencies – essentially, what technology to use and how to use it - have stalled the adoption of existing technology. In fact, in the United States, half the bandwidth reserved for V2V communications was recently released for general usage [4].

The recent, explosive growth of the cryptocurrency sector has followed decades of research in data security that eventually led to blockchain. Interested readers might consult [5] to learn about core blockchain models and their applicability to real-world problems. Certainly, blockchain has received a great deal of attention for processing financial transactions, reflected in an abundance of research output. Security is naturally also a core concern for blockchain research; [6] provides a good introduction to the major security issues in blockchain implementations. In vehicular contexts, researchers have proposed and evaluated adopting blockchain for various building blocks of secure IVSAs, such as:

- Data management via blockchain in vehicular ad hoc networks [7, 8]
- Securely processing payments between electric vehicles and the grid [9]
- Privacy-preserving authentication [10–12]
- Group management: managing blockchain group memberships [13, 14]
- Evaluating the performance of blockchain under the high mobility typical of vehicular networks [15].

The other element of our scheme is the SBSD model for sharing data. SBSD is an alternative to models that manage routing paths in vehicle groups. By including age and distance metrics with packets, SBSD regulates data propagation without directly managing vehicle groups. Compared to [14], no clusters need to be managed and no cluster heads elected. Similarly, in [13], the blockchains are linked to large spatial areas without a mechanism for dynamically changing the covered areas. In contrast, our SBSD model is inherently adaptable to changing conditions of vehicle population, effective transmission distance, and wireless data transmission capacity.

SBSD grew out of an earlier model [16] for ranking data according to factors like age and popularity, as a mechanism for delivering the most interesting data within transmission capacity limits. When data flows exceed network capacity, participants must decide which packets to forward. In SBSD, only high-ranking packets (*e.g.*, new and close their point of origin) are forwarded by receiving vehicles. Analogous to Facebook's EdgeRank algorithm, which ranked the order in which posts would appear in a user's feed, SBSD uses similar methods to regulate data propagation.

3   Model Components

Let us now briefly cover the basic concepts of blockchain and SBSD, in Subsects. 3.1 and 3.2, respectively.

3.1   Blockchain

Fundamentally, blockchain is a data management technology for letting mutually distrustful users share information and quickly verify its correctness. Data is managed in batches called blocks. When a new block is created, database records can be added to it by blockchain users. However, these records must be approved by consensus - if one user tries to insert bad data, other users are expected to reject it and prevent its insertion. In IVSAs, vehicles would advertise their own recent trajectory and others would confirm its correctness. Eventually, the current block will be full - they hold a finite number of records - and it will be permanently added to the blockchain, with a timestamp and hash codes to facilitate detection of any changes to the finished block.

Next, we consider who can use a given blockchain. Blockchains can be public – allowing anyone to read and write data – or private, only allowing access to members of a single organization. An intermediate possibility is the consortium blockchain model, which allows access to members of multiple organizations. However, the larger the pool of users, the more work is entailed in getting a majority of users to approve a record. To ensure the processing needed to prevent vehicular collisions can happen in real-time, each blockchain would be owned by a small, localized vehicle group.

Within the IVSA context, each new blockchain database record would be a fixed-time trajectory segment and each block would let every vehicle add the same number of records. Every block would thus cover a known time interval and every record in a parent block would predate every record in any of its child blocks. This would facilitate recognizing missing records in the block, helping ensure a complete and sequential set of traffic data.

To create a new record, a vehicle announces a set of its own recent trajectory segments. When other nearby vehicles confirm the set, confirmed record would be shared with the rest of the group and be added to their block copies. Within an appropriate time after the expected end of the block's time interval, the block would be confirmed by consensus. This blockchain model would give vehicles actionable data before finalizing each block. In the long term, sources of improperly altered data can be recognized. In cases of disputed data, vehicles might cautiously treat all conflicting data as being possible, but this policy certainly requires further development.

Blockchain does present unique security risks since consensus can be gained through fraud. For example, a single vehicle controlling many phony vehicle identities could confirm bad data. Likewise, a set of malicious users with a simple majority of the group could achieve the same outcome, i.e., a 51% percent attack. Although it would be possible for a trusted authority (such as roadside infrastructure) to provide this security, we envision a system distributed over the vehicles themselves. In this case, a trusted blockchain should have its ownership shared over a large group of users over time, with reliable user verification.

Because blockchain is a novel technology with standards still in development, there are many questions about how a blockchain system with adequate security and speed would be implemented. We do not address that question in this paper nor claim superiority for a particular blockchain implementation, *e.g.*, in the proof-of-work vs. proof-of-stake approaches. In fact, a single system might well use multiple blockchain technologies.

For example, hybrid systems like Decred employ both proof-of-stake (for its low energy consumption) and proof-of-work (to offer security against large but malicious cryptocurrency holders). Accordingly, we believe the membership application should be a modular one, which simply gathers vehicle population data and, when needed, forwards that information to the various blockchain users. Ideally, this application should also be able to automatically regulate bandwidth consumption among a background of other V2V applications.

3.2 Self-balancing Supply/Demand

The SBSD framework provides a low-overhead probabilistic framework for regulating network traffic flows. Fundamentally, SBSD is a controlled flooding protocol which dynamically limits every packet's flooding extent. To limit propagation, vehicles only forward (via broadcast) the most relevant packets within the limits of their transmission capacity. Each packet's header stores its age and hop count from its source to allow calculating the relevance metric:

$$1/\left[(age)(hops)^{1/2}\right] \qquad (1)$$

As a packet travels away from its source, each hop increases the hop count and the packet gets older, decreasing the packet's relevance and making it less likely to be forwarded again.

The relevance metric may be multiplied by a popularity factor, frequency, which tracks the number of times a packet is independently created. For example, an urgent safety message might be simultaneously created by multiple vehicles. Frequency will multiply the relevance metric above, *i.e.*:

$$(frequency)/\left[(age)(hops)^{1/2}\right] \qquad (2)$$

More popular content has higher relevance, all else equal, causing those packets to be forwarded for longer and over a larger area. For a blockchain group, frequency could also be aligned with group populations and areas, so that packets are flooded over the approximate extent of the group.

Finally, to hasten packet delivery in the network, new packets are transmitted according to a binary exponential backoff model. A packet received at a node n with enough relevance to be forwarded will typically be forwarded at n's next opportunity to transmit. Thereafter, subsequent retransmissions will take about twice as long. This approach helps ensure that new data injected into the network will be quickly shared but retransmissions will substantially slow down after most nodes in the vicinity have probably already received it.

4   Model Operation

This section describes how our scheme shares and processes vehicle trajectory data in a blockchain. We assume that the blockchain mechanics – like tracking membership and finalizing each block – are handled outside of our scheme. We also note that our scheme is inherently designed to accommodate vehicles simultaneously belonging to more than one blockchain.

In our scheme, vehicles maintain a table of data for each blockchain, consisting of a list of vehicles, their trajectories, and the sources of that data. We describe the data vehicles generate and transmit (Sect. 4.1), then how recipients process the data (Sect. 4.2), how the data may be forwarded (Sect. 4.3), and beneficial aspects of our approach (Sect. 4.4).

4.1   Generation

Each vehicle will periodically measure and transmit its own trajectory to other nearby vehicles, with itself as the source. Let the transmitting vehicle be v_s and the set of recipients be V. The source v_s will add its own trajectory t_s to the tables for its blockchains. The initial relevance of the packet will be created with *age* and *hops* at 0. Because the packet will have high relevance, it will be transmitted immediately and then given priority in forwarding.

4.2   Processing

When a vehicle v_r in V receives the packet from v_s, it will compare the new data to its own last confirmed trajectory from v_s. If the data appears correct, it will add its own identifier to the packet payload. Ideally, the data verification would use line-of-sight but alternative methods could be used for vehicles that cannot be seen due to terrain obstacles. For example, v_r could verify that the recent trajectory segments connect and any speed changes are plausible for v_s.

The updated trajectory data would be kept as a tree list of verifications for the trajectory. For each vehicle in the blockchain, v_r would maintain entries as a list starting with the root – the source vehicle v_s – and the sequence in which verifications were made. In the tree graph, all vehicles in V would be child nodes of v_s and each vehicle in V could have its own child nodes, vehicles which did not receive the trajectory data directly from v_s.

For any {time interval, vehicle} pair, multiple trajectory measurements could exist. However, without tampering, each vehicle ultimately can only confirm one of them. Thus, the number of votes for a particular trajectory is simply the number of confirming vehicles in the tree. When enough votes for a particular trajectory are obtained (either a majority or some supermajority, depending on the blockchain model), the trajectory can be added to the blockchain as a permanent record.

4.3 Forwarding

Vehicles will packetize the tree lists of trajectory data and forward the data to nearby vehicles. Prior to transmitting, the forwarding vehicle will update the *hop* and *age* metrics so that each transmission is already updated at receipt. To use network transmission capacity more efficiently, tree lists with similar relevance might be bundled together and transmitted as batches.

Recall that each vehicle in a blockchain knows all members of that blockchain and that vehicles may belong to multiple blockchains. To limit superfluous forwarding, vehicles only forward data involving vehicles from their own blockchain group(s). Any vehicle receiving a packet about a vehicle not in its blockchain(s) would simply not forward it.

4.4 Verification

Trajectories that cannot be directly verified by a vehicle's line-of-sight-sensors must, inevitably, accept data from those with direct knowledge. So, our scheme is designed to facilitate detection of bad data received indirectly. An immediate alteration of a new trajectory generated by a vehicle v_s will not succeed because other vehicles directly verify the trajectory of v_s. The alteration would be easily detected. However, later elements of a tree list, which cannot be directly verified, are a more serious concern.

The existence and sharing of multiple copies of trajectory data, received from multiple sources, provides security against isolated incidents of tampering. For example, if a tree list entry shows a vehicle confirming two different trajectories, vehicles can recognize and exclude the vehicle providing the bad data. Two foreseeable malicious actions are altering trajectory data and altering vehicles in the tree lists:

Altering Trajectory Data: If a vehicle v forwards an incorrect trajectory, other vehicles earlier in the sequence will recognize it. They can see that v sent bad data that did not match what they confirmed. Downstream vehicles from v will likewise recognize that v's claims conflict with others from the same source, the parent node of v in the tree list.

Altering Vehicle Identities: Suppose a vehicle v changes the tree list, either altering a vehicle identity v' or changing the sequence of confirmations. Then, v transmits the changed list. Again, recipients will recognize the change. If they received data directly from v', they know that v changed the data and will not confirm it. This will prevent

v from gaining a majority in the blockchain voting process even if all other vehicles confirm both versions of the tree list.

Malicious alteration attempts like the above by single vehicles are typically easily detected. However, coordinated malicious behavior by groups of nodes cannot always be stopped. Still, this is not a disqualifying weakness for blockchain. In any shared database system, some users must be able to make updates and might act maliciously. Blockchain relies on making coordinated malicious behavior prohibitively difficult – there are simpler and more certain ways to cause harm than getting multiple vehicles to travel together and deliberately manipulate vehicular safety data.

5   Conclusion

This paper presented a framework for combining blockchain and SBSD as a secure, scalable, and decentralized solution to sharing information in IVSAs. Certainly, there remain many details to clarify and questions to resolve. Our next steps will be to clearly model blockchain implementations, including security policies and membership management. Then, we will run the corresponding simulations of V2V applications. This will provide better understanding of the tradeoffs from different blockchain models regarding the timeliness, completeness, and security of IVSA data. Many performance comparisons can be made for variables such as:

- Data delivery and confirmation speed: Assuming trustworthy vehicles, how quickly can data be shared and confirmed within the entire group?
- Faulty or malicious group members: How is IVSA performance affected by isolated or small groups of malicious vehicles?
- Group membership convergence: How is IVSA performance affected by frequent changes in group membership?
- Network overhead: How much network traffic is required to deliver group membership information?
- Reliability: What guarantees are given that required information arrives?

In the coming years, vehicular safety technology will continue to be developed and standardized. Growing adoption of 5G technology will alleviate data transmission bottlenecks, allowing more data to be shared faster and over larger areas. Self-driving cars will become more common and perhaps ubiquitous. We look forward to seeing how these trends converge in vehicular safety applications.

References

1. Consumer Reports Safety First: Car Crashes, Innovation, and Why Federal Policy Should Prioritize Adoption of Existing Technologies to Save Lives, June 29 2020
2. Hussain, R., Lee, J., Zeadally, S.: Trust in VANET: a survey of current solutions and future research opportunities. IEEE Trans. Intell. Transp. Syst. 22(5), 2553–2571 (2021)
3. Ouksel, A., Lundquist, D.: Demand-driven publish/subscribe in mobile environments. Wireless Netw. 16(8), 2237–2261 (2010)

4. Federal Communications Commission: FCC 20-164: Use of the 5.850 to 5.925 GHz Band, November 2020
5. Sherman, A., Javani, F., Zhang, H., Golaszewski, E.: On the origins and variations of blockchain technologies. IEEE Secur. Priv. **17**(1), 72–77 (2019)
6. Li, X., Jiang, P., et al.: A survey on the security of blockchain systems. Futur. Gener. Comput. Syst. **107**, 841–853 (2020)
7. Zhang, X., Chen, X.: Data security sharing and storage based on a consortium blockchain in a vehicular ad-hoc network. IEEE Access **7**, 58241–58254 (2019)
8. Arora, S., Kumar, G., Kim, T.: Blockchain based trust model using Tendermint in vehicular adhoc networks. Appl. Sci. **11**(5), 1998 (2021)
9. Gao, F., Zhu, L., et al.: A blockchain-based privacy-preserving payment mechanism for vehicle-to-grid networks. IEEE Netw. **32**(6), 184–192 (2018)
10. Feng, Q., De, H., et al.: BPAS: blockchain-assisted privacy-preserving authentication system for vehicular ad hoc networks. IEEE Trans. Industr. Inf. **16**(6), 4146–4155 (2020)
11. Lin, C., et al.: BCPPA: a blockchain-based conditional privacy-preserving authentication protocol for vehicular ad hoc networks. IEEE Trans. Intell. Transp. Syst. (early access) **22**, 7408–7420 (2020)
12. Ren, Y., Li., X., et al.: Privacy-preserving batch verification signature scheme based on blockchain for vehicular ad-hoc networks. J. Inf. Secur. Appl. **58**, 102698 (2021)
13. Shrestha, R., Nam, S.: Regional Blockchain for vehicular networks to prevent 51% attacks. IEEE Access **7**, 95033–95045 (2019)
14. Joshi, G., Perumal, E., et al.: Toward blockchain-enabled privacy-preserving data transmission in cluster-based vehicular networks. Electronics **9**(9), 1358 (2020)
15. Kim, S.: Impacts of mobility on performance of blockchain in VANET. IEEE Access **7**, 68646–68655 (2019)
16. Xu, B., Ouksel, A., Wolfson, O.: Opportunistic resource exchange in inter-vehicle ad-hoc networks. In: 5th Conference on Mobile Data Management, pp. 4–12, Berkeley, California (2004)

Main Track (TRIDENTCOM 2021)

A Trust-Based and Secure Real-Time Traffic Information Sharing Scheme

Yuhao Wang$^{(\boxtimes)}$ and Chengzhe Lai

National Engineering Laboratory for Wireless Security, Xian University of Posts and Telecommunications, Xian, China
13720736623@163.com

Abstract. Real-time Traffic information sharing can make the transportation more effective, which requires the vehicles on the road to participate in the road condition report actively. However, in the untrustworthy network environment, malicious traffic information dissemination will result in severe traffic issues, meanwhile, the risk of disclosure of users' privacy information may also be increased. To address these problems, we propose a trust-based and secure real-time traffic information sharing scheme. Particularly, the trust value of the vehicle is calculated by the trusted organization, and the system updates the real road conditions according to the calculated results. Moreover, we utilize the improved pairing-free certificateless aggregate signature technique to provide the security service. As shown in the simulation results, the computing cost can be reduced because of using aggregate signature technique. In addition, the reliability of data is improved through trust management of vehicle users, and the sybil attack can be alleviated.

Keywords: Internet of vehicle · Real-time traffic information sharing · Trust · Anonymity

1 Introduction

According to the statistics, licensed vehicles exceed 1 billion around the world, a number that will double in the next 10 to 20 years. The explosive growth of car ownership has caused many serious social problems, such as road safety, traffic congestion and air pollution [3]. In order to make the vehicle driving environment safe and efficient, vehicles can upload the ultramodern traffic information with the various kinds of communication devices and vehicle-mounted transducer [9,16]. At present, the traffic information sharing schemes based on GPS (Global Positioning System) positioning have been widely studied and applied [4], but they can not reflect the accurate traffic information. In these schemes, the reporting vehicle voluntarily uploads its GPS information to a trusted agency, but these schemes lack privacy and data security protection as well as information authenticity judgment. For these reasons, the development of traffic information

© ICST Institute for Computer Sciences, Social Informatics and Telecommunications Engineering 2022
Published by Springer Nature Switzerland AG 2022. All Rights Reserved
W. Bao et al. (Eds.): ADHOCNETS 2021/TridentCom 2021, LNICST 428, pp. 217–228, 2022.
https://doi.org/10.1007/978-3-030-98005-4_16

sharing system has been seriously affected. When the reporting vehicle reports the traffic information, its reporting information is no longer controlled by itself, but calculated and processed by RSU (Roadside Units) and TA (Trusted Agencies). Therefore, how to ensure the integrity of the reported traffic information and the confidentiality of the reported vehicle has become a new challenge for traffic information sharing [10]. In the meantime, due to the lack of verification measures, the exactitude of the traffic information sharing will be reduced when the malicious vehicles distribute the incorrect road condition information deliberately in the system, thus affecting the efficiency and safety of vehicles on the road. Therefore, academic boffins have been aware of the assurance of the security in IoV (Internet-of-Vehicles). In the ordinary way, cryptography-based solutions [15] and trust-based solutions [5] are the two ways to address the security issues in the IoV.

To solve the above problems, this paper introduces the ideas of certificateless aggregate signature and trust management into the traffic information sharing. The general process of the system can be described as follows. RSU send the massage to the nearby verifying vehicles when the RSU receive the road information from the reporting vehicle, and then verifying vehicles will give their feedbacks. After RSU verifying the legitimacy of the vehicles, it will send all vehicles' massages to the TA (Trusted Institutions) by aggregation signatures. After that, to prevent the spread of malicious messages, TA calculates trust value from vehicles by using trust management. During the whole process, the privacy of the user's vehicle will not be disclosed to any party. Underneath, we have summed up the main contributions in this paper:

- An effective trust evaluation scheme is designed. Vehicles can share the traffic information independently in the scheme, which can avert the malicious vehicles diffusing the incorrect information to the scheme.
- To ensure that only legitimate vehicles are certified, a certificateless encryption and aggregate signature technique [6] is equipped, which can also protect the privacy of the user's vehicle.
- By using aggregate signature technique, the computing cost is reduced. In addition, the reliability of data is improved through credit management of vehicle users, and the sybil attack can be alleviated.

2   Related Work

2.1   Trust Management

Currently, trust has become momentous in the IoV. Trust scheme foresee the uers' future behaviour by calculating the past-reputation. Trust management scheme plays an important role in the security and privacy of user information in the Internet of Vehicles. In the traffic information sharing system, the trust value describes the user's expectation also as known as trust level, and employs the user vehicle's historical interaction experience to reduce various threats and risks by trust management. The author proposes a true-filtering algorithm for wireless sensor networks. The basic idea is that if the data of the user's vehicle is closer to the preset credit score, it will be assigned a higher weight, and the data provided by the user's vehicle with a higher weight will be more likely to be considered as the true feedback information [11]. In order to deal with the report of false news, Zhang, C. et al. [13] proposes an artificial intelligence trust management system for vehicle-mounted network based on blockchain technology. Malicious vehicles can occur in the scheme for a longtime because the system don't exist the punitive measure to the evil users. The fatal part in the traffic information sharing scheme is zapping the malicious vehicles [12]. A protocol for anonymously aggregating vehicle notifications in a base station controller is proposed. It uses identities-based group signature technology to achieve conditional privacy. If a malicious vehicle sends a false message, the trusted institution can track its identity in an anonymous announcement through the public address of the blockchain [7].

2.2 Certificateless Aggregate Signature

In 2003, Al-Riyami et al. proposed the Certificateless public key cryptography in the Asian Society of Secrets, and the cryptosystem was gradually studied and applied in the V2N system. A new, efficient, certificateless set signature based on elliptic curve cryptosystem is proposed, and its ability to support conditional privacy protection is proved [2]. In order to deal with the problem that encrypted data is difficult to search after encryption, Du, H. et al. [1] proposes a scheme to grant the cloud server the right to perform equality tests on encrypted data. This scheme can retrieve the results without the cloud server knowing any relevant information of the ciphertext [8]. A lightweight certificateless and pairing-free scheme is proposed, which is feasible without infrastructure. The scheme can resist attacks with a small computational cost. Some studies have proposed a privacy-protected certificateless set signature scheme based on hierarchical trust institutions for message authentication. The scheme does not require key escrow, and any entity within the scheme can verify the messages received by vehicles running under different trust institutions. In this paper, we utilize the improved pairing-free certificateless aggregate signature technique [6] to provide the security service in our scheme.

3 System Background

In this section, we describe the background of the system, including the system model and the adversary model.

3.1 System Model

The system model is mainly composed of three parts: vehicle, TA and RSU.

– Vehicles: These nodes are OBUs (On Board Unit) on the vehicle and have some storage capability. The vehicle can actively report the road condition information to the nearby RSU, and also put forward its own opinion on the road condition information sent by the RSU and report the opinion to the RSU. In this scheme, vehicles are divided into reporting vehicles and verification vehicles.

Reporting vehicle: The reporting vehicle can report its road condition information to the RSU at any time and wait for the system to verify the correctness of the message through calculation.

Verification vehicles: These vehicles receive traffic information from the RSU and choose whether or not to participate in the validation. When verifying the vehicle validation message, it sends its opinion, agree or disagree with the traffic information reported by the vehicle to the RSU and waits for the system to verify.

– TA (Trusted Authority): This entity is responsible for all participants and maintains a database to store the trust value of the user's vehicle. It has full resource storage and data computing capabilities. The trusted agency can calculate the credibility of each vehicle based on the data submitted by the RSU to determine whether the traffic information is true or not. Based on the results of the calculation, the traffic information is updated and the lying vehicle is punished.

– RSU (Roadside Units): The RSU, known as the roadside unit, is a subsidiary of the trusted authority TA. It has limited resources but higher computing power than the vehicle to ensure that the RSU can verify the legitimacy of the user's vehicle identity and perform the aggregation operation to send to the trusted authority TA.

3.2 Adversary Model

Both reporting vehicles and verifying vehicles will attempt to upload false traffic information to the system to interfere with the normal traffic environment. The main attack in this paper is message spoofing attack, in which the attacker covers up the real information of the road condition by reporting false information to the RSU. For example, a malicious vehicle may send a traffic jam to a nearby RSU when the road is clear for its own purposes.

4   Proposed Scheme

A road condition evaluation scheme based on privacy and trust management is proposed, which includes system overview, vehicle reporting and authentication stage, and information management and verification stage (Fig. 1).

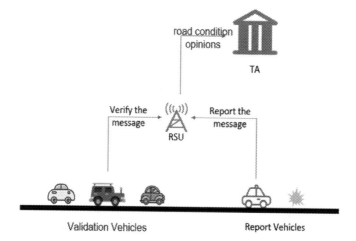

Fig. 1. System architecture

4.1 Overview

The vehicle reports the road condition information to the RSU, which is called the reporting vehicle. The RSU sends the road condition information to other nearby vehicles other than the reporting vehicle, and the other nearby vehicles are called verification vehicles. Verify that the vehicle submits its opinion to the RSU regarding the road condition information, agrees or disagrees. The RSU then verifies the legitimacy of the vehicle through a certificateless encryption scheme. When the verified vehicle passes the verification, the RSU submits the vehicle information and road condition opinions of the verified vehicle to the TA through the aggregate signature. TA calculates and verifies the authenticity of the road condition information submitted by the vehicle with the trust evaluation algorithm based on the historical data of the vehicle. Based on the verification results, TA records the report of the vehicle and verifies the new credit score of the vehicle and updates the latest traffic conditions on the traffic information sharing system according to the results of the trust evaluation algorithm (Table 1).

4.2 System Initialization

Vehicle outputs the following system parameters when it gets the security parameter $k \in Z^+$. Select a group G of prime order q and a generator P of the group G. Compute vehicle's master public $P_{pub} = sP$ which s is master secret key by choosing $s \in Z_q^*$. Pick hash functions $H : G \times G \to Z_q^*$, $H_1 : \{0,1\}^* \times G \times G \to Z_q^*$, $H_2 : \{0,1\}^* \times \{0,1\}^* \times G \to Z_q^*$, and $H_2 : \{0,1\}^* \times \{0,1\}^* \times G \to Z_q^*$ for $i = 3, 4$. Publish system parameters as $params = \{q, G, P, P_{pub}, H, H_1, H_2, H_3, H_4\}$ and keep master secret keys secure.

Table 1. Formalized notations involved in traffic information sharing scheme

Notation	Descriptions
k	Security parameter
q	Prime
G	Cyclic group of prime order q
params	System parameter
Z_q	Finite field
Z_q^*	$Z_q/0$
H_1, H_2, H_3, H_4	Cryptographic hash function
(P_{pub}, s)	Public and private key pair of TA
RID_i	Real identity of V
ID_i	Pseudo identity of V
D_i	Partial private key of V
(PK_i, SK_i)	Public and private key pair of V
ROT	Role-oriented trust
isT	Credit scores for individual vehicles
d	Distance score
ξ	Tier-boundary
Trust	Whether the message is trusted

4.3   Vehicle Registration and Verification Stage

With the input of params and s, the real identity of Vehicle RID_i, TA computes the following vehicles partial private key. Choosing $r_i \in Z_q^*$ and computing $R_i = r_i P$. Compute the pseudoidentity $ID_i = RID_i \oplus H(r_i P_{pub}, T_i)$, which T_i is the validity period of the corresponding pseudo identity. Generate $h_{1i} = H_1(ID_i, R_i, P_{pub})$ and $d_i = r_i + s h_{1i} mod q$. TA send the (ID_i, R_i, D_i) to the homologous vehicle and install $D_i = (d_i, R_i)$. Vehicle will compute the equation $d_i p = R_i + h_{1i} P_{pub}$. If the equation eligible, vehicle will accept the partial private key D_i for ID_i at T_i. Each vehicle performs the following to generate the public and private key pairs when they accept the $D_i = (d_i, R_i)$. Compute $X_i = x_i P$ where $x_i \in Z_q^*$ as the secret key and set $PK_i = (X_i, R_i)$ sa public key and $SK_i = (x_i, d_i)$ as the secret key. When the public key and the secret key set done, vehicle will signature for a given massage $m_i \in \{0,1\}^*$ with the ID_i, SK_i, params and current timestamp t_i. Choose $y_i \in Z_q^*$ and compute $Y_i = y_{1i} P$. Let $u_i = H_2(m_i, ID_i, Y_{1i}) W_i = (u_i(y_i + h_{3i} x_i) + h_{4i} d_i) P$ where $h_{3i} = H_3(m_i, ID_i, PK_i, t_i)$, $h_{4i} = H_4(m_i, ID_i, PK_i, t_i)$. Output a signature $\sigma_i = (Y_{1i}, W_i)$ on the message $m_i \| t_i$. When the RSU get the given massage from the vehicle, RSU computes $h_{3i} = H_3(m_i, ID_i, PK_i, t_i)$, $h_{4i} = H_4(m_i, ID_i, PK_i, t_i)$ and $u_i = H_2(m_i, ID_i, Y_i)$ to accept the signature when the $W_i - u_i(Y_i + h_{3i} X_i) = h_{4i}(R_i + h_{1i} P_{Pub})$ holds. Plus, RSU will generate aggregate signatures σ which collected by n distinct signatures $(\sigma_i)_i = 1, ..., n$

on different messages $(m_i \| t_i)_{i=1,...,n}$ from different vehicles with corresponding identities $(ID_i)_i = 1,...,n$. $\sigma = (Y, W)$, where $W = \sum_{i=1}^{n} W_i, Y = \sum_{i=1}^{n} u_i Y_{1i}$, $u_i = H_2(m_i, ID_i, Y_{1i})$. RSU send $\sigma = (Y, W)$ to the TA. TA check whether the $W - Y - U = \sum_{i=1}^{n} h_{4i}(R_i + h_{1i} P_{Pub})$ holds, where $h_{1i} = H_1(ID_i, R_i, P_{Pub})$. $h_{3i} = H_3(m_i, ID_i, PK_i, t_i)$, $h_{4i} = H_4(m_i, ID_i, PK_i, t_i)$, $U = \sum_{i=1}^{n} u_i h_{3i} X_i$. If it holds, accepts the aggregated signature σ, else rejects.

4.4 Trust Management

After the Verification vehicle entity is evaluated, the next step is evaluate the data sent by the verification vehicle. The trust score is defined as follows:

$$isT = f(d, ROT) \tag{1}$$

The formula describes the two parameters of isT. Since the occurrence of traffic accidents is highly deterministic, the trust function must consider the trust value of the verified vehicle and the accurate geographical location, that is, the trust value of the vehicle Vtrust is represented by ROT and effective distance of the vehicle is represented by d. Further, the formula can be described as:

$$isT = -\sum_{n=1}^{n} e^{-ROT \cdot d} \tag{2}$$

Firstly, TA compute the trust value ROT. When a vehicle is first registered with TA, TA will assign an initial value to the vehicle. Every vehicle is considered as the part of the trust network, which includes official vehicles, public vehicles and private cars. Our trust management scheme integrates all the vehicles on the road and the initial trust value may vary depending on their identity. This article uses the following method to assign the initial trust value

$$ROT = \begin{cases} 0.8-1 & if \ veh = Authority \ Vehicles \\ 0.6-0.8 & if \ veh = Public \ Transport \ Vehicles \\ 0.4-0.6 & if \ veh = Traditional \ Vehicles \end{cases} \tag{3}$$

We divide the cars as three types on account of the relationship with the authorities.

Authority Vehicles: Such vehicles include police cars, ambulances, etc., which are authorized by central authorities, so they are highly credible.

Public Transport Vehicles: Such vehicles include buses as well as taxis operated by government companies, which are considered to be moderately reliable because they are authorized by specific government departments.

Traditional Vehicles: These vehicles are social vehicles with no relationship with the authorities like Uber service cars or other private cars. Such vehicles have no connection with the authorities so these vehicles must remain honest in the network so that their information can make an impact in the network.

$$ROT^{l+1} = \eta \times ROT^l + (1 - \eta) \times ROT^{l-1} \tag{4}$$

We adopt the improved (EMWA: Exponential weight moving average) technique to calculate the future credit value of the vehicle. Where ROT^{l+1}, ROT^l and ROT^{l-1} respectively represent the vehicle's future, current and historical credit values. And we also defines the influence factor η to influence the influence of the credit value in different historical time on the future credit value. A higher weight is given to the first two vehicle (Authority Vehicles, Public Transport Vehicles)

$$\begin{cases} 0.7 \leq \eta < 1.0 & if\ veh\ =\ V_{av}, V_{ptv} \\ 0.5 \leq \eta < 0.7 & if\ veh\ =\ V_{tv} \end{cases} \tag{5}$$

Note that some user vehicles may increase their trust value by performing well at first, but intentionally underperform when the trust value is high enough. For this reason, we further designed a trust circuit breaker mechanism, as shown below:

$$ROT^{l+1} = \begin{cases} ROT^{l+1} & if\ ROT^{l+1} > ROT^{threshold} \\ 0 & if\ ROT^{l+1} < ROT^{threshold} \end{cases} \tag{6}$$

Through the formula, we can calculate whether the future credit value is greater than the predetermined value of the system. Through calculation, we conclude that the predetermined value needs to be satisfied at least $ROT^{threshold} \geq 0.2$ otherwise the newly registered traditional vehicle will not be able to update their scores. Further, when $ROT^{l+1} = 0$, the circuit breaker mechanism is triggered, the predicted trust value will be reduced to $ROT^{l+1} = \alpha \cdot ROT^l$, where $\alpha \epsilon (0, 1)$, called the penalty factor. This will allow the attacker to spend more time to improve their reputation to the previous level.

After that, TA calculates the distance between the verification vehicle and reporting vehicle,

$$dis = \sqrt{\left(m_{Sender_x} - m_{in_x}\right)^2 + \left(m_{Sender_y} - m_{in_y}\right)^2} \tag{7}$$

where m_{Sender_x}, m_{Sender_y} represents the coordinates x and y of the reporting vehicle. m_{in_x}, m_{in_y} represents the coordinate x and y of the i-th verification vehicle. In addition, the distance coefficient ξ is defined. As shown in the Fig. 2, the location of the reporting vehicle v_i is divided into three geographical areas, including high confidence area, medium confidence area and low confidence area. In practical application, the shape of this area may change with the actual situation of the road. For the sake of loss of generality, we assume that all three layers are circular,

$$d = \begin{cases} 1 & 0 < dis \leq \xi_1 \\ 0.6 & \xi_1 < dis \leq \xi_2 \\ 0.3 & \xi_2 < dis \leq \xi_3 \end{cases} \tag{8}$$

Once each parameter (d, ROT) has been calculated, TA divides the vehicle into two groups based on the message $m_i = (1 or 0)$ upload by the validation vehicle $(V_1, V_2, V_3, ..., V_n)$ and calculates the isT of each group, where $isT_1 = -\sum_{n=1}^{n} e^{-ROT \cdot d}$ represents the message as $m_i = 1$, $isT_2 = -\sum_{n=1}^{n} e^{-ROT \cdot d}$ represents the message as $m_i = 0$. Plus, TA compute the Trust $= |isT_1| - |isT_2|$, if Trust > 0, $m_i = 1$ is taken as the opinion of the verified vehicle, else, $m_i = 0$

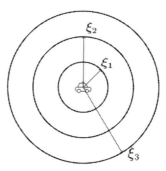

Fig. 2. Threshold approach

is taken as the opinion of the verified vehicle. After TA calculates the truth of the road condition information, TA will increase or decrease the reputation score of the vehicles in the corresponding verification vehicle group and the reporting vehicle according to the result, and carry out the traffic information sharing system update.

5 Scheme Analysis

According to the security objectives of the previous adversary model, the following analysis as follows

5.1 Trust Management

Unregistered vehicles can be effectively excluded from the system through the system initialization phase. When receiving road condition information, TA can score the different opinions on the same traffic accident through the trust management scheme, so as to select the true opinions representing the group. In the calculation of trust value, vehicles with better historical performance and closer to the accident site are given higher weight, so as to ensure that the traffic information provided is true and reliable, and resist the reporting of false news of malicious vehicles.

5.2 Resistance to Sybil Attacks

Because of Sybil attack, the reliability of traffic information and the operation of evaluation mechanism will be greatly damaged [14]. In this scheme, a penalty factor is introduced to make the trust value of the vehicle drop rapidly after the malicious behavior. And since the credit score is related to the historical credit score, it takes more effort for the vehicle to restore its trust score to a higher level after committing a malicious act. Figure 4 shows the status of a vehicle's reputation when it spreads malicious messages. Apparently, the more malicious vehicles spread the false traffic information, the more trust value be deduct.

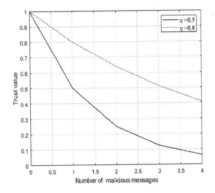

Fig. 3. Trust value changing of malicious messages

5.3   Performance Evaluation

We use a personal computer conduct a test which we put forward in this paper. The computer's core is Intel I5-9300H. RAM is 16.00 GB. The operation system is 64-b windows 10. We accomplish the cryptosystem with Java and the compiler is IDEA. As one shall see from Fig. 3, the time cost of aggregate signature and aggregate signature verification steps increases with the increase of the vehicle number. The total time cost of our scheme is extremely fast. At the same time, compared with single signature verification, aggregate signature verification has the advantages of low computational overhead, so it is more suitable for resource-constrained network environments such as the Internet of vehicles.

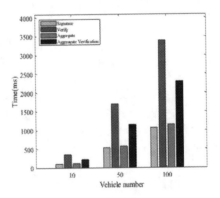

Fig. 4. Total time cost

6 Conclusion

Aiming at the problem of traffic information sharing, this paper proposes a trust-based and secure real-time traffic information sharing scheme. In this paper, the certificateless aggregate signature technique is used to achieve the integrity, identity verifiability and non-repudiation of data. The trust management system is introduced to improve the reliability of data. Using aggregate signature technology, the computing cost is reduced. In order to protect the privacy of users, this paper realizes the anonymity of users by generating pseudonyms for users. Finally, through the simulation, the incentive of the scheme is verified, and the effectiveness of the proposed scheme is proved from the aspect of computational cost.

References

1. Du, H., Wen, Q., Zhang, S.: An efficient certificateless aggregate signature scheme without pairings for healthcare wireless sensor network. IEEE Access **7**, 42683–42693 (2019). https://doi.org/10.1109/ACCESS.2019.2907298
2. Elhabob, R., Zhao, Y., Sella, I., Xiong, H.: Efficient certificateless public key cryptography with equality test for internet of vehicles. IEEE Access **7**, 68957–68969 (2019). https://doi.org/10.1109/ACCESS.2019.2917326
3. Elleuch, W., Wali, A., Alimi, A.M.: Mining road map from big database of GPS data. In: 2014 14th International Conference on Hybrid Intelligent Systems, pp. 193–198 (2014). https://doi.org/10.1109/HIS.2014.7086197
4. Jia, D., Lu, K., Wang, J., Zhang, X., Shen, X.: A survey on platoon-based vehicular cyber-physical systems. IEEE Commun. Surv. Tutor. **18**(1), 263–284 (2016). https://doi.org/10.1109/COMST.2015.2410831
5. Kerrache, C.A., Calafate, C.T., Cano, J.C., Lagraa, N., Manzoni, P.: Trust management for vehicular networks: an adversary-oriented overview. IEEE Access **4**, 9293–9307 (2016). https://doi.org/10.1109/ACCESS.2016.2645452
6. Liu, J., Wang, L., Yu, Y.: Improved security of a pairing-free certificateless aggregate signature in healthcare wireless medical sensor networks. IEEE IoT J. **7**(6), 5256–5266 (2020). https://doi.org/10.1109/JIOT.2020.2979613
7. Liu, X., Huang, H., Xiao, F., Ma, Z.: A blockchain-based trust management with conditional privacy-preserving announcement scheme for VANETs. IEEE IoT J. **7**(5), 4101–4112 (2020). https://doi.org/10.1109/JIOT.2019.2957421
8. Song, J., He, C., Zhang, L., Tang, S., Zhang, H.: Toward an RSU-unavailable lightweight certificateless key agreement scheme for VANETs. China Commun. **11**(9), 93–103 (2014). https://doi.org/10.1109/CC.2014.6969774
9. Sou, S.I., Lee, Y.: SCB: store-carry-broadcast scheme for message dissemination in sparse VANET. In: 2012 IEEE 75th Vehicular Technology Conference (VTC Spring), pp. 1–5 (2012). https://doi.org/10.1109/VETECS.2012.6240177
10. Wang, X., et al.: Privacy-preserving content dissemination for vehicular social networks: challenges and solutions. IEEE Commun. Surv. Tutor. **21**(2), 1314–1345 (2019). https://doi.org/10.1109/COMST.2018.2882064
11. Willink, T.: Possibility-based trust for mobile wireless networks. IEEE Trans. Mob. Comput. **19**, 1896–1909 (2019)

12. Zhang, C., Li, W., Luo, Y., Hu, Y.: AIT: an AI-enabled trust management system for vehicular networks using blockchain technology. IEEE IoT J. 8(5), 3157–3169 (2021). https://doi.org/10.1109/JIOT.2020.3044296
13. Zhang, C., et al.: TPPR: a trust-based and privacy-preserving platoon recommendation scheme in VANET. IEEE Trans. Serv. Comput. (2019). https://doi.org/10.1109/TSC.2019.2961992
14. Zhang, K., Liang, X., Lu, R., Shen, X.: Sybil attacks and their defenses in the internet of things. IEEE IoT J. 1(5), 372–383 (2014). https://doi.org/10.1109/JIOT.2014.2344013
15. Zhong, H., Huang, B., Cui, J., Xu, Y., Liu, L.: Conditional privacy-preserving authentication using registration list in vehicular ad hoc networks. IEEE Access 6, 2241–2250 (2018). https://doi.org/10.1109/ACCESS.2017.2782672
16. Zhou, H., et al.: Chaincluster: engineering a cooperative content distribution framework for highway vehicular communications. IEEE Trans. Intell. Transp. Syst. 15(6), 2644–2657 (2014). https://doi.org/10.1109/TITS.2014.2321293

TuneIn: Framework Design and Implementation for Education Using Dynamic Difficulty Adjustment Based on Deep Reinforcement Learning and Mathematical Approach

Alessio Bonti[(✉)] , Manas Palaparthi , Xuemei Jiang, and Thien Pham

Deakin University, Burwood, VIC 3125, Australia
{a.bonti,m.palaparthi,jiangx,jason.pham}@deakin.edu.au

Abstract. Education, personal self-development, and overall learning have vastly changed over the years as a result of historical events, methodologies, and technologies. As students first, and then as educators, we have only seen slight changes in the delivery of educational content, with the most accepted model being "one system fits all", we have seen content and delivery mediums, but little about differentiating or personalizing the education experience. We challenge this traditional model by implementing an Adaptive Training Framework based on AI techniques through a Dynamic Difficulty Adjustment agent. We have conducted a limited sample size experiment to prove that personalized content allows the learner to achieve more than a static model.

Keywords: Dynamic Difficulty Adjustment (DDA) · DDA deep reinforcement learning · Mathematical DDA · DDA in education · Gamification in education

1 Introduction

As students then and educators now, we are often in the position of following the footsteps of our predecessors in a mission to spread knowledge and educate the next generations. What may start as one of the most exciting professions soon becomes a more significant endeavour that we may have hoped to deal with. As this paper will mainly focus on, university education requires continuous work, which often leaves us with little to no time to improve our coursework beyond the standard.

As we move towards education as a commodity that can be accessed across any media, more questions arise about whether or not standards can be maintained to engage with the ever-increasing student population.

© ICST Institute for Computer Sciences, Social Informatics and Telecommunications Engineering 2022
Published by Springer Nature Switzerland AG 2022. All Rights Reserved
W. Bao et al. (Eds.): ADHOCNETS 2021/TridentCom 2021, LNICST 428, pp. 229–241, 2022.
https://doi.org/10.1007/978-3-030-98005-4_17

An increased number of students have created burdens on the system, reflecting on the quality of life of educators. Watts and Robertson in [1] identify three main characteristics, emotional exhaustion, depersonalization and dissatisfaction, as critical indicators of burnout syndromes in universities and how this impacts not only the personal life but also the quality of teaching.

With these critical findings, how can we guarantee quality and also an exceptional student experience? Under this pressure, the ideals of young educators fall back into 'provide the minimum required standard', or the comfortable, one method fits all.

This has motivated us to go beyond these thoughts and find ways to make students' lives more rewarding and educators' role simpler by applying an adaptive framework that only requires to be developed once and updated less, which can provide a higher level of study experience to our young future professionals. In creating our novel approach, one of the key features was implementing an assessment system based on flow theory. Csikszentmihalyi [2] - the creator of this theory, explains that "there exists a state of mind called FLOW, where the user's engagement and learning are maximized, and that happens when the task ahead is of a well-adjusted difficulty for the user, not to seem too easy, nor too difficult."

This theory is vastly used in creating artificial intelligence for video games to keep the player engaged, making the game neither too difficult nor too easy. We adapt this to allow us to create a personalized experience for each student. Using this method, students always need to face a task ahead of the right difficulty, as we assume that all students are different and learn at a different pace. This way, students who are slower than others do not face tasks so tricky that makes them drop out, and those who are faster are not bored because the tasks are too easy for them. How we implemented, it is better described in the experimental methodology.

In this paper, we have taken a simple approach, by our admission, but further studies will provide more significant insights. Furthermore, as proved by our experiments, we are very optimistic that this is only the foundation of a long-term project which will boldly target changing how we assess students today.

2   Student Engagement and Gamification

2.1   Engagement and Learning Styles

Student engagement is also defined as "students' involvement with activities and conditions", which aim to facilitate high-quality learning [3]. The improvement of student involvement has been one of the primary missions and challenges for higher education regardless of educational formats. While student engagement is derived from many underlying factors, many teaching approaches (e.g., active learning) have been adopted and suggested to either build or enhance student engagement in various higher education fields (Fig. 1).

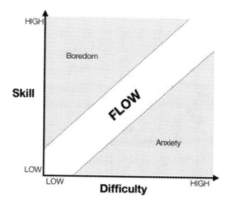

Fig. 1. Flow theory in practice

Given the differences in personality types, professional/educational experience and expectations, and adaptive competencies, individual students have their ways of gaining knowledge and skills [4]. This opinion may raise the question of considering student learning styles to design and improve learning structures and courses. Where several studies suggest the use of learning style theory as a potential tool to assist students in improving their learning performance [5], there are concerns toward the course customization based on learning styles, mainly due to problems of measurement [6].

According to an AUSSE report, 'appropriate levels of intellectual challenge along with sufficient education support' play an essential role in increasing student involvement in their work, and this further gives a positive effect on their learning outcomes [3]. Given the generic learning activities and assessment, it often relies on the individual class tutor or unit chair to generate the 'appropriate levels of learning challenges', which could be challenging for many tutors and unit chairs. This challenge may lead to the hype of using gamification in many educational fields.

2.2   Gamification in Education

The use of game elements/features has been one of the educational trends for the past few years. Although the focus of studies is different, some experimental studies identified the positive impact of using game elements/features in student motivation, attention and learning performance [7]. This positive outcome may have a close relationship with the characteristics of games. According to the literature, one of the most well-known characteristics is the freedom to fail. This approach reduces the fear of failure in learners' experiment process and also resulted positively in student engagement [8]. Besides, the ability to provide frequent and immediate feedback could be beneficial [9], considering the practical restrictions in providing frequent feedback in a classroom setting. Lastly, it also allows adjusting learning activities based on the progression of individual learners, which is known as a Dynamic Difficulty Adjustment system [5]. These characteristics are often discussed as the major benefits of using gamification in education.

3 Dynamic Difficulty Adjustment (DDA)

Much research has been done that points to the fact that computer-based learning is highly effective in comparison to traditional learning and that too from a very initial stage from an individual's learning and development [10]. Yien et al. [11] provides an experimental group of sixth-grade students with a game-based learning curriculum and establishes that it was more effective than the traditional learning curriculum.

Wang and Chen [12] highlighted a fundamental distinction between performance and engagement. According to their research, individuals performed better when they were initially given a game to clarify their concept, followed by a challenge game. However, they showed less engagement or flow as described by Mihaly Csikszentmihalyi [2]. The primary reason could be that participants were asked initial concept clarification questions that required them to differentiate between important concepts and point out examples that might digress individuals from the immersive experience and cause boredom. Therefore, it seems crucial to find the right balance between performance and engagement while developing computer-based learning platforms.

Research supporting computer-based learning has been carried out in recent times. However, the purpose of our study was to go one step further than that and apply Dynamic Difficulty Adjustment to computer-based learning platforms. Most of the research done in Dynamic Difficulty Adjustment has focused on multiplayer games. However, research is now also being done to apply DDA to serious games [13]. Serious games are games that are not designed for entertainment purposes but for the education of other means. In both scenarios, most of the difficulty 'adjustment' revolves around the modification of specific parameters and game scenarios to ensure that the players do not get bored or frustrated while playing the game [14]. Our research is the first of its kind as we aim to apply DDA on purely educational platforms to be used in higher education.

Besides ensuring that users do not get disengaged from the tasks, research has also been conducted to show that DDA techniques can assess the users' current state and adapt to improve performance. This feature helps students maximize their work productivity as well [15]. Despite all these qualitative experiments, it has also been claimed that player expertise has a considerable influence on the perception of the level of difficulty [14]. There were promising results concerning adaptive educational games adjusting their features such as task difficulty, object speed and learning content according to the current state of the player [13,16]. In research conducted by DDA, systems can also be used to facilitate the transition of users from novice to expert [17].

One study has shown that while using DDA in gaming, an AI runtime module called the Experience Engine can dynamically create activities that are actively allocated to the players to ensure that the aims of the author or teacher are fulfilled. The individual's profile includes various features, which include his level of skill, task type preferences, skill needs and preferences, learning styles needs/preferences [13]. For all these reasons and others, DDA is seen to provide personalized learning for the participants. Ung, Meriaudeau and Tang [15] aiming to improve the outcome as shown in Fig. 2. Furthermore, it has been reported in research that this also improves the experience for the players to get quicker performance gains and get the feeling of being in greater control when DDA is used to match their skill level [18].

Another school of thought has tried to assess the participants based on their mental state rather than their performance. This approach showed a more remarkable improvement in the performance of the participants. They seemed to be more immersed in the challenge [10, 19] tries to study when to trigger DDA in a third-person shooter game and used a unique approach of measuring players' excitement level using an Emotiv EPOC headset to read electroencephalography (EEG). If the level of excitement drops down under a certain threshold, DDA is activated to mitigate the problem. This method addresses degraded game experience and uses a proxy for excitement level than a performance scoring level.

Ung, Meriaudeau and Tang [15] in their research proposes the design and subsequent application of a functional near-infrared spectroscopy (fNIRS)–dynamic difficulty adjustment (DDA) system. Their experiment has a total of 25 participants that undergo a control session with Fixed Difficulty Training (FDT) and one with the Neurofeedback Training (NFT) that uses the DDA system. The result showed considerable improvement using the DDA backed system. All of the above researches have opened an avenue for DDA to be used in alleviating medical disorders. This idea can be seen in one research that has claimed that DDA can play a potential role in several fields, including treating cognitive mental disorders such as Attention Deficit Hyperactivity Disorder (ADHD) [21]. They use Visio-haptic training with DDA as they claim that it is the most effective in attention training.

When we talk about educational assessment, we see that the personalization brought by DDA can help mitigate the problem of plagiarism as well [22].

Much research has been done to conclude the most viable and effective way of measuring how difficult the task is for the individual. For example, a "Challenge Function" and "Evaluation function" are two concepts introduced in research by [14]. The functions use various quantitative information from the players and assess the game state and the player's skill level and perform the right adjustments that suit the suitable abilities. Therefore, using heuristic functions is very common in assessing the skill level of participants.

On the other hand, some people believe that difficulty adjustments are required when the individual is mentally fatigued rather than his skill level not being up to the mark. The research assesses that the drop in oxygenation level in subjects might indicate mental fatigue leading to the participant being less engaged in the task at hand. In contrast, the oxygenation levels remained almost constant by NFT subjects throughout the experiment. This finding suggests that the proposed fNIRS-DDA system aided the participants in avoiding mental fatigue [15].

Bayesian statistics may be used to dynamically predict or evaluate the difficulty of specific tasks using the participants' performance measure. Such probabilistic techniques are more commonly applied in multiplayer games, which are mainly stats-based in nature. A neural network, k-nearest neighbours' algorithm linear and nonlinear regression are other standard models used to assess individual skill levels and future states [20]. All these models aim to predict players' current state and make necessary parameter adjustments to keep individuals in engaging interaction loops for a required amount of time.

While it has potential benefits, DDA does not come cheaply. Ultimately, DDA IA systems tend to take control away from the author and give it to the algorithm [20]. [4] does highlight the need for several trials of user performance to predict with accuracy; however, other research claims that since we are just aiming for the best fit of the given current information, several trials may not be necessary.

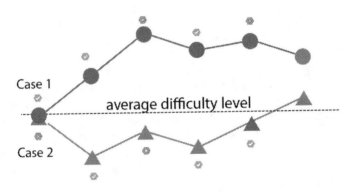

Fig. 2. An example on how DDA is applied to maximise the final outcome of a test.

4   Research Methods

In creating TuneIn, we wanted to make sure that we would be able to test our assumptions;

- Assumption 1: that a study path tailored to keep the student in the flow zone (DDA student) will improve their performance, especially in the amount of content absorbed.
- Assumption 2: Students using the standard method (STD students) will score, overall, less than DDA students.

To run the test, we selected a pool of 500 questions and problems from a Linear Algebra class divided into five levels of difficulty (division already provided by the book used to gather the test questions). To this end, we run a randomised, double-blind trial which we carried out through an app. The test consisted of a pool of 20 questions with a time limit of 2 min for every question. Every time a new student takes the test, the app chooses behind the scenes whether to use the DDA mechanism or not.

The app in DDA mode presents questions of varying difficulty, depending on the student's current level. While the DDA mechanism is not chosen, the question is generated using a pattern from 1–5. The level is chosen randomly with an equal distribution of difficulty to prevent the student from facing a test with only hard questions or easy questions. The result will be a random selection of 4 questions per level (that leads to 20 questions in total).

To run the test and evaluate whether the DDA mode is more efficient than the random picking of the questions, we used two different models of DDA. A simpler one based on mathematics operations (called MathDDA) and a different approach based on Reinforcement Learning (called RLDDA).

4.1   MathDDA

In MathDDA, the level always starts at 1. It is updated depending on whether the last questions were answered correctly or not. Each correct answer increases the updated level by $\frac{1}{3}$, while each mistake decreases it by $\frac{1}{6}$. The two numbers differ, reflecting that a wrong answer is not intended to be a punishment.

The current level (the level of the question the user will face) during the test is the result of the following formula:

$$Y = round(updatedlevel) \tag{1}$$

4.2   RLDDA

On the other hand, RLDDA is based on a DQN feed-forward Neural Network and a custom reward function to extract the best outcome from the student.

The basic concept of this model is to train a network based on a Q-Learning algorithm to automatically select the following question with the final aim to maximize the student grade.

At the heart of Q-Learning is the function $Q(s, a)$, which gives the discounted value of taking an action a in a state s. This value is equal to the reward for taking a specific action a in a state s plus a discounted value for all the future states in which the agent will end up. Shortly is the value of picking the optimal action in a specific state, represented by the formula:

$$Q(s, a) = r + \gamma \, max'_a \Big(Q(s', a') \Big)$$

The goal of this approach is to find the optimal policy that maximises the reward function:

$$\pi(s) = argmax_a \Big(Q(s, a) \Big)$$

Where $\pi(s)$ is the policy at state s in order to let the student achieve the highest possible score compared to his current level.

The reward function has to reward the model whether the student answers correctly and punish it if the answer is wrong, meaning that the model has picked the wrong question's level so that the student can achieve the highest possible score. To prevent the model from converging to a local minimum presenting only low-level questions to maximize its reward, the higher the question's level, the higher the reward/punishment has to be. As a normal Reinforcement Learning approach, the model has to have an observation space (state) and an action space described below.

State. The state provided to the DQN network is an array with the following elements:

- Level of the previous question (from 1 to 5).
- Question index (e.g., 4 if is the fifth question).
- Number of correct answers.
- Number of wrong answers.
- Total reward achieved from the beginning of the test (that has to be also an input since it represents an estimator of the level of the student).

Observation Space. On the other hand, the actions space is a set of 3 actions:

- 0 for decreasing the level of -1 compared to the previous question.
- 1 for increasing the level of $+1$ compared to the previous question.
- 2 for keeping the level the same as the previous question.

Network Structure. The network structure, as shown in Fig. 3, is composed of an input layer with 5 nodes, 2 fully connected hidden layers with 12 nodes each and an output layer with 3 nodes. This last layer will be responsible for output the estimated Q-value for the 3 different actions that the network can perform.

Reward System. In order to provide an evaluator that the network can use to assess the quality of its own decision, a simple reward function is implemented. This reward function aims to direct the network toward its absolute minimum, providing every action with a score (reward/punishment system). The only network objective is to maximize in the long run the value of the reward.

The reward in this experiment is a score corresponding to the coefficient of the question provided (coefficient based on the level), where the sign is positive if the answer is right (reward) and is negative if the sign is negative (punishment). The coefficient is described as follows: level 1: 0.5, level 2: 0.6, level 3: 0.7, level 4: 0.85, level 5: 1.0.

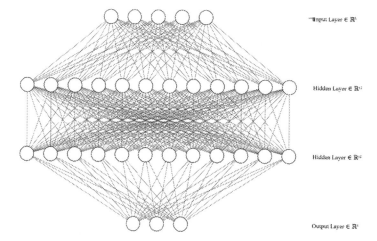

Fig. 3. DNN structure

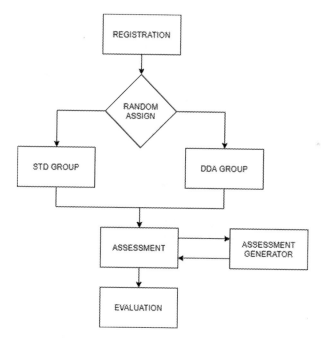

Fig. 4. Application flow, simplified to allow users from different domains to comprehend the end to end solution.

4.3   Application Flow

As shown in Fig. 4, the application developed randomly assigns every user to the selected group and then performs the final assessment on the result. Although simple, the application developed is fully functional and was offered as a service. The participants were chosen from a cohort of people of both genders, between 18 and 23 years of age. All participants have at least completed high school, currently enrolled in a scientific course of a university (to guarantee that all the students used had already covered the fundamentals of Linear Algebra). Coming from a university background and thinking about future adoption, we have strategically decided to look into that part of the education world that is faster at implementing than others, so we picked the university target among others.

5   Preliminary Findings

After conducting our pilot experiment, we cleaned our data. We had a sample of the 99 students who completed their assessment equally split into three groups, each assigned to an approach. Every cluster of 33 students performed the test similarly, with the same time constraint differing only by the algorithm that picked the questions.

As shown in Fig. 5, the Random approach led to an average of 46 points compared to 54 and 57 of the MathDDA and RLDDA. So, the DDA approach is beneficial for the students' outcomes.

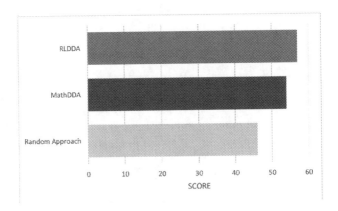

Fig. 5. Visual representation of the final score in the three groups.

The second observation was that the DDA-backed cohort attempted more questions than the control group (8% more on average). The control group attempted fewer questions or even dropped out of the assessments more frequently. The main explanation could be that the students attempting their assessment on the DDA platform felt more engaged and confident. With DDA, the students never faced questions significantly too tricky compared to their actual level.

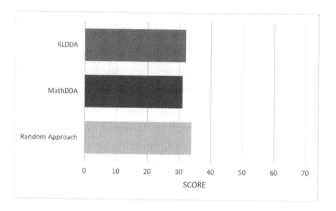

Fig. 6. Visual representation of the average time spent per question in the three groups.

Finally, it was also noteworthy that the DDA groups were spending less time on each question on average, with 31 and 32 s of MathDDA and RLDDA compared to 34 s of the random approach, as shown in Fig. 6. Possible explanations for that fall in line with the flow theory of learning. The student is more engaged and performs much better on the dynamic platform, adjusting the difficulty of questions and ensuring that the student remains within the flow channel.

6   Discussion

This paper has revealed some interesting insights that are bound to become the foundation for much more extensive exploration. The few elements that we have used and the assumptions we have brought forward were proven correct within the limitation of our experiment. The outcomes were relatively straightforward, limiting our current phase to simple validation.

From an early experiment, we showed how a DDA approach could improve student performance, shaping the test to its specific knowledge level and making him comfortable with the test level. Given that the user usually never faces a question too difficult by orders of magnitude, We strongly believe that the psychological factor is the key to keeping him focused on the test and confident about his knowledge.

7   Limitations and Future Research

There are several limitations to this study. Firstly, the sample size of this study is limited because it is only based on the first phase of data collection. Besides, data collection is only focused on capturing time and levels; we did not have information specific to individuals in our cohorts, but only the general information. Given the limitations, this research will be extended to gather another phase of data collection to test student engagement and performance and identify critical factors/features that play an essential role in shaping the student's experience of using the platform.

In the future, we will include more concise information about our participants to fine-tune the difficulty levels. We will also explore different topics beyond mathematics to verify whether or not the theory still proves correct in non-stem subjects.

References

1. Watts, J., Robertson, N.: Burnout in university teaching staff: a systematic literature review. Educ. Res. **53**(1), 33–50 (2011)
2. Csikszentmihalyi, M.: Finding Flow: The Psychology of Engagement with Everyday Life. Basic Books, New York (2008)
3. Radloff, A., Coates, H.: Doing More for Learning: Enhancing Engagement and Outcomes: Australasian Survey of Student Engagement: Australasian Student Engagement Report (2010)
4. Kolb, D.A., Boyatzis, R.E., Mainemelis, C.: Experiential learning theory: previous research and new directions. In: Perspectives on Thinking, Learning, and Cognitive Styles, vol. 1, no. 8, pp. 227–247 (2001)
5. Cagiltay, N.: Using learning styles theory in engineering education. Eur. J. Eng. Educ. **33**(4), 415–424 (2008)
6. An, D., Carr, M.: Learning styles theory fails to explain learning and achievement: recommendations for alternative approaches. Personality Individ. Differ. **116**, 410–416 (2017)
7. Barrio, C.M., Munoz-Organero, M., Soriano, J.S.: Can gamification improve the benefits of student response systems in learning? An experimental study. IEEE Trans. Emerg. Top. Comput. **4**(3), 429–438 (2016)
8. Kiesler, S., Kraut, R.E., Koedinger, K.R., Aleven, V., Mclaren, B.M.: Gamification in education: what, how, why bother. Acad. Exch. Q. **15**(2), 1–5 (2011)
9. Kapp, K.M.: The Gamification of Learning and Instruction. Wiley San Francisco (2012)
10. Liu, C., Agrawal, P., Sarkar, N., Chen, S.: Dynamic difficulty adjustment in computer games through real-time anxiety-based affective feedback. Int. J. Hum.-Comput. Interact. **25**(6), 506–529 (2009)
11. Yien, J., Hung, C., Hwang, G., Lin, Y.: A game-based learning approach to improving students' learning achievements in a Nutrition course. Turkish Online J. Educ. Technol.-TOJET **10**(2), 1–10 (2011)
12. Wang, L., Chen, M.: The effects of game strategy and preference-matching on flow experience and programming performance in game-based learning. Innov. Educ. Teach. Int. **47**(1), 39–52 (2010)
13. Brisson, A., et al.: Artificial intelligence and personalization opportunities for serious games. In: Eighth Artificial Intelligence and Interactive Digital Entertainment Conference, October 2012
14. Silva, M.P., do Nascimento Silva, V., Chaimowicz, L.: Dynamic difficulty adjustment on MOBA games. Entertain. Comput. **18**, 103–123 (2017)

15. Ung, W.C., Meriaudeau, F., Tang, T.B.: Optimizing mental workload by functional near-infrared spectroscopy based dynamic difficulty adjustment. In: 2018 40th Annual International Conference of the IEEE Engineering in Medicine and Biology Society (EMBC), pp. 1522–1525. IEEE, July 2018
16. Chang, D.M.J.: Dynamic difficulty adjustment in computer games. In: Proceedings of the 11th Annual Interactive Multimedia Systems Conference (2013)
17. Bederson, B.B.: Interfaces for staying in the flow. Ubiquity 5(27), 1 (2004)
18. Jegers, K.: Pervasive game flow: understanding player enjoyment in pervasive gaming. Comput. Entertain. (CIE) 5(1), 9-es (2007)
19. Stein, A., Yotam, Y., Puzis, R., Shani, G., Taieb-Maimon, M.: EEG-triggered dynamic difficulty adjustment for multiplayer games. Entertain. Comput. 25, 14–25 (2018)
20. Hunicke, R., Chapman, V.: AI for dynamic difficulty adjustment in games. In: Challenges in Game Artificial Intelligence AAAI Workshop. AAAI Press, San Jose (2004)
21. Peng, C., Wang, D., Zhang, Y., Xiao, J.: A visuo-haptic attention training game with dynamic adjustment of difficulty. IEEE Access 7, 68878–68891 (2019)
22. Manoharan, S.: Personalized assessment as a means to mitigate plagiarism. IEEE Trans. Educ. 60(2), 112–119 (2016)

P-sharding: Streamline Emergency Medical Transactions via Priority Sharding

Akanksha Saini[1]([✉])([iD]), Navneesh Kaur[2], Navneet Singh[2], and Dimaz Wijaya[3]

[1] Deakin Blockchain Innovation Lab, School of Information Technology,
Geelong, Australia
sainiakan@deakin.edu.au
[2] Department of Information, Communication and Electronics Engineering,
Catholic University of Korea, Seoul, South Korea
navneetsingh@catholic.ac.kr
[3] School of Information Technology, Deakin University, Geelong, Australia
dimaz.wijaya@deakin.edu.au

Abstract. In recent years, several blockchain-based access control models have been emerged to give individuals control over their sensitive Electronic Medical Records (EMRs) in the healthcare sector. From our extensive literature review, we observe that currently, these models have no provision of prioritising the emergency transactions. This critically affects the quick and streamline sharing of EMRs in a multi-domain network environment. Further, it restricts the optimal usage of blockchain network affecting scalability. Sharding has arisen as a viable option for addressing the issue of blockchain's scalability and performance. Motivated from this, in this paper, we first propose prioritised sharding (P-sharding), a novel mechanism to streamline the processing of priority or emergency transactions in blockchain-based access control models by improving the throughput of each prioritised shard, in the context of multi-domain healthcare networks. Finally, the performance of the model is verified, validated, and also compared with the existing sharding mechanism. The obtained results are promising and encourage to further sparkle this direction.

Keywords: Blockchain-based access model · Electronic medical records · Healthcare · Priority transactions · Scalability · Sharding

1 Introduction

Blockchain technology is defined as a peer-to-peer decentralised network having distributed ledger of transactions. The network of nodes validates the transactions using cryptography means solving a mathematical puzzle via mining. With its secure features, blockchain has found many applications in various sectors ranging from financial services, supply chain, insurance to healthcare. Our research primarily focuses on the healthcare domain. There exists highly sensitive Electronic Medical Records (EMRs) need to securely access and streamline

© ICST Institute for Computer Sciences, Social Informatics and Telecommunications Engineering 2022
Published by Springer Nature Switzerland AG 2022. All Rights Reserved
W. Bao et al. (Eds.): ADHOCNETS 2021/TridentCom 2021, LNICST 428, pp. 242–259, 2022.
https://doi.org/10.1007/978-3-030-98005-4_18

sharing among healthcare professionals working in multi-domain healthcare facilities. EMRs are conventionally recorded in cloud-based health repositories, with the strategic initiatives of data sharing across different registries. However, it constitutes a very high privacy risk of a security breach to occur posing a major challenge for the digital trust in e-Health where storing, accessing, and exchanging sensitive patient-related data must comply with several regulations, while remaining accessible to authorized health practitioners [1]. Cloud-based access control models [2,3] validate the access right through a centralized entity suffer a single point of failure.

Healthcare is one of the domains with the biggest investment in blockchain technology due to its secure transaction processing to transfer sensitive EMR. Decentralised blockchain technology provides a solution to make the medical data secure, achieves patient-eccentricity, and makes it accessible across the health departments. In recent years, many blockchain-based access control mechanisms have been proposed for EMRs. All these models rule out the validation of access rights by a centralised server. An architecture for scalable access management has been proposed in Internet of Things (IoT) context [4]. Some other methodologies for managing medical records have been proposed in [5] and [6] using smart contracts [7] considering the issue of interoperability and making their system more compatible. In [8], the authors have developed an access control framework based on smart contract, which is built on the top of distributed ledger, to secure the sharing of EMRs among different entities involved in the smart healthcare system.

However, during our study, we identified that among healthcare data, not all are of equal importance, they have different service requirements on the blockchain-based access model. Emergency EMRs need to get processed faster as per their priority in the access control mechanism which the current blockchain is not fully capable to do unless for high transaction fees. In existing blockchain systems, all the transactions are considered evenly and processed as First-In-First-Out (FIFO) invariant of the type of consensus used. We believe that a) it does not only restricts the optimal usage of blockchain's capacity but also selfish (malicious) validators can flood the network with less important transactions preventing emergency transactions from being processed in a timely manner, b) without prioritising the emergency transactions, fatal loss incurs to the patients and hospitals as it hinders the real-time access of patient's EMR in Emergency Medical Services (EMS), c) finally, to optimize OPEX and CAPEX, EMS have to consider the prioritised transactions prior than the regular ones. Some early attempts have been made by [9,10] to analyse the performance of blockchains in the context of scalability without the provision of transaction prioritisation.

To the best of our knowledge, none of the existing blockchain-based access models have the provision of prioritising the emergency transactions which eventually restrict them to get scaled [11,12]. Since existing blockchain platforms like Bitcoin [13], and Ethereum [14] only process limited rate of transactions per second (tps) in FIFO manner leading to the increased overall latency. It takes longer time for emergency transactions to get fetched from the memory pool because there is no provision for prioritized scheduling. Hence it cannot be immediately applied to the healthcare system in its present state. It is of utmost importance to tackle these challenges before commercially integrating blockchain-based access control into the healthcare system. A blockchain-based healthcare system can be optimized in terms of scalability in the following ways to handle a growing number of EMR transactions, a) reducing the communication and computation overhead; b) adding resources to a single node, i.e., vertical scaling; and c) adding more nodes to the blockchain, i.e., horizontal scaling, which include the concept of sharding.

In order to add this provision, we are among the early ones to propose a novel mechanism named priority sharding (P-sharding), fundamentally based on the sharding principle, to prioritise the processing of emergency transactions by applying tags to EMR transactions in blockchain-based access control models. The key idea behind P-sharding is to automatically divide the available computational resources into smaller groups or committees, each processing a prioritised sharded block containing a set of emergency EMRs. The major contribution of P-sharding is to process the transactions faster and alleviate the scalability issues. In sharding [15], data is broken into different shards and instead of all nodes verifying the entire data individually, they verify one shard each side-by-side. The amount of time is saved exponentially through sharding [16]. In this paper, we have applied prioritised sharding on Ethereum-based permissioned blockchain[1]. We take advantage of sharding concept and with our analysis, we observe that the prioritisation of transactions directly impacts the scalability of the system. Hence, our model of P-sharding prioritises the emergency transactions and processes them faster contributing to the development of a streamlined and scalable system. The main contributions of our paper are highlighted as follows.

1. We propose the first-ever novel approach of prioritisation in sharded blockchain to process emergency transactions faster as per their priority. This improves the processing rate of prioritised emergency transactions drastically.
2. We simulate our proposed approach through permissioned blockchain in a controlled environment. Evaluation results signify that our model is scalable and efficient to achieve priority-based weighted fair queuing using a probabilistic approach.
3. We identify a significant use-case of the above contribution in the healthcare sector to have scalable and efficient blockchain-based access control.

The remaining of this paper is organized as follows. Section 2 gives an overview of the related works. In Sect. 3, we introduce our proposed P-sharding model and provide the details. In Sect. 4, the implementation and performance analysis are given. Finally, this paper is concluded in Sect. 5 and provides further discussion.

---

[1] https://github.com/ethereum/sharding.

2   Preliminaries

Before we provide in depth details of P-sharding, in this section we show a typical behavior of blockchain-based access control models. We observe that workflow of the majority of these models [4–8] is relatively the same. Based on this observation, now we present a high-level generic blockchain-based access control framework, as shown in Fig. 1.

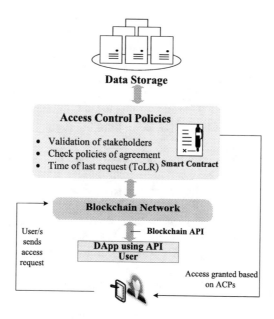

Fig. 1. High level illustration of blockchain-based access control framework.

2.1   Blockchain-Based Access Control Mechanism

There are mainly four entities involved in the blockchain-based access control models. Here, we discuss the functionality of each sub-module as below.

– **Users with DApp.** It is a decentralised web application used by front-end users to render the blockchain-based access control application. It contains peer decision makers, rules, and policies scripted in a specific language (Solidity, Vyper etc.) about how the peers are allowed to access information [17]. The interface between users and DApp is mainly via JavaScript Application Programming Interface (API) to establish communication with the blockchain network. It contains a wallet that manages the cryptographic keys and keeps a record of blockchain addresses. A user sends an access request through the DApp. In DApps, users can directly send requests and access data without a single server controlling it like in client-server model. Once the user has sent the request through DApp, it cannot be tampered or deleted. This leads to secure and open governance. DApps offers various applications in healthcare, financial sectors, gaming, supply chain etc.

- *Blockchain network.* After the user sends the access request, it is broadcasted among each peer in the blockchain network. Then, the network of nodes verifies the legitimacy of access requests based on a consensus mechanism. The transactions are cryptographically signed and appended on the main chain after the consensus. Blockchain consensus can be broadly classified into Proof-based and Vote-based. Proof-based consensus are fully decentralised and permissionless. They elect a leader by introducing a game approach to propose a final block value. For example, cryptocurrencies like Bitcoin and Ethereum utilise Proof of Work (PoW) consensus where miners with varying computational power compete against each other to solve a mathematical puzzle to confirm transactions on the blockchain network, and the miner with sufficient proof gets rewarded. Other such consensus are Proof of Stake (PoS) [18], Delegated Proof of Stake (DPoS) [19], etc. They are hard to scale with the growing number of nodes across the network [20]. While the vote-based consensus are simpler than the proof-based as they achieve consensus based on the round of votes. Byzantine fault-tolerant (BFT) consensus protocols are among the vote-based consensus such as Practical Byzantine fault-tolerance (PBFT) [21]. These consensus protocols have high performance but the degree of decentralisation is low. Due to decentralised consensus, blockchain achieves a great level of security. Blockchain network also famously called distributed ledger technology (DLT) records and replicates the transactions across each node. It provides ledger and smart contract or chain code services to various applications. It records the provenance of a digital asset in a distributed, shared, and immutable ledger. The blockchain network operates across a peer-to-peer network of computers without a central authority or intermediary.
- *Access control policies.* Each peer in the system has a list of Access Control Policies (ACPs) constituting access agreements between the data owner and data requester. In a blockchain-based system, the involved entities define the access control policies in the smart contract and manage access. Smart contract-based ACPs check any kind of misconduct, time of last request (ToLR), etc. and grants access permission to the requester. It also revokes access control in case of any misconduct. The smart contract-based access policies are not only decentralised but also self-executable. It eliminates the threat of any internal or external attack due to the SSL certificates located at each node rather than using the traditional passwords. Multiple smart contract-based access policies have been proposed for Internet of Things (IoT) systems to achieve distributed and trustworthy access control [22].
- *Data storage.* As blockchain is a distributed system, data is stored in computers or nodes across the whole network. Each of these nodes contains a copy of the blockchain ledger. In blockchain-based access control, data can be stored inside or outside the blockchain. Considering the limited block size of the blockchain, some of the existing frameworks come up with the idea of storing data in the cloud while their corresponding hash is packed into

the blockchain. Various existing blockchain platforms have different ways of storing data. For example, Ethereum stores the transaction data in trie only when the transaction is confirmed. Corda [23] uses the concept of states to store data rather than broadcasting to each peer, while Hyperledger [24] uses LevelDB and CouchDB to store the state data. The whole process of data storage can take anywhere ranging from few minutes to hours depending on the congestion in the network.

The bottleneck in the existing [4–6] and our proposed smart contract-based access control model [8] is the slower transaction processing rate for emergency or priority EMR transactions due to the FIFO scheduling, despite having higher importance. In next subsection, we will explain the issue of scalability in detail to get an insight to understand and analyse the performance and scalability of blockchain-based access models.

2.2 Scalability and Performance Issue

Blockchain networks such as Bitcoin avoid the double-spending problem through the consensus protocols where each transaction is recorded and validated by every node on the chain. This ensures transparency, data integrity, and immutability in a decentralised blockchain environment. But, it restricts the scalability as current blockchain systems can process only a few transactions per second. It is mainly affected by key factors, i.e., block mining rate, transaction processing, and waiting time of the transaction in the queue to get processed. This needs to be addressed before blockchain is adopted in real-time systems such as smart healthcare [4]. Blockchain network deals with the mining congestion because of higher transaction generation rate than the transaction processing rate, leading to a longer waiting time for the transaction to get mined. We emphasis that none of the given access models have the provision to process the prioritised transactions or access requests faster and they do not consider the allocation of adequate resources (resource fairness). This factor is of utmost importance and hence cannot be ignored in terms of increasing scalability [25] or optimizing the blockchain network resources. Some of the solutions proposed to address this challenge are a) Off-chain solutions, b) Directed Acyclic Graph (DAG), c) Sharding.

1. *Off-chain:* This approach to tackle scalability in the blockchain network is to store transaction-related data in the local nodes, which are often referred to as off-chain [26]. These local nodes only send a summary or outcome of the transactions to the main chain. Another such solution is creating a network of micro-payment channels to instantly confirm a payment transaction [27]. Such off-chain solutions cannot guarantee the validity or legitimacy of off-chain transactions. To tackle that, often validator nodes are introduced to endorse the transactions but still, the validity is compromised due to the centralisation.

2. *Directed Acyclic Graph:* Another approach is to design blockchain as Directed Acyclic Graph (DAG) network [28,29], where each transaction is linked to multiple transactions rather than the blocks. Theoretically, the higher, the volume of transactions, the faster a DAG network can validate them.

3. *Sharding:* Sharding has been extensively explored in the distributed database systems to alleviate scalability and performance. Database sharding refers to the horizontal partitioning that splits large databases into smaller chunks called shards across multiple servers.

To address scalability problems in conventional blockchain, many blockchain sharding protocols have been introduced. In the standard blockchain sharding, the entire blockchain's state is broken into shards that contain their independent history of state and transaction. Omniledger is among the earliest work conducted to achieve high Visa-level performance in distributed ledgers through parallel intra-shard transaction processing [30]. It introduces a cross-shard protocol to handle transactions affecting multiple shards. Optchain [31] seeks to enhance the placement of transactions in order to minimize the adverse effect of cross-shard transactions on the efficiency of existing sharding proposals. It has implemented the temporal fitness score to measure the probability of transaction should be placed into the shard without causing further cross-shard transactions. However, these sharding techniques enhance scalability by compromising the very core properties of blockchain i.e. decentralisation. Spontaneous sharding has been suggested as a solution where transactions are sharded by the nature of the value transfer system [32]. With each value, a proof is associated that grows with the number of nodes passing. Hence, to keep the transmission costs low, nodes would prefer to keep the transaction in smaller shards than the entire network. It does, however, bring out the downside of low storage capacity.

3   P-sharding: Proposed Framework

In this section, we propose and discuss our novel framework to prioritise and efficiently process emergency transactions in blockchain-based access control mechanisms in smart healthcare. We name this model P-sharding and explain it as follows in detail.

Our proposed model of P-sharding introduces the priority in the sharding mechanism proposed by Ethereum. In this methodology, the transaction is split up among smaller groups of nodes based on the prioritised data, to get validated. Using the assumption that only trauma and emergency departments of any hospital can put priority tag to the EMR transactions. And the emergency EMR transactions get accumulated in the memory pool. The idea behind the P-sharding is illustrated in Fig. 2. The detailed step-wise workflow sequence is given below.

1. Transactions are grouped in the memory pool as they arrive in the system. In every mining iteration, the blockchain is divided into shards. The number of shards which is the length of the transaction array is divided according to

two factors: (a) the transactions load and (b) the number of validators in the network. Then the transactions are randomly divided among all the shards and get collected into their respective sub-block. Each of the shards has its own ledger. These shards process and store a disjoint set of transactions. Validator nodes are randomly assigned to each shard.

2. The transactions with priority are then chosen from the sub-block based on their priority tag. The tag with 0 indicates a non-priority transaction, while 1 represents a transaction of priority. In our proposed model, the transactions are then sequenced as per the priority and held in the respective priority and non-priority mining queues based on FIFO.

3. After sequencing, the randomly selected validators in the network verify the prioritised transactions by allocating their resources prior to the non-priority transactions.

4. Finally, the verified block is generated and added into the sharded blockchain.

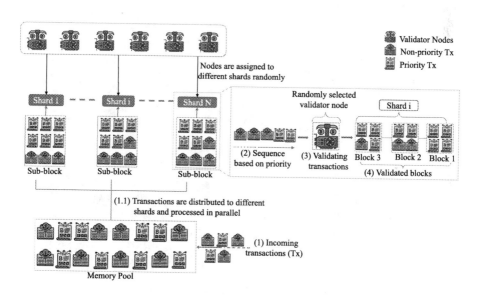

Fig. 2. Proposed P-sharding model.

Since the sharded blockchain has multiple shards, these emergency transactions spend least amount of time to fetch from the memory pool. This results in faster transaction processing and helps in the development of an efficient access control mechanism. Table 1 depicts the structure of the proposed P-shard in which a transaction group is divided into two parts: a) transaction group header and b) transaction group body. The transaction group header is further divided into two sections. The left section is as follows:

- *Shard ID.* Every transaction specifies the ID of the shard it belongs to.
- *Pre-state root.* It represents the state of the root of the shard before the transaction is registered.
- *Priority score.* It is the total count of priority transactions in a block. Our aim of adding a priority score is to reduce the response time and maintain the service quality for the priority transactions.
- *Post-state root.* It shows the state of the root of the shard after the registration of transactions.
- *Receipt root.* It is generated after all the transactions in the shard are registered. It facilitates the cross shard-communication.

While the right part of the transaction group header consists of random validators. They are randomly chosen and responsible to verify the transactions in the shard. And transaction group payload has all the transaction IDs in the shard itself. Each transaction has a field of priority tag of 0 or 1 that represents its non-priority and priority state respectively.

Table 1. Structure of P-shard.

Transaction group header		
Shard ID: 23	<sig #3256>	<sig #4672>
Pre state root: 142c3dfg	<sig #7089>	<sig #8796>
Priority score: 6	<sig #4351>	<sig #2317>
Post state root: 567819ab	<sig #2356>	<sig #6451>
Receipt root: ca4567f7	<sig #1254>	<sig #2478>
Transaction group payload		
Tx a142; PriorityTag:1	Tx a674; PriorityTag:1	Tx a542; PriorityTag:1
Tx a231; PriorityTag:1	Tx a892; PriorityTag:1	Tx a902; PriorityTag:1
Tx a256; PriorityTag:0	Tx a353; PriorityTag:0	Tx a762; PriorityTag:0

Based on the queuing theory principle [33], the incoming shards follow Poisson distribution. Upon arrival, each shard is either in the priority queue with a mean arrival rate of λ_p or in non-priority queue with λ_{np} such that the total rate is

$$\lambda = \lambda_p + \lambda_{np} \tag{1}$$

It is important to notice that the waiting time of the non-priority transactions in the queue is longer than priority transactions, typically depends on the number of transactions waiting to get processed in the priority queue ahead of non-priority queue, such that

$$W_{nq} = \frac{\mu}{\mu - \lambda} W_{pq} \tag{2}$$

where μ is the average processing time of the validators, W_{pq} and W_{nq} are the average waiting time of the transaction in the priority and non-priority queue respectively. General equations for our model where priority transactions are served at the rate μ_1 and non-priority transactions are served at μ_2 are as below:

$$QL_{pq} = \frac{\lambda_p}{\mu_1}\hat{\rho}\frac{\lambda_p/\lambda + (\lambda_{np}/\lambda)(\mu_1^2/\mu_2^2)}{1 - \lambda_p/\mu_1} \tag{3}$$

$$QL_{nq} = \frac{\lambda_{np}/\mu_1}{1 - \lambda_p/\mu_1}\hat{\rho}\frac{\lambda_p/\lambda + (\lambda_{np}/\lambda)(\mu_1^2/\mu_2^2)}{1 - \lambda_p/\mu_1 - \lambda_{np}/\mu_2} \tag{4}$$

where QL_{pq} and QL_{nq} are respective mean queue lengths of prioritised and non-prioritised queue. Total utilization or % system busy time is given by

$$\rho^* = \frac{\lambda_p}{\mu_1} + \frac{\lambda_{np}}{\mu_2} \tag{5}$$

We should observe $\rho^* < \hat{\rho}$ if

$$\frac{\lambda_p}{\mu_1} + \frac{\lambda_{np}}{\mu_2} < \frac{\lambda}{\mu_1} = \frac{\lambda_p + \lambda_{np}}{\mu_1} \tag{6}$$

Both the priority and non-priority mining queues in our P-sharding model preserve non-preemptive scheduling within due to the cases of conflict between transactions of the same priority. The transaction that goes to the head of the shard deemed valid and served first. Non-preemptive priority scheduling is time saving also. Our system is based on the following assumptions.

– Priority and non-priority mining queues are kept of infinite buffer capacity (B) to avoid transactions being discarded in order to maintain Quality-of-Service (QoS).
– In our simulations, we keep all validators of the same capacity for fair play. Although the above assumptions might not be realistic and we will work on this in our future research as queuing is another research domain.

The process of sharding of prioritized blocks containing priority transactions is explained in Algorithm 1.

4   Implementation and Performance Analysis

In this section, we present the implementation setup and analysis of our simulated results.

Algorithm 1. P-sharding: prioritised sharding

Input: *Transactions (Tx), No of validators, Capacity of each shard, Minimum validators per shard, Previous block hash, No. of transactions in memory pool, Current state*

Required: *Queue capacity, Priority tag, Arrival rate of transactions (λ_p, λ_{np}), Service time (t_s)*

Output: *Minedblocks == (M_B), Priority score (PS), Departure time from queue (t_d)*

1. *Set PriorityTx Arrival rate$\rightarrow \lambda_p$, Non-PriorityTx Arrival rate$\rightarrow \lambda_{np}$*
2. *Set Priority MiningQueue capacity$\rightarrow B$, Set NonPriority MiningQueue capacity$\rightarrow B$*
3. *Set Validators$\leftarrow M_T$*
4. *Set Minimum validators per Sharded Block$\leftarrow M_{SB}$*
5. *Set Maximum Sharded Block$\leftarrow S_{MX}$*
6. *Current state$\leftarrow C_{st}$*
7. *Memorypool$\leftarrow$ transactions(Tx), ServTime(ts)$\leftarrow$Start*
8. *Current state$\leftarrow C_{st}++$*
9. *AriTime$\leftarrow t_a$, priority tag$\leftarrow$ 1// 0*
10. **If**(*Tx $\leftarrow$priority tag[1]*)
11. *{*
12. $tx_{p1}, tx_{p2}, tx_{p3} \ldots . tx_{pn} =:tx$
13. **Priority MiningQueue** $\leftarrow tx_{p1}, tx_{p2}, tx_{p3} \ldots . tx_{pn}$
14. *}*
15. **else**
16. *{*
17. $tx_{np1}, tx_{np2}, tx_{np3} \ldots . tx_{npn} =:tx$
18. **NonPriority MiningQueue**$\leftarrow tx_{np1}, tx_{np2}, tx_{np3} \ldots . tx_{npn}$
19. *}*
20. $t_s \leftarrow end$
21. **Result**$\leftarrow (M_B)^{new} \leftarrow tx_{p1} + tx_{p2} \cdots + tx_{pn} \cdots + tx_{npn}$,
    $PS = count(tx_p)$, $DepTime(t_d) \leftarrow t_a + t_s$

4.1   Simulation Setup

We simulate our model on Python in a controlled permissioned blockchain environment. The study designed a blockchain scenario by creating multiple Ethereum virtual nodes on each device with configuration of Lenovo ThinkCentre, Intel(R)CoreTM i5-7500 CPU @3.40 GHz, Windows 10 Enterprise, 64-bit, 16 GB. It mainly aims to measure and compare the overhead of the existing sharding approach [15] and our proposed prioritised sharding model.

Our model consists of a source station: transactions, one queuing station: memory pool, a fork station: P-sharding, two sets of queues: priority mining queue and non-priority mining queue, one join station, and a sink station: discharge block as shown in Fig. 3. The arrival rate for the transactions source station is generated randomly. The memory pool is modeled using M/M/1 where the arrival of transactions is Poisson distributed, service time is exponentially distributed, and the number of server is one. While on the other hand, mining pool is modeled as M/M/c since, in reality, several validators compete in parallel to solve a single block of puzzle. The fork station named P-sharding splits the transactions based on their priority tag. This station is used to achieve fast processing and reduce the service time of transactions in the mining pool. This task is synchronized and forwarded for processing in the priority and non-priority mining queue respectively. After all these tasks are processed and completed, they are joined again to dispatch the final blocks to the blockchain network.

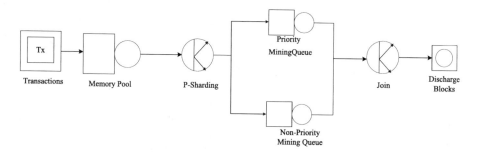

Fig. 3. Simulation model for P-sharding.

4.2 Simulated Results

In this section, we present simulated results of our model and compare them with the basic sharding model. We have utilized updated Ethereum[2] actual data parameters to carry out our simulations. The QoS performance metrics with proposed P-sharding model and basic sharding are shown in Fig. 4 and 5 respectively and explained below.

- *Mining queue count after sharding.* These are the accumulated sharded transactions that are waiting in queue to get mined.
    - *Priority mining queue count after sharding.* Due to the probabilistic approach, the priority mining queue has more priority transactions than the non-priority mining queue. In Ethereum simulation, the average priority mining queue count comes out 0.5772, which improves significantly as compared to the basic sharding where all transactions are considered evenly irrespective of their priority as shown in Fig. 4(a), 5(a) respectively.
    - *Non-priority mining queue count after sharding.* The average non-priority mining queue count comes out to be 0.3837 in Fig. 4(a).
- *Response time.* It is the average mining time of a shard, or mining time of both priority and non-priority mining queue which is almost the same with negligible variations due to dynamic arrival and mining rates. In Ethereum, both queues have an average of 0.0712(s) simulated mining rate with the input or actual mining rate of 0.0714(s) shown in Fig. 4(b) which comes in coherence with sharding results in Fig. 5(b).

---

[2] https://etherscan.io/.

- Throughput: The rate at which transactions depart from a mining queue, i.e., the number of transactions completed in a unit time depicted in Fig. 4(c).
  - *Priority mining queue throughput.* Priority mining queue has higher throughput. In other words, mining of a prioritised transaction is faster as compared to non-priority mining queue. In Ethereum simulation, the average throughput in the priority mining queue is 7.9877 tps (refer Fig. 4(c)) which is faster than the basic sharding where all the transactions irrespective of their priority are treated the same as shown in Fig. 5(c).
  - *Non-priority mining queue throughput.* The departure of transactions in a non-priority mining queue is comparatively slower. In Ethereum simulation, the average throughput in non-priority mining queue is 5.3248 tps.
- *Utilization.* It can be defined as the percentage of time a station is used (i.e., busy). It ranges from 0(0%), when the station is idle, to a maximum of 1(100%), when the station is constantly busy mining transactions for the entire simulation run. The utilization rate with single server S is $U = lS$ and subsequently, utilization with m number of servers is $U = lS/m$ where l is arrival rate.
  - *Priority mining queue utilization.* In the priority mining queue, we set up three servers (validator nodes) mining three sharded blocks simultaneously with utilization $1.86*10^{-3}$ less than 1 (Fig. 4(d)), which means the priority mining queue is not fully occupied. Hence our system achieves $\rho^* < \hat{\rho}$. In the basic sharding model, the system is congested due to a high utilization rate (refer Fig. 5(d)).

To further validate our model, Table 2 shows the comparison between the actual and simulated results of basic sharding and our P-sharding model. The values indicate the significant improvement in the stated parameters with our P-sharding model in comparison with the basic sharding model.

4.3   Performance Analysis

In this section, we evaluate the performance of our proposed P-sharding mechanism as shown in Fig. 6 and 7.

- *Latency per number of shards.* The latency (or average confirmation time) of a transaction is measured by the time the transaction is sent until it is committed to the blockchain. It is a significant factor in block propagation time. A large number of confirmed sharded blocks will multiply this delay as shown in Fig. 6(a). As the latency changes linearly with the increasing number of shards and transaction rate. This shows that the two mining queues are able to streamline the flow of transactions.

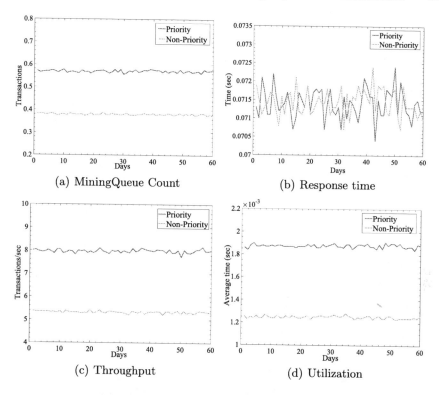

Fig. 4. Simulation results of Ethereum real statistics with P-sharding.

Table 2. Comparison between the simulated results of sharding and proposed P-sharding model.

Parameters	Sharding	P-sharding	
		Priority-mining queue	Non-priority mining queue
Mining queue count (tx)	1.4359	0.5772	0.3837
Response time (sec)	0.0713	0.0712	0.0712
Throughput (tx/sec)	6.4379	7.9877	5.3248
Utilization	0.00479	0.00186	0.00126

– *Latency per transaction rate.* We analyze the latency with respect to the rate of input transactions in the mining queue i.e. the number of transactions coming in unit time for mining. As shown in Fig. 6(b), it increases with the increase in input transactions to the mining queue with respect to the increase in number of shards.

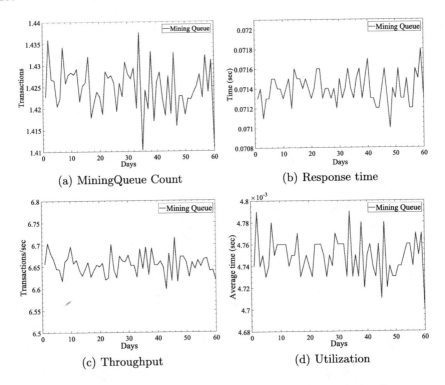

Fig. 5. Simulation results of Ethereum real statistics with sharding.

- *Throughput per number of shards.* The transaction throughput is the rate at which valid transactions are committed by the blockchain at one time, i.e., committed at all nodes of the network, usually measured in transactions per second. Throughput decreases with an increase in the number of shards and input transactions as shown in Fig. 7(a). These results indicate that the proposed scheme achieves its highest throughput with 16 shards, when running with different combinations of transaction rates and number of shards.
- *Throughput per transaction rate.* The results in Fig. 7(b) show that our proposed scheme is capable of handling variable transaction rates as the throughput changes linearly without lagging. It guarantees that there is no backlogging or congestion in the system.

Our idea of prioritised sharding with parallel mining divides the overloaded transactions into shards allowing multiple concurrently maintained sub-chains to record them. In this way, we are able to improve the processing rate of emergency transactions significantly while keeping the whole network less congested. This eventually improves the scalability of the network.

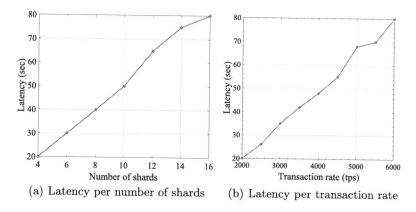

(a) Latency per number of shards   (b) Latency per transaction rate

Fig. 6. Performance analysis in terms of latency.

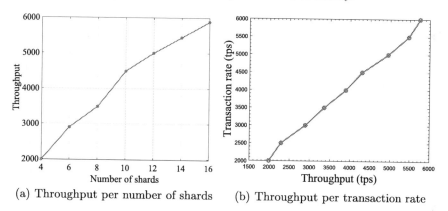

(a) Throughput per number of shards   (b) Throughput per transaction rate

Fig. 7. Performance analysis in terms of throughput.

5   Conclusion and Further Discussion

We propose a framework to streamline the processing of prioritised transactions in a blockchain-based access model. With our method of prioritised sharding, the emergency transactions were divided among smaller shards and mined in parallel. This improved the processing rate of prioritised transactions drastically. Also, the mining congestion got reduced with our proposed P-sharding model as the waiting time for the transaction confirmation time reduces. The QoS improved in our proposed P-sharding algorithm in the context of prioritised transactions as compared to the existing sharded blockchain. In this paper, the performance of a high-level blockchain-based access control model had also been evaluated which provided insights about developing a prioritised, scalable, and efficient decentralised access control framework for healthcare. The simulation results are promising and give valuable insights into our model.

However, in certain ways, the model needs a more in-depth evaluation of how validators come to a decentralised consensus to select the emergency transactions and avoid selfish mining. In real scenario, there exist transactions with varying priorities. Therefore, we should include them with and implement the whole system on a larger scale. Further, to enhance interoperability, it is important to analyse the work on the cross P-shard communication to efficiently share prioritised EMRs across different blockchain-based access control models. Another challenge is how to join these prioritised sharded transactions and dispatch them to the blockchain network in a decentralised manner, which still needs to be deeply explored. We welcome the research community to contribute to alleviate these issues and explore further challenges in this domain.

References

1. Sun, J., Fang, Y.: Cross-domain data sharing in distributed electronic health record systems. IEEE Trans. Parallel Distrib. Syst. **21**(6), 754–764 (2009)
2. Osborn, S., Sandhu, R., Munawer, Q.: Configuring role-based access control to enforce mandatory and discretionary access control policies. ACM Trans. Inf. Syst. Secur. (TISSEC) **3**(2), 85–106 (2000)
3. Hu, V.C., Kuhn, D.R., Ferraiolo, D.F., Voas, J.: Attribute-based access control. Computer **48**(2), 85–88 (2015)
4. Novo, O.: Blockchain meets IoT: an architecture for scalable access management in IoT. IEEE Internet Things J. **5**(2), 1184–1195 (2018)
5. Azaria, A., Ekblaw, A., Vieira, T., Lippman, A.: MedRec: using blockchain for medical data access and permission management. In: 2016 2nd International Conference on Open and Big Data (OBD), pp. 25–30. IEEE (2016)
6. Roehrs, A., da Costa, C.A., da Rosa Righi, R.: OmniPHR: a distributed architecture model to integrate personal health records. J. Biomed. Inform. **71**, 70–81 (2017)
7. Introduction to smart contracts. https://solidity.readthedocs.io/en/v0.5.6/introduction-to-smart-contracts.html/
8. Saini, A., Zhu, Q., Singh, N., Xiang, Y., Gao, L., Zhang, Y.: A smart contract based access control framework for cloud smart healthcare system. IEEE Internet Things J. **8**(7), 5914–5925 (2020)
9. Dinh, T.T.A., Wang, J., Chen, G., Liu, R., Ooi, B.C., Tan, K.-L.: Blockbench: a framework for analyzing private blockchains. In: Proceedings of the 2017 ACM International Conference on Management of Data, pp. 1085–1100. ACM (2017)
10. Pongnumkul, S., Siripanpornchana, C., Thajchayapong, S.: Performance analysis of private blockchain platforms in varying workloads. In: 2017 26th International Conference on Computer Communication and Networks (ICCCN), pp. 1–6. IEEE (2017)
11. Tschorsch, F., Scheuermann, B.: Bitcoin and beyond: a technical survey on decentralized digital currencies. IEEE Commun. Surv. Tutor. **18**(3), 2084–2123 (2016)
12. Decker, C., Wattenhofer, R.: Information propagation in the bitcoin network. In: IEEE P2P 2013 Proceedings, pp. 1–10. IEEE (2013)
13. Nakamoto, S., et al.: Bitcoin: a peer-to-peer electronic cash system (2008)
14. Wood, G.: Ethereum: a secure decentralised generalised transaction ledger. Ethereum project yellow paper, vol. 151, pp. 1–32 (2014)

15. On sharding blockchains. https://github.com/ethereum/wiki/wiki/Sharding-FAQ
16. Dang, H., Dinh, T.T.A., Loghin, D., Chang, E.-C., Lin, Q., Ooi, B.C.: Towards scaling blockchain systems via sharding. In: Proceedings of the 2019 International Conference on Management of Data, pp. 123–140 (2019)
17. Bogner, A., Chanson, M., Meeuw, A.: A decentralised sharing app running a smart contract on the ethereum blockchain. In: Proceedings of the 6th International Conference on the Internet of Things, pp. 177–178 (2016)
18. Saleh, F.: Blockchain without waste: proof-of-stake. Available at SSRN 3183935 (2020)
19. Larimer, D.: Delegated proof-of-stake (DPoS). Bitshare Whitepaper (2014)
20. Xie, J., Yu, F.R., Huang, T., Xie, R., Liu, J., Liu, Y.: A survey on the scalability of blockchain systems. IEEE Network 33(5), 166–173 (2019)
21. Castro, M., Liskov, B.: Practical byzantine fault tolerance and proactive recovery. ACM Trans. Comput. Syst. (TOCS) 20(4), 398–461 (2002)
22. Zhang, Y., Kasahara, S., Shen, Y., Jiang, X., Wan, J.: Smart contract-based access control for the internet of things. IEEE Internet Things J. 6(2), 1594–1605 (2018)
23. Brown, R.G., Carlyle, J., Grigg, I., Hearn, M.: Corda: an introduction. R3 CEV, vol. 1, p. 15, August 2016
24. Androulaki, E., et al.: Hyperledger fabric: a distributed operating system for permissioned blockchains. In: Proceedings of the Thirteenth EuroSys Conference, pp. 1–15 (2018)
25. Goel, S., Singh, A., Garg, R., Verma, M., Jayachandran, P.: Resource fairness and prioritization of transactions in permissioned blockchain systems (industry track). In: Proceedings of the 19th International Middleware Conference Industry, pp. 46–53 (2018)
26. Wood, G.: Polkadot: vision for a heterogeneous multi-chain framework. White Paper (2016)
27. Poon, J., Dryja, T.: The bitcoin lightning network: Scalable off-chain instant payments (2016)
28. Popov, S.: The tangle. White Paper, vol. 1, p. 3 (2018)
29. Churyumov, A.: Byteball: a decentralized system for storage and transfer of value (2016). https://byteball.org/Byteball.pdf
30. Kokoris-Kogias, E., Jovanovic, P., Gasser, L., Gailly, N., Syta, E., Ford, B.: Omniledger: a secure, scale-out, decentralized ledger via sharding. In: 2018 IEEE Symposium on Security and Privacy (SP), pp. 583–598. IEEE (2018)
31. Nguyen, L.N., Nguyen, T.D., Dinh, T.N., Thai, M.T.: Optchain: optimal transactions placement for scalable blockchain sharding. In: 2019 IEEE 39th International Conference on Distributed Computing Systems (ICDCS), pp. 525–535. IEEE (2019)
32. Ren, Z., Cong, K., Aerts, T., de Jonge, B., Morais, A., Erkin, Z.: A scale-out blockchain for value transfer with spontaneous sharding. In: 2018 Crypto Valley Conference on Blockchain Technology (CVCBT), pp. 1–10. IEEE (2018)
33. Kleinrock, L.: Queueing Systems, Volume 2: Computer Applications, vol. 66. Wiley, New York (1976)

BiDKT: Deep Knowledge Tracing with BERT

Weicong Tan[1(✉)], Yuan Jin[1], Ming Liu[2], and He Zhang[3]

[1] Monash University, Victoria, Australia
{weicong.tan,yuan.jin}@monash.edu
[2] Deakin University, Victoria, Australia
m.liu@deakin.edu.au
[3] ZHONGTUKEXIN CO., LTD., Beijing 100020, China
zhanghe@cnpiec.com.cn

Abstract. Deep knowledge Tracing is a family of deep learning models that aim to predict students' future correctness of responses for different subjects (to indicate whether they have mastered the subjects) based on their previous histories of interactions with the subjects. Early deep knowledge tracing models mostly rely on recurrent neural networks (RNNs) that can only learn from a uni-directional context from the response sequences during the model training. An alternative for learning from the context in both directions from those sequences is to use the bidirectional deep learning models. The most recent significant advance in this regard is BERT, a transformer-style bidirectional model, which has outperformed numerous RNN models on several NLP tasks. Therefore, we apply and adapt the BERT model to the deep knowledge tracing task, for which we propose the model **BiDKT**. It is trained under a *masked correctness recovery* task where the model predicts the correctness of a small percentage of randomly masked responses based on their bidirectional context in the sequences. We conducted experiments on several real-world knowledge tracing datasets and show that BiDKT can outperform some of the state-of-the-art approaches on predicting the correctness of future student responses for some of the datasets. We have also discussed the possible reasons why BiDKT has underperformed in certain scenarios. Finally, we study the impacts of several key components of BiDKT on its performance.

Keywords: Educational data mining · Knowledge tracing · BERT

1 Introduction

The Intelligent Tutoring System (ITS) aims to provide students with personalised learning schemes based on their respective proficiency over different teaching concepts/subjects to help them achieve better learning outcomes. Hence, the efficacy of personalisation highly depends on the accurate estimate of students' proficiency. The ITS usually requires the students to become sufficiently knowledgeable about one concept before allowing them to proceed to study the next concept [23].

© ICST Institute for Computer Sciences, Social Informatics and Telecommunications Engineering 2022
Published by Springer Nature Switzerland AG 2022. All Rights Reserved
W. Bao et al. (Eds.): ADHOCNETS 2021/TridentCom 2021, LNICST 428, pp. 260–278, 2022.
https://doi.org/10.1007/978-3-030-98005-4_19

Alternatively, it has also attempted to place the questions/exercises in an optimal ordering such that students with increasing levels of proficiency can tackle them progressively without being discouraged or dropping out from the study [15]. The estimates of the student proficiency can also help the ITS monitor the skill development of the students implicitly and meanwhile, give them explicit feedback on their performance under different skills/subjects on time [2].

A well-known family of approaches that can effectively estimate the student's proficiency is knowledge tracing (KT) [11]. Corbett and Anderson [4] proposed the first knowledge tracing model based on Bayesian statistics and inference, referred to as the Bayesian knowledge tracing (BKT). It estimates the student's proficiency over different teaching concepts based on a student's previous history of performance on interactive exercises [4]. They proposed that if the model could accurately predict students' future behaviours based on their performance history, it can be considered able to capture the students' proficiency on different teaching concepts. They achieved this by modelling the historical performance sequences of each student as a Markov process which tracks the students' learning states on each subject as being either mastered or not mastered. The Markov process is primarily characterised by 1) a transition probability of the subject from being not mastered to mastered, but not vice versa, and 2) conditional probabilities of correctness given different states of the mastery. These two sets of probabilities are estimated using the Bayesian inference method.

After this pioneering work, a plethora of research that aimed to extend the BKT model had been proposed. For example, Pardos and Heffernan have proposed to introduce the difficulty of the questions into the BKT model by conditioning the probabilities of correctness on the specific questions [21]. Yudelson et al. proposed to personalise the two sets of probabilities by making them specific to each student [29]). These extended models have been shown to improve the prediction accuracy on the correctness of responses of the students compared to the original BKT model. However, despite the performance improvements, these traditional knowledge tracing models are developed under the constraints imposed by the Bayesian methods (e.g., the restricted Bayesian update rules on the parameters and the difficulty of being scaled up to handle large and datasets with longer sequences [8]). As a theoretical result, their performance improvements are limited due to the lack of flexibility.

The advent of deep neural networks granted the ITS a competitive alternative for knowledge tracing. In theory, leveraging deep learning techniques for knowledge tracing can 1) avoid the heavy engineering of the input features that are required by many classical models and 2) increase the flexibility and efficacy of the student proficiency and response correctness estimation. The pioneering work of applying deep learning to knowledge tracing is from [22] where a recurrent neural network (RNN) is employed for sequentially predicting the response correctness of each student on the current questions based on their response correctness on the previous questions. In their model, the student proficiency and its transition patterns (e.g. skill mastery transitions) are modelled by the flexible and sophisticated non-linear recurrent layers instead of some statistical models.

The authors reported a substantial gain in performance from this "deep" version of the knowledge tracing, referred to as DKT, compared to BKT models. Following the DKT paradigm, many extensions have been proposed which have focused on using recurrent neural networks for the sequential prediction of the response correctness [16, 19, 22, 28, 30]. Their performance, however, is mostly comparable to that of the original DKT model. This has cast a question to deep learning for knowledge tracing; that is whether the former has the potential to contribute to a further leap in the performance of the latter. In particular, Gervet et al. [8] has found that the DKT model tends to overfit smaller datasets and are less effective than a logistic regression model with hand-crafted features. For larger datasets, DKT tends to perform better than the logistic regression model.

Recently, transformer-style deep learning models start to become prominent and lead the performance in many natural language processing and computer vision tasks. One of the most popular transformer-style models is BERT [5], which leverages stacks of fully connected transformers (as hidden layers) and random masked token prediction (as the objective) for capturing the contextual information of each input token. Unlike the RNN models which endeavour to capture sequential contexts during the training, BERT focuses on the bidirectional contexts which tend to convey more information about each input token than the sequential ones. BERT has had many extensions [18, 24, 27]. Nonetheless, it remains to be the most popular and effective deep learning model whose potential has never been fully exploited in the knowledge tracing domain.

Therefore, in this paper, we strive for filling this research gap by adapting BERT to the domain of knowledge tracing. To achieve this, we seek to answer the following research questions:

- **RQ1**: How can BERT be adapted to 1) take in the knowledge tracing sequential data, which consists of the (correctness of) students' responses, the responded questions and subjects, and 2) perform random masking on the input data, which needs to be specialised for knowledge tracing?
- **RQ2**: How does BERT perform compared to the state-of-the-art DKT models and the classical BKT and logistic regression models in terms of the prediction accuracy on the response correctness?
- **RQ3** Under what conditions does BERT yield better or worse prediction performance, possibly compared with the aforementioned competing models?

Therefore, in this paper, we first reviewed the research that had been done in the knowledge tracing domain especially in how recent new deep learning techniques have been applied to the deep knowledge tracing model to improve model performance. We then proceeded to introduce our proposed deep knowledge tracing with BERT. We introduced how we constructed our model layer by layer and the training and testing strategies for our model. We also introduced a plethora of experiments we conducted to evaluate the performance of our proposed model and discussed in what circumstance our model would perform better and how the changes of some of the important parameters of the model could affect the performance of the model. Finally, we concluded the result of our research and discussed how some of the improvement and future work could be done to the research and the deep knowledge tracing domain.

2   Related Work

2.1   Bayesian Knowledge Tracing and Extensions

Corbett and Anderson [4] proposed the Bayesian Knowledge Tracing model (i.e., BKT), which attempts to capture the knowledge states of students in an ITS. It has the following modelling assumptions:

- The knowledge state is binary for a subject, either "mastered" or "non-mastered", and the state can only change in one direction: from "non-mastered" to "mastered".
- The correctness of response is conditioned on the student's knowledge state on the corresponding subject (as a conditional probability table).

The knowledge tracing is then modelled by BKT as a Markov process. As a student responds to a sequence of questions, each belonging to a subject, BKT maintains the estimated probability that each subject is in the "mastered" state; when the student answers a question, this probability will be updated simultaneously.

Based on the BKT model, there has been further research on proposing extended models or studying the properties and limitations of BKT. Pardos and Hefferman [21] proposed to introduce difficulty (level) variables to different questions. Yudelson et al. proposed to have the probabilities of the knowledge state $P(L_t)$ and the mastery transition $P(T)$ specific to each student [29].

Khajah et al. [13] have studied the limitations of the classical BKT model. They found that the performance of BKT heavily rely on whether the Markov process modelling assumptions satisfy the particular scenario to which BKT is applied. Furthermore, they pointed out that due to the modelling limitations, BKT has failed to fully exploit the recency effects where a student who has (constantly) underperformed in recent timestamps tends to underperform in the current one. Correspondingly, Galyardt and Goldin [7] have shown that integrating features of recent history into their logistic regression model can improve its predictive performance on response correctness. BKT has also failed to capture the effects of the ordering patterns (e.g. interleaved ordering) of the subjects on the response correctness. Moreover, It ignores the inter-subject similarity and its effects on the response correctness; students are more likely to master more similar subjects altogether by practising on questions under these subjects [13].

2.2   Deep Knowledge Tracing and Its Extensions

To address the problems that BKT had, Piech et al. [22] proposed to apply recurrent neural networks (RNNs) [10] to exploit more of the complex characteristics of the sequential student-question interactions in knowledge tracing. They further employed a specialised case of RNN, long-short-term memory (LSTM) networks [12], which is more capable of capturing the long-term non-linear interactions in the sequences.

Ever since the proposal of the DKT model, many extensions with more deep learning capabilities and modelling of more characteristics of knowledge tracing have been proposed. Cheung and Yang [3] proposed to incorporate heterogeneous features, such as the number of hints used and the number of attempts, into the DKT model. They used the classification and regression tree (CART) to predict whether a student will answer a question correctly based on the heterogeneous features. This prediction will be concatenated with the ground-truth value of the response correctness and the result will be encoded into a four-digit one-hot vector. This vector will then be concatenated with the original one-hot vector of the pairwise input as the new input of the model. This model has been shown to have higher AUCs compared to the DKT model.

Minn et al. [19] proposed to incorporate the dynamic clustering of students into the DKT model. They achieved this by segmenting the sequences of students' responses into multiple equal-width intervals. The model will dynamically group the students based on their estimated proficiency in different subjects using the K-means clustering for each interval. The inputs of their proposed model then include the resulting group IDs, the subject IDs, and the responses' correctness. It has been shown to achieve higher AUCs than the DKT and BKT models. This paper has also investigated the impacts of the different number of clusters and the width of time intervals on the model performance.

More recently, the self-attention mechanism has attracted attention from the deep knowledge tracing domain. Pandey and Karypis proposed the first deep knowledge tracing that applied the self-attention mechanism [20]. Ghosh et al. proposed an attentive deep knowledge tracing model that applied monotonous self-attention in the encoder from Transformer to minimise the effect of unrelated subjects and interaction distant, in terms of time, from the position required to be predicted [9].

2.3   Transformer and BERT

A major problem of the RNN is that it performs sequential prediction, which hinders the parallelisation of its training and prediction. To address this issue, Vaswani et al. [26] proposed the transformer model which completely relies on the self-attention mechanism for the sequential prediction. A transformer inherits the classical encoder-decoder architecture. Both the encoder and decoder comprise a stack of composites of a multi-head self-attention component followed by a feed-forward network. In the encoder component, each input element will be used as a query for the self-attention in which the embedding of each of them is attended to the embeddings of all the others to obtain their final latent representations, which will be used in the decoder. To handle the problem that there is no convolution and recurrence in the transformer, a positional embedding specific to each input element is added/concatenated to their embeddings. The Transformer model has outperformed many state-of-the-art sequential sequence-to-sequence deep learning models at the time in several NLP tasks. More importantly, it has provided the foundation for many powerful state-of-the-art bidirectional deep learning models to date.

BERT [5] is one of the most successful bidirectional deep learning models based on the transformer encoder. It comprises the stack of composites of the multi-head self-attention component and the feed-forward network from the encoder part of the transformer model. The output from each layer of the composite serves as the input to the composite at the next layer. Another key feature of BERT is that it is trained to recover a small percentage of randomly masked input elements from the sequences. This training phase of BERT is known as the pre-training, which aims to learn coherent and meaningful latent representations for the data.

3 Proposed Model Architecture

3.1 Problem Formulation

The knowledge tracing problem can be formulated as a sequential prediction problem: given a sequence of a student's interactions $x_1, \ldots, x_T$, a DKT model needs to predict the result of the next interaction x_{T+1}, which is the correctness of the $(T + 1)$-th response. In this case, the t-th interaction is denoted as $x_t = (q_t, a_t)$ where $1 \leq t \leq T$. Here, q_t refers to the t-th subject the student was practising on, and $a_t \in \{0, 1\}$ is the correctness of the student's response to the question under the t-th subject with the value 1 standing for being correct [22].

A straightforward architecture for DKT is based on the RNN-type neural networks which model uni-directional sequential contexts and are trained to use the results of all the previous interactions to predict the result of the current interaction. However, we believe that modelling uni-directional sequential contexts is not sufficient for learning the complex dynamic patterns underlying the sequences of interaction results between the students and the subjects. Instead, we should model the bidirectional contexts surrounding each interaction to let the model better figure out what patterns underlying the preceding (or subsequent) interactions might have contributed to the current interaction result (Fig. 1).

Therefore, we propose to apply and adapt BERT, a transformer-style bidirectional deep learning model, to knowledge tracing. we name the adapted BERT model **BiDKT**. Unlike the current DKT models and the self-attentive knowledge tracing model [20] which are uni-directional and thus only make use of the preceding sequence $x_1, \ldots, x_t$ while predicting a_{t+1}, BiDKT also leverages the subsequent sequence from x_{t+2} to x_T to predict a_{t+1}. In the following sections, we will further introduce the key components of the BiDKT model.

3.2 Input and Embedding Layer

The input layer of BiDKT takes in each interaction in the sequences specific to each student, which consists of two tokens: the correctness token (i.e., a_t) and

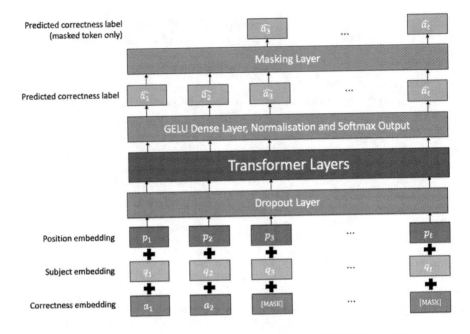

Fig. 1. The network architecture of our proposed BiDKT model.

the subject token (i.e., q_t). BiDKT inherits the transformer architecture which naturally ignores the position information of each interaction in the sequences. However, such information can be useful for revealing the knowledge states of the students. For example, students' earlier responses in their respective sequences are more likely to be erroneous, while their later responses are less likely to be so. Therefore, it is reasonable for the input layer of BiDKT to incorporate the positional information of each interaction. Therefore, the final embedding for the t-th interaction x_t is equal to the element-wise summation of three corresponding embeddings: the subject embedding q_t, correctness embedding a_t and the position embedding p_t. Mathematically, this can be formulated as:

$$x_t = a_t \bigoplus q_t \bigoplus p_t \tag{1}$$

In the following sections, we use X to denote the input matrix for BiDKT where:

$$X = \begin{bmatrix} x_1 \\ x_2 \\ \vdots \\ x_T \end{bmatrix} \tag{2}$$

However, the introduction of the position embedding can limit the length of the sequence for the input layer [25]. When the sequence length exceeds the maximum length allowed by the model, it needs to be split into shorter sequences to fit it into the model [9,25]. More precisely, we denote N as the maximum length of the sequence input for BiDKT, for a sequence with the length $T > N$, we will split it into $\lceil T/N \rceil$ sequences. After the embedding layer, we apply a dropout layer to the output embeddings of each interaction to prevent the overfitting problem before feeding them to the core transformer layers.

3.3   Transformer Layers

The transformer layers of BiDKT are stacks of fully connected composites of two neural network modules: a multi-head self-attention module and a position-wise fully connected feed-forward neural network [26]. The first module is responsible for aggregating the contextual information towards each interaction from the other interactions in the same sequences. The second module takes in the aggregated information and transforms it non-linearly for the inputs of the next layer. We will elaborate on the details of both the modules in the following sections.

Multi-head Self-attention Layer. Self-attention [26] is a mechanism that can compute the embedding for each position in a sequence by relating the embeddings at all the other positions in the same sequence. More specifically, a multi-head attention mechanism with H heads refers to applying the self-attention mechanism to H consecutive chunks of the sequence separately with different sets of trainable parameters, which had been found beneficial to the performance of the model [26]. More specifically, each "head" is responsible for projecting the embeddings of the input matrix $\boldsymbol{X} \in \mathbb{R}^{T \times M}$ into a query matrix $\boldsymbol{Q} \in \mathbb{R}^{T \times M'}$, a key matrix $\boldsymbol{K} \in \mathbb{R}^{T \times M'}$ and a value matrix $\boldsymbol{V} \in \mathbb{R}^{T \times M'}$ respectively via the dot product with the corresponding trainable projection matrix, including $\boldsymbol{W_Q} \in \mathbb{R}^{M \times M'}$, $\boldsymbol{W_K} \in \mathbb{R}^{M \times M'}$ and $\boldsymbol{W_v} \in \mathbb{R}^{M \times M'}$, as follows:

$$\boldsymbol{Q} = \boldsymbol{X} \boldsymbol{W_Q}$$
$$\boldsymbol{K} = \boldsymbol{X} \boldsymbol{W_K} \tag{3}$$
$$\boldsymbol{V} = \boldsymbol{X} \boldsymbol{W_V}$$

In this case, the intermediate dimension for each head $M' = \frac{M}{H}$. For the i-th self-attention head where $1 \leq i \leq H$, its calculation can be formulated as follows:

$$\boldsymbol{A}_i = \mathrm{Attention}(\boldsymbol{Q}, \boldsymbol{K}, \boldsymbol{V})$$
$$= \mathrm{Softmax}(\frac{\boldsymbol{Q}\boldsymbol{K}^T}{\sqrt{M}})\boldsymbol{V} \tag{4}$$

where the result $\boldsymbol{A}_i \in \mathbb{R}^{T \times M'}$. Afterwards, all the attention results across the H heads will be concatenated in the output layer of the multi-head self-attention module as follows:

$$\boldsymbol{Z} = \mathrm{Concat}(\boldsymbol{A}_1, \boldsymbol{A}_2, \dots, \boldsymbol{A}_H)\boldsymbol{W_O} \tag{5}$$

where $\boldsymbol{W_O} \in \mathbb{R}^{M \times M}$ is a weight matrix for computing the final output embeddings $\boldsymbol{Z} \in \mathbb{R}^{T \times M}$ from the multi-head attention module. This module allows BiDKT to capture the bidirectional information from all the positions in each sequence during the training. Moreover, the attention computation of each head can be parallelised, which can reduce the computational complexity of the model.

Feed-Forward Neural Network (FNN) Layer. We then feed the output of the multi-head self-attention module to a position-wise fully-connected feed-forward neural network, which can be formulated as follows:

$$\text{FNN}(\boldsymbol{Z}) = \text{Max}(0, \boldsymbol{Z}\boldsymbol{\Phi}_1 + \boldsymbol{b}_1)\boldsymbol{\Phi}_2 + \boldsymbol{b}_2 \tag{6}$$

where $\boldsymbol{\Phi}_1 \in \mathbb{R}^{M \times L}$ and $\boldsymbol{\Phi}_2 \in \mathbb{R}^{L \times M}$ are the trainable weight matrices for the hidden and output layers of the FNN module, while $\boldsymbol{b}_1 \in \mathbb{R}^L$ and $\boldsymbol{b}_2 \in \mathbb{R}^M$ are the bias vectors for the two layers respectively. Notice that we set the above trainable weight matrices and bias vectors to be specific to each layer of the transformer component.

3.4   Output Layers

The output module of BiDKT starts with a dense layer with GELU (i.e. Gaussian Error Linear Unit) activation function. It is followed by a normalisation layer, whose result is passed onto the softmax function to obtain the predicted probability of response correctness corresponding to each interaction in the sequences. The output embeddings from the activated dense layer have a dimension of 4, where the indices 0 and 1 are reserved tokens respectively for the padding and the masked tokens, the index 2 represents the incorrect response, and index 3 represents the correct response. Finally, the softmax probability outputs for each interaction in the sequences will be multiplied element-wise with a binary masking layer. Its positions corresponding to the masked interactions are set to be 1 and the observed interactions are set to be 0, so that only the predictions for the "to-be-recovered" interactions will be considered in the calculation of the loss. In this case, BiDKT aims to minimise a sparse categorical cross-entropy between the correctness of the target (i.e. to-be-recovered) interactions and the corresponding softmax probability outputs.

3.5   Model Training and Testing

Training. Previous DKT models are primarily based on RNNs. Therefore, their training strategy focuses on predicting one interaction ahead. More specifically, with a sequential inputs $x_1, \ldots, x_t, 1 \leq t \leq T$ for the training, the corresponding outputs are $a_2, \ldots, a_{t+1}$ [22]. As for BiDKT, the ground-truth interactions will be masked at the input layer so that the corresponding predictions in the output layer will not be able to "see" the ground-truths but rather infer them using the surrounding bidirectional information from the sequences. Therefore, a straightforward training strategy for BiDKT is to simply predict the masked interactions at the current timestamps (rather than the ones ahead) based on the corresponding [MASK] tokens in the input layer.

More specifically, during the training, we will randomly substitute a small percentage of the correctness tokens with a [MASK] token, while the corresponding subject tokens are intact and input into BiDKT as they are. As an example, given an interaction sequence with the length of 4, i.e. $(q_1, a_1) \rightarrow (q_2, a_2) \rightarrow (q_3, a_3) \rightarrow (q_4, a_4)$, for the training, its corresponding random masked sequence to be input to the model will be in the form of $(q_1, a_1) \rightarrow (q_2, [MASK]) \rightarrow (q_3, a_3) \rightarrow (q_4, [MASK])$.

Testing. For testing, we adopted a method similar to the one in [25]. More specifically, for any sequence in the test data with the length being T', we generate T' sequences from it. Take a sequence with the length of 4 as an example. We will generate the following four sequences:

- Sequence 1: $(q_1, [MASK])$
- Sequence 2: $(q_1, a_1) \rightarrow (q_2, [MASK])$
- Sequence 3: $(q_1, a_1) \rightarrow (q_2, a_2) \rightarrow (q_3, [MASK])$
- Sequence 4: $(q_1, a_1) \rightarrow (q_2, a_2) \rightarrow (q_3, a_4) \rightarrow (q_4, [MASK])$.

In each of the above sequences, we mask only the correctness token in the last position for the model to predict, given all the previous interactions and the subject token at the current interaction.

It is worth noticing that the training and testing strategies of our model have some inconsistency in that the former one aims to predict the tokens masked at arbitrary positions in the sequences while the latter aims to predict the tokens masked at the last positions. Such inconsistency could possibly affect the performance of BiDKT adversely.

To address the above issue, during the training, we randomly sample a certain percentage of the sequences and only have their correctness tokens masked at the last positions. In other words, their masking strategy is now the same as that used for the test data. This method can be viewed as a fine-tuning step for BiDKT and can potentially improve the performance of the model.

4 Experiments

In this section, we evaluate the efficacy of our proposed model by comparing it with several state-of-the-art BKT and DKT models across 8 real-world datasets. The datasets are provided by Ghosh et al. (2020)[1] and Gervet et al. (2020)[2].

---

[1] https://github.com/arghosh/AKT/tree/master/data.
[2] https://github.com/theophilee/learner-performance-prediction.

4.1   Datasets

The details of these datasets are listed as follows:

- **The ASSISTment dataset in 2009, 2012, 2015, 2019.** The ASSISTment (**ASSIST**ing and assess**ment**) datasets are collected from a system utilised in the United States of America for high school mathematics classes. Each record in the dataset comprises the student's mastery status on the concept, timestamp of the response, the teaching concept associated with the question, etc. [6]. ASSISTment 2009 has been chosen to be the benchmark dataset for knowledge tracing problem in the past decade.
- **Statics 2012.** It is a dataset of the log data of ITS for a college-level engineering subject [14].
- **Algebra 2005 and Bridge to Algebra 2006.** These datasets are originally for KDD Cup 2010, a competition of data mining. The task of the competition was to predict students' correctness on mathematical exercises by learning from their log data from the Intelligent Tutoring Systems[3]. Each record comprises the hierarchy of curriculum levels containing the exercise, the identified concepts that are used in an exercise (where available), whether the student answered it right at the first go, etc.
- **Spanish.** It is a set of log data of high school students learning Spanish on an ITS [8,17]

Tables 1 and 2 summarise the key statistics of these datasets.

Table 1. Details of the data provided by Gervet et al. (2020); The average sequence length is abbreviated in the last row of the table.

	Statics	Assist09	Assist12	Assist15	Assist17	Spanish	Bridge06	Algebra05
Size	189,297	278,336	2,682,211	656,154	934,368	578,726	1,817,393	606,983
# of students	282	3,114	22,589	14,228	1,708	182	1,130	567
# of subjects	1,223	149	265	100	411	221	550	271
Avg_seq_len	636	32	59	31	440	2,924	1,373	581

Table 2. Information of the data provided by Ghosh et al. (2020); The average sequence length is abbreviated in the last row of the table.

	Statics	Assist09	Assist15	Assist17
Size	189,297	325,637	683,801	942,816
# of students	333	4,151	19,840	1,709
# of subjects	1,223	110	100	102
Avg seq len	568	78	34	551

---

[3] https://pslcdatashop.web.cmu.edu/KDDCup/rules.jsp.

4.2 Baselines and Metrics

The area under the receiver operating characteristic curve (AUC) has been widely used as the benchmark score for the comparison of model performance. Therefore, we used AUC as the performance score and compared the performance of our model with the results from Ghosh et al. (2020) and Gervet et al. (2020) by respectively testing our model on the pre-processed data they provided [8,9]. They also respectively re-implemented a plethora of baseline models by themselves. More specifically, the context-aware knowledge tracing model in Ghosh et al. (2020) was the state of the art [9]; and Gervet et al. conducted comprehensive experiments over different existing models and datasets [8]. We listed the datasets they provided and their chosen baselines in Table 3. Non-KT baseline models (e.g., models based on Item-Response Theory and Performance Factor Analysis) evaluated in Gervet et al. (2020) will not be listed, but we kept their proposed logistic regression model and compared it with our model in the experiments.

Table 3. Details and baseline models in Ghosh et al. (2020) and Gervet et al. (2020). Non-KT baseline models are not listed.

	Ghosh et al. (2020)	Gervet et al. (2020)
Dataset	ASSISTment 2009, 2015, 2017 and Statics 2012	ASSISTment 2009, 2015, 2012, 2017, Statics 2012, Bridge to Algebra 2006, Algebra 2005 and Spanish
Baseline models	BKT+ [29], DKT [22], DKT+ [28], SAKT [20], DKVMN [30]	BKT [4], BKT+ [29], DKT [22], SAKT [20]

4.3 Experiment Settings

As mentioned in Sect. 3.5, if a sequence is longer than a certain length, we will split it into several smaller sequences to fit in our model. To conduct 5-fold cross-validation, we have split each dataset into three parts: 60% of the data to be used as the training set, 20% to be used as the validation set for optimizing the hyper-parameters and for performing the early stopping, and the remaining 20% to be used as the test set to evaluate the competing models.

We have implemented BiDKT with Keras[4], and the structure of its transformer layers was adapted from Keras-BERT[5]. Adam optimiser was used for training the BiDKT model [1]. The implementations of all the baseline models are provided by Gervet et al. [8] and Ghosh et al. [9]. All the experiments are

---

[4] https://github.com/keras-team/keras.
[5] https://github.com/CyberZHG/keras-bert.

conducted on an NVIDIA V100 GPU with 16 GB memory on the M3 cluster (a high-performance computing cluster maintained by Monash University)[6].

We conducted a grid search across the hyper-parameter candidate sets specified in Table 4 to find the best one that can optimise the average model performance over the 5 validation folds of each dataset. We found the following best hyper-parameter set with 16 as the batch size, 200 as the maximum sequence length, 0.1 as the dropout rate, 1 as the number of self-attention heads, 2 as the number of transformer layers, 16 as the embedding dimension, 64 as the number of hidden neurons for the feed-forward networks, 0.15 as the masking rate (i.e. the probability of a correctness token being substituted by a [MASK] token) and 0.25 as the fine-tuning rate (i.e. the probability of a sequence only being masked at the last position in a training batch). In the later section, we will have a more detailed discussion about how the masking rate and fine-tuning rate will affect the model performance.

Table 4. Hyperparameters experimented

Hyperparameter	Values experimented
Batch size	8, 16, 24, 32, 64
Maximum sequence length	100, 200, 300
Dropout rate	0.1, 0.25, 0.5
Learning rate	1e−6, 5e−6, 1e−5, 5e−5, 1e−4
Number of self-attention heads	1, 2, 4, 8, 12, 16
Number of Transformer layer	1, 2, 4, 8, 12
Embedding dimension	16, 24, 64, 128, 192, 256
Hidden dimension	64, 96, 256, 512, 768, 1024
Mask rate	0.1, 0.50.2, 0.25, 0.3, 0.4, 0.5, 0.6, 0.7, 0.8, 0.9
Fine-tune rate	0.1, 0.50.2, 0.25, 0.3, 0.4, 0.5, 0.6, 0.7, 0.8, 0.9

4.4 Results and Discussion

In this section, we present the results of the competing models across the different datasets in Table 5 and 6. Ghosh et al. (2020) reported two AKT models similar in the core layers but applied different encoding mechanisms for the input (i.e. one with Rasch encoding and one without) [9]. On the ASSISTment 2009 and 2017 datasets, to which the Rasch encoding can be applied, the AKT model with such encoding had achieved better performance than the one without. Therefore, we only reported the results with the Rasch encoding on these two datasets.

It can be observed from Table 5 that BiDKT has outperformed the BKT model on the Statics 2012, the Algebra 2005 and the Spanish datasets. It has also outperformed DKT and SAKT on the Spanish dataset. It is also interesting

---

[6] https://www.massive.org.au/about/.

Table 5. Performance (AUC) comparison of BiDKT and the experiment result from Gervet et al. (2020). NA refers that the data is not provided or the experiment had not been conducted in the original paper. "LR" stands for "logistic regression".

Dataset	BKT	BKT+	LR	DKT	SAKT	BiDKT
Statics 2012	0.73	0.811	0.819	0.829	0.813	0.772
ASSISTment 2009	0.63	0.759	0.772	0.757	0.756	0.700
ASSISTment 2012	NA	NA	0.751	0.771	0.732	0.689
ASSISTment 2015	NA	0.701	0.702	0.731	0.730	0.674
ASSISTment 2017	NA	0.710	0.714	0.770	0.722	0.632
Bridge to Algebra 2006	NA	NA	0.803	0.790	0.784	0.763
Algebra 2005	0.62	NA	0.83	0.821	0.801	0.777
Spanish	0.83	0.851	0.863	0.832	0.831	0.835

Table 6. Performance (AUC) comparison of BiDKT and the experiment result from Ghosh et al. (2020). NA refers to that the result is not reported in the original paper

Dataset	BKT+	DKT	DKT+	DKVMN	SAKT	AKT	BiDKT
Statics 2012	0.75	0.8233	0.8301	0.8195	0.8029	0.8265	0.7785
ASSISTment 2009	0.69	0.817	0.8024	0.8093	0.752	0.8346	0.7651
ASSISTment 2015	NA	0.731	0.7313	0.7276	0.7212	0.7828	0.6766
ASSISTment 2017	NA	0.7263	0.7124	0.7073	0.6569	0.7702	0.5978

to see that BiDKT has outperformed SAKT on the ASSISTment 2009 dataset provided by Ghosh et al. (2020) but not on the same dataset provided by Gervet et al. (2020) (Table 6).

On the other datasets from the two sources, we can see that there is a notable performance gap between BiDKT and some of the state-of-the-art DKT models (e.g. AKT and SAKT). However, it is also worth noticing that in the original paper of SAKT [20], the authors reported an AUC of 0.848 on the ASSIST-ment 2009 dataset and 0.857 on the ASSISTment 2015 dataset. In comparison, both Ghosh et al. (2020) and Gervet et al. (2020) cannot reproduce the original performance.

Despite the performance gap on some of the datasets, we believe that BiDKT still bears the potential to further improve its performance. BERT has demonstrated its efficacy in the sequential recommendation, a similar domain to knowledge tracing [25]. The only difference is that the datasets used in this case contain hundreds of millions of responses and millions of users and items, which are much larger than popular knowledge tracing benchmark datasets. Both Gervet et al. (2020) and Ghosh et al. (2020) have pointed out that self-attentive models might require a large amount of data to be trained properly [8,9]. In comparison, the datasets used in our experiments are relatively small.

Furthermore, we hypothesise that the gap performance exists because the students' future performance is only dictated by their performance in the recent past but not by any longer one. Another possible reason is that the dynamic patterns underlying the interaction sequences are not sufficiently complex for our model to fully exploit to allow it to outperform simpler models.

4.5   The Impact of Masking Rate

The mask rate refers to the probability of whether a correctness token will be substituted by a [MASK] token. The mask rate will decide how many tokens in a training sequence the model should predict. On one hand, if it were too large, it would impose extra difficulty for the model to capture the pattern of the sequence; on the other hand, if it were too small, the robustness of the model would be impaired [25]. In this experiment, we kept fine-tune rate at 0.25 and changed the value of the mask rate to investigate how it affects the performance of the model.

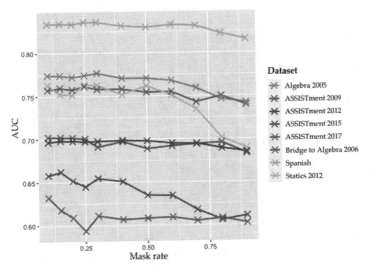

Fig. 2. The performance (AUC) of BiDKT with different masking rates across the different datasets.

As we can tell from Fig. 2, generally, the performance of BiDKT does not monotonously grow or decline within the domain of [0.1, 0.9], which can lead us to the same conclusion that the change of mask rate does not always result in performance improvement or decline, as per [25]. When the mask rate is larger than 0.3, generally speaking, the performance of BiDKT declines when the mask rate continues to grow.

4.6 The Impact of Fine-Tuning Rate

The fine-tune rate refers to the probability in which a sequence will have the correctness token masked only in the last position. Similar to the mask rate, we conjectured that it can either be too small or too large. On one hand, if it were too small, the discrepancy between the training task and the testing task would be large; on the other hand, if it were too large, we cannot fully leverage the power of BERT to capture the learning characteristics of the students by predicting correctness tokens from their upstream and downstream context.

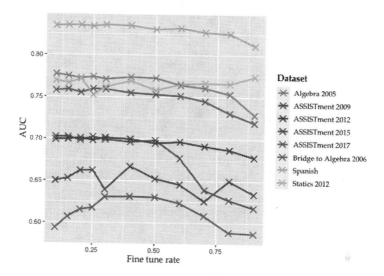

Fig. 3. The performance of BiDKT with different fine-tuning rates across the different datasets.

As we can tell from Fig. 3, when we changed the fine-tune rate from 0.1 to 0.9, the performance of the model did not monotonously grow or decline. This proved our aforementioned hypothesis.

4.7 Limitations of Our Study

Due to the time and resource limitation of this paper, we can only improve and evaluate our work within a certain scope. One of the limitations of this paper is that we did not investigate the root cause of the performance gap. We only empirically analysed why the gap exists. Another limitation of our research is that the granularity of the grid search for optimal hyperparameters was very high.

5   Conclusion and Future Work

In this paper, we proposed BiDKT, a deep knowledge tracing model based on BERT. We introduced the structure of BiDKT in details and how we implemented the model. We conducted a series of experiments to evaluate the overall performance of our model and analyse how some of the important parameters affect the performance of the model. Our model outperformed some of the current deep knowledge tracing models in certain scenarios. To our knowledge, even though a plethora of extensive BERT models have been proposed and have shown excellent performance in their respective settings, most of them are still models for natural language processing tasks. Our work extended the usage of the BERT model to the knowledge tracing domain, and more broadly, the non-NLP sequential prediction domain.

There are many possibilities for future research in the deep knowledge tracing domain. Currently, many DKT models have tried to incorporate more features of a student's response (e.g. the text of the exercise as side information [19]) or a more sophisticated method to encode the input (e.g. the Rasch encoding) [9]) We consider these research directions probable to be integrated with BERT models for higher performance. Another possible research direction could be training and testing the model on the EdNet dataset, which is larger in size and has a larger number of students but has not been widely used as a benchmark dataset.

References

1. Ba, J.L., Kiros, J.R., Hinton, G.E.: Layer normalization. arXiv preprint: arXiv:1607.06450 (2016)
2. Bull, S., Kay, J.: Open learner models. In: Nkambou, R., Bourdeau, J., Mizoguchi, R. (eds.) Advances in Intelligent Tutoring Systems. Studies in Computational Intelligence, vol. 308, pp. 301–322. Springer, Heidelberg (2010). https://doi.org/10.1007/978-3-642-14363-2_15
3. Cheung, L.P., Yang, H.: Heterogeneous features integration in deep knowledge tracing. In: Liu, D., Xie, S., Li, Y., Zhao, D., El-Alfy, E.S. (eds) Neural Information Processing. ICONIP 2017. Lecture Notes in Computer Science, vol. 10635, pp. 653–662. Springer, Cham (2017). https://doi.org/10.1007/978-3-319-70096-0_67
4. Corbett, A.T., Anderson, J.R.: Knowledge tracing: modeling the acquisition of procedural knowledge. User Model. User-Adapt. Interact. 4(4), 253–278 (1994)
5. Devlin, J., Chang, M.W., Lee, K., Toutanova, K.: Bert: Pre-training of deep bidirectional transformers for language understanding. arXiv preprint: arXiv:1810.04805 (2018)
6. Feng, M., Heffernan, N., Koedinger, K.: Addressing the assessment challenge with an online system that tutors as it assesses. User Model. User-Adapt. Interact. 19(3), 243–266 (2009)
7. Galyardt, A., Goldin, I.: Move your lamp post: recent data reflects learner knowledge better than older data. J. Educ. Data Mining 7(2), 83–108 (2015)
8. Gervet, T., et al.: When is deep learning the best approach to knowledge tracing? JEDM—. J. Educ. Data Mining 12(3), 31–54 (2020)

9. Ghosh, A., Heffernan, N., Lan, A.S.: Context-aware attentive knowledge tracing. In: Proceedings of the 26th ACM SIGKDD International Conference on Knowledge Discovery and Data Mining, pp. 2330–2339 (2020)
10. Goodfellow, I., Bengio, Y., Courville, A.: Deep Learning. MIT Press, Cambridge (2016)
11. Hernández-Blanco, A., Herrera-Flores, B., Tomás, D., Navarro-Colorado, B.: A systematic review of deep learning approaches to educational data mining. Complexity **2019**, 1–22 (2019)
12. Hochreiter, S., Schmidhuber, J.: Long short-term memory. Neural Comput. **9**(8), 1735–1780 (1997)
13. Khajah, M., Lindsey, R.V., Mozer, M.C.: How deep is knowledge tracing? arXiv preprint: arXiv:1604.02416 (2016)
14. Koedinger, K.R., Baker, R.S., Cunningham, K., Skogsholm, A., Leber, B., Stamper, J.: A data repository for the EDM community: The PSLC datashop. Handbook Educ. Data Mining **43**, 43–56 (2010)
15. Koedinger, K.R., Brunskill, E., Baker, R.S., McLaughlin, E.A., Stamper, J.: New potentials for data-driven intelligent tutoring system development and optimization. AI Mag. **34**(3), 27–41 (2013)
16. Lee, J., Yeung, D.Y.: Knowledge query network for knowledge tracing: how knowledge interacts with skills. In: Proceedings of the 9th International Conference on Learning Analytics and Knowledge, pp. 491–500 (2019)
17. Lindsey, R.V., Khajah, M., Mozer, M.C.: Automatic discovery of cognitive skills to improve the prediction of student learning. In: Advances in Neural Information Processing Systems, pp. 1386–1394 (2014)
18. Liu, Y., et al.: Roberta: a robustly optimized BERT pretraining approach. arXiv preprint: arXiv:1907.11692 (2019)
19. Minn, S., Yu, Y., Desmarais, M.C., Zhu, F., Vie, J.J.: Deep knowledge tracing and dynamic student classification for knowledge tracing. In: 2018 IEEE International Conference on Data Mining (ICDM), pp. 1182–1187. IEEE (2018)
20. Pandey, S., Karypis, G.: A self-attentive model for knowledge tracing. arXiv preprint: arXiv:1907.06837 (2019)
21. Pardos, Z.A., Heffernan, N.T.: KT-IDEM: introducing item difficulty to the knowledge tracing model. In: Konstan, J.A., Conejo, R., Marzo, J.L., Oliver, N. (eds.) UMAP 2011. LNCS, vol. 6787, pp. 243–254. Springer, Heidelberg (2011). https://doi.org/10.1007/978-3-642-22362-4_21
22. Piech, C., et al.: Deep knowledge tracing. In: Advances in Neural Information Processing Systems, pp. 505–513 (2015)
23. Ritter, S., Yudelson, M., Fancsali, S.E., Berman, S.R.: How mastery learning works at scale. In: Proceedings of the Third (2016) ACM Conference on Learning@ Scale, pp. 71–79 (2016)
24. Sanh, V., Debut, L., Chaumond, J., Wolf, T.: DistilBERT, a distilled version of BERT: smaller, faster, cheaper and lighter. In: The 5th Workshop on Energy Efficient Machine Learning and Cognitive Computing (EMC2) co-located with NeurIPS 2019 (2019)
25. Sun, F., et al.: BERT4Rec: sequential recommendation with bidirectional encoder representations from transformer. In: Proceedings of the 28th ACM International Conference on Information and Knowledge Management, pp. 1441–1450 (2019)
26. Vaswani, A., et al.: Attention is all you need. In: Advances in Neural Information Processing Systems, pp. 5998–6008 (2017)

27. Yang, Z., Dai, Z., Yang, Y., Carbonell, J., Salakhutdinov, R.R., Le, Q.V.: XLNet: generalized autoregressive pretraining for language understanding. In: Advances In Neural Information Processing Systems, pp. 5754–5764 (2019)
28. Yeung, C.K., Yeung, D.Y.: Addressing two problems in deep knowledge tracing via prediction-consistent regularization. In: Proceedings of the Fifth Annual ACM Conference on Learning at Scale, pp. 1–10 (2018)
29. Yudelson, M.V., Koedinger, K.R., Gordon, G.J.: Individualized Bayesian knowledge tracing models. In: Lane, H.C., Yacef, K., Mostow, J., Pavlik, P. (eds.) AIED 2013. LNCS (LNAI), vol. 7926, pp. 171–180. Springer, Heidelberg (2013). https://doi.org/10.1007/978-3-642-39112-5_18
30. Zhang, J., Shi, X., King, I., Yeung, D.Y.: Dynamic key-value memory networks for knowledge tracing. In: Proceedings of the 26th International Conference on World Wide Web, pp. 765–774 (2017)

Vision - An Innovative Management System Based on Private DLT

Thien Pham(✉), Alessio Bonti, Xuemei Jiang, and Manas Palaparthi

Deakin University, Burwood, VIC 3125, Australia
{jason.pham,a.bonti,jiangx,m.palaparthi}@deakin.edu.au

Abstract. Education is a crucial aspect of most nations. It is the backbone of society, but many regulations and multiple actors make it a complex bureaucratic system, lacking transparency and efficiency. Furthermore, the use of central databases in storing academic records raises concerns about security issues. In this paper, issues of the academic processes in the current system are pointed out, and the solution using private distributed ledger technology is proposed accordingly. A brief comparison with Blockcerts, which is a counterpart using public blockchain to facilitate decentralized certificate verification, is made to emphasize the benefits of the proposed system. Based on distributed ledger technologies, the solution we present aims to create a transparent system to support the institutions' processes and lay a solid foundation for lifelong learning.

Keywords: Blockchain · Private distributed ledger · Academic system

1 Introduction

University bureaucracy is complicated and time-consuming, which lower the quality of student experience in higher education. Specifically, in the enrolment process, students have to deal with multiple stakeholders in order to get enough documents and submit them to the right organizations. Figure 1 demonstrates the current enrolment process of international students. Similarly, the process when a student wants to change education provider is also cumbersome. There are, again, various steps to be taken before the student can be enrolled in a new university. However, the process likely ends in frustration when the credits are not recognized correctly or even the student is rejected. Moreover, central databases make the current system prone to long-standing problems, including falsified documents and single point of failure of academic records. While the former has been on debate for a long time, verifying academic qualifications is not simple, given that forged degrees are becoming much more sophisticated. The latter is caused due to the risk of the central database storing academic records being compromised, thus, lead to the loss or leakage of academic records. Furthermore, using central databases also hinders information continuity and consistency.

W. Bao et al. (Eds.): ADHOCNETS 2021/TridentCom 2021, LNICST 428, pp. 279–288, 2022.
https://doi.org/10.1007/978-3-030-98005-4_20

Distributed ledger technology (DLT)'s prominent immutability, transparency, and traceability make it a comprehensive solution to the stated problems. The main idea of applying DLT in managing academic records and university-related bureaucracies is to eliminate a single point of data storage and make data transparent to authorized entities. This means student enrolment and academic credits transfer processes will become much simpler and faster. Additionally, data transparency offered by DLT is a key to connect learning records produced by various education providers. Therefore, a sustainable foundation is set for lifelong learning to evolve. Blockchain is an emerging distributed ledger technology that was introduced in 2008 and become a promising technology that will make noticeable impacts on the world [1]. It has been researched in various sectors, even some of the blockchain-based applications (BBAs) have started making the differences [2]. The application of blockchain in education has been suggested since around the year 2016 when MIT Lab was researching their Blockcerts project [3]. It has been elaborated in multiple papers [4,5], but the topic is still in its infancy, yet the number of researches on this topic has been dramatically increasing in recent years [2,6,7]. Various researches have been conducted to study integrating blockchain into the education field, suggesting a variety of enhancements that could be brought to the current systems [6,7]. According to [6] and [7], majority of them discuss about certificate management and learning outcomes management [8–15], some discuss about evaluating learners' capability [16,17], some suggest securing collaborative learning environment [18–20], and numbers of other problems in education sector [21,22]. Most of those research papers suggest using public blockchains, including Bitcoin and Ethereum, while there is a limited number of papers that proposed private blockchain as the solution.

2   Issues in Student Enrolment and Transfer Processes

2.1   Long Waiting Time

Traditional academic transferring processes are claimed to be time-consuming by Badr et al. [8], Ghaffar and Hussain [24] and Jirgensons and Kapenieks [11] due to the involvement of multiple stakeholders and manifold document handling processes. This significant delay in time is also a cause for hindering learning from becoming lifelong [11].

2.2   Security Risk

Daraghmi considers that academic records are common targets of information theft as they include students' personal information [10]. Ocheja et al. claim in both [18] and [19] that the current process of records sharing is lack protection for learners' confidential data. The traditional system is also considered to be easy to be attacked [17]; thus, prone to the risk of a single point of failure [12].

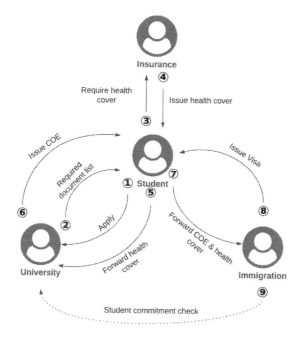

Fig. 1. Current process of enrolment

2.3   Lack of Interoperability

Srivastava et al. [23], Turkanović et al. [15] and Kontzinos et al. [25] claim that different standards in storing academic records lead to the absence of information continuity when records are transferred. Furthermore, [23] and [15] also point out that the barrier of language and script in different countries is another challenge to keeping the seamless stream of learning records. Therefore, lifelong learning is significantly held back.

2.4   Fraudulent Activities

Fake academic documents, nowadays, can be easily forged at a startling speed due to the weak security mechanism of the current system [26] and duplication of records caused by its lack of interoperability [23]. Fake degrees increase legitimate university's expense to compete with "degree mills", conduct investigations and mounting litigation against fake entities to protect their intellectual property rights and protect their reputation against the potential harms caused by those fake qualifications [27]. This problem is also enforced by numbers and examples given by Kazakzeh et al. [28]. From the employer perspective, it may cost them an average of 40,000 US dollars per bad hire [29].

3   Private Distributed Ledger

The private distributed ledger is used because it facilitates the partnership between government and public organizations where optimization of resources utilization is guaranteed [14]. Besides, better scalability, security and privacy are also the main reasons private blockchain is preferred in this use case. In addition, the low computational cost is another advantage of using a private blockchain, which, on the other hand, is the main problem when applying public blockchain in any use cases. In this vision paper, Hyperledger Fabric[1] is the private blockchain considered as the solution so that we can take advantage of its additional features of modularity, configurability and versatility.

3.1   More Scalability

Bitcoin [30], and Ethereum [31] are the most popular public blockchains which have been used in improving educational processes. However, they are known for their problems in scaling due to their limited throughput and costly transactions [8]. Hyperledger Fabric, on the other hand, is a permissioned blockchain which, in default, maintains smaller chains, has a shorter processing time, and scalable to handle more amount of transactions thanks to the ability to leverage non-cryptocurrency consensus protocols. According to the comparison in [8], Hyperledger performs much better than other popular platforms, including Bitcoin, Ethereum, Cardano and Multichain in terms of transactions per second with 2500 transactions in a second. However, [32] has introduced a plug-and-play mechanism to boost the performance of Hyperledger Fabric to a promisingly maximum of 20000 transactions per second.

3.2   Better Security and Privacy

Permissioned blockchain (or private DLT), in their default, are operated on a restricted private network where nodes are known to each other, thus, more trust in the network. Furthermore, the network can be configured so that data can only be accessed or verified by authorised nodes. Thus, it is a good fit for protecting confidentiality and privacy of data on the system [8]. In addition, non-cryptocurrency operation in a private distributed ledger lowers the risks of the system being attacked. Unlike other platforms which propose data encryption or Zero Knowledge Proofs as the mechanism for preserving data confidentiality and privacy with different trade-offs, Hyperledger Fabric, in default, provides the channel architecture and private data feature as solutions.

3.3   Less Computational Cost

As permissioned blockchains do not depend on any costly blocks mining processes, there is no native cryptocurrency needed; thus, less expensive consensus

---

[1] https://hyperledger-fabric.readthedocs.io/en/release-2.2/.

protocols can be used. The computational cost is kept low due to the elimination of cryptocurrency consensus protocols and cryptographic mining processes. Furthermore, end-users are not required to run their own nodes to be part of the blockchain network. In this vision, the Hyperledger Fabric network serves in the web application's backend to which the users communicate to take advantage of the services. Therefore, the system will not cost users anything computational resources, and the use of resources is also reduced from a service provider perspective as no additional nodes are created upon end-users interaction [8].

4 Proposed System Using Private DLT

4.1 Simple Processes

Instead of forwarding required documents from one entity to another, which is time-consuming, the proposed system allows stakeholders to interact directly with each other. By facilitating direct interactions between stakeholders in the university's bureaucracy, students are free from involving in any processes after providing their details to the document issuers; thus, complexity and time are lessened. As shown in Fig. 2, what students need to do is request a document, and the rest of the process is automated by related entities.

After receiving and processing applicants' information, bureaucratic entities issue relevant documents and store them on their ledgers in the Fabric channel where other channel members can have access to those documents. Sequentially, the next stakeholder can continue the process as soon as the document they require is issued and stored on the channel ledgers. Thus, the complexity and long waiting time are significantly reduced.

4.2 A Trusted Network

The system also proposes a collaboration space facilitated by a network with enhanced security and trust. Application of DLT in storing documents and records decentrally eliminates the central database's single point of failure risk. In addition to that, the current problems in sharing academic records can be solved thanks to the immutability and transparency features of blockchain, which make data and transactions viewable by any approved entities, however, unable to be modified after committing. In the proposed system, academic records are viewable and accessible by any external entities of the university as long as they are trusted, thus, included in the channel. Therefore, universities in the system are able to share and exchange academic records effortlessly.

4.3 Support Lifelong Learning

Thanks to the use of blockchain, data is owned by the learners, who also control access to it [33], thus, students are placed in the center of the proposed system, which allows them to make their own decisions on their career path [6].

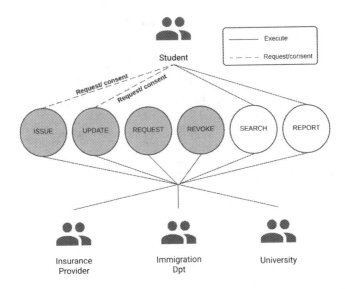

Fig. 2. Proposed DLT solution.

Mikroyannidis et al. [33], in their proposal of a learner-centered approach for life-long learning, have proposed multiple benefits brought by blockchain to ePort-folios, a crucial component of lifelong learning. Furthermore, simplifying and securing enrolment and academic records sharing processes sets sustainable steps for lifelong learning to become the norm and probably beyond that. When these processes are no longer cumbersome and enhanced with a robust data sharing procedure, learners will be more comfortable and confident to acquire new knowledge and skills from diverse institutions.

5   Comparison to Blockcerts

Although some concerns had been raised on data privacy when data is transparent on the blockchain. By taking advantage of Hyperledger Fabric's channel and private data collection features, which are developed for the purpose of conserving privacy on the blockchain network, a university in the proposed system can choose particular entities in the network to share their data in a channel privately; or they can even further choose a subset of entities in the channel to share data with each other using private data collection secretly. As Blockcerts[2] is a system based on Ethereum and Bitcoin, public blockchains, the features for accommodating private information is not available. Also, the consensus rules are also unchangeable on those permissionless blockchain networks. Therefore, there are limited capabilities provided by Blockcerts, which leads to the incompatibility of the system with the variety of business needs. Blockcerts

---

[2] https://www.blockcerts.org/.

only offers the service of qualifications issuance and verification. On the other hand, Hyperledger Fabric is used in order to take advantage of its versatility and modularity. Also, multiple configurations in the Fabric network are pluggable, which makes it a modular and configurable platform facilitating innovation, versatility, and optimization for a variety of applications while still ensure a high level of security. Therefore, the proposed system promisingly provides a comprehensive management system for education providers, government entities, and other related agencies to facilitate collaboration to optimize any processes with interoperability, transparency, and security.

Hyperledger Fabric platform is suggested to perform better, comparing to other popular platforms, including Bitcoin and Ethereum, in terms of transaction per second (TPS), which is a vital attribute to determine the performance of a platform and whether it can scale up to large applications. Specifically, Badr et al. [8], in their comparison, showed that Hyperledger Fabric (2500 TPS) could process 100 times more than the number of transactions that Ethereum (from 15 to 25 TPS) can process within 1 s, while the difference is more than 300 times comparing to Bitcoin (from 3.3 to 7 TPS).

Blockcerts certificates have been found to be vulnerable to impersonation attacks [34]. In details, fake certificates can be forged if an issuer profile is fabricated with an altered certificate resulting in indistinguishability between fake and legitimate certificates [34]. While [34] suggested using public key infrastructure (PKI) or decentralized identity system to mitigate this vulnerability, Hyperledger Fabric, in its default, has been implemented with these features thanks to the Membership Service Provider (MSP) mechanism. Hence, Hyperledger Fabric is ensured with robust identity management, which prevents malicious activities of malevolent entities in the network. Furthermore, in the Hyperledger Fabric network, participants are expectedly known to each other and collaborate under a certain governance model. Thus, the likelihood of intentional malicious codes injected through smart contracts is eliminated (Table 1).

Table 1. Comparison between Blockcerts and proposed system using Hyperledger Fabric

	Blockcerts	Proposed system
Data privacy		✓
Security		✓
Modularity		✓
Versatility		✓
High throughput		✓

6   System Architecture

The system's high-level architecture is illustrated in Fig. 3. External information exchanges occur in the external channel, while each entity's internal information sharing occurs in their own internal ones, separate from the former. By having this blockchain-of-blockchains alike architecture, data sharing is immutable, transparent and traceable, thus, interoperable across different organizations within the system. Therefore, this will be a viable platform for lifelong learning to thrive.

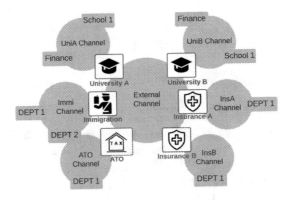

Fig. 3. High level architecture of proposed system.

References

1. Panetta, K.: 3 trends appear in the Gartner Hype Cycle for Emerging Technologies, Gartner (2016). https://www.gartner.com/smarterwithgartner/3-trends-appear-in-the-gartner-hype-cycle-for-emerging-technologies-2016
2. Zou, Y., Meng, T., Zhang, P., Zhang, W., Li, H.: Focus on blockchain: a comprehensive survey on academic and application. IEEE Access **8**, 187182–187201 (2020)
3. MIT Media Lab Learning Initiative and Learning Machine, "Digital Certificates Project". http://certificates.media.mit.edu/
4. Kolvenbach, S., Ruland, R., Gräther, W., Prinz, W.: Blockchain 4 Education (2018)
5. Grech, A., Camilleri, A.F.: Blockchain in Education. Publications Office of the European Union, Luxembourg (2017)
6. Alammary, A., Alhazmi, S., Almasri, M., Gillani, S.: Blockchain-based applications in education: a systematic review **9**(12), 2400 (2019)
7. Malibari, N.A.: A Survey on Blockchain-based Applications in Education (2020)
8. Badr, A., Rafferty, l., Mahmoud, Q.H., Elgazaar, K., Hung, P.C.K.: A permissioned blockchain-based system for verification of academic records. In: Proceedings of the 10th IFIP International Conference on New Technologies, Mobility and Security (NTMS 2019), pp. 1–5 (2019). https://doi.org/10.1109/NTMS.2019.8763831

9. Curmi, A., Inguanez, F.: BlockChain based certificate verification platform. In: Abramowicz, W., Paschke, A. (eds.) BIS 2018. LNBIP, vol. 339, pp. 211–216. Springer, Cham (2019). https://doi.org/10.1007/978-3-030-04849-5_18
10. Daraghmi, E., Daraghmi, Y., Yuan, S.: UniChain: a design of blockchain-based system for electronic academic records access and permissions management. Appl. Sci. **9**(22), 4966 (2019). https://doi.org/10.3390/app9224966
11. Jirgensons, M., Kapenieks, J.: Blockchain and the future of digital learning credential assessment and management. J. Teach. Educ. Sustain. **20**(1), 145–156 (2018). https://doi.org/10.2478/jtes-2018-0009
12. Rachmat, A.A.: Design of distributed academic-record system based on blockchain. In: Proceedings of the International Conference on ICT for Smart Society: Innovation and Transformation Toward Smart Region, ICISS 2019 (2019). https://doi.org/10.1109/ICISS48059.2019.8969849
13. Rasool, S., Saleem, A., Iqbal, M., Dagiuklas, T., Mumtaz, S., Qayyum, Z.: Docschain: blockchain-based IoT solution for verification of degree documents. IEEE Trans. Comput. Soc. Syst. **7**(3), 827–837 (2020)
14. Shrivastava, A.K., Vashistth, C., Rajak, A., Tripathi, A.K.: A decentralized way to store and authenticate educational documents on private blockchain. In: 2019 International Conference on Issues and Challenges in Intelligent Computing Techniques (ICICT), vol. 1, pp. 1–6 (2019). https://doi.org/10.1109/ICICT46931.2019.8977633
15. Turkanović, M., Hölbl, M., Košič, K., Heričko, M., Kamišalić, A.: EduCTX: a blockchain-based higher education credit platform. IEEE Access **6**, 5112–5127 (2018). https://doi.org/10.1109/access.2018.2789929
16. Deenmahomed, H.A.M., Didier, M.M., Sungkur, R.K.: The future of university education: examination, transcript, and certificate system using blockchain. Comput. Appl. Eng. Educ. **29**, 1234–1256 (2021)
17. Zhao, W., Liu, K., Ma, K.: Design of student capability evaluation system merging blockchain technology. J. Phys. Conf. Ser. **1168** (2019). https://doi.org/10.1088/1742-6596/1168/3/032123
18. Ocheja, P., Flanagan, B., Ogata, H.: Connecting decentralized learning records: a blockchain based learning analytics platform. In: Proceedings of the 8th International Conference on Learning Analytics and Knowledge, pp. 265–269 (2018). https://doi.org/10.1145/3170358.3170365
19. Ocheja, P., Flanagan, B., Ueda, H., Ogata, H.: Managing lifelong learning records through blockchain. Res. Pract. Technol. Enhanc. Learn. **14**(1), 1–19 (2019). https://doi.org/10.1186/s41039-019-0097-0
20. Worthington, T.: Blended Learning for the Indo-Pacific (2019)
21. Kanan, T., Obaidat, A.T., Al-Lahham, M.: SmartCert BlockChain Imperative for Educational Certificates (2019)
22. Mohan, V.: On the use of blockchain-based mechanisms to tackle academic misconduct. Res. Policy **48**, 9 (2019)
23. Srivastava, A., Bhattacharya, P., Singh, A., Mathur, A., Prakash, O., Pradhan, R.: A distributed credit transfer educational framework based on blockchain. In: 2018 Second Internationl Conference on Advances in Computing, Control and Communication Technology (IAC3T), pp. 54–59 (2018). https://doi.org/10.1109/IAC3T.2018.8674023
24. Ghaffar, A., Hussain, M.: BCEAP - a blockchain embedded academic paradigm to augment legacy education through application. In: Proceedings of the 3rd International Conference on Future Networks and Distributed Systems - ICFNDS 2019, pp. 1–11 (2019). https://doi.org/10.1145/3341325.3342036

25. Kontzinos, C., Markaki, O., Kokkinakos, P., Karakolis, V., Skalidakis, S., Psarras, J.: University process optimisation through smart curriculum design and blockchain-based student accreditation. In: 18th International Conference on WWW/Internet 2019, pp. 93–100 (2019). https://doi.org/10.33965/icwi2019_2019131012

26. Arenas, R., Fernandez, P.: CredenceLedger: a permissioned blockchain for verifiable academic credentials. In: 2018 IEEE IEEE International Conference on Engineering, Technology and Innovation (ICE/ITMC), pp. 1–6 (2018). https://doi.org/10.1109/ICE.2018.8436324

27. Grolleau, G., Lakhal, T., Mzoughi, N.: An introduction to the economics of fake degrees. J. Econ. Issues **42**(3), 673–693 (2008)

28. Kazakzeh, S., Ayoubi, E., Muslmani, B., Qasaimeh, M., Al-Fayoumi, M.: Framework for blockchain deployment: the case of educational systems. In: 2019 2nd International Conference on new Trends in Computing Science (ICTCS), pp. 1–9 (2019). https://doi.org/10.1109/ICTCS.2019.8923025

29. Tariq, A., Haq, H.B., Ali, S.T.: Cerberus: A Blockchain-Based Accreditation and Degree Verification System (2019)

30. Nakamoto, S.: Bitcoin: A Peer-to-Peer Electronic Cash System (2008). https://bitcoin.org/bitcoin.pdf

31. Wood, G.: Ethereum: A Secure Decentralised Generalised Transaction Ledger (2014). https://gavwood.com/paper.pdf

32. Gorenflo, C., Lee, S., Golab, L., Keshav, S.: FastFabric: scaling hyperledger fabric to 20,000 transactions per second. In: 2019 IEEE International Conference on Blockchain and Cryptocurrency (ICBC), Seoul, Korea (South), pp. 455–463 (2019). https://doi.org/10.1109/BLOC.2019.8751452

33. Mikroyannidis, A., Domingue, J., Bachler, M., Quick, K.: A learner-centred approach for lifelong learning powered by the blockchain. Proc. EdMedia Innov. Learn. **1**, 1388–1393 (2018)

34. Baldi, M., Chiaraluce, F., Kodra, M., Spalazzi, L.: Security analysis of a blockchain-based protocol for the certification of academic credentials (2019)

Value-Aware Collaborative Data Pricing for Federated Learning in Vehicular Networks

Yilong Hui[1], Jie Hu[1], Xiao Xiao[1(✉)], Nan Cheng[1], and Tom H. Luan[2]

[1] State Key Laboratory of Integrated Services Networks, Xidian University, Xi'an 710071, China
xiaoxiao@xidian.edu.cn
[2] School of Cyber Engineering, Xidian University, Xi'an 710071, China

Abstract. Vehicular federated learning (VFL) is a new paradigm that enables the use of data for distributed training under the premise of protecting the privacy of vehicular nodes (VNs). However, due to the heterogeneity of federated learning data, it is a challenge to evaluate the value of data and design an intelligent pricing scheme to effectively motivate the VNs in the vehicular networks (VNets) to complete learning tasks collaboratively. To this end, in this paper, we consider the value of data and propose a value-aware collaborative data pricing scheme for VFL. In the scheme, we first design a data transaction architecture based on the value of data and the cooperation among VNs. Then, by considering the non-independent and identically distributed (non-IID) degree and the age of data (AoD), we develop the data value model to evaluate the quality of data. Next, based on the requirement of the learning task and the data owned by each VN, we formulate the cooperation of the VNs as a coalition game, where the equilibrium of the coalition game is obtained by designing a distributed coalition formation algorithm. The simulation results show that the proposed scheme can lead to higher utility than the traditional methods.

Keywords: Federated learning · Vehicular networks · Data pricing · Coalition game

1 Introduction

With the rapid development of 6G and vehicular networks (VNets), a large number of machine learning tasks have been generated to facilitate intelligent transportation systems (ITS) [1]. As a new learning architecture, federated learning has attracted widespread attention to support various applications and services [2–4]. Different from traditional machine learning which needs to transmit the collected data to a central server for training, federated learning allows each data owner to locally train the collected data and to upload the local update to the central server, reducing the communication overhead and improving the data

W. Bao et al. (Eds.): ADHOCNETS 2021/TridentCom 2021, LNICST 428, pp. 289–300, 2022.
https://doi.org/10.1007/978-3-030-98005-4_21

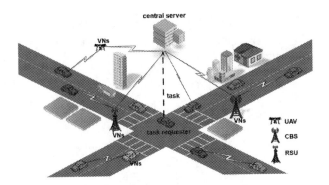

Fig. 1. System model.

security [5]. With these advantages, a new paradigm called vehicular federated learning (VFL) has been proposed to facilitate the applications and services in VNets such as vehicle positioning [6] and vehicle classification [7].

In the VFL, as shown in Fig. 1, a task requester can send its request to the central server which will select a number of vehicular nodes (VNs) including unmanned aerial vehicles (UAVs), cellular base stations (CBSs), roadside units (RSUs) and vehicles to train the learning task locally. After a round of training, the local update will be collected by the central server to update the global model. Repeat this process until a certain precision or the maximum number of the iteration is reached.

Obviously, in the model training process, the VNs with different data have different contributions to the global model training. According to [8], when performing learning tasks, the higher the quality of data, the higher the quality of local model updates. However, VNs usually generate and collect data in different ways. As a result, the number and characteristics of data owned by different VNs may vary greatly. Therefore, the data of VFL is non-independent and identically distributed (non-IID). For neural networks trained on highly skewed non-IID data, the accuracy will be significantly reduced [9]. Furthermore, most of the tasks in the VNs require the timeliness of data. Outdated data may reduce the accuracy of the training model, leading to wrong judgments and low quality of experience (QoE) of the task requester. Taking an autonomous driving task as an example, fresh driving environment data can significantly improve the accuracy of analysis of accident risks [10].

Apart from the data quality, another factor that affects VFL is data pricing. In the VFL, VNs may consume different resources when collecting data and training samples. As selfish and rational nodes, they will not actively participate in the training process of the VFL task. To solve this problem, a collection of mechanisms has been proposed to motivate VNs [11–13]. However, few of them consider the fact that VNs will declare various prices for joining in the VFL. In addition, the existing works typically think that VNs independently price data because they will train local models with their own data, which lacks the consideration of the cooperation among VNs to increase their data value and maximize their utility. Therefore, it is still an urgent problem to design a pricing scheme in VNets to facilitate the VFL by considering the value of data and the cooperation among VNs.

By considering the above issues, this paper proposes a value-aware collaborative data pricing scheme to facilitate VFL. In the scheme, we first establish a data transaction architecture for VFL in VNets by considering the value of data and the cooperation among VNs. Then, we design a value model to evaluate the quality of data by jointly considering the non-IID of data and age of data (AoD). Next, the interactions among VNs are modeled by a coalition game, where a distributed coalition formation algorithm is designed to achieve the equilibrium of the coalition game with the target of maximizing the utility of each VN. The simulation results show that the proposed scheme can bring the highest utilities to the VNs by comparing with the traditional methods.

The remainder of this paper is organized as follows. Section 2 describes the system model. Section 3 designs the proposed scheme. Section 4 formulates the cooperation among VNs as the coalition game. The simulation results are presented in Sect. 5. Finally, we conclude the paper in Sect. 6.

2 System Model

In this section, we introduce the system model which consists of network model and task model.

2.1 Network Model

In the VNets, as shown in Fig. 1. the networks consist of a central server, task requester and VNs.

- **Central Server:** As the controller of the VFL, the central server caches the data and price information of each VN. If a VN intends to update its information, it can send a revised message to the central server. In addition, the central server manages local updates, aggregates global models, and controls the collection of local updates and the distribution of global updates. After the central server receives a learning task, it can assign the task to a number of VNs to train the model locally and cooperatively.
- **Task Requester:** In the VNets, each VN can be a task requester. If a task requester has a learning task that needs to be completed, it can publish the task to the central server. After the central server completes the learning task, the trained model then can be delivered to the task requester.
- **Vehicular Nodes:** Let $I = \{1, ..., i, ..., I\}$ represent all the VNs in the VNets. For VN i, it can decide the price of its data to execute the local training based on the pricing model broadcasted by the central server. If the VN is selected by the central server to train the learning model, the reward will be paid to the VN after the learning task is completed.

2.2   Task Model

The set of learning tasks in the VNets is denoted as $R = \{1, ..., r, ..., R\}$. For task $r(r \in R)$, it can be represented as

$$r = \langle \text{id}_r || \text{des}_r || \text{reward}_r \rangle, \tag{1}$$

where id_r is the unique identification of task r. des_r is the description of task r. reward_r is the reward for completing task r which is provided by the task requester. If a task requester intends to complete learning task r, it can deliver task r to the central server. Then the central server broadcasts a request message to the VNs in its communication coverage, shown as

$$\text{req}_r = \langle r || h_r || \psi_r^0 || E || B || D_r \rangle, \tag{2}$$

where h_r is the machine learning model which is selected by the central server for task r. ψ_r^0 is the initial parameter of the machine learning model. E is the number of epochs. B is the local batch size used for local training. D_r is the requested number of samples in each round for training the learning task.

3   Value-Aware Collaborative Data Pricing for VFL

In this section, we introduce the proposed value-aware collaborative data pricing scheme.

3.1   Data Transaction Architecture

The data transaction architecture designed for the VFL has the following steps.

1) When a task requester has a task r to be completed, it first describes the detailed information of the task as a task requirement message and sends it to the central server.
2) After receiving task r from the task requester, the central server initializes the parameters E, B, and ψ_r^0. Meanwhile, the central server selects the machine learning model h_r for training task r.
3) Based on the information of the task request and the VNs, the central server starts to operate the coalition game. Specifically, for each VN $i(i \in I)$, it decides its data price based on the value of its data, where the price model is determined by the central server. Furthermore, it can form a coalition by itself to train the model individually or form a coalition with other VNs to increase its data value. The details of the designed coalition game among the VNs will be discussed in Section 4-A.
4) Based on the data prices of different coalitions, the central server selects a group of coalitions to form the optimal coalition set (OCS) and complete the learning task collaboratively. The selection of the OCS will be introduced in Section 4-B.

5) After the central server determines the OCS, it broadcasts the task request message and the determined OCS to the VNs within its communication coverage.

6) Once a VN receives the OCS, it then starts to execute the K rounds learning task if the VN is a member of the OCS. Specifically, for round $k(1 \leq k \leq K)$, the VNs in the OCS train the local model with their data sets. The purpose of local training is to minimize the loss function of task r. For VN i, the samples in its data set are denoted as $D_i = \{1, ..., d_i, ..., D_i\}$, where d_i is a pair of input and output $\{x_{d_i}, y_{d_i}\}$. Therefore, the loss function of sample d_i can be defined as $f_{d_i}(x_{d_i}, y_{d_i}, \psi_r^k)$.

Denote by $S_j^* = \{S_1^*, ..., S_j^*, ..., S_J^*\}$ the set of coalitions in the OCS. Then, the samples in the data set of the VNs in coalition S_j^* can be expressed as $D_{S_j^*} = \sum_{i \in S_j^*} D_i$. Similarly, we can define the loss function of coalition S_j^* with data set $D_{S_j^*}$ shown as

$$f_{S_j^*}(x_{d_i}, y_{d_i}, \psi_r^k) = \frac{\sum_{d_i \in D_{S_j^*}} f_{d_i}(x_{d_i}, y_{d_i}, \psi_r^k)}{|D_{S_j^*}|}, \quad (3)$$

where $|D_{S_j^*}|$ is the number of samples in $D_{S_j^*}$.

Based on the loss function of the task, we then introduce the optimization process to find the parameter of (3) with the target of minimizing the value of the loss function.

Similar to [14], we use the Mini-Batch Gradient Descent (MBGD) as the optimization method. The strategy of the MBGD is to reduce the value of loss function along the direction of gradient descent. For each epoch, there are $\lceil \frac{|D_{S_j^*}|}{B} \rceil$ iterations. Each iteration uses B samples to update the parameters. Therefore, the number of local updates of coalition S_j^* is $E * \lceil \frac{|D_{S_j^*}|}{B} \rceil$.

Then, we update the local model of coalition S_j^* according to the gradient, where the local update can be defined as

$$\psi_r^k = \psi_r^{k-1} - \eta_r^k \nabla(\psi_r^{k-1}). \quad (4)$$

In (4), ψ_r^{k-1} is the local model of coalition S_j^* in the k-1th round. η_r^k is the learning rate (step size), $\nabla(\psi_r^{k-1})$ is the gradient of ψ_r^{k-1}.

7) For each VN in the OCS, it sends the local update to the central server if the local training is completed.

8) The central server aggregates the local updates received from the VNs into a new global model Ψ_r^k. We have

$$\Psi_r^k = \sum_{S_j^*=1}^{S_j^*} \frac{|D_{S_j^*}|}{\sum_{S_j^*=1}^{S_j^*} |D_{S_j^*}|} \psi_r^k. \quad (5)$$

9) The central server sends the newly formed global model to the VNs in the OCS.

10) After the VNs in the OCS receive the global model, the $k+1$th round starts. Repeat the above training process until the given precision or the maximum number of iterations is reached, ending the execution process of the learning task.

4   Game Analysis

In this section, we first introduce the value of data. Then, we design the coalition game to formulate the interactions among VNs to maximize their utilities, followed by the coalition selection mechanism to form the OCS.

4.1   Value of Data

In the VFL, VNs with different data values have different contributions to the global model training. In other words, the contribution of nodes is related to the value of data. In general, the data owned by different VNs are heterogeneous. Therefore, we define the data value by jointly considering two factors, i.e., non-IID and AoD.

– **non-IID:** Based on the studies in [9], the average earth mover's distance (EMD) can be used to measure the heterogeneity of data distribution among different VNs. Considering the data sample $\{x_{d_i}, y_{d_i}\}$ follows the distribution P, we define the non-IID of coalition S_j as

$$\overline{EMD_{S_j}} \approx \sum_{c=1}^{Y} ||p_{S_j}(y = c) - p(y = c)||, \tag{6}$$

where y is the label of sample, and $y = \{0, 1, ..., Y\}$. $p_{S_j}(y = c)$ is the proportion of data with label c in coalition S_j's data and $p(y = c)$ is the proportion of data with label c owned by all the VNs. It can be seen from (6) that a high EMD value can result in a high non-IID degree of data.

In order to make EMD and AoD in the same order of magnitude, we adopt the min-max normalization to convert the range of EMD values to $[0, 1]$. The minimum value of EMD is 0. Therefore, (6) can be rewritten as

$$EMD_{S_j} = \frac{\overline{EMD_{S_j}} - \min(\overline{EMD})}{\max(\overline{EMD}) - \min(\overline{EMD})} = \frac{\overline{EMD_{S_j}}}{\max(\overline{EMD})} \tag{7}$$

$$= \frac{\sum_{c=1}^{Y} ||p_{S_j}(y = c) - p(y = c)||}{\max(||p_{S_j}(y = c) - p(y = c)||) * Y}.$$

– **AoD:** AoD can be used to evaluate the freshness of data [15]. For coalition S_j, the AoD can be defined by

$$AoD_{S_j} = \sum_{i \in S_j} \frac{|D_i|}{\sum_{i \in S_j} |D_i|} \triangle_i, \tag{8}$$

where $\triangle_i$ is the AoD of data set owned by VN i, $\triangle_i \in [0, 1]$.

– **Data value:** We measure the value of data by its heterogeneity and age. In this way, based on the non-IID and AoD of the data owned by different VNs, the value of the data owned by coalition S_j can be expressed as

$$VoD_{S_j} = \log(1 + \frac{\rho}{EMD_{S_j}} + \frac{1-\rho}{AoD_{S_j}})$$

$$= \log(1 + \frac{\rho * \max(\|p_{S_j}(y=c) - p(y=c)\|) * Y}{\sum_{c=1}^{Y} \|p_{S_j}(y=c) - p(y=c)\|}$$

$$+ \frac{1-\rho}{\sum_{i \in S_j} \frac{|D_i|}{\sum_{i \in S_j} |D_i|} \Delta_i}),$$

(9)

where ρ is used to balance the importance of the non-IID and the AoD.

4.2 Coalition Game

1) Definition: a coalition game can be expressed as $[I, V(S_j)]$ where I is a set of VNs which take part in the coalition game, S_j is an arbitrary subset of I, and $V(S_j)$ is the characteristic function of coalition S_j.
2) Characteristic function: In the game, the characteristic function $V(S_j)$ represents the utility of the coalition. The data value and data volume of the coalition will affect the global model of VFL. Therefore, we can define the utility of the coalition by

$$V_{S_j} = \alpha_r \log(1 + VoD_{S_j}) * |D_{S_j}|$$

$$= \alpha_r \log(1 + \log(1 + \frac{\rho}{EMD_{S_j}} + \frac{1-\rho}{AoD_{S_j}})) * |D_{S_j}|,$$

(10)

where α_r is the basic price of task r. $\log(1 + VoD_{S_j})$ is the unit price of data.
3) Game rules: The rules of the coalition game consist of coalition conditions and coalition principles.
   – **Coalition conditions:** Considering that VN i is in coalition $S_{j'}$ and intends to split from this coalition and merge in coalition $S_{j''}$. It can join coalition $S_{j''}$, if the following two conditions are satisfied.
   For VN i, the utility after the node merge in the new coalition $S_{j''}$ is larger than the utility of the node in coalition $S_{j'}$. We have

$$U_i(V(S_{j''} \cup \{i\})) > U_i(V(S_{j'})).$$

(11)

The utility obtained by each VN after VN i merged in coalition $S_{j''}$ is no less than the utility obtained by the VN in this coalition. It can be expressed as

$$U_{i'}(V(S_{j''} \cup \{i\})) > U_{i'}(V(S_{j''})), i' \in S_{j''}.$$

(12)

- **Coalition principles:** Given the coalition structure $S = \{S_1, ..., S_{j'}, ..., S_j, ..., S_{j''}, ..., S_J\}$, if VN i switches from coalition S_j' to coalition S_j'', the coalition structure can be updated by

$$S_{j'} \leftarrow S_{j'} \setminus \{i\}, S_{j''} \leftarrow S_{j''} \cup \{i\}. \tag{13}$$

4) Node utility: If VN i in coalition S_j participates in this round of federated learning training and contributes to the global model, it will obtain the corresponding reward. Because the data value of different nodes is not the same, the contribution to the whole coalition is different. Therefore, we can calculate the utility of each VN in the coalition based on its contribution. We have

$$U_i(V(S_j)) = V(S_j) - V(S_j \setminus \{i\}). \tag{14}$$

Therefore, the utility model of the VN can be defined as:

$$U_i = \begin{cases} U_i(V(S_j)), i \in S_j, \\ V(\{i\}), \text{else}, \end{cases} \tag{15}$$

where $\{i\}$ is the coalition consisting VN i itself.
5) Game equilibrium: We can know from the game rules that each VN needs to operate some switches to find its coalition. Therefore, we use the iterative method to design a distributed coalition formation algorithm for finding the equilibrium of the coalition game [16]. The algorithm makes the coalition structure stable through the VNs continuously joining a coalition and leaving a coalition.
6) Coalition formation process: In the process of data transaction, each node tries to merge to form a coalition according to the coalition conditions and coalition principles, and finally forms a stable coalition structure through multiple rounds of the coalition formation process. The process of coalition formation can be described as follows.
   - **Initial coalition:** The nodes are divided into I coalitions, where each coalition has only one VN. The initial coalition structure can be given by $S = \{S_1, ..., S_j, ..., S_J\} = \{\{1\}, ..., \{i\}, ..., \{I\}\}$.
   - **Coalition formation:** For VN $i(i \in S_j)$, there is a candidate coalition sequence SQ_i that includes the remaining coalitions except S_j, shown as

$$SQ_i = \{S_1, ..., S_j - 1, S_j + 1, ..., S_J\}. \tag{16}$$

Based on (16), VN i selects a coalition from SQ_i in turn. If the coalition conditions are satisfied, VN i merges in the coalition according to the coalition principles. In this way, each VN is analyzed by coalition game in turn until the stable coalition structure is achieved.

4.3   Coalition Selection

In the data transaction process, the central server intends to obtain the highest quality data with the lowest rewards. Therefore, we define the coalition type by considering value of data and price of data to help the central server make a decision.

Coalition type: The coalition type represents central server's preference for coalitions. The higher order of the type of S_j implies that the coalition has a larger possibility to contribute its data. Then, the type of coalition S_j can be defined as

$$TYPE_{S_j} = \log(1 + VoD_{S_j}/V(S_j)). \tag{17}$$

Coalition selection mechanism: When the coalition structure is stable, there are J^* coalitions. Sort by the coalitions based on the type in ascending order: $S_1 > S_2 > ... > S_{J^*}$. Central server selects the coalitions to join the training. There are two cases to form the OCS. First, if $D_r < D_{S_j}$, the central server selects D_r data from this coalition, we have $D_{S_j} = D_r$. In this case, the coalition provides D_r data to train the global model. Second, if $D_r > D_{S_j}$, we have $D_r = D_r - D_{S_j}$. Namely, this coalition provides all data to train the global model. Repeat this process until we have $D_r < D_{S_j}$. Then, the case is similar to case 1.

5 Simulation Results

In this section, the performance of the proposed scheme is evaluated by using a simulator in Matlab. We first introduce the simulation setup and then show the simulation results and discussions.

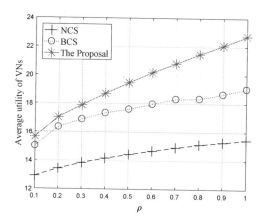

Fig. 2. Average utility of VNs by changing the EMD parameter ρ.

5.1 Simulation Setup

In our simulation, we consider an image classification task. The data set used in our simulation is Cifar-10 data set. Cifar-10 is divided into 5 batch training sets and 1 batch-test set, where the data set contains 10 labels: airport, automobile, bird, cat, deer, dog, frog, horse, ship, and truck. Each image belongs to one of the labels. The occurrence probability of each category of images is essentially equal. Each VN randomly extracts a fragment as its own data set. The values of ρ and α_r are 0.5 and 0.1, respectively. With this scenario, we evaluate the proposed scheme by changing the values of ρ and the number of VNs in the VNets. The performance of our proposed scheme is evaluated by comparing with the following conventional schemes.

- Non-cooperation scheme (NCS): In this scheme, all the VNs provide their data to train the learning model independently.
- Big coalition scheme (BCS): In this scheme, all the VNs form a big coalition and provide their data to complete the learning task collaboratively.

5.2 Simulation Results

Figure 2 is the average utility of VNs by changing the EMD parameter. As shown in Fig. 2, we can see that the proposed scheme can bring a higher utility to the VNs than the conventional schemes. This is because the proposed scheme allows VNs to form distributed coalitions to maximize their utility. In addition, it can be seen in this figure, the average utility of the VNs increases with the increase of ρ. The reason for this is that the importance of EMD increases with the increase of ρ. As a result, the value of data increases and the utility of VNs increases.

Figure 3 is the average utility of VNs by changing the number of VNs participating in the learning process. From this figure, we can see that the utility

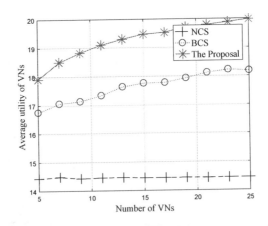

Fig. 3. Average utility of VNs by changing the number of VNs.

of VNs in the NCS is almost stable. In addition, as we can see in this figure, the utility of VNs increases with the increase of the number of VNs in the BCS and the proposal. This is because the increase of nodes promotes the variability of the coalition structure, where the probability of the coalition with low heterogeneity becomes high.

6 Conclusion

In this paper, we have proposed a value-aware data pricing scheme to facilitate the VFL in VNets. In the scheme, we have designed a novel data transaction architecture based on the value of data and the cooperation among VNs. Then, by considering the non-IID and AoD, we have developed a value model to evaluate the quality of data. Next, with different values of data owned by different VNs, a distributed coalition formation game has been designed to promote cooperation among VNs, where the equilibrium of coalition game has been obtained by designing a coalition formation algorithm. Simulation results have demonstrated that the proposed scheme can achieve the optimal strategy for VNs and outperform the conventional schemes in terms of the average utility obtained by VNs. For future work, the integration of blockchain and the proposed scheme will be considered to guarantee the security of the VFL in VNets.

Acknowledgement. This work was supported in part by the National Key R&D Program of China under Grant 2019YFB1600100, in part by the NSFC under Grant 61901341, in part by the China Postdoctoral Science Foundation under Grant 2021TQ0260, in part by the XAST under Grant 095920201322, in part by the National Natural Science Foundation of Shaanxi Province under Grant 2020JQ-301, and in part by the Fundamental Research Funds for the Central Universities under Grant XJS200109.

References

1. Hui, Y., et al.: Secure and personalized edge computing services in 6G heterogeneous vehicular networks. IEEE IoT J. **99**, 1–12 (2021). (Early Access)
2. Qu, Y., Pokhrel, S.R., Garg, S., Gao, L., Xiang, Y.: A blockchained federated learning framework for cognitive computing in industry 4.0 networks. IEEE Trans. Ind. Inf. **17**(4), 2964–2973 (2021)
3. Zhan, Y., Li, P., Qu, Z., Zeng, D., Guo, S.: A learning-based incentive mechanism for federated learning. IEEE IoT J. **7**(7), 6360–6368 (2020)
4. Qu, Y., et al.: Decentralized privacy using blockchain-enabled federated learning in fog computing. IEEE IoT J. **7**(6), 5171–5183 (2020)
5. Liu, Y., Yu, J.J.Q., Kang, J., Niyato, D., Zhang, S.: Privacy-preserving traffic flow prediction: a federated learning approach. IEEE IoT J. **7**(8), 7751–7763 (2020)
6. Kong, X., Gao, H., Shen, G., Duan, G., Das, S.K.: FedVCP: a federated-learning-based cooperative positioning scheme for social internet of vehicles. IEEE Trans. Comput. Soc. Syst. **9**, 1–10 (2021)

7. Abdellatif, A.A., Chiasserini, C.F., Malandrino, F., Mohamed, A., Erbad, A.: Active learning with noisy labelers for improving classification accuracy of connected vehicles. IEEE Trans. Veh. Technol. **70**(4), 3059–3070 (2021)

8. Duan, S., Zhang, D., Wang, Y., Li, L., Zhang, Y.: JointRec: a deep-learning-based joint cloud video recommendation framework for mobile IoT. IEEE IoT J. **7**(3), 1655–1666 (2020)

9. Ding, N., Fang, Z., Huang, J.: Optimal contract design for efficient federated learning with multi-dimensional private information. IEEE J. Sel. Areas Commun. **39**(1), 186–200 (2021)

10. Savazzi, S., Nicoli, M., Bennis, M., Kianoush, S., Barbieri, L.: Opportunities of federated learning in connected, cooperative, and automated industrial systems. IEEE Commun. Mag. **59**(2), 16–21 (2021)

11. Hui, Y., Su, Z., Luan, T.H.: Unmanned era: a service response framework in smart city. IEEE Trans. Intell. Transp. Syst. **99**, 1–15 (2021). (Early Access)

12. Kang, J., Xiong, Z., Niyato, D., Xie, S., Zhang, J.: Incentive mechanism for reliable federated learning: a joint optimization approach to combining reputation and contract theory. IEEE IoT J. **6**(6), 10700–10714 (2019)

13. Hui, Y., Su, Z., Luan, T.H., Li, C.: Reservation service: trusted relay selection for edge computing services in vehicular networks. IEEE J. Sel. Areas Commun. **38**(12), 2734–2746 (2020)

14. Mills, J., Hu, J., Min, G.: Communication-efficient federated learning for wireless edge intelligence in IoT. IEEE IoT J. **7**(7), 5986–5994 (2020)

15. Hu, H., Xiong, K., Qu, G., Ni, Q., Fan, P., Letaief, K.B.: AoI-minimal trajectory planning and data collection in UAV assisted wireless powered IoT networks. IEEE IoT J. **8**(2), 1211–1223 (2021)

16. Ng, J.S., et al.: Joint auction-coalition formation framework for communication-efficient federated learning in UAV-enabled internet of vehicles. IEEE Trans. Intell. Transp. Syst. **22**(4), 2326–2344 (2021)

Dual Scheme Privacy-Preserving Approach for Location-Aware Application in Edge Computing

Bruce Gu[1]([✉]), Youyang Qu[2], Khandakar Ahmed[1], Wenjie Ye[1], Chenchen Tan[2], and Yuan Miao[1]

[1] Intelligent Technology Innovation Lab, Victoria University, Footscray, Australia
{bruce.gu,khandakar.ahmed,wenjie.ye,yuan.miao}@vu.edu.au
[2] Deakin Blockchain Innovation Lab, Deakin University, Burwood, Australia
{y.qu,tanchen}@deakin.edu.au

Abstract. The location awareness capabilities of edge computing (EC) contains large quantity of the physical devices with short coverage range. The possibilities of the potential private data attacks from adversaries increases dramatically through easily accessible location information. The existing research on privacy-preserving schemes cannot meet various privacy-preserving expectations in practice for EC variants. In this paper, we proposed a dual scheme customizable ϵ-differential privacy preservation to provide comprehensive protection. We establish the first scheme by clustering Edge Nodes (ENs) with SDN-enabled EC where SDN enables the capabilities of the programmability. In addition, we customize the ϵ-differential privacy preservation scheme for variant EC services with the employment of modified Laplacian mechanism to generate noise, where the optimal tradeoff been found. The extensive experiments results demonstrate the significance of the proposed model in terms of privacy protection level and data utility, respectively.

Keywords: Edge computing · Privacy-preserving · Software defined network · Differential privacy · Location-aware application

1 Introduction

The Internet of Things (IoTs) is advancing at a breakneck pace, and connection between things is becoming more pervasive [3,7]. Increasingly more objects are becoming intelligent as they are capable of seeing their surroundings, connecting to the internet, and receiving instructions remotely. These intelligence of the objects are derived from data, analysis, and input from a variety of systems or servers connected to a variety of mobile devices [4].

The wireless and decentralized properties of ENs are vulnerable to adversaries in the actual application process of edge computing (EC), resulting in

Supported by Intelligent Technology Innovation Lab (ITIL), Victoria University.

W. Bao et al. (Eds.): ADHOCNETS 2021/TridentCom 2021, LNICST 428, pp. 301–316, 2022.
https://doi.org/10.1007/978-3-030-98005-4_22

major location-aware privacy disclosure vulnerabilities [14]. EC enables computation to take place closer to the user [17]. It evaluates data locally and makes decisions based on it. It decreases the danger of privacy leakage by avoiding long-distance data transfer in the network to certain extent [27]. However, a substantial amount of sensitive private data can be retrieved since attackers can easily access real-time data received by ENs. Higher criteria for privacy protection techniques in EC have been recommended as a result of methodologies that assure users can utilise the service without revealing their sensitive location data [19]. Traditional privacy-preserving solutions are impractical for directly addressing the highlighted problem in an effective manner, despite certain existing privacy-preserving models or algorithms being presented [9]. Furthermore, the location privacy disclosure concern identified in EC will have a significant impact on EC application development. It is critical to investigate location-aware privacy preserving solutions for massive EC applications based on location.

Motivated by this, to establish an optimal trade-off on data utilities with a sufficient accuracy and efficiency, we offer a dual-scheme ϵ-customised differential privacy model (DDSDP) based on software-defined EC (SD-EC) services. SD-EC increases the network's privacy protection capabilities by allowing it to be programmed flexibly and dynamically [11,18]. First, we initiate the EN clustering method. This strategy connects users to EC services through a group of ENs rather than a single reliable service provider, while also increasing the complexity of attacking targets for adversaries. Furthermore, the measurements of ϵ-customised differential privacy was determined by the distance between ENs cluster. To quantify data utilities and privacy protection levels, we create a QoS-based mapping function. Our thorough studies illustrate the efficiency and accuracy in real time.

The contributions of this paper can be summarized as follows:

- We offer a dual-scheme ϵ-customized differential privacy model to retain location-aware private data for users. In addition, to offer first scheme protection for location-aware data from users to ENs, we consider a dynamic clustering strategy. This protects against frontal attacks from adaptable foes. Furthermore, We adapt Affinity Propagation methods to boost the effectiveness of the clustering scheme while retaining the greatest degree of privacy protection.
- We designate our second approach as the ϵ-customized protection model with modified Laplacian mechanism by providing noise to the clustered EN. Moreover, we developed a QoS-based mechanism to measure the distance between privacy levels. DDSDP seeks to enhance the utilities of data while minimising privacy costs.
- To illustrate the proposed models, we perform extensive experiments based on real-world dataset. The evaluation results reveal notable significant performances in data utilities and privacy protection level.

This paper is organized as following. Section 2 summarizes the existing research on EC and related privacy protection approaches. The attacking formulation with two popular attack methods is analyzed in Sect. 3. Section 4 formulates our proposed DDSDP model in both schemes. Section 5 performs evaluation results from our extensive experiments by using the DDSDP protection model. Finally, summarization and future works are discussed in Sect. 6.

2   Related Work

EC benefits from dense geographical dispersion, which accomplished by installing ENs in multiple locations and interconnecting each of the nodes to end devices [22]. Moreover, the geographic dispersion of the ENs enables location mobility for IoTs devices, obviating the requirement for devices to traverse the entire network [10]. Besides the tangible benefits of EC's location-aware capabilities, the most immediate challenge is the preservation of users' privacy when it relates to geographical location data.

The user in the EC environment are not expected to reveal actual location to attackers when obtaining services. Location-aware data includes not only the current specific location, but also the contents of the EN that are saved and processed in EC, such as movement patterns and behavioural patterns. Indeed, the dimensionality to which location-aware privacy protection and Quality of Service(QoS) are the result of a sequence of antagonistic connections [8]. Current research on location-aware privacy protection technology for EC is primarily concentrated on two aspects: 1) the the models of privacy-preserving that utilises reputable third-party entities [24], and 2) the data anonymization technique [16].

Moreover, J. Kang [13] proposed privacy-preserving pseudonym method which addressed privacy concerns associated with location-based EC internet vehicles. While these solutions provide acceptable performance, they are more concerned with maintaining a stable network state than with dynamic and tailored EC restrictions. Lyu [15] performed extensive research on the tailored *epsilon*-differential privacy-preserving technique [12], which Qu [20], Badsha [2], and Wang Wang [25] all effectively demonstrated. These strategies are very successful in social networks, recommendation systems, and location-aware apps. They are theoretically sound and include strong privacy safeguards [23].

Furthermore, we examine two typical attack vectors that adversaries are commonly using to target sensitive location data in the EC.

Wormhole Attacks. This type of attacks are very hazardous since they may occur even when all parties to the communication guarantee the message's validity and secrecy. The attacker creates a secret channel between two cooperating malicious nodes with the intent of transferring data groups acquired at one network point to another. J. Zhang et al. [28] developed the grid clustering routing method (FGC) to protect against wormhole attacks, and it is currently extensively used in industrial IoT.

DDoS Attack. Another popular attack technique in SDN-enabled EC is the DDoS assault, which targets the communication layer. According to the location service provider, it prevents radio signals from being transmitted [21,26].

The literature has examined the feasibility and efficacy of DDoS attacks against a variety of transport protocols, including Bluetooth [5]. Along with active interfering attacks, the adversaries may conduct a denial-of-service (DoS) attack by installing a malicious device or router that intentionally violates the communication protocol in order to cause conflicts or disrupt communication.

3   Formulation of Adversaries Attack in Location-Aware

The volume of information that attackers may extract from the location-aware privacy data for the users after its broadcasting influences the effectiveness of the adversary attack model in the EC. The location data captured by the adversaries from user encapsulated within the context of a collection of spatiotemporal data $\{r : r = (P, t)\}$, where r determined a single adversary-collected location data, and P defined the specific location of the user, and the accurate timing of the collection determined as t. Moreover, the disclosure of sensitive location data is structured as a set of $\{s_1, s_2, ..., s_n\}$, where s_n denotes the nth position after numbering.

Adversaries can deduce users' privacy information based on location data by predicting the probability p when user is in a sensitive location s_i at time t. We describe location data that users supply at any point in time t where it does not reveal the θ privacy of users in a sensitive location. Therefore, it will quantify the adversary location data collection in order to identify the user in a specified sensitive location information.

Definition 1 *(Location-Aware Data Privacy)*

In any time t', it represents the rate of probability for each user at the time of t' at location s_i, we use $P\left\{U_i^{t'}\right\}$. We also use Ld_t to represent the data at specific location which collected by attackers at certain time t. As a result, we have

$$P\left\{U_i^{t'} \mid L_t\right\} - P\left\{U_i^{t'}\right\} \leq \theta \tag{1}$$

where θ denotes the user's privacy requirement, $P\left\{U_i^{t'} \mid L_t\right\}$ denotes that the adversary acquires location data subsequent to the user at time t and evaluates the posterior probability of the user being in a vulnerable position s_i at specific time t', and $P\{U_i\}$ denotes the adversary's prior probability of speculating that the user is in a perilous position s_i. According to Def 1, the adversary's collection of user location data cannot surpass θ in order for the attacker to deduce the user's sensitive location. Therefore, after aggregating the position sequence from the users, the discrepancy in probability values between the posterior and prior probabilities of the user being in a specific sensitive position at a given moment is less than θ. At each moment t', the adversary has $-\sum_i P\left\{U_i^{t'}\right\} log P\left\{U_i^{t'}\right\}$ of previous knowledge about the user's location.

Thus, the amount of sensitive user location data exposed to attackers in ENs can be estimated as follows:

$$Comp(s) = \sum_i P\left\{U_i^{t'}\right\} log P\left\{U_i^{t'}\right\}$$
$$- \sum_i P\left\{U_i^{t'} \mid L_t\right\} log P\left\{U_i^{t'} \mid L_t\right\} \tag{2}$$

As defined in Definition 1, a privacy-preserving technique that meets θ privacy may guarantee the quantity of information included in the published data in the EN is less than $n\theta$, where n is the quantity of sensitive locations. At any point in time, users with strict privacy needs may set *theta* to 0. As a consequence, users must ensure the location data they post does not jeopardise their θ privacy in any sensitive location. They only need to adhere to the $\frac{\theta}{n}$ standard of the privacy level.

4   System Modeling and Analysis

Figure 1 illustrates the proposed DDSDP model utilised in the SDN-enabled EC service. Both schemes secure the data privacy in location-aware applications between users and ENs. We begin with a customized SDN control layer. This novel control layer attempts to offer a real-time clustering solution. It uses the modified affinity propagation (AP) clustering technique. As the clusters are constantly updated, attackers cannot identify the source of the first connected EN. As a result, clustering protects privacy. The security level is also increased by modifying the Laplacian mechanism. We utilise QoS mapping to assess data utility and privacy protection. Thus, SDN-enabled EC services provide the highest privacy level and data utility protection.

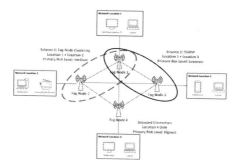

Fig. 1. DDSDP framework in SD-enabled EC.

4.1   Edge Nodes (ENs) Clustering Modelling

We use EN clustering to conceal the real position data from users in the first scheme of proposed DDSDP model. This preservation approach successfully avoids the opponent from quickly invading and allows for more complex attack measures. Each cluster is composed of at least two or more ENs. Instead of direct connections, users are assigned to EN clusters that span a larger region under the adversary attacking paradigm. Adversaries need necessary analytical stages as precise selection gets increasingly difficult.

Weight Factors and Unification Process. Distance-based location is a popular location-aware privacy-preserving technique in EC. We determine the distance based on the user situation by analysing the arrival time and the its difference between the arrivals. Typically, each EN calculates the user position via a distance-based location method. If location information is exposed, user privacy will be jeopardised. Moreover, in order to establish the current location of the user, the selected EN must be aware of the location of each reference node. The geolocation information for the reference node are revealed if the adversary perform spoofing on the location data and other attacks against the reference node.

We calculated the position distances between specified ENs and the initial anchor node using the matrix S where $S = S_1^1, S_2^1, S_3^1, S_\beta^1$ denotes distinct factors associated with the same EN, whereas the elements $S = S_1^1, S_1^2, S_1^3, S_1^\alpha$ denotes the same factor for all ENs. As a result, we construct the matrix as

$$S = \begin{bmatrix} S_1^1 & S_2^1 & S_3^1 & \dots & S_\beta^1 \\ S_1^2 & S_2^2 & S_3^2 & \dots & S_\beta^2 \\ & & \dots\dots \\ S_1^\alpha & S_2^\alpha & S_3^\alpha & \dots & S_\beta^\alpha \end{bmatrix} \tag{3}$$

ENs have a variety of indices based on their features, such as access points and servers. Before the aggregate indicator can be computed, a unification procedure is needed to identify the distances. To address the issue of differing absolute values for various indices, the absolute values must be transformed to relative values. S' denotes the matrix S after the unification procedure.

$$S' = \begin{bmatrix} \dfrac{S_1^1}{\sum_{i=1}^\alpha S_1^i} & \dfrac{S_2^1}{\sum_{i=1}^\alpha S_2^i} & \dfrac{S_3^1}{\sum_{i=1}^\alpha S_3^i} & \cdots & \dfrac{S_\beta^1}{\sum_{i=1}^\alpha S_\beta^i} \\[2ex] \dfrac{S_1^2}{\sum_{i=1}^\alpha S_1^i} & \dfrac{S_2^2}{\sum_{i=1}^\alpha S_2^i} & \dfrac{S_3^2}{\sum_{i=1}^\alpha S_3^i} & \cdots & \dfrac{S_\beta^2}{\sum_{i=1}^\alpha S_\beta^i} \\[2ex] & & \dots\dots\dots\dots \\[1ex] \dfrac{S_1^\alpha}{\sum_{i=1}^\alpha S_1^i} & \dfrac{S_2^\alpha}{\sum_{i=1}^\alpha S_2^i} & \dfrac{S_3^\alpha}{\sum_{i=1}^\alpha S_3^i} & \cdots & \dfrac{S_\beta^\alpha}{\sum_{i=1}^\alpha S_\beta^i} \end{bmatrix} \tag{4}$$

Cluster Triggering Process. Primarily, all ENs are geographically allocated. When the potential attacks are detected, we initially propose a cluster triggering technique by allocating measurements according to the entropy weight determination. The EWM's fundamental premise is to derive objective weights of certain variables. The EWM determine the weight of each element in each factor of the attacking formulation. In general, lower e^j value indicates the importance of the element including dataInformation, quantity of the data, and therefore merits a greater weight in the relevant factor. In comparison, a higher entropy e^j implies that an element has a lower value, offers less information, and contributes less to the overall assessment, and therefore should have a lower weight. Due to the unification procedure, the weight factor for each component j in each dimension i must be computed, where $j = 1, 2, 3, ..., m$, and $i = 1, 2, 3, ..., n$.

$$P_{ij} = \frac{S'_{ij}}{\sum_{i=1}^{n} x_{ij}} \tag{5}$$

Each factor j must have an entropy value computed, where $j = 1, 2, 3, ..., m$. $k = 1/\ln(n) > 0$ in this case, and $e_j >= 0$.

$$e_j = -k \sum_{i=1}^{n} P_{ij} \ln P_{ij} \tag{6}$$

A redundancy rate is determined throughout this procedure to minimise variance. The redundancy rate for $j = 1, 2, ..., m$ is $d_j = 1 - e_j$. Following the redundancy correction, the following weight factors are calculated:

$$w_j = \frac{d_j}{\sum_{j=1}^{m} d_j} \tag{7}$$

After assigning weights towards each element per dimension, the clustering procedure is carried out by the weight factors. Assume that t_{tg} is the threshold value for clustering that is dependent on the edge network's distance. T_{tg} is the outcome of the triggering process and is determined by the weight factor computed for each element. Clustering process is defined by the unique EN factor abstracted with the maximum value.

$$T_{tg}^1 = \frac{S_1^1}{\sum_{i=1}^{\alpha} S_1^i} \times t_{tg}$$

$$T_{tg}^2 = \frac{S_2^1}{\sum_{i=1}^{\alpha} S_2^i} \times t_{tg}$$

$$\ldots$$

$$T_{tg}^\beta = \frac{S_\beta^1}{\sum_{i=1}^{\alpha} S_\beta^i} \times t_{tg}$$

$$T_{tg} = max(T_{tg}^1, T_{tg}^2, ..., T_{tg}^\beta) \tag{8}$$

4.2   Affinity Propagation-Based Clustering

On the basis of a modified AP mechanism, we develop a clustering model. AP is a semisupervised clustering method based on closest neighbour propagation developed by Frey et al. [6]. In comparison with other clustering techniques, AP does not need a final number of clusters to be specified. Rather of creating new data points, the cluster centres are chosen using existing geographical data points. AP approach is less reliant on the initial location information input and does not require a symmetric data similarity matrix. In EC, the input data may be of various types as a result of our triggering mechanisms weight factor-based selections. As a result, the AP method is the optimal choice for grouping ENs.

Preference. We begin by examining the parameter for the preferences. The similarity between each cluster centres is stated as $sim(d, p)$, which reflects the similarities between the data points p and d. The Euclidean distance is used to determine this similarity:

$$sim(d, p) = \sqrt{\sum_{r=1}^{n}(d - p)^2 \times T_{tg}} \tag{9}$$

Responsibility. $sim(d, p)$ indicates the degree to which data point p is appropriate for designation as the cluster centre for data point d and represents a message sent from d to p, where $p \in 1, 2..., N$ and $p \neq p'$.

$$r(d, p) = (s(d, p) - max\{a(d, p') + sim(d, p')\}) \times T_{tg} \tag{10}$$

where $a(d, p')$ is the value showing the accessibility of point i to all points except k with a starting value of 0. $s(d, j)$ denotes the responsibility of a point by points other than p, where points other than d are in rivalry with d for ownership. $r(d, p)$ denotes p's cumulative duty to act as the cluster centre for d. When $r(d, p) > 0$, it indicates that p has a greater responsibility to act as the cluster centre.

Availability. To analysis the availability aggregration, $a(d, p)$ indicates the probability that data point d should always choose data point p as its cluster centre and is equivalent to a message delivered from p to d.

$$a(d, p) = min\left\{0, r(d, p') + \sum_{p}\{max(0, r(d', p))\}\right\} \times T_{tg} \tag{11}$$

$$a(p, p') = (\sum_{p}\{max(0, r(d', p))\}) \times T_{tg} \tag{12}$$

where $r(d', p)$ indicates the responsibility value of point p as the cluster centre for points other than d. We aggregate all responsibility values greater than or equal to 0, and we also include the responsibility value p as a cluster centre in its own right. Specifically, all data points with matching responsibility values larger than 0 support point p, and data point d chooses p as a cluster centre based on its cumulative value.

λ *Damping Factor.* A damping factor is used as the algorithm repeatedly updates the availability and responsibility values. This factor λ enables the AP method to converge more quickly. The damping factor may take on values ranging from 0 to 1. λ operates on the responsibility and availability values throughout each iteration of the algorithm to weight the update in relation to the previous iteration.

$$d_n = (1 - \lambda) \times d_n + \lambda \times r_{n-1} \tag{13}$$

$$p_n = (1 - \lambda) \times p_n + \lambda \times p_{n-1} \tag{14}$$

4.3 ϵ-Customized Differential Scheme

Each user in EC exposes their sensitive location data during connection establishment. However, before this location data is released, it must be protected from disclosure. We developed the first clustering method in order to enhance the difficulty level when an opponent intends to attack. Additionally, the model secures the released data with a tailored degree of protection based on the cluster distances. Additionally, our second scheme seeks to offer consumers with the utmost in privacy protection. To get the greatest protection, we compromised ϵ-customized differential privacy and introduced Laplacian noise to the cluster.

QoS Data Utility Mapping. The previous paragraph specified the distance between each cluster as $sim(i,k)$, and the Softmax function was utilised to describe the data utility with QoS and privacy preservation level as ϵ in the DDSDP model. In a multi-class problem, the Softmax function assigns decimal probability to each class. Moreover, it is often used to visualise the utility of data and the level of privacy protection provided by the QoS mapping. The mapping function is represented as follows:

$$\text{QoS}(\epsilon_i) = k \times \frac{\exp(\theta_i^t sim_{ik} \cdot x)}{\sum_{k=1}^{K} \exp(\theta_k^t sim_{ik} \cdot x)} \tag{15}$$

where $k \in K$ is the parameter used to modify the maximum amplitude value, θ indicates the curve's steepness, and x indicates the position.

Laplacian Mechanism and Laplacian Noise. On preserve anonymity of location, we use probabilistic clustering to the initial results of the single clustering query. To protect users' privacy when it comes to location-aware information, we utilise the Laplacian technique to change the actual value by adding Laplacian noise to the original clustering result data, guaranteeing differential privacy both before and after noise addition.

$$M(D) = f(D) + Y$$

s.t.

$$Lap(\alpha) = \frac{p_x(z)}{p_y(z)} = exp(\frac{\epsilon \cdot \| f(x) - f(y) \|}{\triangle f})$$

(16)

where ϵ specifies the privacy budget and ϵ may be adjusted to obtain a better privacy budget outcome owing to the clustering requirement. The Laplacian distributed noise is determined by Y. $Lap(\alpha)$ denotes the mechanism's probability density, while α denotes the noise's magnitude.

ϵ-Customizable Differential Privacy Formulation. To prevent data release in ENs, we model the ϵ-customized differential privacy method. We map the privacy protection level using the clustering method and multihop with QoS. Users submit sensitive location data under the EC clustering paradigm. These data must be protected against attackers. ENs also vary in capacity and processing capability. As a result, we construct the second scheme as follows.

We utilise ϵ-customizable differential privacy. In the case of $M \rightarrow \theta(\chi)$, we defined the mechanism as follows:

$$Pr\left[M(D) \in \Omega\right] = \exp(QoS(\epsilon_i)) \cdot Pr\left[M(D') \in \Omega\right]$$

$$= \exp(k \times \frac{\exp(\theta_i^t sim_{ik} \cdot x)}{\sum_{k=1}^{K} \exp(\theta_k^t sim_{ik} \cdot x)}) \cdot Pr\left[M(D') \in \Omega\right]$$

(17)

s.t.

$$\forall \Omega \subseteq \chi,$$
$$\forall (D, D') \subseteq \psi,$$

where χ represents the result of the nosied location and D denotes the location sensitive data's storage space. $\epsilon \geq 0$ signifies the proximal relationship between the data, and $\psi \subseteq \forall(D, D') \subseteq \psi$ denotes the proximal relationship between the data. We treat D_t and D_{t+1} as changeable datasets to allow the proposed model to include additional dynamic characteristics.

Three criteria are defined in order to undermine the configurable privacy protection approach and clustering model. Initial ϵ-customizable protection is provided by the first qualifier. Each piece of sensitive location data is referred to as p_i, and $\epsilon(\frac{1}{d_{ik}})$ should be fulfilled by anticipations $\{y_{ik}\}$ from p_k. The second qualification's purpose is to specify a maximum degree of privacy protection for the upper bound EN which where the sources are.

The second requirement specifies the degree of privacy protection that the upper limit EN should be maximum. As stated above, the composition in its entirety represented as:

$$com(\epsilon) = \sum_{i=1, k \neq 1}^{n} M_D(\epsilon(\frac{1}{d_{ik}}))$$

(18)

In the third qualification, we optimise user-published data utilities. The response of the real output x_d should be the most accurate noisy n from mechanism M. Additionally, various approximations $\{y_{dp}\}$ result in a range of data utility optimisation values. Thus, we can represent the total usefulness of the data as follows:

$$\sum_{d=1}^{n}\sum_{p \neq 1}^{n} E\| y_{dp} - x_i \|_2^2 \tag{19}$$

Thus, optimal tradeoffs will be evaluated based on the anticipated greatest degree of privacy protection and lowest data usefulness.

$$\epsilon = k \times \frac{\exp(\theta_i^t sim_{ik} \cdot x)}{\sum_{k=1}^{K}\exp(\theta_k^t sim_{ik} \cdot x)}$$

$$\sum_{i=1, k \neq 1}^{n,n} M_D(\epsilon(\frac{1}{d_{ik}})) \leq max M_D(\epsilon(\frac{1}{d_{ik}})) \tag{20}$$

$$\sum_{i=1}^{n}\sum_{k \neq 1}^{n} E\| y_{ik} - x_i \|_2^2 \geq min(DU)$$

5   Performance Evaluation

To evaluate the performance of our proposed DDSDP model, we examine a series of simulations in this section. We first assess data utilities by sampling time periods at various places, then privacy protection levels at different locations. Finally, the experiment assesses the clustering approach's performance, including clustering, transmission and loading outcomes for the total ENs. We used the VicFreeWiFi Access Point Locations dataset [1] to validate these findings. The dataset covers over 300 kms distances geographically and minimum of 250 MB data flow per device every day. In the dataset, it contains 391 nodes are located in the city centre, 44 nodes are located in the northbound zone, and 82 nodes are located in the west-northbound region. This data impairs adversaries ability to identify the location of users.

Due to the fact that SDN-enabled EC should allow more customization choices without sacrificing original performance, we begin by analysing clustering efficiency and evaluating network performance as a result of SDN-enabled clustering. Furthermore, we evaluate our DDSDP model against a range of ϵ values in order to optimise the ϵ-specific differential privacy protection technique. Additionally, two additional methods are compared: classic customisable differential privacy (CCDP) and classic ϵ-differential privacy (CDP). In CDPs, the Laplacian process produces noise. The CCDP provides a customizable degree of privacy and adheres to Laplacian noise.

5.1   Clustering Analysis

Figure 2 illustrates the node clustering results from our DDSDP model's initial scheme clustering technique. The expected number of clusters is 16, created from

517 accessible ENs. We assess system performance using three similarity values. The lowest similarity is 2.00000e-9, the median is 0.017874, and the highest is 1.276488. Likelihood is dependent on location, length, and connection speed. The homogeneity rate is 0.513, which shows how closely related nodes are grouped. This dataset's rate is heavily influenced by connection speed. It has a V-measure and completeness of 0.333 and an adjusted Rand index of 0.080. The first scheme clustering system produces excellent clustering results.

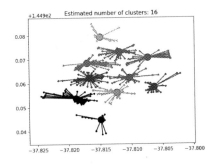

Fig. 2. Edge Node (EN) clustering results.

5.2   Data Utilities Performance

Figure 3 illustrate the outcomes of our DSDP data utilities. The figure depicts the overall QoS functionality. We compare our findings with raw data values for $\epsilon = 0.1$, $\epsilon = 0.5$, and $\epsilon = 1$, which makes it relevant to different situations. We begin by aggregating 20 clustered EC nodes based on QoS metrics derived from the distances between cluster. The Laplacian process generates a large amount of noise in the form of responses. As illustrated in the figure, decreasing the value of ϵ results in improved overall data utility performance. When $\epsilon = 0.1$, we use clustering time slot 5 to achieve the peak value of 1.7.

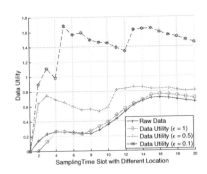

Fig. 3. Data utilities performance with three ϵ values.

Furthermore, we examine various clustering scenarios in terms of privacy protection performance. To build up the customised ϵ, we enable three sample parameter values from the data utilities evaluation. In order to mimic the Laplacian mechanism's unpredictability, three ϵ values were chosen. Figure 4 compares privacy protection levels in terms of configurable ϵ. It achieves a maximum privacy protection level of 1.5 while sampling time slot 7, while sampling time slot 20 maintains the greatest degree of privacy protection. Although the performance for three parameters varies across clusters, it demonstrates the significance of customisation. Moreover, we set $\epsilon = 1$ for the cluster in time slot 4.

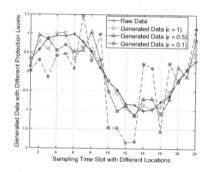

Fig. 4. Different locations privacy levels.

5.3 Performances Against Attacking Scenarios

Figure 5 demonstrates the performance level of privacy protection in a wormhole attack scenario against solitary and clustered ENs. The DDSDP model is compared to the other two classic models. Two dotted green lines show the adversary's data's ϵ value. A lower ϵ results in greater privacy protection. Since our approach relies on ϵ-customized differential privacy, a lower value of ϵ indicates less data given to adversaries. ϵ has two values. When ($\epsilon = 0.45$), the adversary can identify most of the location data and familiar with the other attacking models. ($\epsilon = 2.05$) is the point when CDP and CCDP are completely functioning and can offer comprehensive protection for consumers. All ϵ values between the dashed green lines except DDSDP model provide optimum protection. As a result, DDSDP can offer stronger protection strategies when assaults occur where CDP and CCDP suffer.

Figure 6 illustrates the performance of proposed DDSDP model against a DDoS attack. We utilise ϵ values of 0.45 and 2.05 from previous figures. Because the composition process is still free, CDP is unaffected by DDoS attacks. On top of that, the ϵ rises from 0.45 for DDSDP and CCDP. However, DDSDP shows that two or more opponents will not collect any additional information following an assault. *epsilon* total = maximum ϵ value at time of assault. As a result, the DDSDP model we presented above outperforms both common attacking techniques.

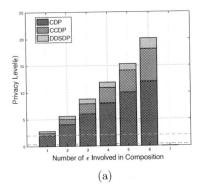
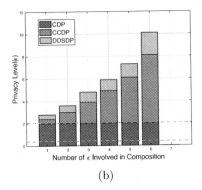

(a)   (b)

Fig. 5. Attacking Scenario 1: (a) Location data shared by multiple users to individual Edge Node (EN); (b) Location data shared by multiple users to clustered Edge Nodes (ENs).

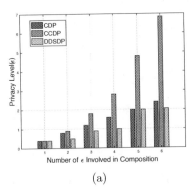
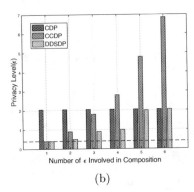

(a)   (b)

Fig. 6. Attacking Scenario 2: (a) Location data shared by multiple users to individual Edge Nodes (ENs); (b) Location data shared by multiple users to clustered Edge Nodes (ENs).

6   Conclusion and Future Works

In this paper, we proposed a privacy protection mechanism (DDSD) for SDN-enabled EC. Our proposed model includes two schemes: SDN based clustering EN and ϵ-customized differential privacy to defend against two common attacker techniques. As a first step, we created our first clustering-based protection system. As a result, attackers cannot identify the location data in the first place. Furthermore, we integrated ϵ-customizable differential privacy model where adding noises into the SDN based EN cluster. Our extensive experimental findings established that the proposed model and clustering approach not only exhibit high reliability in specified situations, but also offer configurable location-aware data privacy protection. More over, we consider to further optimize the data utilities and privacy loss by considering Markov Decision Process

(MDP) where will provide optimal tradeoff solutions. Moreover, reinforcement learning methods will also be tested to optimize the convergence speed.

References

1. Vicfreewifi access point locations - victorian government data directory, July 2017. https://discover.data.vic.gov.au/dataset/vicfreewifi-access-point-locations
2. Badsha, S., et al.: Privacy preserving location-aware personalized web service recommendations. IEEE Trans. Serv. Comput. **14**(3), 791–804 (2018)
3. Bonomi, F., Milito, R., Natarajan, P., Zhu, J.: Fog computing: a platform for internet of things and analytics. In: Bessis, N., Dobre, C. (eds.) Big Data and Internet of Things: A Roadmap for Smart Environments. SCI, vol. 546, pp. 169–186. Springer, Cham (2014). https://doi.org/10.1007/978-3-319-05029-4_7
4. Dang, T.D., Hoang, D.: A data protection model for fog computing. In: 2017 Second International Conference on Fog and Mobile Edge Computing (FMEC), pp. 32–38 (2017)
5. Deepali, Bhushan, K.: DDoS attack defense framework for cloud using fog computing. In: 2017 2nd IEEE International Conference on Recent Trends in Electronics, Information Communication Technology (RTEICT), pp. 534–538 (2017)
6. Frey, B.J., Dueck, D.: Affinity propagation (2007)
7. Xia, Q., Tao, Z., Li, Q.: Privacy issues in edge computing. In: Chang, W., Wu, J. (eds.) Fog/Edge Computing For Security, Privacy, and Applications. AIS, vol. 83, pp. 147–169. Springer, Cham (2021). https://doi.org/10.1007/978-3-030-57328-7_6
8. Gu, B., Wang, X., Qu, Y., Jin, J., Xiang, Y., Gao, L.: Context-aware privacy preservation in a hierarchical fog computing system. In: 2019 IEEE International Conference on Communications (ICC), ICC 2019, pp. 1–6. IEEE (2019)
9. Gu, B.S., Gao, L., Wang, X., Qu, Y., Jin, J., Yu, S.: Privacy on the edge: customizable privacy-preserving context sharing in hierarchical edge computing. IEEE Trans. Netw. Sci. Eng. **7**, 2298–2309 (2019)
10. Hasan, K., Ahmed, K., Biswas, K., Islam, M.S., Kayes, A.S.M., Islam, S.M.R.: Control plane optimisation for an SDN-based WBAN framework to support healthcare applications. Sensors **20**(15) (2020). https://doi.org/10.3390/s20154200. https://www.mdpi.com/1424-8220/20/15/4200
11. Hasan, K., Ahmed, K., Biswas, K., Saiful Islam, M., Ameri Sianaki, O.: Software-defined application-specific traffic management for wireless body area networks. Future Gener. Comput. Syst. **107**, 274–285 (2020). https://doi.org/10.1016/j.future.2020.01.052, https://www.sciencedirect.com/science/article/pii/S0167739X19322587
12. Ho, S., Qu, Y., Gu, B., Gao, L., Li, J., Xiang, Y.: DP-GAN: differentially private consecutive data publishing using generative adversarial nets. J. Netw. Comput. Appl. **185**, 103066 (2021)
13. Kang, J., Yu, R., Huang, X., Zhang, Y.: Privacy-preserved pseudonym scheme for fog computing supported internet of vehicles. IEEE Trans. Intell. Transp. Syst. **19**(8), 2627–2637 (2018)
14. Lu, R., Heung, K., Lashkari, A.H., Ghorbani, A.A.: A lightweight privacy-preserving data aggregation scheme for fog computing-enhanced IoT. IEEE Access **5**, 3302–3312 (2017)
15. Lyu, L., Nandakumar, K., Rubinstein, B., Jin, J., Bedo, J., Palaniswami, M.: PPFA: privacy preserving fog-enabled aggregation in smart grid. IEEE Trans. Ind. Inf. **14**(8), 3733–3744 (2018)

16. Ma, L., Liu, X., Pei, Q., Xiang, Y.: Privacy-preserving reputation management for edge computing enhanced mobile crowdsensing. IEEE Trans. Serv. Comput. **79**, 500–513 (2018). Part 2

17. Mouradian, C., Naboulsi, D., Yangui, S., Glitho, R.H., Morrow, M.J., Polakos, P.A.: A comprehensive survey on fog computing: state-of-the-art and research challenges. IEEE Commun. Surv. Tutor. **20**(1), 416–464 (2018)

18. Nafi, N.S., Ahmed, K., Gregory, M.A., Datta, M.: Software defined neighborhood area network for smart grid applications. Future Gener. Comput. Syst. **79**, 500–513 (2018). https://doi.org/10.1016/j.future.2017.09.064, https://www.sciencedirect.com/science/article/pii/S0167739X17311007

19. Ni, J., Zhang, K., Lin, X., Shen, X.: Securing fog computing for internet of things applications: challenges and solutions. IEEE Commun. Surv. Tutor. **20**(1), 601–628 (2018)

20. Qu, Y., Yu, S., Gao, L., Zhou, W., Peng, S.: A hybrid privacy protection scheme in cyber-physical social networks. IEEE Trans. Comput. Soc. Syst. **5**(3), 773–784 (2018)

21. Rasool, R.U., Ashraf, U., Ahmed, K., Wang, H., Rafique, W., Anwar, Z.: Cyber-Pulse: a machine learning based link flooding attack mitigation system for software defined networks. IEEE Access **7**, 34885–34899 (2019). https://doi.org/10.1109/ACCESS.2019.2904236

22. Stojmenovic, I., Wen, S.: The fog computing paradigm: scenarios and security issues. In: 2014 Federated Conference on Computer Science and Information Systems, pp. 1–8, September 2014. https://doi.org/10.15439/2014F503

23. Wang, Q., Chen, D., Zhang, N., Ding, Z., Qin, Z.: PCP: a privacy-preserving content-based publish subscribe scheme with differential privacy in fog computing. IEEE Access **5**, 17962–17974 (2017). https://doi.org/10.1109/ACCESS.2017.2748956

24. Wang, T., Zhou, J., Chen, X., Wang, G., Liu, A., Liu, Y.: A three-layer privacy preserving cloud storage scheme based on computational intelligence in fog computing. IEEE Trans. Emerg. Top. Comput. Intell. **2**(1), 3–12 (2018)

25. Wang, W., Zhang, Q.: Privacy preservation for context sensing on smartphone. IEEE/ACM Trans. Netw. **24**(6), 3235–3247 (2016). https://doi.org/10.1109/TNET.2015.2512301

26. Wibowo, F.X., Gregory, M.A., Ahmed, K., Gomez, K.M.: Multi-domain software defined networking: research status and challenges. J. Netw. Comput. Appl. **87**, 32–45 (2017). https://doi.org/10.1016/j.jnca.2017.03.004, https://www.sciencedirect.com/science/article/pii/S1084804517300991

27. Yannuzzi, M., Milito, R., Serral-Graci, R., Montero, D., Nemirovsky, M.: Key ingredients in an IoT recipe: fog computing, cloud computing, and more fog computing. In: 2014 IEEE 19th International Workshop on Computer Aided Modeling and Design of Communication Links and Networks (CAMAD), pp. 325–329 (2014)

28. Zhang, J., Feng, X., Liu, Z.: A grid-based clustering algorithm via load analysis for industrial internet of things. IEEE Access **6**, 13117–13128 (2018)

Survey on Bridge Discovery in Tor

Fucai Yu[1]([✉]), Ruoshui Zhou[1], Xuemeng Zhai[1], Youyang Qu[2], and Gaolei Fei[1]

[1] University of Electronic Science and Technology of China (UESTC), Chengdu, China
fcyu@Uestc.edu.cn
[2] Deakin University, Burwood, VIC 3125, Australia

Abstract. To prevent users from using Tor for anonymous communication, many regulatory agencies have blocked the IP addresses of public Tor routers in Tor networks, resulting in the interception of traffic to Tor public routers. Existing research solves this problem by introducing bridge nodes into the Tor network to avoid supervision; The bridge node is usually the entrance node of the Tor network, and its information is not completely public on the network, so it cannot be intercepted completely. This allows anonymous users to access the Tor network through the bridge node, which can effectively avoid Tor censorship. Nevertheless, many studies still focus on the discovery of Tor bridge nodes. The technology of bridge node discovery in Tor networks within recent years is summarized in this paper.

Keywords: Tor networks · Bridge · Tor relay nodes

1 Introduction

A Tor network [1], as shown in Fig. 1, is an overlay anonymous network in which each Tor router runs as a normal user-level process without any special privileges. Each user runs local software called an onion proxy to fetch directories, establish circuits across the network, and handle connections from user applications. These onion proxies accept TCP streams and multiplex them across the circuits. The Tor router on the other side of the circuit connects to the requested destinations and relays data. A Tor network relies on onion routing to guarantee anonymity. Onion routing [1], as shown in Fig. 2, is a distributed overlay network protocol designed to anonymize TCP-based applications like web browsing, secure shell, and instant messaging. Clients choose a path through the network and build a circuit in which each onion router in the path knows its predecessor and successor but no other nodes in the circuit.

Normal clients access the Tor core network directly through public Tor entry routers listed in the consensus file available at the official Tor website. To anonymously communicate with a web server, a normal client uses source routing and chooses a series of onion routers (generally three) from a downloaded consensus file. The selected onion routers construct an anonymous path along which a circuit will be set up incrementally by applying onion routing. Figure 1 depicts a circuit created incrementally along the path Source → Router A → Router B → Router C. Here, Routers A, B, and C also refer to entry, middle, and exit nodes, respectively.

W. Bao et al. (Eds.): ADHOCNETS 2021/TridentCom 2021, LNICST 428, pp. 317–326, 2022.
https://doi.org/10.1007/978-3-030-98005-4_23

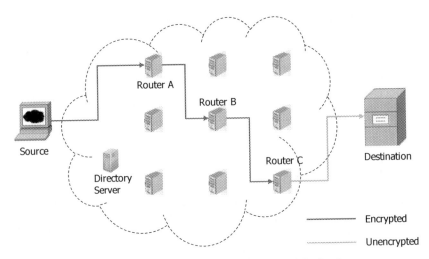

Fig. 1. Sample Tor circuit between source and destination.

Tor has been commonly used for resisting various forms of censorship [2]. However, Tor uses source routing for communication privacy, and the information of all Tor routers is available to clients and publicly listed on the Internet [3]; thus, blocking Tor is as simple as blocking connections to those known Tor routers. To resist the censorship blocking of public Tor routers, bridges were introduced in Tor. A bridge can act as the first hop relaying user traffic into the core Tor network, i.e., entry node (Router A) in Fig. 1. The bridge information is not listed on the Internet. As described in [4], the bridge population significantly varies over time: It has steadily grown from 2.8K active public bridges in July 2012 to a maximum of 12.7K in July 2014; it began declining in January 2015, falling to 5.3K by April 2016. A few bridge pools exist and some are stored on the bridge https and email servers. A user can access the bridge https server or send a Google/Yahoo email to the bridge email server to retrieve three bridges at one time. Bridges are also distributed through various social networks.

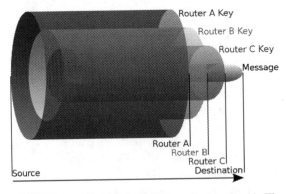

Fig. 2. Tor onion routing, Routers A, B, and C correspond to those in Fig. 1, respectively.

For subjects such as blocking Tor, Tor censorship, finding available bridges, Tor network analysis, performance improvement, and bridge concealment, a number of studies have focused on bridge discovery. Although Arma presented 10 possible ways to obtain bridges on Tor's official website [5], he did not describe the exact bridge acquisition method in detail. In this paper, a brief survey of bridge discovery with respect to bridge categories and discovery schemes is conducted.

2 Background

The components of Tor and bridges are reviewed in this section. As described in [6], a Tor client runs an onion proxy (OP) to anonymize the client data into Tor. Tor uses a multi-hop proxy mechanism to protect user communication privacy: The client first uses a weighted random routing algorithm to select three relay nodes from the consensus file as the Tor network entry, middle, and exit nodes and then establishes a circuit with these relay nodes hop by hop. As shown in Fig. 2, the client encapsulates the sent data with three-layer encryptions. In the process of data transmission, the entry, middle, and exit nodes sequentially decrypt and restore the plaintext and then send it to the destination. The client's user privacy is guaranteed by using onion routing, under which any relay node cannot know the IP address of both the client and the destination server, and the client IP address is also unknown to the destination server. The public relay node list is stored in the accessible consensus file; therefore, to block Tor network communication, one only needs to block the IP address of the public relay node IP obtained from the accessible consensus file. Bridge nodes were introduced into the Tor project to resist such supervision. The Tor project provides all the source code of the Tor system. Users can create bridge nodes by downloading Tor source code and use bridge nodes instead of public relay nodes as entry nodes. Since the bridge node information is not accessible, under this situation, regulatory agencies cannot block Tor communication effectively. Bridge nodes are classified into two categories: public bridge nodes and private bridge nodes [4]. Public bridge node information is stored in the Tor network directory server, which only provides three public bridge nodes to a user at a time. Therefore, it is not easy to obtain the information of all bridge nodes. Of course, users can obtain a large amount of bridge node information through distributed enumeration. The private bridge node information is only kept by the creator and cannot be obtained by other users.

Although Tor can use bridge nodes to circumvent the supervision based on IP blocking, supervisors can still identify Tor traffic through deep packet inspection (DPI) technology [7]. To make Tor communication characters fuzzy in using bridge node environments, a transmission plug-in called an obfs, or obfuscation, proxy was developed by the Tor project. The latest version of obfs4 [8] uses BridgeDB to implement key exchange based on bridge authentication. The client queries the bridge node through BridgeDB and obtains its IP address, node ID, and public key information. Only by matching these three conditions at the same time can it pass the identity verification of the obfs4 node and establish a connection. obfs4 not only effectively confuses Tor traffic but also realizes, with bridge authentication, that it can resist active detection attacks and man-in-the-middle attacks.

3   Bridge Discovery Schemes

The discovery methods of bridge nodes are classified and summarized in this section. The specific methods are as follows.

3.1   Normal Bridge Enumeration Mechanism

Ling *et al.* elaborated on and verified the method of obtaining bridge node information in batches through email and http requests in [6]. An attacker can use a Yahoo or Gmail account to send an email to the bridge email server (bridges@torproject.org) with the line "get bridges" in the body of the mail. The bridge email server promptly replies with three distinct bridges. To avoid malicious enumeration, the bridge email server only replies with one email to an email account each day. Alternatively, the user can access the bridge website (https://lbridges.torproject.org) to obtain three bridges. To avoid malicious enumeration, the https server distributes three bridges to each 24-bit IP prefix each day as well.

The authors verified the effectiveness of the above method of obtaining bridge nodes through emails and http requests. Since each mailbox can only obtain three bits of bridge node information per day, obtaining more bridge node information requires a large number of mailboxes to send bridge node request emails, but an IP address can only apply for one Yahoo mailbox. To solve this problem, the authors applied for Yahoo mailboxes through more than 500 PlanetLab nodes and also used more than 500 exit nodes of the Tor network as agents to apply for Yahoo mailboxes. In the end, the authors applied for more than 2,000 Yahoo mailboxes in total and enumerated more than 1,500 bridge nodes within 22 d through these mailboxes. In addition, the authors also used these PlanetLab nodes and Tor exit nodes to retrieve the bridges from the bridge website (https://lbr idges.torproject.org) and obtained more than 550 bridge nodes within 37 d. McLachlan described a similar method in [9]. The advantage of the above bridge node enumeration method is that the fingerprint information of the bridge node can be obtained. With the fingerprint information, these bridge nodes can be used to construct anonymous communication links for anonymous communication. To avoid the information of all bridge node being enumerated, the bridge website may only provide part of the bridge node information for users to obtain within a period of time. In addition, only public bridge nodes can be obtained in this way; private bridge nodes cannot be obtained using this method.

3.2   Bridge Inference by Malicious Tor Middle Routers

Ling *et al.* also described a method of using malicious middle nodes to infer bridge nodes in [6]. The anonymous circuit of the Tor network is composed of entry, middle, and exit nodes. The entry node may be a general public Tor router or a bridge node. The anonymous traffic received by the middle node comes from the entry node. A malicious middle node can obtain the IP addresses of all entry nodes by extracting the source IP of the received data packets. By excluding the IP addresses of the known public routers, an attacker obtains the IP information of the bridge nodes. This method requires that the middle node be a controlled node, and the identified bridge nodes only include those transmitting anonymous communication traffic through the controlled middle node. To identify more bridge nodes, the controlled middle node must have a higher bandwidth to attract more anonymous communication traffic.

3.3 Tor Bridge Discovery Through Internet-Wide Scans

Ports 443 and 9001 are common ports for Tor bridges and relays, and the TLS protocol is used for encryption and authentication between bridges/relays. Based on the above characteristics, Durumeric *et al.* [10] and Tsyrklevich [11] successively proposed a bridge node discovery method based on Internet-wide scans. Durumeric *et al.* exploited the ZMap tool to perform Internet-wide scans on ports 443 and 9001 and applied a set of heuristics to identify likely Tor nodes. For hosts with one of these ports open, they performed a TLS handshake using a specific set of cipher suites supported by Tor's "v1 handshake." When a Tor relay receives this set of cipher suites, it will respond with a two-certificate chain. The signing ("Certificate Authority") certificate is self-signed with the relay's identity public key and uses a subject name of the form "CN = www.X.com," where X is a randomized alpha-numeric string. This pattern matched 67,342 hosts on port 443 and 2,952 hosts on port 9001. Durumeric *et al.* then calculated each host's identity fingerprint and checked whether the SHA1 hash appeared in the public Tor metrics list for bridge pool assignments. Hosts that were found matched 1,170 unique bridge fingerprints on port 443 and 419 unique fingerprints on port 9001, with a combined total of 1,534 unique fingerprints (some were found on both ports). From the bridge pool assignment data, they found that 1,767–1,936 unique fingerprints were allocated at any given time in the recent past, which suggests that they were able to identify 79%–86% of allocated bridges at the time of the scan. The unmatched fingerprints in the Tor metrics list may correspond to bridges missed, offline bridges, or bridges configured to use a port other than 9001 or 443. Based on the work of Durumeric *et al.*, Tsyrklevich [11] identified pluggable transport (PT) [4]-enabled bridges. A PT is just a wrapper for the Tor protocol that transforms the Tor traffic flowing between clients and bridges to prevent DPI attacks. Experimental results have also proven the effectiveness of the Internet-wide scan method in bridge recognition. Wilde also described a similar method in [12]. The advantage of the above method is that there is no need to deploy malicious Tor relay nodes. It only needs to detect the 443 and 9001 ports of a large number of IP addresses and further verify the detection results. The disadvantage of this method is its poor timeliness. Because the set of active bridges is constantly changing, the data would be stale by the time a long-running scan was complete.

3.4 Tor Bridge Identification Through DPI

In 2011, Iran added a filter rule to its border routers that recognized Tor traffic and blocked it. Arma investigated the situation in [13] and found the following. (1) Tor tries to make its traffic look like a web browser talking to a https web server, and the characteristic of Tor's SSL handshake was the expiry time for SSL session certificates. (2) Tor's SSL handshake rotates the session certificates every 2 h, whereas normal SSL certificates received from a certificate authority typically last a year or more. The fix was to simply write a larger expiration time on the certificates, so the current certificates in use have more plausible expiry times. Another DPI-based method developed by Winter *et al.* [14] and Wilde [12] is to check a special cipher list in the Tor TLS handshake. The cipher list is part of the TLS client hello, which is sent by the Tor user to the relay or bridge after a TCP connection has been established. This particular cipher list appears to be unique to Tor: c0 0a c0 14 00 39 00 38 c0 0f c0 05 00 35 c0 07 c0 09 c0 11 c0 13 00 33 00 32 c0 0c c0 0e c0 02 c0 04 00 04 00 05 00 2f c0 08 c0 12 00 16 00 13 c0 0d c0 03 fe ff 00 0a 00 ff. Through these methods, a Tor TLS handshake can be detected, thereby determining whether the entry node is either a public relay or a bridge.

3.5   Tor Bridge Detection Based on TCP SYN Connections

Yang *et al.* [15] proposed a bridge detection method based on the following observation: When connecting to a Tor network via bridges, the client first creates a series of non-blocking sockets and then connects those sockets one after another in a short period for establishing TCP connections to chosen bridges. The chosen bridges include two parts: bridges configured by users and bridges cached by Tor software. As with most applications, the Tor client does not bind pre-determined source ports for those connections. Conversely, it is the operating system that assigns ephemeral source ports for connections to chosen bridges. Such ephemeral source ports are usually consecutively allocated in widely used operating systems like Windows platforms. As a result, multiple SYN packets with consecutive source ports will be sent almost simultaneously, destined for different bridges. Therefore, if multiple SYN packets from the same IP address with consecutive source ports are observed, then the destination IPs are extracted, and, if at least one destination IP belongs to a known bridge set, then all the other destination IPs are inferred to be bridges. This is called the opportunism bridge detection method and requires a large known bridge set.

3.6   Tor Bridge Detection Based on Flow Classification or Identification

The idea of the bridge identification method based on Tor traffic classification and identification is to identify Tor anonymous communication traffic, extract the source and destination IP addresses of the traffic at first, and then exclude the IP addresses of the known public routers from the accessible consensus file to obtain the bridge node information. Several studies have focused on Tor flow classification [16, 17]. In [16], Shahbar *et al.* aimed to analyze the amount of information that can be extracted from the encrypted Tor traffic without decrypting the traffic. They employed two different approaches for the classification of user activities. The first approach is flow level classification, and it depends on analyzing the TCP communication between the user and the Tor relay to predict the type of user activities in the encrypted traffic. The second approach is circuit-level classification. The encrypted circuits have characteristics that can be extracted and calculated to classify the type of traffic in the circuits.

In [18], traffic analysis was used to discover the identity of the user using the Tor network. The analysis depends on the size of the packet transmitted on the network from the web server through the router to the user. Tor has a fixed cell size, but the packet size can vary. The authors of [18] used padding with one bit to mark the packets so that they could be traced back at the receiver side. They reported that 10 packets are enough to get reasonable detection with a low number of false positives. The length of the padding will force the Tor router to use the known number of cells. The Tor cell size is 512 bytes, which means if the data size is more than 512 bytes, then it must be fragmented to fit into the cell size. This enabled the authors to mark the client receiving these cells as the client having access to the server.

To avoid censorship, obfs4 has been widely deployed to obscure the flow between a Tor client and bridge. In [19], He *et al.* proposed a scheme for obfs4 traffic detection based on two-level filtering. They sequentially utilized coarse-grained fast filtering and fine-grained accurate identification to achieve high-precision, real-time recognition of obfs4 traffic. In the coarse-grained filtering phase, they used a randomness detection algorithm to detect the randomness of the handshake packet payload in the communication and used the timing-sequence characteristics of the packet in the handshake process to remove other interference traffic. In the fine-grained identification phase, they analyzed its statistical feature on a large amount of obfs4 traffic and used classification algorithms to identify the obfs4 traffic. Their experimental results show that the accuracy for identifying obfs4 traffic is above 99% when using a support-vector-machine algorithm, which indicates that obfs4 cannot effectively counteract traffic analysis attacks in practical applications. Once an instance of obfs4 traffic was identified, the corresponding IP address could be further confirmed as whether it was a bridge based on the port.

Through the above methods, one can first identify which users are using a Tor network for anonymous communication, then extract the destination IP addresses of anonymous traffic sent by these users, and finally remove public relays from them to obtain the bridge node information.

4 Discussion

Among the above studies on bridge recognition, only the bridge node information obtained based on http and e-mail requests described in [6] contains the fingerprint of the bridge nodes. According to the obtained bridge node fingerprint information, the obtained bridge node can be used to construct a circuit for anonymous communication. In addition, the connection configuration window of the Tor browser also provides the function of obtaining three bridge nodes and their fingerprints. Although other bridge nodes cannot obtain the fingerprint information of a bridge node, the obtained IP address and port information of the bridge nodes can meet the requirements of blocking Tor, Tor censorship, finding available bridges, Tor network analysis, performance improvement, bridge concealment, etc. The above-mentioned bridge node discovery algorithms are summarized in Table 1. In the table, "bridge availability" indicates that the method can obtain fingerprint information of bridge nodes and that the fingerprint information can be used to construct an anonymous communication circuit; "bridge comprehensive" indicates the proportion of bridge nodes that can be discovered by the particular method in the total bridge nodes of the Tor network; "discovery efficiency" indicates the efficiency of the method, i.e., the number of bridge nodes discovered per unit time; "method effectiveness" indicates whether the bridge node discovery methods are still available; and "method precision" indicates the proportion of real bridge nodes among the bridge nodes discovered by the listed methods.

Table 1. Comparison of bridge discovery methods.

Study		Bridge availability	Bridge comprehensive	Discovery efficiency	Method effectiveness	Method precision
Normal mechanism	Ling *et al.* [6]	Yes	Middle	High	Yes	High
	McLachlan *et al.* [9]	Yes	Middle	High	Yes	High
By Tor middle router	Ling *et al.* [6]	No	Low	Low	Yes	High
Internet-wide scans	Durumeric *et al.* [10]	No	High	Low	Yes	High
	Tsyrklevich *et al.* [11]	No	High	Low	Yes	High
Through DPI	Arma [13]	No	Low	Low	No	High
	Wilde [12]	No	Low	Low	No	High
	Winter *et al.* [14]	No	Low	Low	No	High
TCP SYN based	Yang *et al.* [15]	No	Low	Low	Yes	Low
Flow classification or identification	Shahbar *et al.* [16]	No	Low	Low	Yes	Middle
	Shahbar *et al.* [17]	No	Low	Low	Yes	Middle
	Ling *et al.* [18]	No	Low	Low	Yes	Middle
	He *et al.* [19]	No	Low	Low	Yes	Middle

Through the above comparison, one can find that the bridge node discovery methods mainly include the following: 1) The actual and available bridge node information can be obtained by using http and email requests; 2) the method of middle malicious forwarding nodes requires the attacker to deploy controllable middle forwarding nodes and can only identify the bridge nodes based on the monitored traffic; 3) although more comprehensive bridge node information can be obtained through Internet-wide scans, this takes a long time and requires further verification of suspected bridge nodes, so the real-time performance is poor; 4) the extraction of bridge node information through DPI depends on the particular cipher list used in Tor TLS negotiation; 5) the TCP SYN–based bridge node discovery method relies on the allocation of ephemeral source ports for connections to the operating system-chosen bridges, and if the operating system modifies the source port allocation strategy, this method will then not achieve the expected effect; and 6) the method based on flow classification or identification mainly realizes bridge node identification based on anonymous communication traffic classification, and its accuracy depends on the accuracy of the flow classification or identification method.

5   Conclusions

This article focuses on the discovery of bridge nodes in the Tor network, and several bridge node discovery methods are analyzed and summarized. Analysis results show that although the Tor project tries to conceal anonymous users through bridges, the concealment of bridge nodes is not perfect, and the existence of bridge nodes can still be discovered through a variety of methods. Future research should further enhance the concealment of bridges, with the following goals: 1) Improve the distribution mechanism of bridge nodes, increase the verification mechanism, and reduce the risk of public bridge information being obtained through a large number of enumerations through http and email servers; 2) encourage users to establish and use bridges, so that the greater the number of bridge nodes, the stronger the concealment; 3) in addition to Meek [20] and obfs technology, new Tor traffic camouflage methods should be studied to reduce the risk of Tor traffic being identified; and 4) many web services prohibit Tor access by blocking the IP of the Tor exit node, the information of which is public. Therefore, the use of exit bridges [21, 22] to bypass server-side censorship—which has rarely been researched—should be studied.

References

1. Dingledine, R., Mathewson, N., Syverson, P.: Tor: the second-generation onion router. In 13th USENIX Security Symposium, San Diego, pp.1–17 (2004)
2. Phobos: Tor and Censorship: lessons learned. https://blog.torproject.org/tor-and-censorship-lessons-learned
3. Tor Node List. https://www.dan.me.uk/tornodes
4. Matic, S., Troncoso, C., Caballero, J.: Dissecting tor bridges: a security evaluation of their private and public infrastructures. In: Conference of Network and Distributed System Security Symposium 2017, San Diego, pp. 1–15 (2017)
5. Arma: Research problems: Ten ways to discover Tor bridges. https://blog.torproject.org/research-problems-ten-ways-discover-tor-bridges
6. Ling, Z., Luo, J., Yu, W., et al.: Tor bridge discovery: extensive analysis and large-scale empirical evaluation. IEEE Trans. Parallel Distrib. Syst. 26(7), 1887–1899 (2015)
7. He, G., Yang, M., Luo, J., Gu, X.: A novel application classification attack against Tor. Concurr. Comput. Pract. Exp. 27(18), 5640–5661 (2016)
8. Angel, Y.: obfs4 (The obfourscator). https://github.com/Yawning/obfs4/blob/master/doc/obfs4-spec.txt
9. McLachlan, J., Hopper, N.: On the risks of serving whenever you surf: vulnerabilities in Tor's blocking resistance design. In: Proceedings of the 8th ACM workshop on Privacy in the electronic society, Chicago, pp. 31–40 (2019)
10. Durumeric, A., Wustrow, E., Halderman, A.: ZMap: fast Internet-wide scanning and its security applications. In: the Proceedings of the 22nd USENIX Security Symposium. 14–16 August 2013, Washington, D.C. pp. 605–619 (2013)
11. Tsyrklevich, V.: Internet-wide1976 scanning for bridges. https://lists.torproject.org/pipermail/tor-dev/2014-December/007957.html
12. Wilde, T.: Great Firewall Tor Probing. https://gist.github.com/da3c7a9af01d74cd7de7
13. Arma.: Iran blocks Tor. https://blog.torproject.org/iran-blocks-tor-tor-releases-same-day-fix
14. Winter, P., Lindskog, S.: How China Is Blocking Tor. 2012. https://arxiv.org/abs/1204.0447v1
15. Yang, M., Luo, J., Zhang, L., Wang, X., Fu, X.: How to block Tor's hidden bridges: detecting methods and countermeasures. J. Supercomput. 66(3), 1285–1305 (2012). https://doi.org/10.1007/s11227-012-0788-4
16. Shahbar, K., Zincir-Heywood, A.N.: Benchmarking two techniques for tor classification: flow level and circuit level classification. In: 2014 IEEE Symposium on Computational Intelligence in Cyber Security (CICS), Orlando, pp. 1–8 (2014)
17. Shahbar, K., Zincir-Heywood, A.N.: Traffic flow analysis of tor pluggable transport. In: 2015 11th International Conference on Network and Service Management (CNSM), Barcelona, Spain, pp.178–181 (2015)

18. Ling, Z., Luo, J., Yu, W., Fu, X.: Equal-sized cells mean equal-sized packets in Tor? In: Proceedings of IEEE International Conference on Communications ICC 2011, Kyoto, Japan, pp.1–6 (2011)
19. He, Y., Hu, L., Gao, R.: Detection of tor traffic hiding under obfs4 protocol based on two-level filtering. In: 2019 2nd International Conference on Data Intelligence and Security, South Padre Island, pp.195–200 (2019)
20. Fifield, D., Lan, C., Hynes, R., et al.: Blocking-resistant communication through domain fronting. Proc. Privacy Enhan. Technol. **2015**(2), 46–64 (2015)
21. Zhang. Z., Subramanian, K., Zhou, W., Sherr, M.,: Ephemeral exit bridges for tor. In: 50th Annual IEEE/IFIP International Conference on Dependable Systems and Networks (DSN), 2020, Spain, pp. 253–265 (2020)
22. Zhang, Z., Zhou, W., Sherr, M.: Bypassing tor exit blocking with exit bridge onion services. In: The ACM Conference on Computer and Communications Security (CCS'20), Virtual Event, 2020, pp. 3–16 (2020)

Author Index

Printed in the United States
by Baker & Taylor Publisher Services